The Development of Cross-Border Economic Relations

The Development of Cross-Border Economic Relations

A theoretical and empirical study of the influence of the state border on the development of cross-border economic relations between firms in border regions of the Netherlands and Belgium.

Proefschrift

ter verkrijging van de graad van doctor aan de Katholieke Universiteit Brabant, op gezag van de rector magnificus, prof. dr. L.F.W. de Klerk, in het openbaar te verdedigen ten overstaan van een door het college van decanen aangewezen commissie in de aula van de Universiteit op vrijdag 3 juli 1998 om 16.15 uur

door

Henricus Jacobus van Houtum

geboren op 14 mei 1969 te Geldrop.

Promotores:

Prof. Dr. J.G. Lambooy
Prof. Dr. F.W.M. Boekema

De man en zijn proefschrift
Ze dansen de tango
Laat ze dansen en draaien in dit spel voor twee
Zij die kunnen dansen, dansen zacht mee.

Ingrid Veldhuizen,
december 1997

Foreword

It is common practice to begin a dissertation with what is in reality its conclusion, the foreword. In the foreword, the PhD student expresses his gratitude towards all those who have assisted him in completing his book. Often, it is the only part of the dissertation that is read with any true interest. A foreword contrasts sharply with the remainder of a dissertation. Where the foreword ceases, science commences. Then scientific and academic standards apply to what is written. Up to and including the foreword, one can actually understand what the author is talking about.

The fact that the foreword is written by PhD students makes it all the more interesting. By now, I have discovered that PhD students are rather a peculiar type of people. Very peculiar indeed. During the most important years of maturing adulthood and self-awareness, these people plod on in absolute seclusion for the sake of Science. Their unremitting effort stands under the auspices of their desire to pass the Test of Competence, so that they will be admitted to the select elite of individuals called 'Scientists'. From the very first day, therefore, the PhD student has only one objective: to write a scientific book. Yet not a single human being will actually really read the work to which the PhD student has devoted so many years of his life. Why should you? Each line of reasoning is stopped up completely. A dissertation provides no surprise, no excitement, and its conclusion is known in advance - 'Further research is necessary'. A dissertation is the common opinion of a multitude of educated people concerning a certain subject. It is a reference work for a very few specialists. Moreover, even the process of writing itself is not taken seriously. The ambiguous name by which the PhD student is called, research assistant ("Assistent In Opleiding"), assistant research fellow ("Onderzoeker In Opleiding") - or even worse, bursar ("Beurspromovendus") -, is interpreted unambiguously in scientific circles. A PhD student has absolutely no responsibility for, or authority over other people at all. The PhD student is being educated, and that is meant literally. What he does is not regarded as 'real work'. Not even by 'outsiders'. So many times, people asked when I would finish studying, and when this graduation thesis ("afstudeerscriptie") would finally be completed. The dissertation period is truly a trial period.

Only in the foreword is the upcoming Doctor allowed to write a text without being obliged to live up to scientific *mores*. In the foreword he can finally shake off the heavy burden of his scientific needs and obligations and ignore the lifelessness of 'the language of sources' that he has for so long enslaved himself to. The words may flow; his brain, half-dead from reading, is finally allowed to dish up any string of words without having to justify their provenance. His friends and his life outside science as their only source.

In the foreword, the PhD student comes to life, becomes human after all. Finally, he is able to express what the University and Science have promised him, but never truly allow: freedom of speech and spirit. For those who know the PhD student best, the foreword is therefore the most exciting part of the whole thing. For them, the foreword is like a detective novel. Who is thanked, and especially, who is 'forgotten'? Am I in there? And how? What does he write about me? What did he think of his supervisor? To whom does he dedicate his dissertation?

Now that my dissertation is finished, I know that I do not like studying. Studying is reproducing. Reading, reflecting upon what was read, and writing about it, to the contrary, are wonderful things to do. The past years in my life have been fascinating, enlightening, and intense. An intense period usually brings you friends and colleagues. In my case, a girlfriend even. To them, I dedicate this foreword.

Scientifically, two people especially have truly exerted themselves to show me around in their profession and their currents of thought. These people are Prof. Dr. Jan Lambooy (Universiteit van Amsterdam and Universiteit Utrecht), and Prof. Dr. Frans Boekema (Katholieke Universiteit Brabant and Katholieke Universiteit Nijmegen). Both have taught me that a quest for the innovative questions begins with learning to understand the questions that specialists ask themselves.

Frans Boekema has become more than a good acquaintance. When I was still a student in economics, he is the one that gave me the enthusiasm to specialise in Regional Economics. When I had become a research and teaching assistant, he taught me the first steps in the world of academic research and education. After I graduated, taking my PhD seemed to follow naturally. Frans also enabled me to teach and to guide students in writing their thesis, both of which I experienced as pleasant and interesting. Frans, I am very grateful for the space you allowed for my own initiatives, for the chances and opportunities you provided. Your open mind and warm support, your charisma, enthusiasm and guidance have been very valuable to me all these years.

Professor Jan Lambooy is a regional economist full of inspiring ideas. Each visit to him proved stimulating and interesting. Professor Lambooy, I thank you for your interest in my work and our illuminating discussions concerning the direction and emphases of border-regional economic research. The possibility you provided of teaching at the Universiteit van Amsterdam I have also experienced as very enriching. But most of all, I wish to thank you for the freedom of thought that you have allowed and stimulated in me.

I thank Prof. Dr. Jan Buursink (Katholieke Universiteit Nijmegen), Prof. Dr. Dirk-Jan Kamann (RijksUniversiteit Groningen), Prof. Dr. Jules van Dijck (Katholieke Universiteit Brabant), and Prof. Dr. Karel Veraghtert (Katholieke Universiteit Brabant) heartily for their willingness to be in the committee that evaluated my dissertation.

I now want to thank the people who were not responsible for the supervision or evaluation of the contents of the dissertation that lies before you, but without whose help I would doubtless have been unable to complete this work.

I first thank everyone at the Chambers of Commerce in Zeeland and Gent/Eeklo, who have enabled me to complete my empirical research in their regions. I hope my final report and summary of the research will prove useful to them. My gratitude goes out especially to the members of the project team; Nynke van der Ploeg of the Chamber of Commerce of Zeeland Flanders, who acted as project leader for the survey, Chantal de Schepper and Cor Helmendach in Central and North Zeeland, and Patrick de Klerck and Philip Verstraete in Gent/Eeklo. My collaboration with these people was always open, constructive, and stimulating. I also wish to thank Margot Westerweel, who is responsible for most of the data entry. I am equally grateful to the directors and managers of the companies in the three regions who took the trouble to answer and return the questionnaire.

If this dissertation is written in impeccable English, it is due to Mrs. I.H. Havona-Ockerse in Amsterdam. Should you discover any errors in either spelling or style, she is not to blame, for they are the result of my own irrepressible tendency to keep on changing the text.

While working at the Economic Institute of Tilburg (EIT) at the beginning of my PhD studies, I collaborated with John Dagevos. Thanks to you, John, I was made aware of the meaning and depth of scientific research. I also want to express my gratitude for the valuable comments you gave with regard to the questionnaire I made for my survey. I also worked together with Leon Oerlemans, both at EIT and at the University's department of regional economics. Leon, thank you for our inspiring academic discussions about our field of study, for your suggestions and advice relating to the questionnaire, and for your comments on an earlier version of the empirical part of the dissertation. Willem de Graaff, with whom I worked in the department of regional economics at the University as well, thank you for your interest in my work and the enthusiasm and dedication you devoted to helping me in making the geographical maps in this work.

John Bell, thanks for your suggestions concerning my hypotheses and my research approach. Your expert dissertation made me enthusiastic for the scientific research on cross-border economic alliances.

Walter Manshanden, thank you for many fascinating and amusing exchanges of ideas relating to the field of regional economics we had in Tilburg, in Amsterdam, and by e-mail.

Martin van der Velde, thank you very much for the inspiring discussions about 'Borders and Interaction' I have had with you since my appointment as Post Doc researcher at the Katholieke Universiteit Nijmegen. I consider it a loss not to have had you earlier as a sparring partner. I hope that we will be able to continue profiling the research on cross-border interaction now that I have completed this dissertation.

Richard Raap, thanks for assisting me with a part of the data entry, for the interesting discussions we had about the importance of networking for starting entrepreneurs, and for your friendship. I want to thank Maarten Donkers for the stimulating discussions we had about the internationalisation process of firms. I thank Paul van 't Veer for the animating and enlightening conversations we had about cooperation and networking between entrepreneurs in the border zones of Growth Triangles. I thank Giovanni Kerkhof for his bright and charismatic ideas during our talks about entrepreneurship and social (inter)action in general.

Erwin van der Krabben was my roommate during the first few years of my research. These were very pleasant years together, in building U of the University. Erwin has shown me around in the world of PhD students. Moreover, Erwin, being an inhabitant of Nijmegen, has prepared me, without our being aware of it, for my actual function at the Katholieke Universiteit Nijmegen.

Ton Langenhuijzen was my roommate during the last few years of my research. Ton, thanks for a wonderful time at B517. The daily coffee breaks with you, Talitha Feenstra, and of course with Paul Driessen provided a very welcome and highly amusing relief from my daily occupations. Paul and Ton, I also want to thank you for untiringly listening to my rambling about 'borders', for commenting on parts of my dissertation, for your support and friendship, and for allowing me to use your offices at the Katholieke Universiteit Brabant during the last few weekends of the writing process.

Noemi Padrón-Fumero was my colleague at the University in Tilburg for several periods. She personalises my love for Spain. She taught me the meaning of the idea of friendship at a distance. Friendship knows no borders, only distances. We human beings are the true countries, not the borders drawn on maps. Noemi, the tape with the cello music of Rostropovich you gave me for my birthday turned out to be a very important and inspiring present. I wrote my dissertation with the player on auto-reverse. The banana tree you gave me when you left the Katholieke Universiteit Brabant is now growing up in Nijmegen.

Erwin de Wolff, I hope you will allow me to thank you for your creativity and efforts with regard to the layout of this book and other books and reports during the work for my PhD. Your work has been invaluable. The many hours we spent together working on the design, after which we drank a beer in the café, meant more to me than just the aesthetic appeal of the result. Thank you for your friendship and tranquillity. Thanks in advance, too, for making the photographs during the degree ceremony. I have told you before that, with your skills in photography and design, you should start your own bureau. You are *very* welcome for this first advertisement.

Gert-Jan, Marck, Marloes, Paul, Sander, Sanne, and Willemijn, editors of OIAaa, the magazine for PhD students at the Katholieke Universiteit Brabant, thanks for the wonderful time we spent together; it was a relief to get away from *academic* writing sometimes. We, especially we, know now, that the saying is right. Who writes, stays. So tell me, when will the new OIAaa appear?

Rob Aalbers, I am happy to have met you at the University at an early stage of my time as a research student. For a moment there, I was afraid that there would be no 'normal' PhD students. I also found in you a friend for philosophising about the knowledge I gathered. René Zoon is the Master of Ceremonies of laughter. We go way back together. René, for me you personalise the relaxation from it all, and putting it all into perspective. Woe betides those who take themselves too seriously! René and Rob, thanks for your willingness to act as 'paranimf' at my degree ceremony. You regard it as an honour. I regard it as a greater honour to know you will be beside and behind me.

In spite of the relatively short time I have now been working at the Katholieke Universiteit Nijmegen, I already have the pleasure of being on friendly terms with the people who work there. Thanks especially to the people of the 'regular breaks club', Arjan O., Arjan S., Froukje, Jeroen, Karel, Marco, Roelof, Tim, Ursula, and Willem, for the pleasant atmosphere and the interest you have shown. I thank Karel Martens and Daphne Kooistra, my companions at dinner and after drinks, for our most amusing and interesting talks on the life and work of PhD students and many other subjects.

Of course, I do not do justice to all the colleagues whom I do not name personally. They determine, to an important extent, the atmosphere at work. I thank you all, my colleagues at EIT, ERAC, the Katholieke Universiteit Brabant, and at the Katholieke Universiteit Nijmegen, where I am but a newcomer, for your support, interest, and the agreeable, informal atmosphere you all created.

To the family of my girlfriend, Ingrid, that is, José, Dick, Robert, and Sandra, thanks for your warm interest in my work, your personal support, and the pleasant homely atmosphere that always helped me to relax entirely.

The last words I reserved for my parents, Mieke and Henk, my sister Jolanda, and my love, Ingrid. Expressing my gratitude to them is most difficult for me. For how can I thank them, who love me unconditionally? Know that the good you saw and see in me has come into being and remained part of me thanks to you.

Finally, my words of love go to Ingrid. More than ever, I have come to realise that love is a mutual sacrifice. I know now, my brain has been enriched with many thoughts these past years. My heart, though, often wondered what the trouble was for, for it was already illuminated.

Henk van Houtum

Contents

Chapter 1

Introduction

If the world is a global village, then the nations are the houses, and the people living in these houses are the villagers. In this village, there are now some two hundred houses and around five billion people. The houses protect the inhabitants against undesired influences from outside, such as storms and insecurity. Moreover, they offer privacy. They demarcate a territory, which is controlled to a large extent by its inhabitants. These consider themselves sovereign with regard to their own homes. Above all, there exists a strong feeling of affection towards the own home. The inhabitants of the houses, furthermore, have set up rules for themselves that differ from those set up by the people living in neighbouring houses. The rules and opinions governing one's neighbours are not necessarily one's own.

Living together, therefore, requires tolerance and solidarity. Most of the people in these houses live next to each other peacefully. As the saying goes, good neighbours are important. But the fences surrounding the houses are also considered important. Products, money and services flow in and out of the various homes quite easily. For people, the thresholds are somewhat higher. Tolerance and solidarity, quite literally, have boundaries sometimes. First of all, not everybody is welcome. The house is soon felt to be too small for people who do not belong to one's own family. Anything affecting the privacy within the home, affecting one's ability to be in complete control, is soon experienced as irritating. Neighbourhood quarrels still constitute environmental problem number one in the global village. Secondly, the crossing of a fence is a move out of one's own, familiar culture into a different and strange one. Imagining oneself in another culture requires a great deal of tolerance and solidarity as well. Seen in this light, truly 'global citizens' still seem hard to find in the global village.

This dissertation studies the influence of fences upon the economic relationships between firms belonging to the various neighbours in one specific 'global district' in which people have decided to unite, the European Union. The dissertation approaches this subject from an economic-geographical point of view.

1.1 The notion of borders

Borders tend to prevent freedom of movement (cf. Jones, 1945; Clark, 1994). Within the European Union, however, with the implementation of an internal market in 1993, free traffic of commodities, services, persons and capital has been made possible. In actual practice, small hindrances with regard to persons and services still exist, but the ambitions of the European Union are clear: to achieve a common European Economic and Monetary Union, with one common currency.

The creation of the European Union has spawned a vast amount of literature on the economic consequences of the unification of the various countries. Surprisingly little however, has yet been written about *the influence* of national borders and national identity, as an offshoot of national borders, upon the interactivity between entrepreneurs of different nationalities. Surprisingly, because it would seem that this influence specifically may be of importance to the economic integration process.

Moreover, the issue of the perception of individual entrepreneurs of cross-border economic integration has rarely been considered the focal point of the analyses on economic integration. Attention mostly tends to focus on the history or the (macro economic) pace and potential gains of European (economic, monetary and political) integration (see, e.g. Tinbergen, 1991). Especially in economics, borders tend to be considered in relation to tariffs, quotas, duties and so on - their study is mostly narrowed down to the discussion of free trade versus protectionism and the consequences of economic integration. In international economics, as a consequence, a border - if defined at all - is therefore considered a (deliberate) barrier to free trade (see, e.g. Balassa, 1961; Tella, 1982). The border is an instrument, used in the interest of economic policies: which policy with regard to our national border yields the best results in terms of welfare, nationalisation, or internationalisation? Moreover, terms such as 'border', 'boundary', or 'frontier' are to be found in practically none of the text books on economics; the same holds true for terms such as 'nation', and 'national identity'. This terminology seems to be reserved exclusively for political and social geographers, political philosophers or historians. Apparently these terms are not fitting in the picture international economics and international business theories have built for themselves. I disagree with this state of affairs. In this work, it shall be argued that the exclusion of the study of the phenomenon of borders from international economics is a strange neglect that ought to be repaired. Borders are more than just barriers to free trade and are more important to economic (inter)activity than economics is apt or willing to tell us. Rumley and Minghi (1991) stated that traditional border landscape research has not attracted any significant amount of attention from other, non-geographical scholars. I therefore agree with them in as far as economic theory is concerned. It appears that the study of the economics of borders has much to do with the study of the borders of economics.

On the other hand, in *geographical* studies on borders one may discern an inclination to stick to case studies. For the most part, the geographical studies on borders are politico-geographical (cf. House, 1981, p. 456). Minghi (1963) enumerates the most important fields of study with regard to borders, which remain valid today (see also Rumley and Minghi, 1991; Prescott, 1987; Paasi, 1996). These mostly concern the study of borders in disputed areas, the study of the evolution of borders, and the effects of changes in the demarcation of boundaries. The concept of borders is thus translated to indicate functional territories; the social and psychological explanation of the existence of borders and their impact is much less often investigated.
It would go beyond the scope of this dissertation to treat all of the fields of political geography extensively. I therefore refer to Minghi (1963) for a more elaborate discussion on the subject. After having touched upon the progress made in the various fields he concludes that, in political geography, the emphasis increasingly tends towards function-oriented studies. In these studies, the exceptions are highlighted rather than the rule; the effects of boundary changes and disputes are disproportionally accentuated in comparison to the influence and evolution of borders. Minghi recommends that more attention should be given to the 'normal situation' of borders. The fact that borders, as political dividers, separate peoples of different nationalities, identities, and of a different iconographic make-up should be more widely recognised. A measure must be sought for

> *...a boundary's viability as such a divider. For this, we must concern ourselves with the role of the boundary in determining spatial patterns of selected behavioural activity, which is itself an indicator of iconographic attitudes.* (Minghi, p. 428)

This is why, he argued, in determining the impact of a border, investigations into the spatial pattern of social behaviour should be made at the primary level, in the sociological field as well as in the cultural and economic areas.

In 1991 Minghi, this time together with Rumley, continued to argue that politico-geographical studies, having introduced the border as a subject of study, tend to be 'overly descriptive and classificatory'(p. 3). There have been quite a few descriptive studies of borders and border regions (particularly in North America and Western Europe). These analyses are, in general, not trying to test theoretical assumptions. Most border studies therefore suffer from what Rumley and Minghi call 'the descriptive/unique case syndrome' (1991, p. 3). 'There has been a lack of real concern with the development of border landscape theory, the implicit assumption of uniqueness, and even a general disinterest in theoretical and conceptual questions' (*idem*, p.4).

In economic geography, the spatial impact of borders (and border regions) was already an issue in classic works like that of Christaller (1933), Giersch (1949) and Lösch (1940/1954). The attention was nevertheless mostly focused on the impact of borders on (the choice of) the locations of firms in border regions of the home country. The focus was not so much on cross-border economic integration between firms. In recent years, probably triggered by the creation of an internal market in Europe, new promising theoretical concepts on cross-border integration are coming up in geography. Especially the works of Ratti (1993ab) and Paasi (1996) must be mentioned in this respect. Ratti makes a plea for a transaction-costs based theory on cross-border economic alliances and Paasi includes the issues of consciousness and identity in the geographical developments across borders. These works will be dealt with in this study.

In present times, most of the studies in geography include in their definition of 'borders' the legal borderline between states as well as the frontier of political and cultural contest which stretches away from the borderline (see, e.g. O'Dowd and Wilson, 1996). This definition makes clear that a study of borders cannot neglect these topics of political and cultural power. In principal, the study of borders is interdisciplinary (Rumley and Minghi, 1991; Clark, 1994).
Still, much of the research on the influence of borders has remained, as Clark recently said it, '...strictly within the domain of a particular discipline, without reference to or knowledge of efforts in other fields' (Clark, 1994, p. 68). While an interdisciplinary approach of borders is necessary, it is difficult to realise. Maybe as a consequence, interdisciplinary theory development explaining the influence of borders and the position of border regions still have been relatively scarce (Clark, 1994). As House put it:

> *There is a need in border landscapes studies to move away from a fixation with visible function toward a consideration of border landscapes as the product of a set of cultural, economic, political interactions and processes occurring in space.*
> House (1982), cited in Rumley and Minghi (1991), p. 4

In this dissertation I will try to further the insights on entrepreneurial perceptions of borders and economic interactions across borders and test the theoretical hypotheses used in the analysis. I believe, there is a need to integrate the macro-level of the influence of borders on the economic integration processes with the micro-level of perceptions on the influence of borders in international economic interactions. In order to study these international economic interactions on a micro-level, I will focus on the development of *cross-border economic relations between firms*.

1.2 Cross-border economic relations

The discipline of economics studies the development of exchange activities or transactions in the light of scarcity of resources. These exchange activities, in our modern world, are handled financially, by means of the transfer of money. Transactions occur between two parties: customers and suppliers, or what is generally called demand and supply. The transaction may be one-off. In that case, the transactions are effected on markets. When the transactions are not effected on a market, but between customers and suppliers within an organisation, economic theory, *i.e.* the transaction costs theory (Williamson, 1975, 1985), speaks of the emergence of an enterprise. The present study examines the formation of bilateral economic relationships between firms across national borders. An economic relationship is not an independent organisation. It is not an enterprise. Still, it is more than a one-off transaction between parties. Thus, it is not a market form either. In this study, the relationship is regarded as involving a financial transaction, which moreover takes place between two enterprises. An economic relationship is here defined as: *An agreement between two different enterprises, which may or may not have been put in writing, that provides for the regular occurrence of a commercial activity or transaction, or for the placement of the commercial activity or transaction under a certain division of joint administration or management.*

The perspective of economic relationships has been chosen for two reasons. In the first place, economic relationships are essential to the individual company. A business needs a (number of) stable client(s) and/or supplier(s). Economic relationships, moreover, offer businesses the possibility of outsourcing certain parts of the production process, thereby achieving cost savings. The point is therefore not so much whether a company has economic relationships, but how these are structured and spread in space. Both these last aspects render the study of economic relations in an international context interesting. Moreover, the degree of clustering of business relations (and networks) is generally regarded, in economics, as an indication of flexibility and dynamism (Boekema and Kamann, 1989). Economists point to the influence of close-knit networks on the creation of a stable environment, and the possibility of responding in concert to rapidly changing market demands (see, e.g. Porter, 1990; Storper, 1993). Finally, recent literature also refers to the improved opportunities for developing and diffusing innovative activities as a consequence of economic relationships between companies (Oerlemans, 1996).

The second reason is that the European Commission expects the formation of economic relationships between companies to have numerous positive effects for the European Union. The Commission aims principally at the positive effects the economic relationships may have on the *cross-border* interaction and *cohesion* between the economies of the member states and (border) regions in Europe. National borders in Europe have often forced a rupture between neighbouring - and previously often closely related - regional identities in many such border regions. Border regions are generally nationally oriented, giving only little attention to 'the other side'. The idea, then, is that border-regional economies could benefit from the increase of the amount of cross-border networking. The formation of economic relationships could lead to a more cost-effective and efficient spatial division of employment (Church and Reid, 1995; Nijkamp, 1993ab; Von Malchus, 1975). In the so-called INTERREG programme, the commission has explicitly declared itself in favour of the stimulation of economic relationships across the borders (European Commission, 1990). The policy aims at 'providing stimuli for the foundation and development of co-operative networks across internal borders, and to link these networks to larger community networks.' (*idem*, 1990).

1.3 Euregions

In the meantime, many cross-border co-operations have come into existence along most of the internal borders, for example along the Dutch-Belgian border (Kessen, 1992; Van Houtum, 1993, 1994). On the Dutch side of the border, these co-operations are mostly institutionalised in so-called *Euregions* (see figure 1.1). These Euregions, which embrace municipalities and parts of provinces on both sides of the internal borders, have approached the state border as a reason and challenge for co-operation and networking (Beek, 1996; Corvers *et al.*, 1994ab; Van Houtum, 1993, 1994). The European Commission, meanwhile, attempts to encourage the formation of Euregional networks through its INTERREG programme.
The Euregions are to provide the institutional framework within which economic and social actors may come to formal and informal contacts and relations across national borders. One of the objectives of the INTERREG programma is to aid border regions with peculiar development problems, and to provide stimuli for the emergence of co-operations across national borders.

Recent empirical research in border regions at the Dutch border has shown that cross-border co-operation in border regions, as for the international co-operation between medium-sized and small businesses, should not be overestimated (Dagevos *et al.*, 1992; Corvers *et al.*, 1994ab; Van den Tillaart *et al.*, 1994; Van Houtum *et al.*, 1996). Despite the research already conducted, it must be concluded that the role of the state border has remained unclear from the empirical point of view. Moreover, it has not yet been examined in a systematic manner which mechanisms lie at the source of the formation of bilateral cross-border economic relations. Most of the articles and books that have been published on Euregions focus on the administrative and legal aspects of the European Commission's administration, and on the functioning of organisations within the border regions. A connection with the theory concerning the internationalisation process among companies and the organisation of transnational or Euregional networks is seldom drawn. Verification of the - mostly voluntary - administrative concepts in the light of empirical reality is all too often neglected.

Figure 1.1 - The Euregions along the Dutch border

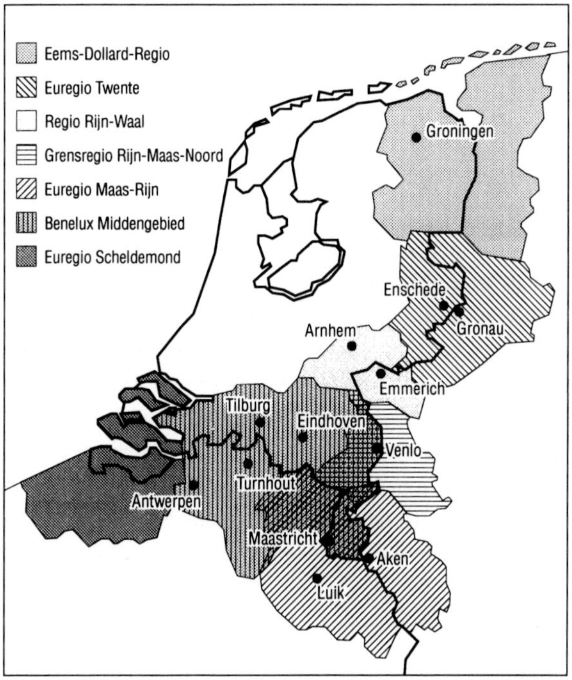

Illustratie: DGS Visueel

The present study aims to achieve a better understanding of the influence of the border in the economic exchange patterns in these Euregions. It makes an effort to indicate the 'blank spots' on the map of the formation of cross-border economic relationships in these Euregions and, where possible, to fill them in. To this end, existing views and concepts of the realisation of cross-border economic relationships will be analysed. Where possible, these will be integrated into a more comprehensive whole. Furthermore, new ideas and concepts will be introduced and tested for their relevance with regard to the existing border-regional context. Finally, directions for further study shall be indicated.

Because of the limited time allowed for the composition of a dissertation, it has proved impossible to survey all the companies functioning in European border regions. For this reason, the research results described in this dissertation have been derived from a number of regions along the border between the Netherlands and Belgium; other border regions within the European Community have not been studied as intensively. The border regions between the Netherlands and Belgium are especially interesting because a strong historical relationship exists between these two neighbouring countries (Kossmann, 1976; Mulder, 1994). Within this framework, it is very interesting to examine and discover how contemporary companies in the border regions of the Netherlands and Belgium relate to each other, and to study the relative importance of the border in the mutual economic relationships between them.

1.4 Objectives of the dissertation

The objective of this study is fivefold.

- In the first place, this study attempts to define the term 'border' within an economic-geographical context. An effort is made to achieve a categorisation of the influence of borders on the cross-border actions of and interactions between entrepreneurs of different societies.
- Secondly, this study examines and elucidates the degree to which a border is a dividing line between businesses in neighbouring regions of differing nationalities.
- The third objective of the present study is provide a critical overview of the dominant economic theories on cross-border economic relations.
- Fourthly, it attempts to provide insights into the determinants of the having or not having and the number of international economic relations between firms.
- The fifth and final objective of the present study is to explore and explain the process of the emergence of successful cross-border economic relationships between enterprises.

1.5 Definition of the central question treated in the dissertation

The question central to this research project is defined as follows:

What is the economic-geographical influence of the state border upon the frequency and number of economic relationships between enterprises in border regions of the Netherlands and Belgium, and what explains the successful formation of these cross-border economic relationships?

1.6 Structure of the dissertation

This dissertation comprises three parts.

The first part, embracing chapters 2 to 4, contains a discussion on the existing theories and aims at constructing a theoretical model of the development of cross-border economic relations on the basis of relevant literature. The discussion on the existing theories is divided in two parts: *the influence of a state border* and *the formation of cross-border economic relations between firms*. The influence of state borders is explored in chapter 2. A distinction is made between four possible influences. In chapter 3, the most influential economic theories on the formation of international economic relations are discussed and evaluated. Concretely, the transaction costs approach, the international network approach, and the psychic distance approach will be submitted to critical analysis. Subsequently, in chapter 4, a comprehensive model will be developed that will serve as a descriptive and explanatory model of the development of cross-border economic relations between firms. On the basis of this model, the research hypotheses are formulated.

In the second part of the dissertation, embracing chapters 5 to 7, the theoretical model that is proposed in chapter 4 will be empirically tested against firms located in Dutch and Belgian border regions. In chapter 5, the design and delineation of the empirical research will be discussed. In chapter 6, the factual pattern of the sales and economic relations of the responding firms will be described. This overview of the factual activities the firms are engaged in makes clear to what extent the border is to be seen as a dividing line in international economic space. In chapter 7 the results of the model and the tests of the hypotheses will be discussed and explained.

The third and final part of this dissertation, chapter 8, touches upon the confrontation between the research hypotheses and the empirical results. Disparities between the expectations and the results will be indicated and where possible, explained. The most important insights and results gained in the course of this dissertation will be summarised in an epilogue.

Part 1

Theory

Chapter 2

The influence of borders

2.1 Introduction

Borders are human artefacts, lines in space, drawn on a map by human beings, at a certain moment in time and for certain political or military purposes. Yet borders ought not to be regarded as an epistemological subject alone. Their impact stretches far beyond political or military affairs. The consequences of that line are often less manifest as their marks in space. National borders, for instance, may represent natural, cultural, psychological, economic, political, or geographical dividing lines. It cannot be stated *a priori* and with great certainty that all these different types of borders will follow the same pattern in space. To the contrary, it may be assumed that each type will have a different impact on a certain territory and the people that live in it. In order to fully comprehend the influence of borders on economic interaction between enterprises across borders, one first has to study the very essence of borders. Questions like what are borders, why are there borders and what are the consequences of borders on social identity and behaviour of entrepreneurs, then come into play. This first chapter of the dissertation deals with these topics.

In spite of their unique character, it is possible to define a typology of the influence of borders on human interaction by combining the various theoretical insights put forward in the relevant literature. Four typologies may in fact be distilled from contemporary literature. Moreover, I will demonstrate that, in order to be able to grasp the content of the current discussions to its full extent, an appeal has to be made to other sciences than economics and geography alone.
In the following sections, four distinctions shall be analysed, *viz.* natural versus artificial borders (section 2.2); open versus closed borders (section 2.3); functional versus affective borders (section 2.4); and concrete versus abstract borders (section 2.5).

2.2 Natural versus artificial borders

The distinction traditionally made is that between natural and artificial or man-made borders (see, e.g. Boerman, 1923; Hartshorne, 1933; Pounds, 1954; Leimgruber, 1980, 1991). It is based upon the following line of reasoning: all borders that have not come into existence through nature, *i.e.* that do not follow seas, rivers, mountains and the like, are made by human beings. Such territorial borders are then usually described as 'artificial', as opposed to natural borders. See for an excellent overview of the notion of 'natural borders', Rykiel (1995).

I believe, essentially agreeing in this respect with Broek (1941), Jones (1943), Racek (1983) and Leimgruber (1980, 1991), that the term 'natural borders' is a false and misleading one. The term 'natural border' suggests that there exists such a thing as a 'God-given' border that cannot possibly be crossed. The idea of natural borders then takes on a strongly ideological character. It should be noted that the term 'natural borders' is most often used by states and dictators who want to enlarge their territory. It is significant in this respect, according to Glasner and De Blij (1980), that while territories have often been expanded because 'they ought to follow their natural borders', they have never been willingly restricted or reduced to their 'natural borders'.

The political geographer Ratzel, most notably, interpreted the term 'natural borders' in a very literal manner (1897). He regarded the state as an organism with natural borders, in which the borders form the 'epidermis' of the state-organism, providing protection and allowing for exchanges with the outer world. Ratzel's evolutionary concept of borders led to his conviction that every state has an idea of the natural borders of its territorial dominion (what he called 'the space conception'). Because of the dynamics of inflow and outflow, the fixation of a border's position is to be regarded as temporary - meaning that the state-organism's process of expansion and contraction has come to a temporary standstill.

However, as Broek already argued as early as 1941, a natural border according to the above definition refers to a natural obstacle, and obstacles cannot be equated with borders. While natural obstacles may lead to a low density of interaction across that obstacle, borders imply the exclusion of people from and inclusion of people within a certain territory by means of the enforcement of power and control.

On a satellite map, no borders can be discerned - the entire area is natural. At most, something that might be called 'territorial variation' can be found in the natural world. Human beings and other animals, however, create and perceive territorial borders. The term 'territorial borders' refers to differences in membership of a species or group, not to differences in natural space. The distinction between 'natural' and 'artificial' therefore is at best an odd one. If 'natural' is equated with 'biological', then political borders ought to be defined as 'natural' since the urge to establish territorial borders for self-preservation is a fundamental aspect of animal existence, displayed in the behaviour of all living creatures. Natural borders, in reality, are *physiographic* barriers to human interaction in space - such as mountains, seas, or rivers (see also Leimgruber, 1980).

It may be concluded that either one should speak only of natural borders since all borders are natural, i.e. inspired by nature, or the term 'natural borders' should not be used at all. In the latter case, which is the view adhered to in this work, use of the term 'border' should be restricted to the territorial demarcation constructed by living creatures that are able to categorise, and that are conscious of their environment.

2.3 Open versus closed borders

The whole issue of borders would not be so challenging and interesting a subject if man would not want them to be changed. Borders are subject to continuous change. The urge to make conquests in terms of territory, to obtain the right to own a stretch of land, is an intriguing drive in man. Once the mountains are crossed, the seas have been dared and the sky has been conquered, outer space is waiting patiently. Once the moon has been explored, a desire to search for a new human territory in the universe comes into existence as a sign of dissatisfaction with the present territories, all of which are referred to as conquests. This implies that over time, many exploratory expeditions on earth have been undertaken, small and big wars have been fought, tribes have been chased, inheritances have been distributed to divide power, and many marriages have been concluded to obtain power - all for the sake of a perceived or hoped-for improvement in the demarcation of a certain space.

The nowadays popular concept of 'globalisation' could be seen as the modern economic version and modern case in point for the intrinsic search for new territories and the opening of borders. Over the past few years, the notion of globalisation has gained rapidly in importance. The image of a new, globalised world order is presented to us primarily by the media, by multinationals and politicians. This often mentioned concept of 'globalisation' in economics and politics has come to carry a mythical connotation: We are living in 'a global village'.

On the other hand, the very reason that there still are borders, is not meaningless either. Apparently they serve a purpose. This section of chapter 2 deals with the second main typology of borders that is of interest to this study, that is between open and closed borders. The question to answer is what influence is more important, the opening of borders or the conserving of them? These two different views on borders will be analysed into more detail in the next two subsections.

2.3.1 Globalisation, the case in point for open borders

In combination with mankind's ever present longing to explore and go beyond known borders, it is said that nowadays the 'closedness' and rigidity of state borders is decreasing at a higher speed than ever before, mainly because of the emergence of new means of communication and transport. The immense technological developments in transportation, whether by plane, boat, automobile, train, the media, e-mail or the Internet, are said to have significantly increased the

time-space convergence on a global scale these past decades. If he has the time and means, modern man seems capable of travelling the world, be it physically or through communication media. By 'zapping' to another channel on television or radio, or by changing sites on the Internet, the whole world seems to be within modern man's reach. Holiday trips to 'exotic' regions are not exceptional anymore, a fact that contributes to the global integration view. The globalisation of information, moreover, contributes to this view as well. Noise and chatter can be heard from all over the world.
Finally, and most importantly for this study, capital in search of the highest profits is nowadays said to travel the globe massively and more intensively than ever before. Multinationals and their deployment of technological advances are indicated as the driving forces behind these developments (see, e.g. Dicken, 1992; Johnston 1984; Levitt, 1983; Lubbers, 1995). It is argued that traditional methods of analysing economies, on a global, national, regional as well as individual level, are coming together unremittingly. Economies and related issues, such as environmental problems, politics, and the exchange of information (telecommunications) no longer seem to acknowledge borders or distances. The literature on globalisation argues that all these different worlds are being interlinked, thus encouraging the formation of 'one world'. Despite the pleonastic sound of it, 'a global world' is said to be formed; 'The world is our village', 'a global marketplace', 'a borderless world' all according to Ohmae (1990), 'The world is our oyster', according to Levitt (1983). The advocates of the globalisation view maintain that this means that regions and states are in permanent contact with other regions and states, a situation that is known as 'the welding effect' (Maillat, 1991).

Obviously, institutions and organisations founded for the purpose of integration try to stimulate this effect. Illustrative is that the Dutch government (Ministerie van Economische Zaken, 1990ab) published two memoranda at the beginning of this decade, one entitled *Economy with Open Borders*, the other *Regions without Borders*. These clearly show that there is no space left for a one-sided analysis and exercise of policies in contemporary economics. According to the authors of these documents (the Dutch Ministery of Economic Affairs), it is essential that specific account be taken of the trends accompanying an economy on its way to internationalisation, and that these demand an adequate response (see also De Smidt, 1991;Van Dijck, 1992; Van Dijck *et al.*, 1994).

The European integration process is both an excellent and ongoing example of a situation in which governments have agreed to relax national borders so as to encourage economic growth for all members of the Community. European integration is meant to create a *de facto* unified and borderless economic space.

Translated to human activities, an 'open border' situation refers to a *centrifugal* orientation of the actors contained within the border. It is a move towards and beyond the external limits of the demarcated territory (cf. Leimgruber, 1991). In the case of centrifugal orientation, free movement is prevalent. The border is then seen as a contact line, as a meeting place between nations or economic subsystems.

Other scholars (cf. Gottmann, 1973; Prescott, 1987; Ratti, 1993a) refer to open borders as *frontiers* (Prescott, 1987, p.1). Before the delimitation of land and the demarcation of borders started to become an issue, there were frontiers. The word '*frontier*' stems from the notion of 'a front', pointing to the spearhead of civilisation (Taylor, 1993). The frontier is, therefore, oriented towards the outside and is in fact a zone of contact. 'Frontiers are zones of varying widths which were common features of the political landscape centuries ago', wrote Prescott in 1987 (p.1). For the people contained within these frontiers, the possibilities towards the exterior are more important than the demarcation line *per se*. In this view, therefore, borders are 'outward-oriented', flexible limits.

On the other hand there are closed borders, which refer to the force countering that which functions in an open border situation. This is called the *centripetal* effect of borders - the orientation towards the interior of the people inhabiting the enclosed territory. The demarcation of a territory with a boundary line results in a tendency on the part of actors within the new unity to turn away from the borders, see figure 2.1 (Heigl, 1978). Distancing and segregation between the newborn spatial units is the result (Johnston *et al.*, 1994).

Figure 2.1 - The centripetal effect of borders

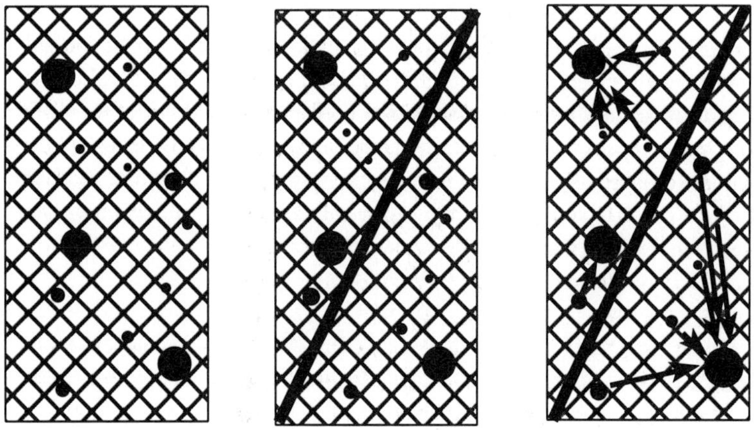

Adapted from Heigl (1978)

The centripetal effect, as shown in figure 2.1, is the effect borders are known for in the first place: as sovereignty marks of state, as limits of jurisdiction. The centripetal effect points to the cut-off effect of borders. This type of border is also referred to as *boundary* (cf. Gottmann, 1973; Prescott, 1987; Ratti, 1993a; Taylor, 1993). The use of boundaries is very recent. Prior to the twentieth century, the rulers of territories did not define the edges of their territories in terms of fixed boundaries (Johnston *et al.*, 1994). However, under the global tide of human settlement, the emergence of citizenship and the growth in economic development, frontiers have now been replaced by boundaries (*idem*, 1994). The word 'boundary' is derived from 'bounds', implying the existence and administration of territorial limits. Boundaries, therefore, are political lines in space.

In terms of centripetal versus centrifugal forces, the notion of globalisation suggests that the centrifugal effect of borders is setting in at a higher speed than ever before.

2.3.2 The raison d'être of borders, the case in point for closed borders

Why are all borders not open? To put it differently, why are there any borders at all? The simplest answer to this question, of course, is that borders serve a purpose - they have a function. Borders are identifying marks in space, made by humans; they are expressions of sovereignty, of power and independence. Borders express the controlling of space. That is the *raison d'être* of borders. As a consequence, they have military, juridical, welfare, fiscal, and ideological functions (Guichonnet and Raffestin, 1974; Raffestin, 1974).

A more comprehensive answer to this particular question must however be sought in the aspect of social cohesion associated with territoriality (Van der Wusten, 1997). Mankind has an inherent tendency to form social groups. Human spatial borders are the result of the differentiation of groups in space. Socialisation in group membership is intrinsically spatial (Johnston, 1994). Human actions (or those of groups) are irreversible in space as well as in time; these actions are manifested in *a place in space*. In his philosophical essay, *The Production of Space*, Lefebvre emphasises man's inherent desire to demarcate this space and the inevitability of his doing so (1991):

> There is no stage however, at which 'man' does not demarcate, beacon or sign his space, leaving traces that are both symbolic and practical; changes of direction and turns in this space always need to be presented, and 'he' meets this figurative need either by taking his own body as a centre or by reference to other bodies. (Lefebvre, 1991, p. 192).

Leimgruber stated it as follows: 'Boundaries are human creations of territoriality, reflecting a basic human need to live in a bounded space' (1991, p. 43). Mankind (as well as every other living creature) is able to, and will, demarcate this space explicitly to create his territory. Hence, for human beings, space ought to be seen as a collection of places (cf. Sack, 1986). Sack defines territoriality as 'the attempt by an individual or group to affect, influence or control people and/or phenomena, by delimiting and asserting control over a geographical area' (1986, p. 19). Spatial units, therefore, only become territories when borders are used to affect behaviour by controlling access to the spatial unit (Sack, 1986). The role of the government is obviously of great importance in this process. For the construction of a demarcation line in the activities of the unit's inhabitants marks the beginning of territoriality, of the explicit marking of space. It also marks the beginning of protecting that territory, since territoriality by definition means (the attempt to) control. Seen in this light, a classification of borders as more open versus more closed is the outcome of the interference of a controlling power in a community.

The exclusive right to use a certain territory combined with the inner belief that one should take care of one's own citizens and protect them from extra-territorial hostility, makes it difficult for the controlling power to relax its borders, the marks in space that delimit its territory. This need to take care of and wish the best for the inhabitants of one's territory could well be combined with a relaxation of border control, but then the governing power would lose some of its strength. Political power depends on continual reinforcement for sustenance. This is what Lefebvre (1991) refers to as 'the vicious circle of political authority'. For this reason, it is in the interest of the state to promote cohesion, in a form fitted to the ideas and ideology of the government, within the territory. The dominance of a state over a certain domain is therefore an important means of manipulating the social relationships within that territory (Van der Wusten, 1997). In his article on the functions of the state, Van der Wusten (1997) refers to the publication of Michael Mann, *The Autonomous Power of the State* (1984), in which this social aspect of the state is also emphasised. The state, according to Mann, has the possibility to determine to an important extent the degree to which the borders are open or closed, and to steer or even direct social circulation, because of its connection with the territory (cf. Mann, 1984, as cited in Van der Wusten, 1997). The marking of borders must therefore be considered the most distinctive and dominant political expression of modern-day territorialism.

2.3.2.1 The consequences of centripetal behaviour

Man's inherent urge to push the limits, that is, to expand his territory, does not always harmonise with his desire to delimit his territory. Exploration and demarcation go hand in hand. A rather ambivalent attitude is noticeable in this respect. Throughout the history of Europe, there have always been such dialectic processes of both integrationism and protectionism. To put this in terms of borders: borders have been both more open and more closed. They cannot be 'frozen' in time, one can only freeze them on a map. But the map is not the territory. A state border will be open for certain kinds of activities and closed to others, but the specific activities for which it is open or closed will vary over time (see Giaoutzi and Kamann, 1993; Kamann, 1993a; Ratti, 1993a). This 'filtering' function of the border reflects human nature. The crux about borders is therefore that the implicit desire to change the borders, the desire to discover and/or to conquer, to annex the neighbouring land to one's own or to lure its inhabitants to do so voluntarily goes hand in hand with the need to consolidate one's own community, and to secure a sufficient degree of unity and power to protect the community against undesirable influences from the outside.

The consequences of this centripetal behaviour are twofold. The first consequence of the centripetal pressure upon national space is that areas along the borders are considered the edges of the community, that is, they are regarded as peripheral (see, e.g. Gottmann, 1980; Rumley, 1991). Border regions may be called peripheral in more than one sense (see Rokkan and Urwin, 1983). The most obvious reason is their geographical position. The territorial centre wishes to secure itself against undesired influences from the outside. Such securing occurs at the borders. As a consequence, large and politically important cities are rarely located in the direct vicinity of a country's borders. Those cities that do lie at the edge of a country have usually come into existence for commercial reasons (trade). Important waterways and motorways near a border usually play an important role in such developments.
Culturally, border regions are what could be called 'zones of overlap' between two neighbouring countries. The national feelings of identity and loyalty for one of those two countries are not always manifest *a priori* (Augelli, 1980). Border regions are often considered as culturally 'peripheral' by the inhabitants of the home country, and as foreign by the inhabitants of the neighbouring country.
Moreover, the influence of the border regions in national politics and policies is most often limited. Finally, the centre-periphery relationship also reigns in economic matters and is recognisable in the often unbalanced division of wealth between the centre and the periphery of a country (Crush, 1980; Hansen, 1977b, 1983).

The second consequence is at least as important. Especially in view of the consideration that border regions may be peripheral in more than one way, it would seem reasonable for border regions to associate themselves with border regions on the other side of the border, which after all have to face the same problems. The difficulty is that the border - that may sometimes function as a true barrier - hampers this kind of association. Seen in this respect, a border can be viewed as a barrier to interaction (see Giaoutzi, Suarez-Villa, and Stratigea, 1993; Kamann, 1993a; Ratti, 1993a; Suarez-Villa, Giaoutzi and Stratigea, 1992). Barriers, in the words of Nijkamp *et al.* (1990, p. 239), are obstacles in space or time that -apart from normal average distance friction costs in spatial interaction - impede a smooth transfer or free movement of information and activities. These barriers can cause nonlinear shock-wise *discontinuities* (*idem*). Below, in figure 2.2, the effect of the border functioning as a barrier on interaction between border regions, is represented schematically (*idem*).

Figure 2.2 - Discontinuity in interaction between border regions

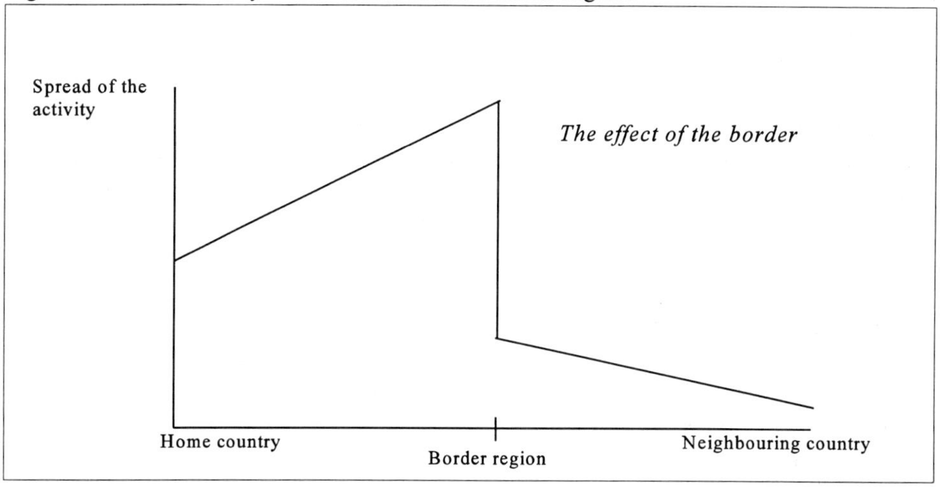

The great challenge for research is to analyse to which extent the pattern suggested in figure 2.2 is empirically valid. There have been several attempts to quantify the inhibiting impact of borders on the interaction pattern. Bröcker (1984) estimated the impact of national borders as trade barriers in Europe by means of a gravity model. In his approach, two determinants of international trade barriers were taken into account: the costs of covering geographical distance and the costs of crossing the border. Bröcker found that the average impact of borders in Western European countries equalled the effect of 375 kilometres' distance, implying a reduction of international trade to one-sixth of the value normally expected if the respective trade flows do not have to cross a border. In Bröcker's model, borders are thus regarded as an element of distance costs. Regions that are geographically close to each other may therefore be separated by large 'economic distances' due to the presence of a border.

The argument that the presence of borders between two regions can be regarded as an increase in the distance between them can be traced back to the classical works of economic geographers, like Giersch and Lösch, who theorised on the economics of locations (see also, Hansen, 1977ab). Giersch (1949/1950) developed a locational theory including an analysis of the consequences of the location of political borders. He argued that, the lower the transportation costs of a product and the greater the internal economies of large-scale production, the larger the market areas would be and the fewer the firms who choose a location near the border. Hence, the network of firms would be denser in the centre.
Lösch, in his influential work *The Economics of Location* (1940/1954), saw a border region as a desert, a wasteland in which many products can only be obtained from a distance or not all (p.205). According to Lösch, state borders cut through regular market networks, which would result in economic losses. 'Tariffs are like rivers, which separate their banks economically more

than would correspond to their actual width' (p.200). 'Thus', he argues, 'tariffs are equivalent to a lengthening of transport routes' (p.200). In short, according to Lösch and Giersch, borders can be seen as a distance value.

In his study of 1984, Bröcker concluded that commodity flows and professional passenger travel between cities on either side of a border are as much as 75% below those between domestic cities of a comparable size. This is confirmed by Nuesser who indicates that the interaction between two cities on either side of a border is reduced to 25% of the interaction that exists when no border needs to be crossed (Nuesser, 1985). He argues that the outward expansion of cities as a result of population and economic growth is also curbed by borders. For telephone traffic, similar results have been found (Rietveld & Janssen, 1990) - the interaction declines to 30%. The proportion of international calls compared to the total number of calls per country is usually slight. For the Netherlands, it has been found that international calls amount to no more than 2% of the total (Bruinsma, 1994).

Bruinsma, in his dissertation, affirms that borders should be considered as barriers in infrastructural networks on the European continent (1994). His analysis and results are interesting. It appears that infrastructural density (measured for motorways and railways) is significantly lower in the vicinity of European borders than in the interior of the investigated countries. This seems to indicate that the 'opening up and therefore the orientation of the border regions is directed, from the borders, towards the national economy' (*idem*, p. 205).
From his analysis of the average accessibility of urban agglomerations in Europe, it appears that the average accessibility, in a situation in which account is taken of the inhibiting influence of borders upon interaction, is approximately 30% lower than in a situation in which no correction is made to account for this effect. In other words, the restraining effect of borders upon the mutual accessibility of European cities amounts to approximately 30%, which is considerable.

Bruinsma adds the important comment that the barrier impact of borders is not primarily physical (see also Nijkamp *et al.*, 1990). Other factors, such as economic and socio-cultural influences, play a more important role (see also Lewe, 1995). In this respect too, the borders of a territory belonging to a certain group of people may be barriers to other groups. Still, he concludes, little research has been devoted to the non-physical barriers to interaction.

2.3.3 Discussion: Open or closed borders?

The distinction between open and closed borders has gradually turned into a debate in itself. The distinction however, is not as obsolete as might seem. It is as yet not entirely certain whether interdependence is indeed growing; it might be a chimera - are the flows merely increasing, or does it just seem so because we know more about them just because of the increase in communication and transport? What is more, entirely open borders do not exist, they are a

contradiction in terms. The desire to achieve sovereignty and to obtain the power to protect oneself and one's people against alien and undesired influences from the outside often proves stronger than the desire to look beyond one's own territory. To open the border is more difficult than to close it. As long as there are living creatures, and as long as there is land to divide, there will be territories. As long as there will be territories, human beings will continue to create borders.
One the other hand, fully closed borders do not exist either. There will always be some degree of interaction between two neighbouring states. No state can be sealed hermetically. Not even the iron curtain, that ultimate effort to create a fully closed border, could be sealed entirely, as Ritter demonstrated for the two former German states (Ritter, 1982). The matter at hand, therefore, is to determine *the degree* to which openness and border-crossing interaction are involved.

Borders are phenomenons associated with states. States begin and end at the borderline. The state, therefore, has a strong hand in deciding its relative openness. Nevertheless, the openness of a border also depends upon the way in which a society deals with its national borders, and the degree to which that society puts the territorial demarcations into perspective. The question is therefore not whether borders will disappear (for they will not), but how they are shaped and enter into space. Moreover, the question of how borders are controlled, how they are given their meaning, and how they change over time is equally important. The reproduction of borders is as important as their production (cf. Lefebvre, 1991; Paasi, 1996).

In short, the debate open and closed borders cannot be an either/or discussion - the distinction covers a continuous scale (see also Ratti, 1993a). The closed border side of this scale will be dominant most of the time because if it were not, one could not speak of territories nor could one speak of identities. To the latter I will turn next.

2.4 Functional versus affective borders

The third distinction made here is that between functional and affective borders (cf. Leimgruber, 1991; Paasi, 1996; Riedel, 1994). I am of the opinion that this third distinction is vital to the understanding of the functioning and influence of borders. Functional borders, according to this standpoint, are indicators of the limits of an organisation's jurisdiction, while the term 'affective borders' refers to the emotional tie people have with a certain territory.

It is crucial to the understanding of the functioning and influence of borders that mankind's activities in space do not only make up places (which may lead to territories), but that his activities may also be affectively guided and even obstructed by these borders. State borders may then become *affective borders*. Functional borders not only provoke the emergence of national institutions but may become institutions by themselves, adding to the cut-off effect of borders.

Falk put it in his article on border symbolism, published in a collection of writings entitled *Maps from Mind* in 1974 as follows, 'It is clear that the emotional meaning of one country's borders, unconsciously, is fused with that of one's own boundaries' (Falk, 1983). Similarly, the political geographers Ratzel (1897) and Prescott (1987) emphasise that a people's self-image (space conception) and their pride are important factors in the demarcation, opening up and closing of borders. According to this view, border disputes might be considered a barometer for the condition of relationships between two neighbouring states.

2.4.1 States and nations

One of the most important types of distinction arising from the functional/affective characterisation is that between states and nations.
It may be considered typical that the term 'nation' is much more common in the language we use, and appeals more strongly to our consciousness, than 'state', even where the interaction with other states is concerned. Expressions such as national income, national policy, national interest, international relations, internationalisation, transnational, supranational and so forth may suffice to illustrate this remarkable tendency. One would expect terms like 'state policy', 'state income', 'interstatualisation' *etc.* to exist. In all these cases, nation and state appear to be used interchangeably, as synonyms. They should however be clearly distinguished (see, *e.g.* Connor, 1978; Habermas, 1996; Hobsbawm, 1990; Weber, 1948). Terms like internationalisation, national policy, and others used in daily practice are imprecise. Borders identify states, but not necessarily nations. The institutionalisation of the border does not necessarily institutionalise the space within these borders. Various 'nationalities', or groups united by one identity, may co-exist within one state. A state is not necessarily the same as a nation, nor is a nation necessarily the same as a state.

Quite obviously, borders clearly demarcate a state in space; it can be shown on a map and has public institutions exercising a monopoly of coercion within the demarcated territory (Smith, 1991). 'Nation' is a much more ambiguous term (cf. Couwenberg, 1994). Nations do not simply *occupy* a certain space; they claim that space, they *possess* it. In the words of Boesch, a German cultural psychologist: '*Wir erleben nicht nur den Raum...sondern wir gestalten ihn auch*' ('We do not only experience space...we also shape it') (1963, p. 145). Nations are the institutionalisation of a territory; represent the common mentality of that territory, and locate a community in space and time. Nations and national identity can therefore never be seen apart from space. In this respect, Lefebvre's argument is thought-provoking (1991). He makes a plea for the inclusion of the existence of imaginative illustrations of space in the explanation of the establishment of constructs like nations.

> Ideas, representations or values which do not succeed in making their mark on space, and thus generating (or producing) an appropriate morphology, will lose all pith and become mere signs, resolve themselves into abstract descriptions, or mutate into fantasies.
> (Lefebvre, 1991, p.417)

As with all abstract concepts, 'nation' is very hard to measure, both quantitatively and qualitatively. The term is a product of the human mind - a construct created to refer to a certain mental concept that is difficult to define, and therefore liable to free interpretation, misinterpretation, and the influence of societal ideals (Knippenberg en De Pater, 1988). In short, whereas the state refers to a territorially-based power over people, the nation refers to a territorially-based ideology of a people.

2.4.2 Nationalism

To learn more about the meaning of the difference between states and nations, one has to study the topic of nationalism. Hutchinson and Smith, in the foreword to their marvellous collection of writings on nationalism by various scholars, argue that nationalism did not constitute a collective power of importance in Europe until the Sixteenth Century, when commercial competition and wars between states drove rulers to mobilise and 'standardise' their subjects in terms of religion, military training, education and language (1994). It was, therefore, a threat from the outside, whether commercial or military, that created a perceived need to unite the people domestically.

In the Twentieth Century, the notion of nationalism has been narrowed down to a movement strongly associated with war. Nazi 'nationalism' rendered the concept of nationalism especially odious. After the Second World War, nationalism became something that must be quickly forgotten - something with which a people preferred not to be associated. It had become something that referred to other peoples, not one's own (Van den Boogaard, 1997).

Despite the fact that it has been declared an archaism many times over, nationalism appears to be a persistent phenomenon. Since the 1960s, the openness with regard to the devotion to nationalism has slowly gained ground again (Hutchinson and Smith, 1994). The claim for ethnic autonomy in Scotland, Wales, Flanders, Brittany, Corsica, Catalonia and other European 'ethno-regions', and the recent events in Eastern Europe and the former Soviet Union are illustrative examples of the renewed flourishing of nationalist sentiments on the European continent. The attention devoted to immigrants and ethnic purity in recent years, mainly by conservative political parties in various countries belonging to the European Union; and more importantly, the renewed interest in national sovereignty and the concern for the nation-state in relation to the European integration process that has arisen in many member states, should also be seen in this light. The threat from the outside, in this case the European integration, or even the appeal to or assumption of it, apparently remains an important stimulus for the activation of nationalism. Hutchinson and Smith speak of the revival and the survival of nationalism in Europe as a consequence of these new developments (see also Milward, 1992; see also section 2.4.7.1).

The feeling of national belonging is, for a large part, an emotional involvement with the ancestors of one's community. The ethnic past of a nation, however, is nothing more and nothing less than an invention of the few and a subjective reconstruction by the many. It is the mobilisation of individuals and certain groups in terms of annexation or attraction to a core ethnic community that makes a nation. The 'ethnic homeland' is made into a nation due to its appeal to 'the people' (Taylor, 1993). It follows that the study of ethnicity and nationality is in large part the study of induced cultural change (cf. Brass, 1979). The imposition of nationalism cannot be based on nature. Nationalism is an ideology (cf. Paasi, 1996). Some even argue that nationalism is a civil religion, in which the nation is seen as sacred (Rokkan and Urwin, 1983).

It may be clear, however, that there have been cases (a number of recent examples can be cited in Eastern Europe) in which nations were often created, even without unambiguous historical precedents, to unite different immigration currents or ethnic communities. Smith (1991) lists the cases of America, Australia and Argentina to exemplify this particular way in which nations are formed. He also mentions the sub-Saharan African states, many of which were first created as colonies and later had to foster nationalism to prevent tribes from warring with each other.
Not all states, therefore, can claim to be true 'nation-states' in the sense that the borders of the state coincide with the nation's, and that the population of the state share a common ethnic culture (Smith, 1991). Ethnic problems within a state indicate the non-acceptance of the nation. National freedom movements are eager to fight for an order in which the borders of the state are identical to the borders drawn by nationality or nationalist sentiments. However, this wish can but very rarely be realised, if one is to judge by the rather arbitrary territorial borders that states have been wont to draw throughout history.
Clearly, it is difficult to reign a territory if a dominant sense of national identity is lacking within the territorial limits. In such cases, there is no basis for the acceptance of sovereignty. On the other hand, nations need a territory to exist, not necessarily an all-encompassing power, but a territory surely. One might say that states need nations, and that nations need states.

2.4.3 The institutionalisation of nations

An interesting issue is the question of order in the spatial formation of affectively bond people, the institutionalisation of nations. Before the demarcation of the majority of Europe's borders was acknowledged as such, the reality one was familiar with consisted of one's daily environment and the language of one's community. To many people, the nation was merely an abstraction, alien and in some respects hostile to everyday habits (military service and taxes, for instance). The emergence of democracy, most notably after the French Revolution, and the development of capitalism contributed greatly to the formation of nations.

Knippenberg and De Pater (1988) describe how the Netherlands were unified as a consequence of these processes of democratisation and capitalism. The realisation of democracy and capitalism meant an enormous enlargement in the scale of space for potential interaction. They distinguish four dimensions of forces of integration.

The first impetus to national integration is infrastructural expansion within the state. Expansion can be communicational (post, telegraph, radio, cinema, telephone, telefax, television, the Internet) as well as physical (waterways, railroads, motorways). In this respect, infrastructure may in fact be regarded as the material condition for the development and growth of social interchange.

Secondly, the gradual scale enlargement of firms and markets adds to the removal of regional institutional barriers (such as toll fares, different currencies, etc.) and the breakdown of peasant economies. This, taken together with increasing industrialisation, specialisation and the territorial differentiation of economic functions, furthers the unification of the territory, which is further encouraged by the increasing penetration of the state into society, the third stimulus of national integration. Nationalisation of the media and the educational system is mentioned as an important factor in this respect. The authors also mention the creation of symbols such as a name, a national flag, and anthem, and the right to vote as factors contributing to the gradual coming together of state and nation.

They list a fourth category of factors that contribute to integration, namely cultural factors. The (space) formation of a single, national language, literature and reading behaviour; the alphabetisation of the people; the exchange and merging of food characteristics and customs; and an increase in the level of education belong to this category.

The authors emphasise that this summing-up of integrative factors does not exclude the involvement of erratic and non-intended developments in the integration process. Integration, they caution, should not be mistaken for homogenisation.

Furthermore, the social geographer Anssi Paasi has recently made a meaningful contribution to the discussion on the institutionalisation of nations (1986, 1991, 1996). In his impressive work of 1996, which is actually one of the very few theoretical contributions on the link between consciousness, borders and territories, he defines the institutionalisation of nations as follows:

> The process through which various territorial units are produced and manifest themselves in various social and cultural practices, such as politics, economy and administration, which in turn will be produced and reproduced consciously and unconsciously by people. (p. 34)

During the institutionalisation process, the territory provides security and an identity for its inhabitants. Power-holding actors in the group define and symbolise the social and spatial limits of membership in order to establish the control which will serve to increase security and territorial identity (cf. Paasi, 1986). According to Paasi, therefore, territories are most often produced 'from the top down'.

The 'reproduction' of borders, however, is a process of interaction between the people and their rulers depending on the solidarity of the group. A nation is not an 'idée fixe', a static phenomenon. Institutionalism is never unchanging. It is a dynamic and ongoing process, through which the collective consciousness of citizens and nationalists may be strengthened. The opposite might also occur, in which case separatism is the logical consequence. It does help if the state supports and encourages nationalism, but it is not a *sine qua non*. A national identity is not born through the exertion of power alone. There are many non nation-states.

The people's solidarity with the state, as well as with each other, is crucial to the 'reproduction' of the borders. It is that solidarity, or rather, the degree of trust that reigns in a society that is vitally responsible for the 'glue', the cohesion of the social system within a territory (Durkheim 1893/1933; Fukuyama, 1995). As Massey (1984), Buursink (1987), and Murphy (1991) put it, the national space is 'a social construct'. The result of the process of the institutionalisation of a nation is therefore more than merely a product; it is an 'imagined community' (Anderson, 1983/1991). A nation is not just 'produced'; it is also *mentally reproduced.* Nobody can know all his fellow citizens, but each has an image of the other within the state borders, and of what they have in common. The belief in a common descent is central. It is only within the context of this collective imagination that the nation is the same and sovereign for all.

In short, the institutionalisation of nations and the creation of a national identity can be subdivided into the following phases (cf. Paasi, 1986, 1991, 1996; Durkheim, 1933; Smith, 1991):
a) Constitution of territorial demarcation
b) Symbolic configuration, language, stories (myths & legends) and institutions
c) The growth of solidarity
d) Identification with the territory
e) Acknowledgement in the global system

Paasi qualifies this summary by remarking that the steps in the institutionalisation process may vary for individual countries and be interchangeable or act in concert; most often, they will be operating simultaneously. Moreover, several feedback moments may occur during the process. The scheme should therefore not be regarded as a manual, but rather as an inventory of the most likely course the formation of a national identity will follow.
Note that the willingness to demarcate and institutionalise the borders was also inspired by the development of cartography, which made such sharp demarcations possible (Harley, 1989). Maps are more than mirrors; by reproducing the world they also construct it (Wood, 1992). Geographical science therefore also produces and reproduces borders in space.

2.4.4 The assimilation and contrast effect of nations

The idea of living in a nation, of living in an 'imagined community', may lead to the emergence of a common social identity. National identity, is just another form of social identity, a term described in the social identity theory of Tajfel (1982), Tajfel *et al.* (1971), and Tajfel and Turner (1979ab). Social identity is that part of the self-perception which is based on the membership of (the 'belonging to') a social group or groups (Tajfel, 1982; Jenkins, 1996). It implies that self-determination and self-evaluation partly occur through social comparison. A positive social identity, then, helps to attain a positive self-perception. Social identity and conformity are mutually reinforcing, since the conformity of the group is positively correlated with the cohesion and negatively correlated with the estimation of one's own contribution to the group.
Applying this theory to the affective term 'nation' puts the discussion in a different light. The theory posits that the identity of a group in fact constitutes an 'in-group' - the 'we' as used in 'We Americans', 'We Arabs' or 'We Israelis'. This is generally referred to as the *assimilation effect* (Koomen, 1988). In the case of nations, as discussed above, the borders of the territory are 'socialised and institutionalised'. The personification of collective units as states also indicates that people often think of a mental entity when referring to 'a state'. The collective unit is regarded as 'one's own': 'The Netherlands have beaten Germany' and 'The United States of America have won many Olympic medals last year' are characteristic examples of such personified states. Still, it is not entirely clear who is the subject in such examples of collective representation (Paasi, 1996). In the distinction between functional and affective borders, the big question is: Who is this 'We'?

An important point in this respect is that the 'we' is both necessary and voluntary. Necessary, because individual members of the group are to a large extent dependent on its other members - which is why policies concerning safety, language, education, culture and economics are primarily formulated on the national level. Voluntary, because it gives the group members a sense of an internal space open to movement, and of security *vis-à-vis* the outer world. It also provides a common background and frame of reference that is recognisable for group members who travel or work outside of the territory. Mutual cognition is thus made easier, contributing to the integration of the in-group.
These effects should also be explained with regard to the incremental process of the sharpening of borders. It is not only the political power that wants to know its (territorial) borders; human beings in general feel the need to have a place in a territorially-bound group. Some scholars regard this social need for reward, identity and security as one of the basic needs of mankind (*e.g.* Johnston, 1989).

The value of the 'we' itself is mostly determined by social comparison - with other groups in this case (Koomen, 1988; Delwaide, 1996). In this sense, the borders that are created become *relational*; they represent the lines of interaction and dissection of neighbouring social identities. Demarcating the 'We' simultaneously demarcates the 'Other'. Another group is necessary to be able to value the characteristics - such as status, intelligence and performance - of the own group. The national identities of two neighbouring countries will grow stronger if the differences between them are pronounced. This causes a sharpening of the identities. Members of the in-group increasingly tend to value the characteristics of their own group above those of the other group. This effect is known as the *contrast effect* (Koomen, 1988).

The two socio-psychological phenomena, assimilation effect and contrast effect, must be understood as perceived differences between the members of two distinct social groups. The perceived homogeneity of individual members in the out-group (the 'Other', also referred to as 'Them') is much greater than that of the in-group - conversely, a greater variety and heterogeneity is perceived among the people of the own nation. Often, this perception results in mutually persistent stereotypes. These stereotypes, these 'simplified beliefs' (Paasi, 1996), depersonalise the members of the other group 'by assuming stereotyped collective features that are common to all members' (*idem*, p. 59). It should be noted that these stereotypes do have a function. They ratify the cohesion of the in-group, provide peace of mind to the individual members of the group, and further the formation or evolution of their social identity. Thus, stereotypes are a necessary part of people's views on the world. Individual decision-making is based upon their own perception or insight and upon their conviction and/or judgements of other group members. A study focussing on the affective influences of borders should therefore not ask whether these stereotypes exist (for they do), but rather how persistent they are and what impact they have on the actions and interactions of a people (see, e.g. Paasi, 1996).

On the basis of Koomen's work (1988/1992) I have identified five distinct determinants of the differences in social identity:

The number of perceived differences
The assumption is that there exists a positive correlation between the differences in social identity and the number of perceived differences in group characteristics, such as language, religion, economic position and culture. Unfamiliarity of one territory's inhabitants with the empirical facts about the Other's characteristics plays an important role in this perception. Language in particular appears to be an important determinant in group bonding and group differences. Most European minorities have their own language although 'standard' or 'national' languages are commonly taught at schools and used by mass media in most European countries.

The homogeneity of the in-group
It is postulated that there exist a negative correlation between the homogeneity of the in-group and the contrast effect. The more similar and coherent the group, the stronger the assimilation effect and hence the contrast effect will be. A group of factory workers on strike, for example, may be expected to have a strong assimilation effect within the group and a strong contrast effect towards the factory's management.

The size of the in- and out-group

The next assumption is that the number of members in the two groups is positively correlated with the contrast in social identity between them. The larger the groups, the greater the perceived necessity to distinguish between them.

The level of co-operation and competition between the two groups

When groups are competing functionally, social identity is stressed more than when the groups are working together to achieve some common goal. Where severe economic, cultural or social competition or even military hostilities are involved, social identities will be strongly emphasised and there will be an important degree of stereotypisation. When the continued existence of a national unity is threatened in some way, the perceived need for resisting the threat will be great. Thus, when one group claims a certain territory with an appeal to ethnicity, other groups will be 'forced' to define a counter-identity. This factor inspired the Dutch social scientist De Swaan to utter the following statement: 'Social identity is the thing you emphasise when it is threatened' (1992).

The permeability of the border

An open border is less threatening and creates a less definite division between the 'We' and 'Them' than a closed border. The amount of barbed wire is not always a reliable indicator, however, to the openness or closedness of a border. The gradations are usually far more subtle. A wide river may divide the population more, in an affective sense, than a stretch of meadows several kilometres wide (Boesch, 1963).

It may be concluded that the concept of social identity, approached through social psychology, allows us to gain considerable insight into the constitution and 'upgrading' of national identity in different situations. Moreover, the vantage point of social identity and its determining factors make it possible to define the terms 'nation' and 'nationalism' more clearly, facilitating empirical verification.

2.4.5 'Us' versus 'Them' and 'Here' versus 'There'

Borders have been defined as lines that separate states from each other. The differing make-up of the political and administrative systems in the separated states may lead to difficulties in the compatibility of matters of sovereignty and power. It is under these circumstances that the states meet at the border. As explained before, borders may also constitute cut-off lines when they separate nations. Strong national identities may lead to a strong contrast effect, which in turn may cause great difficulties when an attempt is made to integrate the national identities of the neighbouring states.

Paasi (1996) offers an explanatory scheme of the specific characteristics of the geography of borders and border landscapes. The analytical framework incorporating the differences between

'Here' and 'There' and 'Us' and 'Them' is used to illustrate how the construction of territorial identities occurs in relation to social distinctions (see table 2.1).

Table 2.1 - Socio-spatial integration and distinction

	Here	There
Us	Integration within a territory	Integration over borders
Them	Distinction within a territory	Distinction between Us and the Other *across* borders

After Paasi 1996, p. 14

'Integration within a territory' refers to the creation of a national identity based on the characteristics of a core ethnic community. The nation is more or less a reproduction of the state. 'Integration over borders' points to people of the same group, for example ethnic minorities living in different states, who are trying to re-unite. The third category, 'Distinction within a territory', characterises a situation in which minorities are living together in one territory. One might think of territorially-bound 'Them' and 'Us' groups in one country, such as the North-South relationship in Italy or that between Flanders and Walloon in Belgium. Paasi himself puts forward the example of refugees, so typical of our modern world.
It is the last category, namely the distinction between the 'Them' and 'Us' groups in different countries, that is most important for my purpose, the study of the development of cross-border relationships. Paasi describes the impact of the confrontation between 'Us' and 'Them' on the relationship between two neighbouring countries at the Finnish-Russian border. The difference between an action in the 'here with one of us' and the 'there with them' is an expectational difference: the opinion is formed on the basis of expectations rather than facts. The state's influence in this perception is certainly an important one. The borders delimit the space in which the state's sovereignty rules. It would be a worthwhile exercise to try to establish some kind of empirical measurement of the state's influence on the border's degree of openness for interaction. If the nation grows stronger, the borders become more clearly perceivable as social institutions and the centripetal orientation becomes more distinct, which leads to a greater degree of institutional and affective divergence. Edward Said describes this affective divergence in his impressive work, *Orientalism* (1978), in a quite elegant manner:

> ...this universal practice of designating in one's mind a familiar space which is'ours' and an unfamiliar space beyond 'ours' which is 'theirs' is a way of making geographical distinctions that can be entirely arbitrary. I use the word 'arbitrary' because imaginative geography of the 'our land-barbarian land' variety does not require that the barbarians acknowledge the distinction. It is enough for 'us' to set up these boundaries in our minds; 'they' become 'they' accordingly, and both their territory and their mentality are designated as different from 'ours'. (Said, 1978, p. 54, as quoted in Paasi, 1996)

2.4.6 Spatial layers in social identity

Identification with a spatial unit is not restricted to the national scale. There are several spatial layers to be discovered in social identity. The psycho-social identification of individuals is greater on the local and regional level than on the national level, but the latter in turn is greater than the identification with the international level. A stimulating contribution to this field has been made by Moles and Rohmer (1972). They argue that identification with territory is hierarchical. Their original figure of geographical identity scales, which was later modified by Leimgruber (1991), offers useful insight into the distribution within spatial identity (figure 2.3).

Figure 2.3 - Human shell-like 'spatial identity' hierarchy

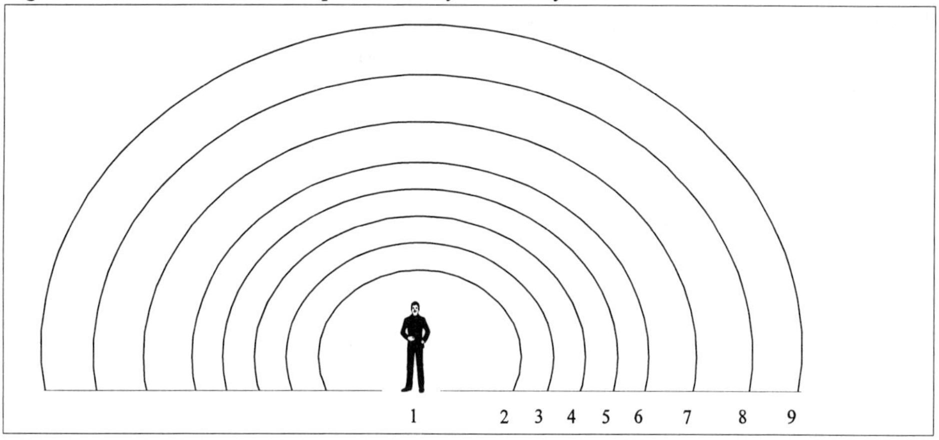

Shells: 1=The human body and gestures, the personal space; 2=The room; 3=The house; 4=The neighbourhood; 5=The town; 6=The region; 7=The country; 8=The continent; 9=The world
After Moles and Rohmer, 1972; Leimgruber, 1991

Identity markers are made in terms of distance. The institutionalisation of space is what human geographers tend to refer to as the creation of a 'sense of place'. The lives of most people are limited to a relatively small number of different environments. The more limited the spatial area occupied during a lifetime, the stronger will be the identification and association with this area. The identification with space is most important in an individual's personal space, from there diminishing as geographical reach is extended: the family, the own yard, the own home, the neighbourhood, the city and the region. The identification with personal space and the direct environment is dominant, for the simple reason that social interaction, in an extensive area, is more difficult to achieve. These direct surroundings are soaked with privately experienced history (Paasi, 1996). These spaces become the history of his life, his homeland full of memories.
Domestically, the private yard and the adjacent pavement are strictly demarcated and linked to a very high degree of spatial association. It is illustrative that the most important threat perceived in the neighbourhood is not an environmental problem, but neighbour's disturbances (Lambooy,

1992). Mostly, however, closed systems are to be found in personal space. People who come within 'breathing distance' are considered highly irritating for that reason. In public spaces such as camping sites, beaches, trains and office halls, where space cannot be privately appropriated, the demarcation of personal space is clearly noticeable. Everyone builds a field of protection around themselves into which none but truly beloved persons are allowed.

This type of institutionalisation has its geographical limits; it gradually becomes blurred as spatial range is extended. On the regional or local level, the connection with borders will be lower than on the local level but stronger than on the national level. Regions, because of their more limited geographical range and resulting, more active socialisation, are better able than countries to structure their life in space and time in a concrete manner. State borders, therefore, do not necessarily imply homogeneity:

> Each state claims to produce a space wherein something is accomplished - a space, even, where something is brought to perfection: namely, a unified and hence homogeneous society. In fact, and in practice, what state and political action institutes, and consolidates by every available means, is a balance of power between classes and fractions of classes, as between the spaces that they occupy. (Lefebvre, 1991, p. 281)

Regionalism appeals more to people than nationalism (see figure 2.3). In terms of identification, the feelings of nationalism will be stronger than those associated with Europeanism or globalism. In comparison with nations and supra-nations, regions are more suitable for active socialisation. Regions are the main arenas (in terms of time) in which people interact with others; they provide a structure of activities for the day-to-day routine that characterises the larger part of most people's lives (Thrift, 1983). The regional arena as a society, in which collective modes of behaviour are constantly being negotiated and renegotiated and in which habits are being learned and created, is closer to our personal spatial identities than Europe or the world.

One must, however, be wary of overly deterministic argumentation. Social identity is not always built up hierarchically in space. There is more dynamism in the hierarchy of identification scales than the figure can show, for several reasons:
1. The circles may overlap to some extent. The transition from one sphere to another is more gradual than is shown. The demarcation of the different scales, the personal spatial borders, is more permeable in most cases than the lines in the figure are able to show. Moreover, not all of the spatial volumes are of equivalent size.
2. The generalisation in this figure does not allow for layers to be biased by personal interest and interaction patterns. Due to considerable variations in personal characteristics, such as age, spatial customs, preferences, sex and culture, the interest or interaction in space may at some stages shift towards a different direction. Besides, due to external factors such as the European integration process or due to changes in personal activities or preferences, the identification is

dynamic, which may change the hierarchy in the different layers.
3. What is more, there is always more than one layer active around and within one person. There is a balance of power between the various layers; it is a matter of and/and, not either/or. Gradations will vary per situation and per person. During international sports games, for instance, the feelings associated with their national identity will supersede the regional background of the sportsmen and women.
4. In daily life, individuals do not usually choose the layers of spatial identity in which they are functioning consciously. The layers are not thought of reflectively. Although one could not live without them, people just tend to occupy spatial identity layers without further reflection. Their region is 'not a region, but simply their home' (Paasi, 1996, p. 258). As Cohen (1982) quite eloquently argues, 'People are not aware of their culture unless they stand at its boundaries' (quoted in Paasi, 1996).
5. The figure, finally, does not incorporate the possibility of overlapping layers. It is unclear where one's own region ends, and where that of the country begins. Border regions are a highly illustrative example of such overlaps of scale, since they combine three scales: the regional, the national, and the international.

These qualifications, however, do not affect the basic proposition concerning the existence of spatial gradations of identification illustrated by the figure. The point I wish to make here is that it does not suffice, in a study that tries to discover the impact of state borders on the behaviour of individuals, merely to enter social identity as an independent category. The discussion on social identity should keep account of individual differences in experiencing social identity, at different spatial levels of scale.

2.4.7 Discussion: functional versus affective

Thus far, the existence of a difference between functional and affective borders has been demonstrated. Both types of borders can change over time. In our present time, the most dramatic changes may be expected from the increase in time-space convergence. It is plausible that this 'globalisation' will upswing the scale of spatial affection. The various identity layers might well become more closely interwoven than before, thereby creating 'global citizenship', although this is far from certain. Relaxation of state borders will not necessarily lead to the increase of international identification. As Kamann put it: '...official elimination of a border does not harmonize the cognitive belief sets at the two sides of the border! The effect of this difference should not be underestimated.' (Kamann, 1993a, p.81; see also Kamann, 1993b). National identity may even be emphasised more strongly when the density of the mutual pattern of contact is high.

As with nationalism, identification at hierarchically higher levels must be recognised as a long-term process. Regions have not yet lost their distinctiveness, though; most individuals still follow the well-worn paths during most of their daily existence. International events and experiences are still mediated according to distinctly local references (Thrift, 1983). Moreover, national and supranational space cannot truly be institutionalised for individuals since it is physically impossible for them to translate all that space into meaningful places and interactions. An equal distribution of identification would equalise all spatial borders, but identification implies spatial limitation. The space of a national or international community can therefore only be imaginative. It is in this sense that the term 'imagined communities' coined by Anderson (1983/1991), which was referred to above to define nations, becomes concretely meaningful.

2.4.7.1 Defunctionalisation versus re-affectivation

When applying the above theoretical reflections to the border situation in the European integration process, there appears to be a twofold tendency, *defunctionalisation* on the one hand and *re-affectivation* on the other. The actual European borders are slowly dissolved but at the same time, new borders are emerging. Thus, for instance, the open border policy leads to emotional problems with regard to the integration and fitting-in of immigrants in a society and the regional discrepancies between rich and poor in countries such as Italy or Spain appear to be emphasised by an open border policy stressing free traffic of trade. The call for the preservation of national culture and sovereignty should also be seen in this light (see, e.g. Scheffer, 1996). Nations have always been looking for ways and arguments to distinguish themselves from other nations. It might be that the emphasis on national identity has become even stronger than before, despite a high degree of co-operation, since the property rights and sovereignty over the territory are at stake. What is more, the member states feel that their identity itself is at stake.

The European Commission attempts to foster a certain kind of 'Europeanisation', the creation of a European identity that will encourage interaction between member states. European policy, similar to that of a newborn state that wants to unify its territory, aims at the gradual replacement of nationalist sentiments with European sentiments. Changing the identity of a nation, and certainly that of a number of greatly diversified nations, is a long-term process. It cannot be managed exogenously alone, which is why in the short run, it often leads to disintegration. When an attempt is made to merge two identities from the top-down, as has been discussed earlier, it might well result in the pronunciation of the differences between them. As such, the newly developing regionalist and nationalist movements might well be the logical consequence of the integration pressure felt in the EC.

It should also be noted that states, from beyond and within the borders, are also facing supernationalism and regionalism. I have already remarked that identity could be seen as that part of the self that emerges the stronger when it feels threatened. Seen in this light, one might argue that the state re-emerges exactly *because* its continued existence is threatened from above and below. Milward too argues, in his celebrated publication *The European Rescue of the Nation-*

State (1992), that it is not despite but due to the European unification that national identities and nation-states have survived and are now experiencing a remarkable revival. The relatively weak European identity might then be blamed on the fact that Europe has nothing to resist, whereas the separate European regions (or countries) are feeling the need to resist the threat of European unification. The increased migration of capital, culture and labour has put the integrative capacity and interdependence of many nations to the test. To conclude, in Europe, it appears that a need is felt to achieve a balance between 'utilitarian' (transnational /international/multinational) networking and integration on the one hand, and the territorial identity movements of separatism and regionalism on the other.

2.4.7.2 Globalisation and glocalisation

Linked to this discussion of global (European) versus regional, the discussion has emerged, which deals with the significance of the so-called 'path dependency' of economic developments (Dosi *et al.*, 1988). This dependency means that one cannot examine the economic developments in a certain area without considering the economic history of that area. Contemporary and future developments in that area, some scholars reason, could be referred back to their roots, that is to the original characteristics of the area. Authors such as Castells, Scott, Storper, Porter and Enright, most notably, argue that, in spite of the influence of internationalisation and globalisation on the enrichment of a body of ideas, the roots of the economic developments in a region or country remain fundamentally important in the determination of the competitive force of the sectors and companies in that region or country. They speak of a paradoxical development, arguing that the import of the local/regional level has accrued, not in spite but because of growing internationalisation (Van Houtum and Boekema, 1994; Boekema, 1996). The adage 'think globally, act locally' takes on new meaning from this vantage point. According to Porter:

> The more competition becomes global, ironically, the more important the home base becomes. Differences in values, traditions, histories, economic structures and institutions are not threatened by the increasing globalisation of competition but they are vital to success in it.
> (Porter, 1990, p. 145)

Enright says it in the following manner:

> Regions and nations will matter as long as the determinants of competitive advantage differ from place to place. (...) Even if differences in institutions, tastes, cultures, entrepreneurship characteristics, firm strategies and structures, local competition and related and supporting industries are eliminated, regions and regional identity will still matter. Economic development is an intensely path-dependent process. It cannot be divorced

> from history, and in particular local economic history.
> (Enright, 1992, pp. 21-2)

The discussion may be summarised as *'globalisation'* versus *'glocalisation'* (Ruigrok and Van Tulder, 1993). 'Glocalisation' in their context refers to the growing significance of the *loc*al level as a consequence of *glob*alisation. The question that remains to be answered is, 'Are we localising globalisation or are we globalising localisation?' This discussion is not new for economic geography. As early as 1940(1954), Lösch, one of the founders of economic geography, stressed that the import of the concept of space is underestimated and will only grow over time, against the apparent repression by the economic spirit of the age. In the epilogue to his important work, he confers meaning on the concept of space in economics in an impressive manner:

> If everything occurred at the same time there would be no development. If everything existed in the same place there could be no particularity. Only space makes possible the particular, which then unfolds in time. Only because we are not equally near to everything; only because everything does not rush in upon us at once; only because our world is restricted, for every individual, for his people, and for mankind as a whole, can we, in our finiteness, endure at all. The extent of this horizon differs, of course, from man to man. But in economic affairs, as in all other affairs, our ken is limited for acting intelligently and for finding our way through the complexities of life. And even within this little world, we are familiar with not more than its innermost circle. Depth must be bought with narrowness. Particularity is the price of our existence. (1954, p. 508)

Like Porter, Lefebvre (1991) refers to the impossibility of theorising about social or economic space without theorising about society. For society produces that space. In this sense, a spatial theory is a social theory and vice versa. Lefebvre emphasises the imaginary and symbolical character of global space, which is what politicians appeal to. They may not own the space beyond their sovereignty, but it is there nevertheless. This may appear as a threat, or on the contrary as a stimulus that may be appealed to as a justification for political actions:

> It may be asserted with reasonable confidence that the process of producing things (the range of so-called consumer goods) tends to annul rather than reinforce homogenisation. A number of differentiating traits are thus permitted to emerge which are not completely bound to a specific location or situation, to a geographically determinate space. The so-called economic process tends to generate diversity - a fact which supports the hypothesis that homogenisation today is a function of political rather than economic factors as such; abstract space is a tool of power. (1991, p. 390-391)

To conclude, the removal of functional borders in Europe may, but does not necessarily imply that the affective borders will become united. The twofold concept of integration versus differentiation is necessary to the consideration of any border movement. There will always be borders because there will always be some kind of social, spatial identity. A borderless world would be an identity vacuum. The divergence between national identities may lead to large socio-cultural and economic differences, causing integrational obstructions. The question is not whether the economic map will become borderless, but to what extent the borders have (had) an impact on the shaping and direction of economic activities. Spatial affection towards the home country and the borders might well then be a factor unjustifiably neglected in the theory of international economic trade. So as to obtain clarity concerning the interest and size of the impact of spatial identity in international economic trade traffic, it must be verified by empirical research. In the empirical part of this study, the degree and impact of the differences in social identity on individual interactions shall be examined.

2.5 Concrete versus abstract borders

The fourth and last distinction that I want to discuss here is that between concrete and abstract borders. Concrete borders are in essence the equivalent of functional borders - they are perceivable jurisdictional borders. Abstract borders are cognitive borders, borders that have been mentally conceived by people. This distinction originated in the work of Koffka (1935), who distinguished between 'things as they "really" are and things as they look to us' (Koffka, 1935, p. 35).

Perception is then defined as the subjective sensory experiencing of reality as it presents itself to us (see, among others, Veitch and Arkkelin, 1995). It is not necessarily visual. Other sensory impressions of stimuli in one's environment also belong to perception as it is defined here. The individual feeds his brain with information about the perceived impressions. That is where the cognitive process begins. The new perception will be referred to what is known, or is directly recognised. The knowledge and recognition of stimuli perceived in the environment is called *spatial cognition* (cf. Veitch and Arkkelin, 1995). Spatial cognition must be regarded as the subjective 'knowing of a space'. Spatial cognition, therefore, is subjectively constructed - it results from the interaction between appearance and personal perception (see Piaget and Weill, 1976). It should be noted that spatial cognition is not the same as spatial affectiveness. The latter refers to the experience and valuation of a space. Still, the processes of spatial cognition and affectiveness presuppose each other and interact in a complex manner (Riedel, 1994). Literature on the subject however, does not yet present a single, unified view on the exact correlation between the two.

The border may sometimes function as a true barrier in a cognitive sense. This is clearly illustrated by the fact that information about events on one side of the border reaches the other side rarely, or not at all. Newspapers and television programmes focus primarily on the country or region in which they are made. Even in areas near the border, national emphasis characterises the flow of information. In this respect the border functions as a dividing line. Spatial cognition, the frame of reference for economic, socio-cultural and political activities in space, clearly declines across the border. Lundén (1973) has transformed this process into a theoretical diagram for different kinds of spatial cognition by the inhabitants of a country (figure 2.4).

Figure 2.4 - Spatial cognition in a border region

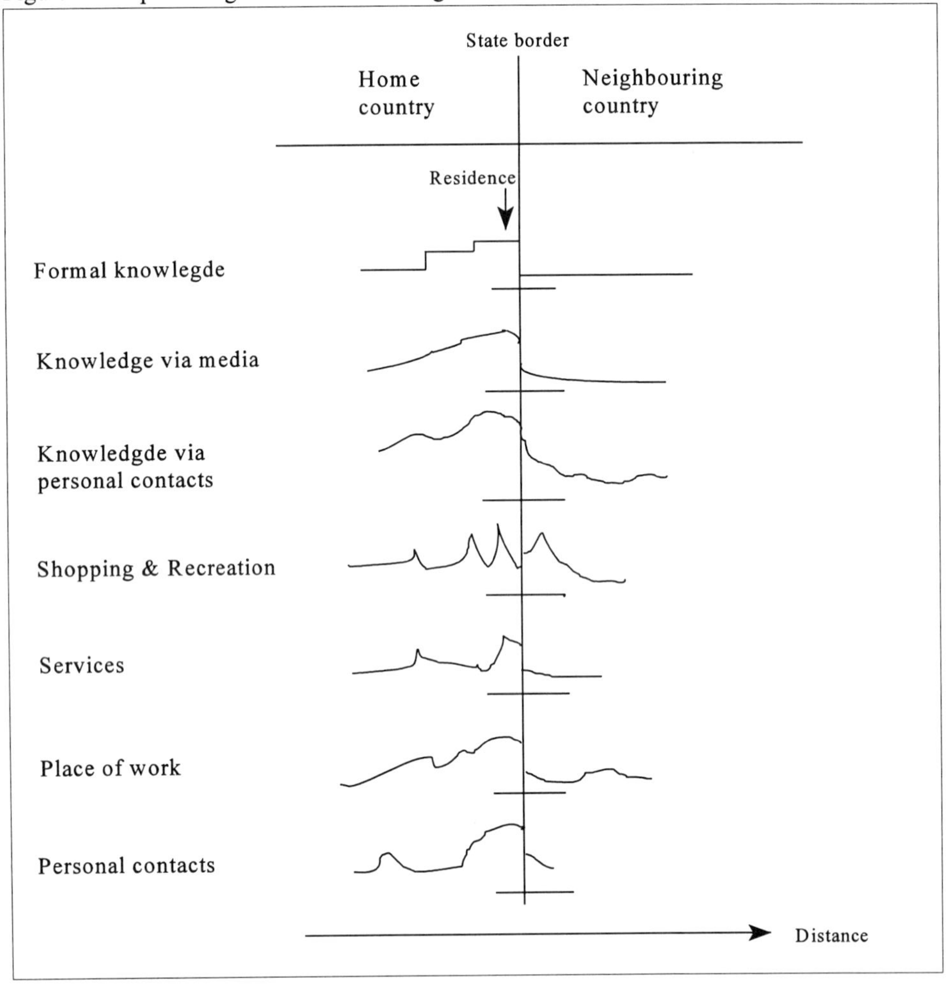

It is clearly discernible that the border can cause a true division. The orientation on recreational activities and shopping (tanking up included) alone profit from the division; all other activities show a negative curve in the diagram as a result of the border's presence.

Cognitive space is for a large part determined by *personal experience-based reality*, by the environment in which the individual is rooted and in which environmental recognition is at its maximum. In environmental psychology, an important topic of research concerns the place of experience in cognitive development. Experiencing and learning about the environment enable a human being to develop assumptions about reality (cf. Veitch and Arkkelin, 1995). These assumptions make it easier for man to act in everyday life. The assumptions are turned into a routine and habits that may reduce investment costs in terms of time, money and energy as a consequence of learning to cope with the new environment. Experience-based reality, therefore, creates a build-up of routine and habits in actions and behaviour. Experience-based reality is most often organically interwoven with the individual's community. The inhabitants of two territorial units, separated by a border, are likely to develop different cognitive spaces (Kamann, 1993a).

In modern societies however, yet another factor determines spatial cognition, *i.e.* knowledge-based reality. Because of more extended information flows (media, science, tourist offices etc.) and increased mobility, modern man can expand his *knowledge-based reality* enormously, thereby making a positive distinction between the borders of the mind and territorial borders. The most recent development in this context is, of course, the Internet, which operates by a separation of mind and body. While the body is local, intellectual exchange can be global.

Nowadays, it is difficult to draw definite dividing cognitive lines in space. This contrasts with concrete borders, which by definition can be drawn on a map. Still, it is possible to render cognitive borders on a map as well, '*the cognitive map*' (Tolman, 1948). This construct has taken on the meaning of a metaphor of the product of internal psychic representation of concrete 'reality' (cf. Gould *et al.*, 1974; Klaue, 1985; Pocock *et al.*, 1978; Riedel, 1994). A cognitive map may be defined as the cognitive representation of an environment (Veitch and Arkkelin, 1995).

A striking illustration of the impact of cognitive maps is the research on the connection between entrepreneurs' behaviour of orientation and the choices they make with regard to their place of business (Pellenbarg, 1985, 1991). Pellenbarg puts forward the hypothesis that spatial cognition, being the basis for a potential valuation of certain spatial units, may be visually rendered in a 'cognitive map'. He demonstrates that entrepreneurs still regard border regions as relatively unattractive for investment. Their peripheral location, in the national context, appears to be responsible for this view.

2.5.1 Discussion: concrete versus abstract

It is interesting to analyse the extent to which cognitive maps resemble concrete maps. In the literature on this subject, discrepancies between concrete reality and cognitive reality are called '*cognitive distortion*' (Riedel, 1994). Cognitive distortion takes on a special meaning in border research, since borders form a political dividing line that may have a cognitive influence. It may

be assumed that the world outside the own state borders, in comparison with the world inside the borders, has been explored less extensively from the cognitive point of view - also in comparison with the regional living space. This is often expressed in terms of the estimation of distances to places beyond the state border (see, e.g. Cohen, 1982; Riedel, 1994). An individual's estimation of a distance between two points in space is called *cognitive distance* (Golledge and Stimson, 1987) or *subjective distance* (Thompson, 1963; Riedel, 1994). The geometrical distance between points A and B will rarely coincide with the cognitive distance between the two points. The idea is to predict or elucidate the discrepancy between concrete reality ('truth') and cognitive reality, which indicates the space of action of the individual that made the estimation. The geometrical distance is intersubjective, the cognitive distance is subjective. That makes that the latter is individually dependent and therefore may be influenced by several factors, of which Evans (1980) enumerates the following: age, sex, familiarity with the space and culture, socio-economic status, and physical structure of the space in question. Riedel adds that, the more the individual is actively involved or has ties with a place, the more accurate will be his estimation of distance (Riedel, 1994). The presence of borders generally leads to an overestimation of distances (Kossylin, 1974; Evans and Pezdek, 1980; Ewing, 1981; Riedel, 1994).
Another way to examine the differences between concrete and abstract reality in the study of borders is the comparison of the concrete map of borders and the cognitive map of the location of borders. This method permits the elucidation of the question 'When and how do the maps of concrete and cognitive borders overlap?' Again the idea is to predict or elucidate the discrepancy between concrete reality and cognitive reality. Both these methods shall be more extensively discussed in chapter 4, where the theoretical model of the development of cross-border economic relations will be formulated. The empirical results of the confrontation between concrete and abstract reality will be discussed in chapter 7.

2.6 Conclusions

In this chapter, the various possible typologies concerning borders that are source of discussion in contemporary literature have been discussed. The following types of borders were distinguished: artificial versus natural borders; open versus closed borders; functional versus affective borders; and concrete versus cognitive borders. For each of these, it has been shown that there exists a paradox with regard to the role and significance of the borders. Summarising this chapter leads to the following paradoxes:

- Borders are functional as well as affective
- Borders are concrete as well as abstract
- Borders are open as well as closed

The *cognitive* (or 'abstract') and *affective* borders of the inhabitants one the one hand and the *concrete, functional* borders of the state on the other are not necessarily identical, neither in permeability, nor in territorial impact. To be able to evaluate the openness of borders, one must examine the mutual divergences of the types of spaces distinguished. Looking at the difference between *cognitive and functional,* and *affective and functional*, I posit the following:

1. The positive divergences may be regarded as opportunities, as challenges for integration. The overlap between active/cognitive/affective space and functional space is a (potential) 'action centre' (Boesch, 1963, p. 139).

2. The negative divergences shall be regarded as barriers to the integration of regions on either side of the border. The active/cognitive/affective space is smaller than the functional space: the overlap is the 'taboo zone' (Boesch, 1963).

The divergences between political dividing lines and cognitive and affective borders are important indications for the degree of openness of borders, the cross-border action space. As it has been made clear, the distinction between open and closed borders is not as obsolete as might seem. Fully closed borders do not exist. There will always be some degree of interaction between (the inhabitants of) two neighbouring states. One the other hand, there are territorial borders still, and there always will be. As it has been stated above, the matter at hand, is not whether the map will become borderless (for it will not), but to what degree the borders have (had) an influence on the shaping and direction of economic interaction and activities across borders.

In this study, I hope to provide a clear picture of the influence of borders in the formation of border-crossing economic relationships between firms. With this end in view, this chapter has explored the first part of the focal point of this dissertation, the influence of borders. As for the second part of the problem, dealing with the development of economic relations across borders, which might lead to a deeper understanding of the process of the initiation and the intensity of cross-border economic relations, the next chapter will evaluate the dominant economic business theories on this point.

Chapter 3

Economic theories on the development of cross-border economic relationships

3.1 Introduction

In chapter 2, I have dealt with the geographical economic and socio-psychological impact of borders. I have indicated the ways in which the border functions as an institutional, active, affective, and cognitive dividing line in space. The objective of this dissertation is to evaluate the role of state borders in the development of *cross-border economic relations* between businesses. As a next step in achieving the solution to this problem, the present chapter examines the existing theoretical insights in economic literature with regard to economic relationships. Special attention will be devoted to the development process and success of cross-border economic relationships with other companies, starting with the beginning and evolution of a firm's internationalisation[1].

In principle, internationalisation is nothing more, and nothing less, than the territorial expansion of a firm's activities. Basically, according to Nordström (1991), it is a simple concept. The company enters new areas to exploit its specific advantage(s). Two reasons conspire to make this difficult theoretically.

Firstly, by internationalising part(s) of its activities, a company crosses the state border and enters another state. Crossing a national border is more than just crossing a community border. In fact,

---

1 The models that have been developed to study the internationalisation process of businesses are mostly oriented towards large firms or multinationals. Here, the type of business remains undefined, as the matter discussed here applies to firms of all sizes. However, not defining the company size in fact revolves to a study of medium-sized and small businesses (all companies employing less than 250 active persons, European definition), since approximately 98% of all companies in most countries are included in this category (Atzema and Wever, 1994).

a double border is being crossed. In reality, therefore, it might not be such a straightforward passage as might seem at first glance. As argued in chapter 2, all kinds of entrepreneurial, managerial, and knowledge-related constraints and perceptions enter into play.

Secondly, different modes of internationalisation exist, which require different strategies and decisions (Louter, 1993). When a company decides not to sell directly to the new market, or to start up a new company in that market, but wishes to enter it via relationships with other companies, new problems arise. The theories presented in the literature on internationalisation are in essence theories about the firm, not theories about the development of economic relations[2]. The question of the development of a relationship between two companies brings new elements into the study of the internationalisation process. Now, matters such as attraction and negotiation between the two companies emerge. In fact, there are few theoretical approaches available that treat the entire process of relationship-formation exhaustively, from the beginning to the success of a cross-border economic relationship between two companies. A conclusive theory on the development of international economic relationships is not available.

This chapter, therefore, searches the literature on the internationalisation of businesses for theoretical clues to explain why and how companies enter into economic relationships across borders. Three theoretical points of departure have been considered most appropriate to elucidate this matter. These are the transaction costs approach, the international network approach, and the psychic distance approach. The transaction costs approach, most notably, is regarded as a highly important current, which is capable of explaining the existence of international economic organisations (section 3.2). The theory is forceful. However, I will demonstrate that it still exhibits many shortcomings for the purposes of this study, even though it is often stretched to fit various objectives (section 3.3). The relatively recent network approach is applied less often internationally, but it offers new, fresh handles for the study of cross-border economic relations. The most important features of this approach are its dynamic nature, its dependability, and the learning perspective (section 3.4). The shortcomings of the theoretical concept of the international network approach are discussed in section 3.5. The third approach, that of psychic distance, endeavours to explain what factors companies take into account when selecting a specific country for investment. An important role is played here by the perceived equality of foreign conventions (section 3.6). The weaknesses and imperfections of this theory are discussed in section 3.7. On the basis of the relevant theories presented in this chapter, the lessons from this overview of approaches in the study of the internationalisation process of economic relationships

2 As defined in chapter 1, economic relations here are not those economic activities executed by the company itself, but those which involve another person or company. The first prerequisite for the existence of economic relationships is that they have continuity. This means that there exists more than a one-off co-operation between two companies to produce or deliver a specific product or activity. A second prerequisite is that there exists agreement concerning the contents of the relation. This agreement may, or may not have been put down in writing.

will be presented (section 3.8). These form the basis for the construction of a theoretical model in chapter 4.

3.2 The international scope of the transaction costs approach: Why do international governance structures exist?

The transaction costs approach is the theory focusing principally on the explanation of economic transactions between parties. This popular, much-cited approach by Coase (1937) and most notably Williamson (1975, 1985) also brought new inspiration to the internationalisation debate within industrial organisation science. Until this theory was proposed, the portfolio diversity of international firms was mainly explained in terms of a difference in the rates of return between countries. In order to understand the international translation of the transaction costs approach, it is necessary to examine the conceptual framework of the original approach.

In apparent contradiction to the dominant approach at that time - the neo-classical, micro-economic approach, which described firms in terms of a production function - Coase (1937) desired to discover the possible *raisons d'être* of a company. In short, he asked himself why all transactions were not simply executed through the market and attempted to answer the question: *Why do firms exist?* To answer this fascinating question, he defined the firm as a governance structure for transactions. He argued that the main reason why it is profitable to establish a firm would seem to be that there is a cost of using the price mechanism. The most obvious cost of 'organising' production through the price mechanism is that of discovering what the relevant prices are' (1937, p.390). To put it differently, Coase regarded the existence of market imperfections as a valuable point of departure towards the explanation of a firm's existence. A firm would then tend to expand its activities 'until the costs of organising an extra transaction within the firm become equal to the costs of carrying out the same transaction by means of an exchange on the open market or the costs of organising in another firm' (*idem*, p.341). In fact, the basis of this line of thinking in transaction costs derives from the need to co-ordinate economic transactions. A division of labour and the specialisation that emerges along with it needs to be co-ordinated. A transaction can be defined as the transfer of goods or services between at least two actors, whereas a market, defined in terms of the transaction costs paradigm, is defined as a co-ordination mechanism through which ownership rights are transferred. Hierarchy, finally, can be regarded as synonymous with 'organisation'. In Coase's model, it stands for the structure within which the transaction takes place while ownership is maintained.

Williamson (1975, 1985, 1991ab, 1993, 1996ab) updated the approach. He focused particularly on the element of the efficiency of a governance structure for a given type of transaction. He tried to predict for which type of transaction, and under what kind of circumstances, which type of organisation is most efficient. In fact, it is this effort of Williamson that turned Coase's approach into a theory, for with the introduction of the possibility to predict, Williamson created the possibility to derive hypotheses suitable for empirical testing.

Assumptions
In order to explain the existence of transaction costs, Williamson assumed that economic agents are 'boundedly rational', a term he derived from Simon (1961). To clarify this assumption, he uses Simon's most-quoted phrase: 'Human behaviour is intendedly rational, but only limitedly so' (Williamson, 1975, p.21, quoted from Simon, 1961, p. XXIV). Simon meant to say that human decision-makers might attempt to maximise their goals, but that they are not always able to do so. It is impossible to gather all data required to make an entirely rational choice. Reckoning with this limitation, decision-makers exhibit a satisfying, rather than a maximising, behaviour. It is important to note that the mere postulate of bounded rationality is unproblematic when the transaction is embedded in a situation without uncertainty. In such a case, satisfying behaviour will equal maximising behaviour. What turns the limitation of the decision-maker's rationality into an issue is the fact that in most cases, the economic environment is characterised by *uncertainty*. Thus, it is costly to compile and sign a contract, and detailed, explicit specifications are necessary to avoid uncertainty concerning the product that is being bought or sold.

According to Williamson, the degree of uncertainty is increased if the economic actors are considered opportunists. Opportunism is generally interpreted as allowing oneself to be guided by chance or circumstances rather than by regard for principles. Williamson translates this definition of opportunism in terms of the strategic behaviour of entrepreneurs. He believes that *some* economic actors *sometimes* make use of a situation with their own advantage as the only *modus operandi*, 'self-interest with guile', one might say. Opportunism, therefore, is of a stronger form than self-interest. Self-interest is usually constrained by morality - opportunism is not. The latter allows for 'the making of false or empty, that is, self-disbelieved, threats and promises in the expectation that individual advantage will thereby be realised' (Williamson, 1975, p. 26).

Not *everybody* is to be regarded as an opportunist *all of the time*, according to Williamson, which means that the uncertainty, and consequently the transaction costs, could be lower. However, as it is impossible to know *a priori* which economic actors are opportunists and which are not, the mere fact of reckoning with this kind of economic behaviour will augment transaction costs. Without opportunism in economic behaviour, unforeseen contingencies would be met in a spirit of trust and towards mutual benefit. In such a context, transaction costs would be very low, or even nil. This postulate about economic behaviour is even more important in a situation where the exchange occurs between a small number of actors. In this case, the transaction costs can be relatively high, since there are only a restricted number of alternatives.

A definition of transaction costs
The premises about economic behaviour discussed above make it possible to explain the existence of transaction costs. In his works of 1975 and 1985, Williamson was not quite clear which costs should be regarded as transaction costs. In 1996, however, he offered the following definition in his mechanisms of governance:

> Transaction costs are the ex ante costs of drafting, negotiating, and safeguarding an agreement and, more especially, the ex post costs of maladaptation and adjustment that arise when contract execution is misaligned as a result of gaps, errors, omissions, and unanticipated disturbances; the costs of running the economic system.
> (Williamson, 1996b, p. 379)

The definition Williamson offers is actually twofold. The first half covers all costs involved in the writing, negotiating, safeguarding, enforcement and control of a contract in decisions to buy on markets. This is the micro-economic definition. In the second part - the alternative definition - transaction costs are much less precisely defined as the costs of running the economic system. This is the macro-economic definition (cf. North, 1990). Whenever I speak of transaction costs in the remainder of this study, I refer to the micro-economic definition.

Criteria
According to Williamson, the choice for a market or hierarchy depends upon three aspects of the transaction, that is to say its asset specificity, the degree of uncertainty involved and its frequency.

Asset specificity, the first determinant, can be described as the degree to which an asset can be used for alternative purposes without losing any of its value. Whenever asset specificity is high, the transaction costs will be high as well. Finding a transaction partner is rather difficult, and the contract must enter into great detail. Moreover, due to the high asset specificity, the transaction partners will be 'locked in', that is, they will become interdependent - meaning that the price to change transaction partners, in terms of transaction costs, will be high. Williamson argues that in this kind of situation, the best solution is to establish a new joint hierarchy (1975). In his later work, however, Williamson suggests that relational long-term contracting - what he called 'hybrid governance structures' - is also a possibility for overcoming such transaction's uncertainty (1985, 1996). Integrating the transaction vertically is efficient, not through ownership, but through co-operative agreements. Then, the dependency between the two partners cannot be regarded as a market transaction, nor can it be seen as a newly born hierarchy. It may be said that Williamson thus opened the way towards intermediate structures of governance, between the archetypal structures of market and hierarchy.

The second factor determining the height of transaction costs is the uncertainty or complexity of a transaction. It is possible to safeguard the intangible investments and uncertainty related to the transaction by using a hierarchy. Causes of high uncertainty in a market transaction could be opportunism, information asymmetry (buyer uncertainty), poor quality of the enforcement system, and/or the costs of information-seeking. The greater the uncertainty or complexity of a transaction, the higher the transaction costs will be.

The third factor determining the height of transaction costs is the frequency of the transaction, which has the same positive relationship with transaction costs. The issue, then, is whether the volume of transactions utilises the governance structure to capacity. The more frequently a transaction occurs, the more efficient a transaction-integrated firm will be.

Decision rules

The essence of Williamson's theory is to find the balance between market transaction costs and internal organisation costs. Williamson argued that in some cases, internalising the transaction in a hierarchy or a hybrid governance structure may be efficient. The uncertainty, in combination with the opportunist stance of the parties involved, incomplete information, and small numbers bargaining on the market, may lead to market failure. The high transaction costs cause the market failure, in this case. The remedy to this type of market failure is vertical integration, either forward (buying out one's representatives), or backward (buying out your suppliers). In other cases, Williamson argues, it may be more efficient not to internalise the transaction in a governance structure, but to buy the commodity or service directly on the market. Then, the transaction costs on the market are lower than the internal organisation costs.

The international extension

The transaction costs approach, which defines a firm or a market transaction in terms of administrative costs, has opened up a new research agenda for economic theory. The insights provided by the transaction costs approach made it possible, among others, to indicate very clearly what had to be subsumed under markets and companies. In the theorisation of international business, numerous scholars have used this framework in the analysis of transnational organisations (see, e.g. Anderson and Gatignon, 1986; Gatignon and Anderson, 1988; Rugman, 1986; Teece, 1981, 1986). Furthermore, many theoreticians have developed conceptual frameworks for the explanation of international governance structure that are in line with the transaction costs approach (see, e.g. Caves, 1982; Hennart, 1982; Solocha *et al.*, 1994; Teece, 1981, 1986). These authors argue that the line of reasoning used to explain the emergence of national firms could also be applied to explain the rise of international firms located in more than one place, the multinationals. The market, in these approaches, is generally regarded as the foreign market, and the hierarchy in Williamson's approach is translated into 'Wholly Owned Subsidiaries' (WOS).

Other theoreticians have combined the transaction costs theory with other concepts to explain the existence of economic governance structures. One of these major contributions to the international extension of Williamson's transaction approach was the work done by Buckley and Casson (1976, 1985, 1988). Analogous to Coase's reasoning (1937), Buckley and Casson argue that multinational corporations expand their activities to the point where the benefits of internalisation are outweighed by the costs. When market imperfections exist, such internalisation is necessary. Buckley and Casson combined the transaction costs approach with the 'firm-specific advantage' approach, which was advocated by Hymer (1960/1976). This last is often referred to

as the first theoretician to give an acceptable explanation of cross-border economic activities. His firm-specific advantage theory generally focuses on the explanation of the existence of multinational enterprises (MNEs). Unlike neo-classical economic theories of that time, Hymer did not assume markets to be perfect, firms to be rational economic agents, and information to flow freely and at no cost. In fact, Hymer was interested in the specific movements of the firm itself and the rationales for its strategies in the course of its market expansion. In other words, he wanted to get into the 'black box' of the firm to find arguments for its locational behaviour. He established that firms who want to expand their activities across the border must have specific advantages over native firms, since cross-border starters must be able to compensate for the 'information disadvantage' concerning (elements of) the newly entered country. They must have a certain product, knowledge, organisational method or technology that is innovative and competitive in other markets, not just in the home market.
This is the 'firm-specific advantage' concept that can be recognised in the industrial organisation theory proposed by Buckley and Casson and by many others who argued following this line of thought (see, e.g. Rugman, 1981, 1986; Rugman and Verbeke, 1992, 1993). Buckley and Casson were one of the first to combine both concepts, the transaction costs theory and the firm-specific advantage theory. They advanced the following line of reasoning: by internalising a specific asset, such as knowledge, technology or human capital, a firm gains and sustains its unique advantage. Direct foreign investments will then be made whenever the internalisation process induces the firm to extend its activities across the national border. The firm-specific advantage theory was used to explain *why* a specific governance structure, and the transaction costs theory was used to explain *which* governance structure would be chosen in international transactions.

Dunning (1977) wanted to propose an approach encompassing the most important contributions to the explanation of international business transactions. He postulated that a foreign direct investment must fulfil three conditions. In the first place, the firm should possess one or more firm-specific advantages, which he called owner-specific advantages. Secondly, if these specific advantages are to be exploited in other markets than the home market, the firm should have location-specific advantages, meaning that some firms are better equipped for foreign expansion because of the political and/or economic environment within which they are located. According to Dunning, 'today's ownership advantages of enterprise may the inheritance of yesterday's country-specific endowments' (1979, p. 283). In the third place, Dunning argues analogously to Buckley and Casson's theory described above, there will have to be advantages in internalising the international transaction whenever a foreign direct investment is considered. Therefore, where and why a firm internalises which transactions depends crucially on the specific advantages that are to be exploited in the foreign market. The opportunities offered to the firm, and the governance structure for transactions that the firm chooses, are all consequences of market imperfection. Efficiency then determines the mode of the international transaction.

If the firm, compared to the foreign market, possesses only owner-specific advantages, export would be the proper mode for foreign investments (cf. the market option in the transaction costs approach). If the firm also possesses location-specific advantages, licensing would be the best option. According to Dunning, when a firm has all three types of advantages, the establishment of a firm (hierarchy) in the foreign market would be possible. These possibilities are outlined in table 3.1.

Table 3.1 - Dunning's eclectic paradigm

	Firm-specific advantages (FSA)	Country-specific advantages (CSA)	Internalisation-specific advantages (ISA)
Export (Market)	●		
Licence	●	●	
FDI (Hierarchy)	●	●	●

Adapted from Dunning, 1977, 1988ab

Dunning's 'Ownership-Location-Internalisation' concept (OLI), which he himself referred to as an 'eclectic paradigm', has become the dominant approach in the explanation of the existence of international business.

A recent and interesting theoretical elaboration of the transaction costs approach concerning the study of cross-border make-or-buy decisions can be found in Ratti's work (1993a). As one of the few theoreticians working within the transaction costs paradigm, Remigio Ratti explicitly discusses the effect of the border. In the first instance, he chooses to elaborate a difference analysis between hierarchy and market (figure 3.1). The 'integration degree' is a function of the transaction costs and the control costs. The control costs of the interfirm organisation are regarded as a positively correlated with the 'integration degree'. Transaction costs are presupposedly exogenous.

Figure 3.1 - Cross-border make-or-buy decision

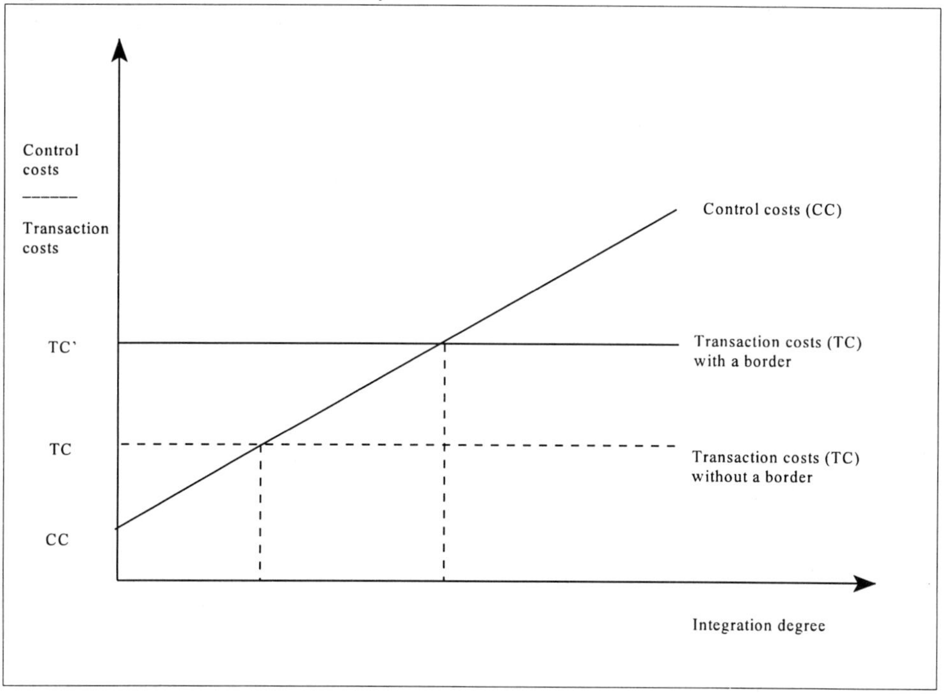

Adapted from Ratti, 1993a

Beneath the line TC executing the transactions within the firm is more attractive (the hierarchy). Above this line, according to Ratti, is it more economical to outsource the transaction to the market. In summarised form: if CC>TC, then there is a market, if CC<TC, then there is a hierarchy.

Ratti demonstrates that the introduction of a state border leads to greater uncertainty and therefore higher transaction costs (TC'), which influences the deliberations in the choice between hierarchy and market organisation. According to Ratti, the consequence of the cost increase is that the break-even point between hierarchy and market is shifted towards the right. Above the line TC' outsourcing the transaction on the foreign market is more attractive; beneath, 'some intermediary solutions with an integration as high as the market distortion' are possible (Ratti, 1993a, p. 44).

The choice of the integration degree made by the company, according to Ratti, depends furthermore on the integration demand, the preferential curve for the degree of integration. The demand for integration links negatively to the integration or control costs. The optimal situation is reached at the point where curve DD intersects with curve CC (see figure 3.2). Please note that Williamson's theory does not incorporate a similar demand curve. Williamson departs from the assumption that the balance of the market transaction costs and the control costs of the internal organisation determines what the entrepreneur will ask for.

Figure 3.2 - Integration demand versus costs of integration

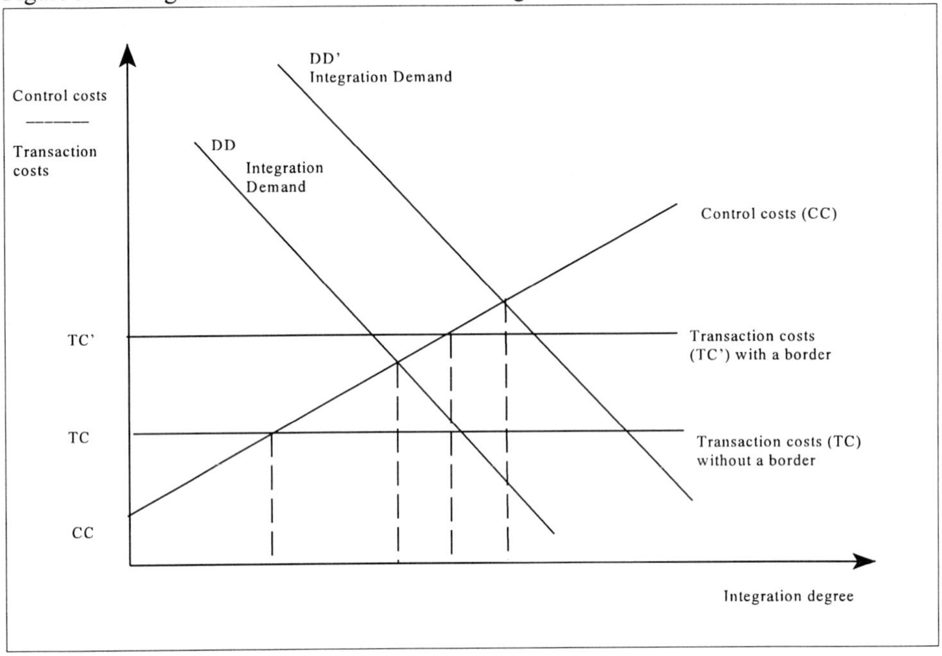

Adapted from Ratti, 1993a

The optimal point between demand (DD) and offer (CC) may be lower than the transaction costs in the case of a border (TC'). This means that the firm will not choose to handle the transaction in the firm, but prefers to outsource it on the market. Space is opened up for intermediate forms of hierarchy and market - the interfirm organisation, in which a form of integration emerges that is nearer the market than hierarchy. If the demand curve (DD') is higher than the transaction costs curve (TC'), an integration form emerges which tends more towards hierarchy than market. Unfortunately, Ratti does not provide further insight into the underlying considerations that offer arguments for the choices between market, hierarchy, and their intermediate forms. Questions such as: How do the control costs differ from the transaction costs, are control costs not part of the transaction costs, according to Williamson's theory; what is the difference between the control costs of intermediary integration forms and those of hierarchies in his model; what is the influence of asset specificity in his line of reasoning; what factors determine the demand for integration; why does the border generate increased uncertainty, and why does this lead to higher transaction costs, remain unanswered.

Concluding, Ratti has elaborated the transaction costs theory to explain the existence of *international* economic governance structures. While there are many questions to be answered, his explicit attention and inclusion of the border in the explanation of international governance structures is refreshing and inspiring.

The approaches presented so far have raised new, important questions in the field of international business economics. Moreover, they have become the dominant way of thinking in international business. However, the approaches present some major shortcomings, which will be discussed in the following section.

3.3 A critical assessment of the Transaction Costs Approach

It would go too far to evaluate, in this study, all international business theories that have the transaction costs theory as a basis or highly important component. I will try to arrive at a common factor of judgement by evaluating the transaction costs theory alone. My principal criticisms are enumerated here.

The problem of defining the costs of transactions

The first shortcoming of the transaction costs theory, as it is used in the explanation of international economic relationships, is that it remains unclear exactly what belongs to a transaction. Contrary to the definition given above, the costs for searching out contracting partners, and obtaining information about them, are not directly part of the transaction costs. It remains unclear why not.

Furthermore, it is unclear whether the transaction costs only apply to activities in the market, or also to production costs and the costs of the internal organisation (the management). If one would want to pursue the reasoning of the transactions costs approach '*in extremis*', one might argue that the production and internal organisation costs should be counted as transaction costs, especially in a large firm. This is because, within an organisation, one has to include a number of transformation processes, deliberations concerning production activities, the costs of accountants and lawyers, and so on. If the internal organisation is regarded in terms of actors that mutually execute transactions, this means that *the costs of internal allocation are weighted against the market transaction costs of the external allocation of means*. Here, it becomes important to determine what is internal and what is external, or, put differently, where are the boundaries of the transaction costs theory? The difference must reside in the rights of ownership. A transaction between two actors involving a hand-over of goods or services without transferral of rights of ownership is internal, a transaction involving partial or complete transferral of rights of ownership is partly or wholly external to the company. Transaction cost economics, then, turns principally into a legal study of the allocation of rights of ownership.

Within Dunning's international eclectic approach as well, there are a number of definitional ambiguities, which offer space for extensive theoretical exercises and speculations. In particular, it has appeared to be very difficult to achieve consensus on what the conditions for the specific advantages would have to be. Measuring owner-specific, location-specific, and internalisation advantages is extremely difficult. Moreover, the relationships between the various types of advantages are complex and difficult to pin down. Unquestionably, the various types are interrelated, as Dunning argues, but the question is *how* they are related (Dunning, 1989). An important contribution, from quite a different corner, has recently been made by Porter (1990) (see chapter 2). His theory, interpreted in terms of Dunning's paradigm, results in the following relationship: the firm-specific advantage is the outcome of the country-specific advantages: FSA = F(CSAs), (see Rugman and Verbeke, 1993; Van Houtum, 1991; Van Houtum and Boekema, 1995).

Bounded rationality and uncertainty

A second criticism on the measurement of the efficiency of the transaction costs approach relates to the concept of bounded rationality. As discussed above, Williamson tried to extend Coase's definition into a theory by introducing prediction mechanisms and postulates on economic behaviour. Yet to assume bounded rationality seems paradoxical with the best choice, in terms of efficiency. How can the rather simple postulate of human behaviour in economic transactions, bounded rationality, be combined with the implicit strategy of cost minimisation? Are the results of the transaction always efficient, then? In fact, one can only state afterwards, with a degree of certainty, what *was* the best choice - and even then it is not entirely certain what the most efficient choice would have been. How should one measure, for instance, the costs of disintegration of an organisational mode? Moreover, how should one measure the institutional setting of the markets in which the managers/entrepreneurs operate? In fact, this setting is one of the main causes of their bounded rationality. Given this uncertainty, the conclusion must be that managers/entrepreneurs cannot and do not rely entirely upon the reasoning offered by transaction cost economics in dealing with transactions. Thus, there *must* be some kind of compensation for the uncertainty of the height of the transaction costs when decisions are made. There must be a trade-off between the uncertainty surrounding the transaction and the certainty with which the (inter)action must be taken. The rational abilities of entrepreneurs are therefore overestimated in transaction costs analysis. Moreover, the importance of the perception of both certainty and uncertainty are thereby underestimated. Berger, Noorderhaven and Nooteboom (1995) said on this subject:

> In our view, received TCE does insufficient justice to the fundamental uncertainty managers of business firms face, and falls short of acknowledging the stringent boundaries to the rational capabilities of human decision-makers [...] However, there is no unambiguous information, nor a simple algorithm, for managers deciding on the optimal governance structure for inter-firm relations. Managers can only advance on the basis of their own imperfect perceptions, using trial-and-error, and making the most abundance of equivocal signs. Given the importance of these perceptions, they should explicitly be taken into account in a theory of inter-firm relations (cf. Dietrich, 1994 in: Berger, Noorderhaven, Nooteboom, 1995, p. 197).

TCE and the exchange process

The transaction costs theory analyses the optimal organisation structure of the exchange at a given point in time (Nooteboom, 1992). The moment of the transaction however, is often a passing moment in a *process* of interaction that has led to that transaction. The static character of the transaction costs theory does no justice to this complexity of the dynamic reality of learning, expectation, and experience. The costs of learning and the costs of trial and error could of course, in theory, be incorporated into the transaction costs theory. Besides the question whether all actions and transactions should and/or could be interpreted in terms of transaction costs, which would mean that the theory in fact explains nothing anymore, incorporating such learning costs into the theory would not change the essence of this specific criticism. Costs are the result of a process. Decision-making can therefore not be analysed merely in static comparative steps, without looking at the 'process variables' and the 'entrepreneurial/ managerial qualities, perceptual and social preferences' that grow and evolve within and through human interaction. The transaction costs theory is unable to analyse the development, growth and eventual ending of the one-off transaction. If the one-off transaction leads to a relationship, the transaction costs theory also lacks most of the tools to study the process in any meaningful way. Thus, when one tries to provide a more complete and dynamic, and therefore more complex picture of the interaction process between entrepreneurs, the theory is less applicable and more difficult to verify empirically (Blois, 1990).

Efficiency as strategy?

In the fourth place, one should bear in mind that existence due to efficiency by no means guarantees survival. Cost minimisation does not necessarily equal profit maximisation, nor does it necessarily mean the firm's survival. Efficient does not necessarily mean effective. Moreover, the organisation's existing structure is not always the most efficient one. Of course, its existence will be more profitable than its non-existence, or the firm would not exist at all. However, if this were the only statement, the definition of the firm would be no more than a tautology (see also Douma and Schreuder, 1991).

Williamson argues that an internal organisation is nothing more than a different type of 'contractual instrument, a continuation of market relations, by other means' (Williamson, 1991a, p. 162). I believe, however, with Ghoshal and Moran (1996), that the persistence of so many organisations cannot be explained merely by virtue of avoiding high transaction costs. Organisations do not just exist because they are governance structures that are more efficient and better equipped than markets to control the opportunist behaviour of economic agents. They have other advantages as well. According to Ghoshal and Moran, these advantages are to be found in the differing logic of markets and firms. The logic of firms reaches deeper than a simple, single gain of efficiency in an interaction.

The relaxation of binding constraints of efficiency gains of the current period allows firms to pursue innovative activities (*idem*). What may appear opportunist beforehand, might be intended to pursue creativity, initiative or leadership ex post, which in its turn may stimulate innovation.

Trust and commitment ('the moral factor') are needed for this behaviour to fiat. It is characteristic of a well-running organisation that it is not over-eager to protect itself against deceit and guile, as Williamson assumes, but that it regards the open spaces in the safeguards, to the contrary, as a 'lubricant' in the interactive links between management, employees, customers, and suppliers. What is more, rational and strict control over compliance with the contract might incite opportunist behaviour, which would lead to the opposite of what is to be attained. The moral factor of interaction is therefore used in an organisation to permit it to adapt itself flexibly to changing circumstances in the longer term. Ghoshal and Moran argue that it ought to be recognised that it is the quality of the organisational structure and of the internal relations within an organisation that determine the characteristics of the transactions. Williamson ignored the potential power and intent of organisations to influence the direction of progress, and the motivation of individuals to contribute to that progress (Ghoshal and Moran, 1996; Moran and Ghoshal, 1996). This, not (just) the efficiency advantage, provides the organisation with its *raison d'être*. As Coase, the founder of the transaction costs approach, put it some time before Ghoshal and Moran:

> I consider that one of the main weaknesses of my article ('The Nature of the Firm') stems from the use of the employer-employee relationship as the archetype of the firm. It gives an incomplete picture of the nature of the firm. But more important, I believe it misdirects our attention... the way in which I presented my ideas has, I believe, led to or encouraged an undue emphasis on the role of the firm as a purchaser of the services or factors of production and on the choice of the contractual arrangements which it makes with them. As a consequence of this concentration on the firm as a purchaser of the inputs it uses, economists have tended to neglect the main activity of a firm, running a business. (Coase, 1988, pp. 37-8, quoted in Ghoshal and Moran, 1996).

Ghoshal and Moran conclude that the economy should not be regarded as a 'market economy'. They argue that much modern-world business is carried out in an 'organisational economy', in which it might be more realistic to assume that the market begins where organisations fail (Ghoshal and Moran, 1996, p. 30).

TCE and its assumptions on human nature

The fifth criticism concerns Williamson's assumptions regarding human nature: opportunism and bounded rationality. An advantage of Williamson's theory is that it put human nature back on the agenda of neo-classical economics. He has attempted to open the 'black box' of organisations by means of the regulating motivations of entrepreneurs in transactions. Nevertheless, the assumptions he uses propose a very restrictively defined image of human behaviour in economic traffic, namely that of the *homo contractis* or contracting man (Williamson, 1985). This assumption is crucial to his theory, it determines the structure and outcome of his theory. A different image of man would change its theoretical structure.

In fact, transaction costs theory creates a new 'black box' by exogenously presupposing a certain human behaviour, which is the typically neo-classical method (cf. Holton, 1992, p. 73). Bounded rationality and opportunism are regarded as given facts, as constants - they are not variables. I believe this is a major weakness in Williamson's theory. I am far from claiming that man cannot be boundedly rational or opportunist - to the contrary, everyday life more than suggests the actual existence of such behaviour. The point is that human characteristics should be considered in a broader light, and most importantly that they are not exogenous. The human characteristics in Williamson's 'main case' consider only a restricted part of human interaction, and are assumed to be independent for the specific characteristics of the interaction, the situation within which the transaction occurs, or social and historical influences. In his attempt to reintroduce society into economics, Holton (1992) speaks of pre-social behaviour in the general assumption of economic man:

> One of the most striking features of Economic Man is the considerable degree to which his wants and basic personality structure are taken as 'given' elements, which exist prior to entry into society. This pre-social emphasis is typified in the assumption that individual wants are arrived at independent of social interaction, and that such wants represent choices freely made by individuals (Holton, 1992, p. 70)

Benshop (1996) also attacks the image of man used by Williamson. In his survey, he lists four objections to that image: Human rationality is reduced to a strategic rationality, affective and normative orientations are underestimated, human behaviour lacks incentives to collective action and knows only material or financial stimuli, and the supposed self-interest is a selfish variation of Utilitarianism.

Williamson takes an extreme standpoint, a fact admitted even by other theoreticians who have worked to perfect the transaction costs theory (see, e.g. Milgrom and Roberts, 1992). From the 'moral' point of view, economic sociologists in particular had already questioned whether mankind is indeed (sometimes) opportunist, acting with 'guile' and 'deceit' (see, e.g. Weber, 1961). Yet Williamson needs this extreme postulate on human behaviour to be able to demonstrate the existence and power of transaction costs. What he actually does, is suggest that economic interaction might bring out the simplistic and evil in people: beware of Economic Man - sign contracts and incorporate safeguards!

I must state here that I do not share Williamson's viewpoint. The assumptions of bounded rationality and opportunism are not useless - but they are desperately incomplete (cf. Holton, 1992). I believe that man, as a biologically adaptive creature, is turned into a caricature of himself where it concerns economic behaviour - in spite of all his advanced capacities to learn, experience, feel, and reflect. In Williamson's theory, economic man is consciously reduced to an

incompletely informed and often untrustworthy, selfishly calculating human being. From such an image of mankind, it is but a logical consequence that a study of the most efficient contract structure follows in traditional economic terms. This becomes less evident, and the scope of possible viewpoints of economic studies grows, if a more realistic, less simplistic image of mankind is used.
To exemplify the limitations of the transaction costs approach, Ghoshal and Moran (1996) tell a story often told in business circles and bearing, so they say, great resemblance to the assumptions of the transactions costs theory. It goes as follows: Two hikers wake up one night and discover a great big tiger lurking near their tent. One of them immediately puts on his running shoes. His fellow hiker reminds him that running is not a good strategy, as he cannot possibly outrun the tiger. The first then answers that outrunning the tiger will not be necessary at all. All he has to do is to outrun him, *i.e.* his fellow hiker.

This somewhat macabre story is usually interpreted as a case in point for the theory of the survival of the fittest. However, according to Ghoshal and Moran, it ought to be regarded as representative of the transaction costs approach. The assumptions underlying the story are twofold. In the first place, the hiker who considers outrunning the tiger is not considering any collaborative action, but is simply thinking opportunistically. He assumes his only option is to run for dear life. *Ex ante*, he does not have any certainty that his partner will *not* behave opportunistically and *ex post* discovery will be costly, that is, will cost him his life. Secondly, what matters is the speed of running, his efficiency. No other strategies are taken into account. Ghoshal and Moran argue that in the world of tigers (the markets) and hikers (the entrepreneurs) - given the assumptions above - the tigers will always triumph. One of the two hikers might escape, but then he would have to go on alone and might be outrun some day by another hiker. Ghoshal and Moran, therefore, reject the transaction costs model and make a plea for the inclusion of both long-term efficiency as a criterion, and for the adoption of opportunism as a variable in combination with the building of the social context (the 'moral factor') of economic behaviour - such as trust, routine and commitment - into economic modelling.

Transaction cost economics (TCE): Not the why, but the how
The sixth criticism brought forward is that, although proponents of the transaction costs approach state that the theory is useful for answering the question why multinationals own and control operations abroad, I believe that it does not provide a satisfactory answer to that question. I posit that the transaction costs approach does not focus on the *why*, but rather on the *how,* that is, on the explanation of the existence of different modes of entry. Efficiency motivations (alone) will not push or pull a firm across the border. To TCE, international expansion does not differ from national expansion. Within TCE, the optimal situation remains the minimisation of total transaction costs, whether in a national or an international context. Economic reasoning according to TCE leads to the optimum market or location, given the uncertainty of the circumstances. When international circumstances lead to greater uncertainty, the transaction costs will simply rise. However, as was stated in the introduction of this chapter, growing nationally is not quite

the same as growing internationally. I am convinced that to assume a rise in transaction costs because of international involvement is all too simple. A different culture and institutionalisation demand an approach that includes aspects of business that have not been considered in the transaction costs theory. A rise in transaction costs is the neo-classical answer corresponding to the implementation of an augmentation of tariffs in the trade model, as a consequence of the crossing of borders. Especially for small and medium-sized firms, it has been empirically established that many kinds of non-economic borders are to be uncovered in the economic landscape (see, e.g. Dagevos *et al.*,1992; Boekema and Van Houtum, 1994; Ratti, 1993b; Van Houtum, 1994).

Missing elements

Although the theory is now generally applied in all kinds of fields, TCE lacks a number of vital elements. A first shortcoming is the absence of consumers in the theory. It deals with make-or-buy decisions - the perspective is that of the company that searches the most efficient governance structure for a transaction: is it going to buy or produce itself? The market side of doing business is thereby ignored entirely. Objecting to this critique that buying also means selling is possible, but this objection does not consider reality. A theory of selling is not equivalent to a theory of buying. It follows that reasoning in terms of governance costs therefore misses arguments concerning market opportunities. In short, the transaction costs theory does not link to one of the vital elements and motivations for a firm's behaviour: the consumer.

A second missing element is that the theory fails to elucidate the other side of 'market failures', that is, the bureaucratic failure. Not only markets fail, which is why transaction costs exist; companies fail too - which is why firms also have bureaucratic costs. Such costs include more than the costs for internal organisation.

To summarise: In Coase and Williamson's approaches, firms are seen as the result of market failure. However, there is more to economic co-operation than this transaction-oriented theory is capable of incorporating. The international implementation of the transaction costs approach involves a static-comparative, efficiency-based, 'ex-post bounded rationale', a deviation from the market equilibrium. The neo-classical transaction costs position is increasingly regarded as untenable (Nooteboom, 1993). It is based on an old-fashioned epistemology of exogenous preferences and unworldly human psychology. Within TCE, economic reality is too drastically simplified, and it is isolated from its social context. Among businessmen, the importance of long-term and resilient relations with clients and suppliers is generally admitted, but within this field of economic science, it is regarded as difficult to come to terms with this basic observation (Knorringa, 1995).

Apparently, Coase's theory has not only constituted a major source for the analytical exploration of firm transactions and interaction, but also a major obstacle to overcome. In fact, the transaction costs approach is so narrow in its assumptions on human nature and economic objectives that this might well be what seduces its proponents and causes its apparently 'hard-to-beat' character. Its reasoning is simple, seems straightforward, and is therefore attractive. This is why it is not surprising that the theory has spread so widely. Partly because of this widespread and extensive use of the transaction costs theory, it has received a great deal of criticism too. There is some suspicion that almost anything can be rationalised with transaction costs as a base (Fisher, 1997).

An economic researcher in this field, however, cannot, and should not, neglect the core argument of this powerful and analytically elegant theory. The transaction costs approach can be used for what it is meant to do: elucidating the emergence of contracts in economic deliberations. However, as I have argued above, the research on cross-border economic transactions and interaction should not focus on the transaction costs approach alone, but look beyond it as well. To fill the theoretical gap left by TCE, the contribution of the international network approach is discussed in the next section.

3.4 Internationalisation and the International Network Approach

The second approach concerning the formation of international economic relations that has been studied in the context of this dissertation is the international network approach. Although network approaches have not been translated directly to explain the internationalisation of firms as yet, the importance of this kind of theory is increasingly emphasised in literature on the subject. Network approaches are increasingly regarded as an alternative to the transaction costs approach. As a consequence, there exists a growing tension between the concept of the transaction costs approach and newly emerged network and institutional-economic theories. From the transaction costs perspective, the network is seen as an intermediate governance structure existing between the classical market and hierarchical structures. In this respect, networks are explained as a variety of structures in the field of organisation, which do not fully equal a typical one-shot auction market or a newly established firm. The transaction-specific investments will be safeguarded through private ordering, and opportunism will be suppressed without the extensive use of contracts. A ranking then occurs, ranging from a completely independent co-operation between the actors with a very loose contract that more closely resembles a market transaction, to a co-operation in which the actors are more or less 'locked in', the nearly hierarchic situation. The social interaction features involved, notably trust, are regarded as inversely proportional to the transaction costs (Hosmer, 1995). The greater the trust between the parties, the lower the transaction costs will be. The network approach therefore regards networks as intermediate governance structures that lower transaction costs in the market. The choice of governance structure is thus extended to make, buy, or collaborate.

Richardson was actually one of the first to see the interfirm co-operation model for describing economic structure as an alternative to the transaction cost economic structures of market and hierarchy. He argued that the traditional market hierarchy presented by the transaction costs approach was 'our simple picture of capitalist economy' (1972, p. 883). According to Richardson, firms ought not to be regarded as islands of planned co-ordination in a sea of market relations.

Instead, firms are to be viewed as linked together through patterns of co-operation and affiliation. Thus, he judged that the traditional dichotomy of 'Market and Hierarchy' was misleading as 'it ignores the institutional fact of interfirm co-operation and assumes away the distinct method of co-ordination that this can provide' (1972, p. 895). Other economists, too, have recognised that co-ordination is insufficiently taken into account in economic analyses (see, e.g. Akerlof,1983; Arrow, 1974). Co-ordination, and especially trust in economic co-ordination, is necessary, they argue, or a Hobbesian situation will evolve in which economic life is filled with attempts at deceit. The efficiency of the market is better off with a certain amount of trust existing between the parties involved. Arrow in particular, has argued that societies have developed implicit agreements to certain kinds of regard for others, agreements which are essential to the further evolution of society or at least contribute greatly to the efficiency of its working (1974).

In an overview of the contribution of the transaction costs approach to the explanation of vertical interfirm relations, Noorderhaven (1994) expresses his doubts regarding the adequacy of existing explanations of economic interaction based on transaction costs. He argues that the simple framework of transaction costs economy has been stretched in order to accommodate hybrid relations, but that in the process, some of the seams of the theory seem to have come under severe pressure. This is illustrated by the limited number of empirical studies within the transaction costs approach giving attention to hybrid relations. Noorderhaven argues that this discrepancy between conceptualisation and empirical evidence is unacceptable. He therefore calls for improvements of, and additions to, the framework of transaction costs, which should be sought in the domain of 'trust and expectations; the significance of human and organisational limitations to the collection and processing of information; and the dynamics of creation, development, and decline of hybrid vertical inter-firm relationships' (*idem*, p. 33). He then goes on to say that 'such additions and adaptations are no small measures, and go to the heart of the assumptions underlying TCE' (*idem*, p. 34).

The alternative view to the neo-classically oriented concept of networking in the transaction costs approach is mostly championed by Scandinavian researchers stemming from the University of Uppsala and Stockholm School of Economics in Sweden. This view, is usually referred to, despite small differences between the various approaches, as the research tradition of the 'Swedish network approach' (see, amongst others, Anderson *et al.,* 1994; Håkansson, 1982, 1987; Håkansson and Johanson, 1988; Håkansson and Snehota, 1989; Johanson and Mattsson, 1987, 1988, 1994). The Swedish network approach was developed from the 1980s and initiated by the presentation of the Interaction Approach by the Industrial Marketing and Purchasing Group (IMP) led by Håkansson. This approach focused on the determinants of buyer-seller relations and interactions. The interaction paradigm they use is based upon the following assumptions: buyers and sellers are active participants; the relationship between them is frequently long-term and complex; and the links between buyers and sellers often become institutionalised (Håkansson, 1982). The interaction approach was heavily influenced by the Inter-Organisational theory (Van de Ven *et al.,* 1975) and the transaction costs approach (Williamson, 1975). The Interaction Approach, may be seen as one of the first network approaches in the Swedish research tradition.

The two most important findings in this research field were that (1) patterns of exchange and adaptation processes vary between actors depending on the interaction strategies and the history of the relationship, and (2) the interaction in dyadic relations is frequently influenced by interaction in relationships with third parties (Johanson and Mattsson, 1987). The attention explicitly devoted to indirect relations (partners of partners) may be regarded as typical to the network approach. It generates an extra dimension for bilateral exchange. The line of reasoning is that the implications (gains or losses) for indirect relations are considered both at the beginning of a bilateral exchange with a partner and at its break-off.

Later on, Johanson and Mattsson (1988) presented a hypothesis on the internationalisation of firms, in which the interaction between firms is examined as a network of relationships. This approach favoured the theme of 'the market as network'. Johanson and Mattsson's model has become one of the most elaborate and influential network approaches focusing on the internationalisation of firms. In all references to the network theory in this work, I will follow their approach, hereafter referred to as International Network Approach (INA).

Johanson and Mattsson (1988) were of the opinion that the existing concept of networking had too narrow a base in economic rationality. Moreover, it was found that empirical evidence did not sufficiently support the transaction costs theory. The need for adjustment of that theory was deeply felt by the two Swedish authors and has been the most important impetus for them to develop their alternative approach. In their theory, markets are networks, and networks are institutions themselves.

Assumptions

The inclusion of the effect of learning in the assumptions on human behaviour is crucial to the postulates of economic behaviour presented by the INA. Economic behaviour, in their view, is therefore not objective, nor is it stable; to the contrary, it is path-dependent and dynamic. The learning effect is a to a large extent a consequence of the interaction with others. This provides a point of departure for economic interaction that differs radically from the transaction costs approach in that the latter, according to Nooteboom, 'is in the habit of taking preferences, capabilities, knowledge and perception, as stable, and as given exogenously and objectively as 'underlying realities' (1993, p. 14). In contrast, the INA emphasises 'dynamic, individual, and interconnected exchange relationships of both a complementary and substitutive nature' (Johanson and Mattsson, 1994, p. 325). One could argue that whereas the transaction costs approach is firmly rooted in neo-classical economics, the INA takes a more sociological perspective (Nooteboom, 1993).

The INA departs from the idea that four commodities are exchanged during a transaction. There is product or service exchange, information exchange, financial exchange, and social exchange. The addition of the last category, that of social exchange, is characteristic of the INA. It is argued that organisations and entrepreneurs do not exist in a vacuum; they are embedded in a social context of relationships. In a relationship, more than just tradable goods and/or information are exchanged. Non-tradable goods are also exchanged.

In the exchange occurring between the two actors, the INA speaks of an adaptation process (Johanson and Mattsson, 1987). The two actors will test whether there is a 'fit'. In this adaptation process, the role of trust between the partners is considered crucial. Trust checks opportunistic behaviour, leads to network stability, and serves as a source of network co-ordination (see also Ford, 1980, 1984). The adaptation may occur at several levels - financial, technical, economic, and/or social. According to Johanson and Mattsson, this adaptation is important for several reasons, and they name three: adaptation strengthens the bond between the actors; it generates a lasting bond; and mutual orientation emerges.

Theoretical foundations

For its assumptions on social exchange, the international network approach is closely related to social exchange theories (Blau, 1964; Homans, 1958). These posit that everyone strives to achieve a maximum positive difference between the rewards and costs of the relation. In social exchange theories, too, the idea is that the advantage of the exchange is obtained through the other. The dependence is mutual. The expectations with regard to the rewards and costs of the relation are, in this case, based on experience and learning. People learn from previous situations of deliberation and will continue to apply successful strategies and choices in new situations. Here, too, it is possible to discern an adaptation process.

For its assumptions on control, the international network approach is closely related to resource dependence theory (see, e.g. Pfeffer and Salancik, 1978). In this theory, the environment is regarded as a source of resources, which are deployed on behalf of the continuity of the company (De Groene, 1995). The continued existence of the company depends on the availability of resources and the efficiency and creativity with which these are distributed. These resources belong to other actors. The ownership of resources generates power. So as to gain access to these resources, be it directly or indirectly, relations with actors in the environment of the company will have to be developed. At that moment, an exchange of, for example, money and commodities is made. As noted, this theory heavily influenced the international network approach, a fact witnessed by the following quotations from the work of Johanson and Mattsson: 'A basic assumption in the network model is that the individual firm is dependent on resources controlled by other firms. The firms get access to these external resources through its network positions' (1987, p.36). And in 1988: the reason for internationalisation of business is that 'a firm wants to utilise and develop resources in such a way that its long-run economic objectives are served. Firms then internationalise if that strategy increases the probability of reaching the general objectives' (Johanson and Mattsson, 1988, p.297)

As in the international network theory an important theme in the resource dependency theory is the degree of dependency of the actors in the environment, as opposed to the degree of control. According to Pfeffer and Salancik (1978) the interplay between dependence and control determines the choice of the inter-organisational relation of a firm.

In the INA, firms are considered as interdependent; their activities are co-ordinated through interaction. Markets are described as sets of interconnected exchange relationships. This means that the competitive position of a single firm on the market is determined by its interaction with other firms, *i.e.* how and to what extent the firm extracts value from the co-operative environment. As Håkansson and Johanson (1988) put it: 'Interaction is a stream of acts' (p. 462). The environment is thereby seen in terms of resources. Firms are not regarded as driven by opportunism in the hunt for efficiency, but as interaction-driven in the hunt for resources. Competence building is crucial. The market position of the firm, the strategic or network identity (Anderson *et al.,* 1994; Håkansson and Johanson, 1988), is therefore defined in terms of potential and active network contacts and relations: 'Much of the uniqueness of a firm lies in how and with whom it is connected' (Anderson *et al.,*1994). In other words, the openness, the degree to which and how the economic relations of the firm are structured in order to achieve a certain exchange, is the measure for its market position. These factors, and not the transaction costs of the exchange, are subject to analysis in the INA. This implies that within the INA the boundaries of the firms are unclear and cannot be seen as the proper focus of study such as in the transaction costs theory.

Finally, the international network approach of firm behaviour is closely related to the social embeddedness approach. Grabher (1993) and Granovetter (1985ab), most notably, have constructed a socio-economic model of firm behaviour. They argue that the personal and professional network relations in the direct environment of entrepreneurs should be incorporated in the analysis of economic actions and interactions. Firm/manager decisions and actions should be set within their social context variables. Granovetter's retort (1985ab) to TCE, therefore, is the 'under-socialisation' of that approach. By under-socialisation he means the atomised utilitarian view of economic actions. He argues that economic actions should instead be regarded as a form of social action and that economic actions are socially situated. Another point Granovetter criticises is a situation of 'over-socialisation', in which the established values dictate economic behaviour (*i.e.* the emphasis lies on the state). One should avoid both under- and over-socialisation; Granovetter himself favours the 'embeddedness' approach. He argues that 'social relations between firms are more important, and authority within firms, less so, in bringing order to economic life than is supposed in the markets and hierarchies line of thought' (Granovetter, 1985b, p. 501). And elsewhere, he stresses 'the role of concrete personal relations and structures (or 'networks') of such relations in generating trust and discouraging malfeasance' (1992, p. 60).

In 1993, Grabher, put it differently: 'Embeddedness refers to the fact that economic action and outcomes, like all social action and outcomes, are affected by actors' dyadic relations and by the structure of the overall network of relations' (1993, p. 4). Granovetter argues that, in the ongoing interaction of economic parties, gathering information about the other party costs money and time. In such circumstances, reputation is important. A firm's reputation is best served by the parties with whom the firm has a good relation, or may emerge from the experience of its past dealings with the other party. Reputation helps to bring trust into economic relationships. Thus,

Granovetter argues that the identity and past relations of individual transactors play an important role in dampening the distrust, opportunism, and disorder that may occur in economic transactions. The concept of social context in the interaction does not have a one-and-for-all influence, but is an ongoing process. The link with the dynamic process of learning and the building of trust in economic relations as postulated by the INA is evident.

Argumentation

The internationalisation of a firm, according to Johanson and Mattsson (1988), means that 'the firm establishes and develops positions in relation to counterparts in foreign networks' (p. 296). They argue that this can be done in three ways:

- By international extension, that is, through the establishment of positions in relation to counterparts in foreign sets that are new to the firm
- By penetration, *i.e.* by developing the positions and increasing commitment in already existing nets in the foreign country
- By international integration, increasing the co-ordination between different national sets

It is often argued that small and medium sized enterprises (SMEs) especially, which are often unable to internalise tasks due to a lack of resources, may have to rely upon the 'network-embeddedness' of their environment. In gaining access to these resources, network contacts are considered essential. These are most effective if they are socially embedded, be it personally or professionally (Dubini and Aldrich, 1991; Larson, 1992; Lorenz, 1991). Table 3.3 lists the most important differences between the transaction costs approach and the international network model.

Table 3.2 - Transaction Cost Economics (TCE) versus the International Network Approach (INA)

	TCE	INA
Theoretical foundation	Neo-classical economic theory	-Social exchange theory -Resource dependency theory -Social embeddedness approach
Argumentation	-Analysis of the boundaries of the firm -Firm is market failure; firm is a governance structure for transaction(s) -Economic exchanges are transactions	-Analysis of the firm's openness -Firm is a social unit with a unique network position in the market; firms are socially embedded -Markets are networks -Economic exchanges are relations
Problem orientation	Explanation of the existence of governance structures (static, equilibrium)	Explanation of the dynamic interaction and adaptation between firms in industrial systems
Strategy orientation	Efficiency	Competence building
Assumptions	-Opportunism -Bounded rationality -Uncertainty -High asset specificity -Small numbers exchange -High frequency of transactions	-Trust -Dynamic boundaries of knowledge, learning by experience and interaction -Uncertainty -High asset specificity -Small numbers exchange - High frequency of transactions
Nature of transaction	-Markets, bilateral governance structures, hierarchy (MBH) as dyadic transaction structures -Transactions as efficient operations	-Relationships as multiple dyads -Exchange and adaptation processes as investments in relations

Adapted from Johanson and Mattsson (1987); Nooteboom (1993)

For the reasons mentioned here, the INA argues that the resource-seeking behavioural and social features of transactions cannot be aligned with the postulates on economic behaviour of the transaction costs model. This conviction is based upon the fact that the transaction costs approach has just not been constructed to theorise about co-operation outside the hierarchy of the firm and social/affective dimensions in relationships.

Above, I argued that the transaction costs approach on international governance structures has important shortcomings (section 3.2). It has no eye for the potentially important behavioural differences between (small and medium-sized) companies, nor does it devote any attention to social and psychological stimuli to or constraints on economic decisions, or the social embeddedness of economic actions. The most important reaction, and the most attractive alternative to the framework provided by the transaction costs theory, the network model, has been discussed in this section. The aspects emphasised by the latter, such as the social conditions of trust and reputation involved in an interaction, are evocative and appear important. Yet the international network approach too has its shortcomings, which will be examined in the following section.

3.5 A critical assessment of the International Network Approach

Analytical sharpness

The first criticism is that the international network model presented here possesses too many characteristics of a reaction still. It has remained rather offensive and as yet has not developed its analytical potential. As Johanson and Mattsson themselves state, 'the Swedish tradition is different from mainstream research. It is less quantitative and more qualitative, less deductive, and more inductive, less theory testing and more theory developing, less specifically oriented to marketing management and more holistic, less prescriptive and more descriptive' (1987, p. 336). Or as Oerlemans recently put it: 'The economic network approach embraces a number of small and great hypotheses that are seldom combined to form a systematic, verifiable explanation of causes and effects of economic networks between organisations' (Oerlemans, 1996, premise 5, my translation). A more balanced and analytically sharper view on economic exchange is yet to be developed. Moreover, despite the efforts of Johanson and Mattsson (1988), the network approach has been elaborated little in an international context. Too little attention is paid to the extent to which the inclusion of borders in the theory may influence the geographical distribution and depth of a network.

The disadvantages of relations and networks

My second criticism is that networks may fail. The degree of dependence is crucial to networks. Above, I already mentioned that people, including entrepreneurs, are interdependent. Economic exchange is founded on dependencies. The reduction of uncertainty is an important stimulus to enter into alliances with others. An economic relation, moreover, may lead to the creation of a joint surplus, either through the reduction of the joint costs, the growth of market shares, or through the increase of knowledge (cf. Commandeur and Den Hartog, 1991). The issue is what degree of dependency is chosen. The reduction of uncertainty, one must keep in mind, is not only an advantage; it may also function as a disadvantage. The reduction of uncertainty through entering into an economic relation also leads to an implicit lock-in. The new community that is created may cause a lock-in so strong that it begins to suffocate the parties involved and thereby reduces flexibility and creativity. The stability of the network then leads to staleness (see, e.g. The Economist, 1992). The very same factors that are the causes and advantages of economic relations may also, therefore, become their disadvantages.

The network concept

In the third place, the term 'network' remains indefinite. The question that remains unanswered is: what degree of dependence turns an interaction into a relation or network? The INA moreover does not distinguish clearly between oft-used terms such as 'contact', 'interaction', 'co-operation', 'relation', and 'network'. For these reasons, the term 'network' has remained more of a chaotic conception than a rational abstraction (Sayer, 1982). The network concept now appears principally an instrument or a (call for) strategy, rather than a theory. This stands in sharp contrast to transaction cost economics, which is not a strategy (cf. Ghoshal and Moran, 1996) but a rational abstraction. Another problem is that the literature on the subject makes little effort to determine which network strategy is most effective. The debate is not helped by the ambiguity concerning the term and the implications of the network concept.

Missing elements

The first element that is crucially absent in the INA is that of *space*. The environment is not just social; it is also spatial. And it is clear that networks between firms are strongly diversified spatially. Many scholars believe that the spatial variations in networks are structural, locational determinants. In this context, they speak of the 'path dependency' of regional network characteristics (see chapter 2), which strongly influences, if not determines, even the performance of individual firms. Authors such as Porter and Storper, most notably, have striven in the past years to validate this postulate (Porter 1990; Storper, 1993).

In my view, incorporating spatial context into network analysis, moreover, implies that the context rationality of entrepreneurs must comprise two components: the social context and the spatial context. Entrepreneurs, in their behaviour, are not only determined or driven by whom they know, but also by what they know. This concerns their spatial cognition and affection, as demonstrated in chapter 2. Therefore, in the economic rationality of entrepreneurs, an important endogenous component of their environment is present. Proshansky *et al.*(1983) put it like this:

> 'The subjective sense of self is defined and expressed not simply by one's relationship with other people, but also by one's relationships with the various physical settings that define and structure day-to-day life' (1983, p.58)

The rationality of entrepreneurs is anchored in space, or path dependent, to an important extent. One should think of national educational systems and media, which strongly form people's cognition (and attitude). But differences in language and the acquisition of knowledge also exist on the regional level. Where it concerns the affective component of spatial dependency, one might think of the processes of spatial identity formation, which might influence economic behaviour, as discussed in chapter 2.

In the second place, the psychological elements of human (international) interaction are missing. The unit of analysis in the INA is paired relationships and/or the structure of the cross-border networks, not individual economic behaviour as such. The INA thereby neglects the dynamics of the actions and attitudes of individual actors that enter into a relation, which do seem to be important. INA looks only at the result of the relationship's dynamics. The *process* character that appears so important in the creation and breakdown of relations and networks, in which a great number of psychological factors seem involved, is given little attention. The behaviour of people towards, for instance, the organisational culture or national identity of partners in cross-border economic relations, can therefore be better understood from the viewpoint of socio-psychology, which tells us that group identities are important mediators for people to live and to act.

In short, considering the number of criticisms presented here, I argue that a more integrated approach should be considered, in spite of the valid criticisms of the INA on the transaction costs approach. The distinction between the two approaches is based on an oversimplified notion of economic reality. Certainly, all kinds of social processes occur during the transaction that cannot be ignored, as the proponents of the INA argue. But networks and economic relations are tools, not the reasons for economic exchange. Relations are the means to an end, and that end is of an economic character. The distinction, therefore, is artificial and blocks a more synthesised view of (economic) interaction.

Another important factor is involved. Both the transaction costs approach and the international network approach seem unable to give a more integrated view of the *strategy* of firms and individual *psychology* of the entrepreneurs in *entering* a foreign country. These factors are, however, prominent in the psychic distance approach, which will be discussed in the following section.

3.6 The 'Psychic Distance' Approach

In section 3 of this chapter, I argued that the prominent field of research, the 'static approach' of TCE, as it is often called, is unable to answer all questions about the existence of cross-border capital flows. In the previous two sections, the alternative model of the INA was presented and evaluated. Now, I will discuss the 'Psychic Distance Approach' (PDA) elaborated by Johanson and Wiedersheim-Paul (1975) and Johanson and Vahlne (1977, 1990). These proponents of the PDA posit that the decision to internationalise should be regarded as a major *strategic decision*. The theory of the static choice at a certain moment in time between the alternative modes determined by relative transaction costs and benefits, is regarded as unsatisfactory. The psychic distance approach is perhaps one of the most prominent 'dynamic' approaches to the study of international business movements.

Theoretical foundations and assumptions

In addition to the strategic behaviour approach of Cyert and March (1963), this model has used elements of Aharoni's decision approach to internationalisation (1966), the phase approach to export marketing (Cavusgil, 1980), and literature on the theory of the firm (Penrose, 1959). These contributions have led to three basic assumptions, on which the model is founded (see, e.g. Nordström, 1991).

In the first place, the PDA posits that the firm's internationalisation is a consequence of its growth (cf. Penrose, 1959). Home market saturation is a stimulus to the search for new markets. If the firm does not wish to diversify, geographic expansion might prove the best option. The size of the potential market is thereby considered the most important factor in the beginning and expansion of international operations.

Secondly, it is assumed that firms are uncertain about the outcome of their (inter)actions. (Managers of) firms are supposed to be boundedly rational (cf. Decision approach, Behaviourism, TCE). The decision process, based on Cyert and March (1963) and Aharoni (1966), underlines the importance of 'lateral rigidity' between the stages in the decision process, the limited perception of alternatives, and selective search in the choices.
Contrary to the transaction costs approach, however, where there is no assumption of a learning-by-doing process, and the preferences and behaviour of economic agents are exogenous and constant, economic agents are believed to learn from their past actions - they possess incremental learning. Thus, it is not the boundaries of their rationality that is important, but their speed of learning. The learning effect, resulting from dealing with cultural differences, constitutes what is called 'objective experiential knowledge' (cf. Penrose, 1959). The degree of uncertainty caused by the trade-off between the need for accurate market knowledge and the lack of such knowledge in a new market, is therefore regarded as central in understanding the dynamics of the internationalisation process of firms. The explicit difference, in this respect, with neo-classical economics (like TCE) is striking. In a neo-classical economic world, there is no psychic distance, since the economic actors are not assumed to differ in their preferences and their knowledge over time (Nordström, 1991).

In the third place, the PDA is a stage model. Firms will evolve internationally according to an 'establishment chain' (Johanson and Wiedersheim-Paul, 1975, p. 307; see also Håkanson, 1979), that is, the internationalisation process gradually evolves according to four stages of foreign involvement (Johanson and Wiedersheim-Paul, 1975; Johanson and Vahlne, 1977):
1. Expansion on the national market, no regular export
2. Export via independent representative (agent)
3. Sales subsidiary
4. Production/manufacturing facility

According to the PDA, the speed at which the path is followed is determined by the experiential knowledge that has been gathered about the foreign country.

Although the approach was explicitly developed for the study of the evolution of large multinational corporations in international business, this approach might be of great relevance for small and medium sized enterprises (SMEs). This is because it may explain why the attempts to move into areas of great potential demand where economies of scale are prevalent are fraught with danger. This is consistent with the observation that smaller firms are, from the international point of view, vulnerable rather than market-sensitive because of the relatively great importance of both internal and external constraints and the relatively great dependency on institutional and market changes of SMEs (United Nations, 1993).

Definition

Psychic distance was originally defined as 'factors disturbing the flow of information between potential or actual suppliers and customers' (Wiedersheim-Paul, 1972). In the measurement of psychic distance, the following principal factors were listed: level of development, difference in level of development between the home and foreign country, business practices, level of industrial development, cultural differences, everyday language, and the links existing between the home country and the foreign market (Johanson and Wiedersheim-Paul, 1975; Johanson and Vahlne, 1977). Recently, this definition was updated by Nordström and Vahlne to 'factors preventing or disturbing firms learning about and understanding a foreign environment' (1992, p. 3). In practice, this means that firms are predicted to start their internationalisation, in a successive order from export to foreign direct investment, by moving into those markets about which the entrepreneur/firm has the greatest experiential knowledge. Thereafter, the firm will learn incrementally about, and enter, more distant markets. As Johanson and Wiedersheim-Paul argued (1975), it is for this reason that psychic distance is not constant; 'it changes because of the development of the communication system, trade, and other kinds of social exchange. In general we expect most changes to take place rather slowly.' (*idem*, p. 308).

Line of reasoning

The clue of the psychic distance model is that firms are assumed to begin their internationalisation in markets about which the entrepreneurs/firms have the lowest market uncertainty, that is, the highest experiential knowledge level. Often, these markets are neighbouring countries as the experiential knowledge, or what is sometimes called the 'tacit knowledge', of these environments is larger.

The problem focus of this theory is therefore how the psychic distance of managers /entrepreneurs relates to the decision-maker's choice of the mode of entry.

Note that although *a priori* there seems to be a strong positive relationship between physical distance and psychic distance, this does not necessarily have to be true in all cases. There may, for example, exist inverse relationships between the United Kingdom and Australia, between the Netherlands and the Dutch Antilles.

O'Grady and Lane (1994), on the other hand, have found in their empirical research on the international interaction between the United States and Canada that a small geographical distance does not necessarily imply a small psychic distance. In their research they even found an inverse relation between the assumed cultural and the actual psychic distance. They established that, although the USA and Canada are generally assumed to be close or similar, the observed cultural distance that underlies and guides the business interactions between them is, in reality, larger than the assumed cultural distance. They named this phenomenon the 'psychic distance paradox'.

3.7 A critical assessment of the Psychic Distance Approach

The attention explicitly devoted to the existence of a 'frontier problem', as well as the process-wise character of economic expansion in international business operations, are convincing aspects of the psychic distance approach. Moreover, the model has a practical and common-sense appeal. Yet, several shortcomings are to be found in this approach.

Leapfrogging and inertia

The first important criticism is that it does not account for leapfrogging on the one hand, and stasis and inertia on the other. There are firms who leapfrog certain stages, either in the 'establishment chain', or in the predicted move according to a 'psychic distance' list of countries. The increasing engagement in this approach is presented as somehow inevitable and mechanistic. This does not appear to conform to economic reality (see Buckley, 1989; Lambooy, 1993; Leonidou and Katsikeas, 1995, 1996; Melin, 1992; Miesenbock, 1987; Young, 1987). Not only are some phases skipped, but some stages may prove 'sticky' for some firms. Thus, no room has been left for inertia in the various stages, nor has 'de-internationalisation', that is, regressions to former stages, been accounted for. Firms experienced in doing business abroad, for example, may well be expected to depart from the theoretical predictions of stages and markets, as their uncertainty regarding foreign markets has decreased (Nordström, 1991, p. 25). The approach does not account for cumulative experience. Nordström (1991) mentions another reason for leapfrogging in the various stages of internationalisation, namely that firms may be under severe pressure from competitive factors and actors, such as often happens in highly internationalised industries.

In such situations, the heterogeneous pattern of entry opportunities might be the economic reality.

Definition and indicator

The definition and indicator of psychic distance are both ambiguous. Apart from the erroneous associations that the word 'psychic' may evoke, the term 'cognitive distance' would express the intentions of the psychic distance approach more accurately. The term cognition, namely, refers to the experience and knowledge gathered by an individual. The psychic distance model departs from such an individual evaluation of countries on the basis of knowledge and experience. The absence of the required knowledge is considered the most important obstacle to the development of international operations.

Besides, the definition of psychic distance can be and has been interpreted in more than one way. The latest update of the definition of psychic distance by Nordström and Vahlne, 'factors preventing or disturbing firms learning about and understanding a foreign environment' (1992, p.3), leads to several questions that all remain unanswered, such as which factors are important for 'learning and understanding', how is the assumption of bounded rationality combined with that of incremental learning, and why are the obstacles that hinder learning about doing business in other countries not mentioned and analysed? The knowledge and experience, so crucial in the approach, is fed by information about that country, but how this information is really gathered, or how it is interpreted, remains unclear. It seems plausible to suppose that the individual interpretation of the information to subjective knowledge, and therefore *the image* of a certain country, plays an important role in its evaluation.

Moreover, one would expect, if the concept were interpreted rightly, that psychic distance would not be measured at the level of the country but at the individual level. But in general, actual practice shows otherwise. Psychic distance is now mostly measured through 'cultural distance' on an aggregative level.

In the literature on international business, it is often argued that the empirical validity of the psychic distance model has proved to be rather low. Most of the empirical models (e.g. Kogut and Singh, 1988; Benito and Gripsrud, 1992) were based directly or indirectly upon Hofstede's much-cited research (1980, 1991) for measuring the psychic distance between countries. By *cultural distance* between country A and country B is meant the size of the objectivated differences in culture between the two countries. In the analysis of cultural differences between countries, it is not individuals but societies that are compared for symbols and the patterns of values, norms and habits. In his research Hofstede measured the ruling cultural pattern for around forty countries. He presented identical, culture-independent questionnaires to employees of IBM, a multinational with one or more subsidiaries in all of these countries. By concentrating on a multinational, the effect of organisational culture was eliminated. One wonders, though, whether the multinationalist basis did not also eliminate part of the cultural differences, which seems very likely. The final factor analysis of the outcome of the variables led to the establishment of two cultural dimensions, 'Power Distance' and 'Uncertainty Avoidance'. The subsequent country analysis led to the identification of the dimensions of 'Individualism' and 'Masculinity'. 'Power Distance' indicates the actual power divergences between individuals in a society. 'Uncertainty Avoidance' is the degree to which individuals attempt to avoid risks and/or uncertainty in a society. 'Individualism' stands for the degree to which a society values individual freedom and personal initiative. By 'Masculinity', finally, Hofstede meant the 'masculine toughness' of a society. In a masculine society, assertivity and materialism are prominent values. Masculinity stands opposed to Femininity, which indicates the degree to which a society's members are caring and serviceable towards each other.

The countries were compared for these four cultural dimensions, allowing the measurement of the cultural distance between two countries by adding the absolute differences between the scores for the four dimensions for those countries.

Kogut and Singh (1988) proposed a more advanced index of cultural distance. Based on Hofstede's four dimensions, they introduced the cultural distance index. The differences between countries are corrected in this index for the variance of each dimension, after which they are arithmetically arranged. Each dimension is equally weighted. This index is often used in studies of the internationalisation processes of businesses as an approximate of psychic distance. Mathematically, the Kogut and Singh' index has the following form:

$$Cd_j = \sum\{(I_{ij} - I_{iN})^2/V_i\}/4 \qquad i = 1$$

in which

- Cdj = the cultural distance between the home country and the host country/countries
- I_{ij} = the index value for cultural dimension i of country j
- V_i = the variance of the index of dimension i
- N = home country

In concert with O'Grady and Lane (1994), I would like to argue here that most of these 'cultural distance' models interpreted the essence of psychic distance approach incorrectly. Cultural distance is not the same as psychic distance. With cultural distance not the individual perception is measured, which is the essence of PDA, but the objectivated cultural differences between countries. An aggregate fallacy may result, that is, the country level of aggregation might veil important differences on the managerial and/or regional and/or local level. Moreover, the original concept of psychic distance proposed by Wiedersheim-Paul (1972) and Johanson and Wiedersheim-Paul (1975) aims not only at the cultural characteristics of countries. That concept is far broader (see above).

The studies of Kogut and Singh (1988) and Benito and Gripsrud (1992) interpreted psychic distance purely in terms of culture, relying mainly on Hofstede's research. It must be said, however, that the lack of clarity of the proper indicator of psychic distance is also fed by Nordström and Vahlne themselves, who used Hofstede's data later on as well, be it only in part (1992). They stated that cultural and psychic distance are 'different but overlapping phenomena' (1992, p. 10). In Nordström and Vahlne's view, psychic distance embraces cultural, structural (*e.g.* legal and administrative), and language differences (Nordström and Vahlne, 1992; O'Grady and Lane, 1994).

In my view, psychic distance should be measured as an indicator of knowledge and experience, *i.e.* the *individual* knowledge and experience of a firm's managers or directors of the characteristics relevant for doing business in a foreign country. Using the indicator of psychic distance may lead to the formulation of a 'ranking list' of countries. In the original concept of PDA, as proposed by Johanson and Wiedersheim-Paul, such a ranking list has been used for Sweden in the analysis of the psychic distance between four Swedish companies (1975). It remained unclear however, exactly how this ranking list has been constructed. But it did make clear that the psychic distance approach explicitly concerns the evaluation of foreign markets by individual entrepreneurs, and that this judgement is based upon knowledge and experience.

Missing elements

In the psychic distance approach presented here there is no room for social exchange, for interaction behaviour in international economic strategy. The PDA does not explain why a firm would choose to interact with a specific foreign agent or firm, and what the conditions of the relation would be.

In addition, Sullivan and Bauerschmidt (1990) and Nordström (1991) have argued that the approach has lost most of its relevance because of the enormous changes in the economic map. This is what they call the 'time boundedness' of the theory. They refer to the growing belief in an economically homogeneous world (see, e.g. Levitt, 1983; Ohmae, 1985, 1990). Because of the acceleration of the globalisation of business, firms have quicker and easier access to knowledge about doing business abroad. According to these authors, the borders on the economic map are increasingly transparent; they are losing importance. As a consequence, cultural differences are evened out, thereby reducing the relevance of the psychic distance approach. Others, however, point to the increase of the relevance of local, regional, or even national economic and cultural characteristics, exactly because of that globalisation (see, e.g. Porter, 1990; Enright, 1992). The debate on this subject is becoming more intense, as mentioned in chapter 2.

3.7.1 Comparing the Transaction Costs Approach and the Psychic Distance Approach

The TCE-oriented approach and the 'strategic phase model' have been compared several times. In 1994 we made a comparison between them and used it to discuss the empirical research in the field of cross-border economic networking in north western Europe (Van Houtum *et al.*, 1996). Before that, Benito and Gripsrud (1992) labelled their comparison 'discrete rational location' process versus 'cultural learning' process. Barkema, Bell and Pennings (1994) and Bell (1996) compared what they referred to as the 'static' versus the 'process' approach. 'Static' approaches here indicated those models in which a firm's foreign expansions are evaluated as alternative choices dictated by relative costs and benefits. As examples, they listed studies like Dunning (1981, 1988ab), Hennart (1982), Hymer (1960, 1976), Buckley and Casson (1976), Teece (1981, 1986), Rugman (1981), and Hill, Hwang and Kim (1990). In contrast, the 'process' models focus on internationalisation as a developmental process during which firms move farther away from their home country at each stage. Among these are distinguished the Swedish school (Johanson and Wiedersheim-Paul (1973), Johanson and Vahlne (1977, 1990), the 'export' models like that of Bilkey and Cesar (1977), and Cavusgil (1980), and the product life-cycle theory of Vernon (1966, 1979).

To conclude this section, on the basis of the comparisons as mentioned above, I have summarised the fundamental principles of the TCE and the PDA in table 3.3.

Table 3.3 -Transaction Costs Economics (TCE) versus the Psychic Distance Approach (PDA)

	TCE	PDA
Theoretical foundation	-Neo-classical economic theory -Analysis of the boundaries of the firm	-Theory of the firm -Strategic behaviour approach -Decision approach - Analysis of the importance and gaining of knowledge in international expansions
Problem orientation	Explanation of the existence of national/international governance structures	Application of 'psychic distance' as the explanation of the internationalisation process of firms
Assumptions	Human/firm behaviour: -Bounded rationality, opportunism Context: High asset specificity, uncertainty, small numbers exchange Outcome: Static, equilibrium	Human/firm behaviour: -Bounded rationality: lateral rigidity and selective search -Learning, experiential knowledge Context: Uncertainty, different cultures and institutional settings Outcome: Dynamic, process
International involvement	Discrete foreign structures: -Export -Licences -Foreign Direct Investment	Step-wise expansion: -Expansion on national market, no regular export -Expansion through an independent representative -Sales subsidiary -Production/manufacturing facility

3.8 Conclusion

In this chapter, three dominant theoretical insights in economic literature with regard to the development of cross-border economic relationships have been examined - the transaction costs approach, the international network approach and the 'psychic distance' approach.

Allocation versus co-ordination

As far as transaction cost economics is concerned, it may be said that it is well in line with the traditional definition of economics - 'the study of the relationship between the optimisation of the ends and scarce means that have alternative uses'. Transaction cost economics is focused upon the optimal governance structure of a transaction. The *allocation mechanism of the market*, central in neo-classical thinking, also occupies a central place in the transaction costs approach. Internally, the efficiency of the transaction within the firm is determined by the organisational costs. Externally, the uncertainty of the market determines the height of the transaction costs. In the past decades, many alternative, convincing sets of explanatory variables have been developed.

In this chapter, two new, important concepts have been treated. The international extension of the Swedish network school most notably stresses the aspect of trust and learning in the interaction. Attention is not so much focused on the characteristics of *allocation*, but more on the characteristics of *co-ordination* in economic life. Firms, institutions, and relation features like trust and commitment are subjects of study, not their allocative interplay. The Psychic Distance Approach posits that the knowledge and experience with regard to doing business in a foreign country may vary per entrepreneur; as a consequence, the degree of internationalisation will also vary. The question has been raised to what extent the newly developed relevant insights can be combined with the two basic general assumptions underlying the transaction costs theory - (bounded) rationality and maximisation of utility with a time- and space-consistent set of preferences.

Within neo-classical economic thinking, the abstract, fictive point of view exists that markets are under way to achieve their equilibrium. Markets are efficient. In the two alternative models, markets are approached from a more concrete, realistic point of view - as being dynamic and therefore never in balance. The tension between these two viewpoints on markets is growing, which indicates that the classical definition of economic science, as given above, is put to the test. According to Granovetter: 'the notion that rational choice is derailed by social influences had long discouraged detailed sociological analysis of economic life and led revisionist economists to reform economic theory by focusing on its naive psychology' (Granovetter, 1992, p. 75). Economic science is now apparently regarded as a broader field of study than the archetypal definition suggests. There seems to be more to economics than the cost optimisation for the allocation of means to certain ends.

Human nature

A crucial question in the theoretical developments in the explanation of international business, is how economists see *human nature*. The transaction costs theory, and neo-classical economics in general, regard human behaviour and preferences as given facts, as exogenous. More importantly, economic reality is seen as a given fact (cf. Nooteboom, 1993). In view of the presupposed behaviour and preferences, these theories primarily aim at how an allocation of resources leading to a state of equilibrium between economic agents can be achieved. The economic agents are regarded as individual, atomist structures with certain preferences and a certain objective. Economic development, however, is not generated by individuals alone. In reality, the factors that matter as well are the interaction, the expectations with regard to the interaction, the co-ordination and outcome of the actions, of both parties involved. As a consequence, the course and outcome of an interaction is and remains fundamentally unpredictable, at most describable process-wise.

My opinion is that those pleading for the incorporation of social embeddedness of economic actors in economic analysis do have a point. Economic actors do not, as Williamson's neo-classical transaction costs approach would have it, behave as atomised individuals outside a social context. It is important to incorporate the social embeddedness of economic relations in a study concerning the how and why of economic behaviour (see, e.g. Oerlemans, 1996).

Especially in the case of economic exchange between SMEs, where there is little difference between the entrepreneur and his firm, relations should be enriched by theories based on the principals of social exchange (see also Christensen and Lindmark, 1993; Eskelinen, 1994).
Economic agents are not boundedly rational (calculating) machines. To employ a more complete picture of human nature implies that businesses, technology and preferences are no longer seen as 'black boxes', which leads to a more realistic account (see, e.g. Hodgson, 1988). The machine paradigm of TCE departs from a constant, exogenous reality that influences human choices and preferences from the outside. It is more realistic to assume that there may be a divergence between objective reality and how we perceive and describe reality. Human beings construct and reconstruct 'reality' in their minds. No two human beings live the same reality. And such personal reality cannot be transferred to other men's minds. It is an individual mind construct. Men, at most, can agree upon the assumptions and/or the results of economic behaviour and developments. Economic behaviour and preferences should therefore be regarded as endogenous. So as to make that possible, the image, the personal perception of reality - which depends on a great number of external factors - should be incorporated as an assumption in the rationality and behaviour of economic actors.

In addition, it should be recognized that social interactions direct the mindsets, the perception and the social behaviour of actors in a society. Human decisions are therefore not detached and do not function autonomously, without links to the brain's associational logic. Human beings are associational creatures, both consciously and unconsciously so. This means that there is no such faculty as pure reason that functions as a detached, objective and dispassionate observer.
The firm and its managers do not only exist in a sea of market relations but also within a social network of established bonds and relations which are partially of their own making (cf. Hodgson, 1988; Christensen and Lindmark, 1993). Economic behaviour is no *deus ex machina*. It is firmly rooted within the context of the social environment. Examples of social contacts that are regarded as important in economic transactions are the relations with friends, business associates and colleagues, and other non-commercial private and semi-public organisations. The direct social environment of the firm/manager is the environment from which they learn, with which they associate, in which they act, and to which they respond. No man is an island. In so far, I agree with the results presented by social psychologist Martin Kilduff (1992) that:

> '...even in conditions, approaching those of perfect information and equal opportunity, individuals differ systematically in the extent to which they rely on the social network in making decisions [...] In a world in which such an excess of information is increasingly becoming a burden to be borne, the social network, as a decision-making resource, may be as much an expression of personality as it is a constraint on choice' (p. 179).

There exists a large variance in the actors' rationality, which can mainly be accounted for through the various socialisations of that rationality. What is rational for some, may be irrational for others. Rationality, in its practical form, is therefore often nothing more (or less) than a reasonable response to an actual situation. And what *is* reasonable, then, is socially dependent. Rationality is therefore not just bounded because of the restricted capability of man to gather all relevant information, but also by his environment. Human rationality is a contextual rationality.

In short, economic rationality ought to be translated into a contextual rationality, meaning that the rationality of economic agents is not a datum *per se*, but that it is dependent of genetic determinants on the one hand, and social and physical environmental influences on the other, all of which are not given facts for mankind, but dynamic factors. What rationality really is depends of where you are and when you are.

In his work of 1975, Williamson himself, as one of the last assumptions in his theory, posits that one should account for the atmosphere within which the interaction takes place. To prove this, Williamson provides the example of blood donorship as a transaction between two parties. Very different attitudes are involved than those appropriate to a calculating involvement. He concludes that theories and models should provide for differences in attitude vis à vis the transaction. It does not suffice merely to examine the interactions and transactions in a strictly neutral, instrumental manner. According to Williamson, 'reference to atmosphere is intended to make allowance for attitudinal interactions and the systems consequences that are associated therewith' (1975, p. 37). He concludes that 'transactional attitudes are greatly influenced by the socio-political system in which exchanges take place' (1975, no. 22, p. 39). Unfortunately, this postulate is not implemented in the theorisation presented in the remainder of his work, nor does he elaborate it. He regards the environment as exogenous. As he himself admitted in 1993, the assumptions of bounded rationality and opportunism remain central to his work: 'A colleague noted that the economics of atmosphere plays a larger role in *Markets and Hierarchies* then in *The Economics Institutions of Capitalism* and asked about the de-emphasis. I replied that I thought atmosphere at least as important to an understanding of economic organisation in 1985 as I had in 1975. Not having made more headway, however, I had little to add' (1993, p. 480). It is against the assumption of the exogenous environment that theorists such as Granovetter and Grabher rebelled.

The discussion between authors stressing the embeddedness of economic action and proponents of the transaction costs model may be compared to a discussion, at least as profound and important, currently under way in social philosophy. The rebels there aim at the Utilitarian tradition. Utilitarianism in fact resembles the neo-classical transaction costs theory. In its simplest formulation, it tries to establish the societal structure which produces the greatest happiness for the largest number of individuals in society. In transaction costs theory too, human beings are supposed to act in the interest of their own happiness, *i.e.* efficiency. Because there are a limited number of resources available for satisfying people's personal preferences, the economic system was developed to distribute the available resources through the market mechanism. Allocation, not co-ordination is emphasised. In socio-philosophical terms, each different individual has a set of given preferences that he strives to realise. Utilitarianism, in this context, is a standard for aggregating and trading off individual interests and desires. The rule established by Utilitarianism to do this, is to give equal weight to each individual's preferences (see, e.g. Hare, 1984; Singer, 1979), which implies that Utilitarianism makes no difference between human beings: all are equal. This is why Rawls (1971) calls it a 'teleological' theory. What counts is the state of affairs, the distribution of the commodity. Human beings are regarded as producers and consumers of that commodity, and the duties of society are to serve that commodity, not people (Kymlicka, 1990).

Opponents to this philosophical theory (the Communitarianists) argue that Utilitarianism 'atomises' human beings (see, e.g. Taylor, 1992). According to Taylor, a theory in which human beings are 'atomised', that is, free at will and (boundedly) rational, denies the requirement of a complex and integrated society that is able to support and promote this freedom and individualism. Freedom requires a certain understanding of the self, and this understanding, this identity is for a large part defined through the interaction with others or through the habitual practices of a society. In short, freedom presupposes restraint since optimal freedom for all implies respecting the freedom of others.

Within political philosophy, a lively debate is therefore going on between the proponents of different views on the structure of society: those emphasising the community (Communitarianism) and those concentrating on the individual and his/her preferences (Utilitarianism) (see, e.g. Kymlicka, 1990). Moreover, the methods of analysis differ. Economists working in the neo-classical tradition appeal to the distinct intuition human beings are presumed to share, that is, the intuition as to 'utility'. This term is used to reckon the aggregations and trade-offs (Taylor, 1992). The method of Utilitarianists seems more straightforward than that of Communitarianism. Proponents of the latter view argue that the Utilitarian view of mankind equals 'conscious blindness', and attempt to turn the discussion to the nature of the subject and the conditions of human agency. The talk of Communitarianists however, about identity, social action, and values is highly speculative and indefinite. This means that most of the time their postulates on human behaviour are more difficult to measure.

In my opinion, this interesting but sometimes little differentiated debate in political philosophy has much in common with the economic debate discussed above. Over the past decades, a number of interesting books and articles on economics have appeared, which deal with the importance of institutional elements in economic behaviour. I mention Hodgson (1988), Etzioni (1988), Eggertson (1990), North (1990), and Zukin and DiMaggio (1990).

Towards a synthesis

The Psychic Distance Approach, in spite of very different basic assumptions, predicts an internationalisation result comparable to that provided by the Transaction Costs Approach. Both predict that the firm will select those countries that generate the least uncertainty (transaction costs), that are closest to the home country with respect to entrepreneurial mores (highest experiential knowledge). It does seem possible, therefore, to construct a synthesis. In my view,

both approaches, however, have to be 'enriched' in their postulates regarding, and elaboration of, human nature. That is, the perception of individuals who act and interact has to be included. Firms in culturally close countries do not necessarily interact much; nor is it necessarily so that firms in countries that are far apart from the cultural point of view interact proportionally less. The contacts managers/entrepreneurs may have in another country influence their perception of, and undoubtedly also their decision to get economically involved in, that country. The macro-economic cultural distance may correspond with that personal perception, but this is not necessarily the case.
Regarding the structure of the relation that is developed, a synthesis of the network and transaction costs models does not seem impossible either. Transaction cost economics provides important insights into the uncertainty that is associated with a transaction, and into the economic consequences of built-in safeguards. The International Network Approach (INA), to the contrary, by including experience, trust and competence in its analysis, generates insights into the economic importance of common conventions in the bonding of individual actors. While the perspective and assumptions of TCE and the INA differ considerably, their results can be aligned: the merits of trust as opposed to the safeguards against opportunism. The INA lacks an efficient analytical instrument to prevent potential opportunism and the dangers of 'lock-in' within a relation; TCE, with its utilitarian theory on human behaviour and its static approach, ignores the potentially positive effects of bonding and learning.

In the separate currents of TCE and the INA, theorists often speak of an irreconcilable opposition between trust and transaction costs because of opportunism. Yet this opposition is superficial, as both aspects are present in an economic relation. My point of view is that networks and economic relations are tools, not the reasons for economic exchange. Relations are the means, not the end. The development of an economic relation is a striving to achieve higher profit. Opportunist behaviour of one of the actors hampers the relation's development. This implies that the tie within the relation is estimated, tested and evaluated for the chances or risks of opportunist behaviour. It is crucial to cross-border economic relations that estimating those chances is generally more difficult when the other is from a different country. The uncertainty is greater, in that case, and the importance of personal experience and the experience with others increases. Interpersonal trust between entrepreneurs across borders is then essential to reduce the uncertainty involved and to make the relationship successful. Looking at it this way, the views of TCE, the INA, and even the PDA are coinciding. I therefore believe that there is a need, and that there is room, to combine the international network approach with the transaction costs model and the psychic distance theory into the conceptualisation of a new framework, a new rationale of the explanation of the international movement of SMEs. This approach should be both holistic and process-based. Only then can the history of a transaction be clarified, with a clear difference between a transaction and a relation, and especially incorporating the determinants in the various phases of the developmental process. The theories discussed above may provide handles for such an approach. In the following chapter, chapter 4, an attempt will be made to construct such an approach to the creation of bilateral cross-border economic relations between two firms.

Chapter 4

The INTERFACE model

4.1 Introduction

At the outset of this study, I introduced my subject from a geographical economic perspective, indicating what importance borders have in human circulation, and how economic relationships are developed across borders according to various economic insights. The role of borders was elucidated in chapter 2, and the theoretical handles with regard to economic relationships across borders were introduced in chapter 3. Because the problem analysis in this dissertation examines individual economic interactions, it became clear that it is necessary to fall back regularly on studies and reports dealing with human behaviour in general, that is, beyond economic traffic. Entrepreneurs make decisions on the basis of incomplete perceptual visions of, and attitudes towards, economic and non-economic relations (see also Tallman and Shenkar, 1994). For this reason, a model based on a single theory is not suitable to adequately represent the process of developing relationships. It was concluded, in chapter 3, that the construction of a synthesis is required. In the present chapter, such a synthesis is proposed.

The purpose guiding the framework of the model is that it should be capable of providing a description of the process of the development of relationships at the level of individual companies and entrepreneurs. It must therefore be an *actor model*, within which the perceptions and attitudes of actions and interactions of and between entrepreneurs will find their explicit place. The level of enterprise sectors is insufficient to allow for the formulation of postulates regarding the developmental process of cross-border bilateral relationships.
Moreover, it should be a *process model*. The model should indicate on a step-by-step basis how and why two entrepreneurs get acquainted, how they enter into deliberations, and finally, how they come to the decision to formulate formal or informal working agreements.
The model proposed in this study is presented in section 4.2; section 4.3 will formulate research hypotheses based on the model, which will be put to the test in part II of this dissertation.
In section 4.4 the hypotheses are summarized in a table.

4.2 The INTERFACE model

This section will explain the descriptive model proposed here that represents, in separate stages, the process of the development of cross-border relationships between two enterprises. The model is concerned with the organisational form that the transaction costs theory regards as the form intermediate to export and foreign direct investment, and which the network theory regards as the essence of economic markets - economic relationships. The model deals with the question how cross-border *contacts* may grow into or lead to cross-border economic *relationships*.

Rationality

I depart from the usual assumption in economics that actors that are 'boundedly rational' in their actions (cf. Simon, 1961). It is important, however, to note that the boundaries of rationality not only develop because the entrepreneur *cannot* prevent it, but partly also because, consciously or unconsciously (cf. Hodgson, 1988), he does not *want* it otherwise. His embeddedness in the local social context provides him with security, because of its familiarity and identity, on which he can fall back and from which he operates. However, it can prove inefficient from the economic point of view. His maximum capacity for gathering and processing information is not used entirely because there are, on the one hand, *physical boundaries* to this capacity ('the traditional principle of bounded rationality') and, on the other hand, *mental boundaries*. These last should be taken to mean the limitations of the *representation of reality* in the mind of the actor. Reality is experienced not objectively but subjectively, at most inter-subjectively. It is assumed that this mental model of physical reality provides an important input for the actor's rational frame of thinking.

A second supposition is that it is possible to enhance the utilisation of the actor's maximum capacity of gathering and processing information through a *learning* process, both from others and from his own experience. The actor 'matures' by linking new information to already existing structures in his pattern of thought. This 'maturing' may result in a modification of his mental representation of reality. In short, the context rationality is mentally and physically bounded, and can be utilised to greater advantage or expanded through a learning process.

Phases in the development process of an economic relationship

I distinguish the following phases in the development process of a cross-border relationship: *contact, attraction, interaction, transaction, relation,* and *success*.

Together, these stages compose the hereafter called INTERFACE model. INTERFACE is an acronym for *INTERnational Formation of Autonomous Co-operation between Enterprises*. The model is concerned with the construction of international economic relationships between independent companies. The actors in the model are entrepreneurs, people with companies. In the first instance, the model applies to companies in all sectors and of all sizes. But, since about 98% of all firms in a country or region are small and medium sized (<250 active persons), both the theoretical and the empirical analysis *de facto* apply principally to small and medium-sized enterprises. In the empirical analysis, I have decided to focus on enterprises in the sectors of building and construction, the manufacturing industry, and wholesale trade (see chapter 5). Please note that this study deals exclusively with bilateral, or 'dyadic' relationships, that is, relationships between two actors.

The complete INTERFACE model is represented in figure 4.1. In this scheme, it is illustrated that the developmental potential of a professional contact, once established, with a company in the neighbouring country may vary considerably. Enterprises may consider the possible modes of development of the contact of varying importance. This is associated to a great extent with the preference of the other company and of the exchanges between the two. Each step towards a subsequent stage in the formation of a relationship is, in fact, a dichotomous variable: yes or no.

Figure 4.1 - The complete INTERFACE model

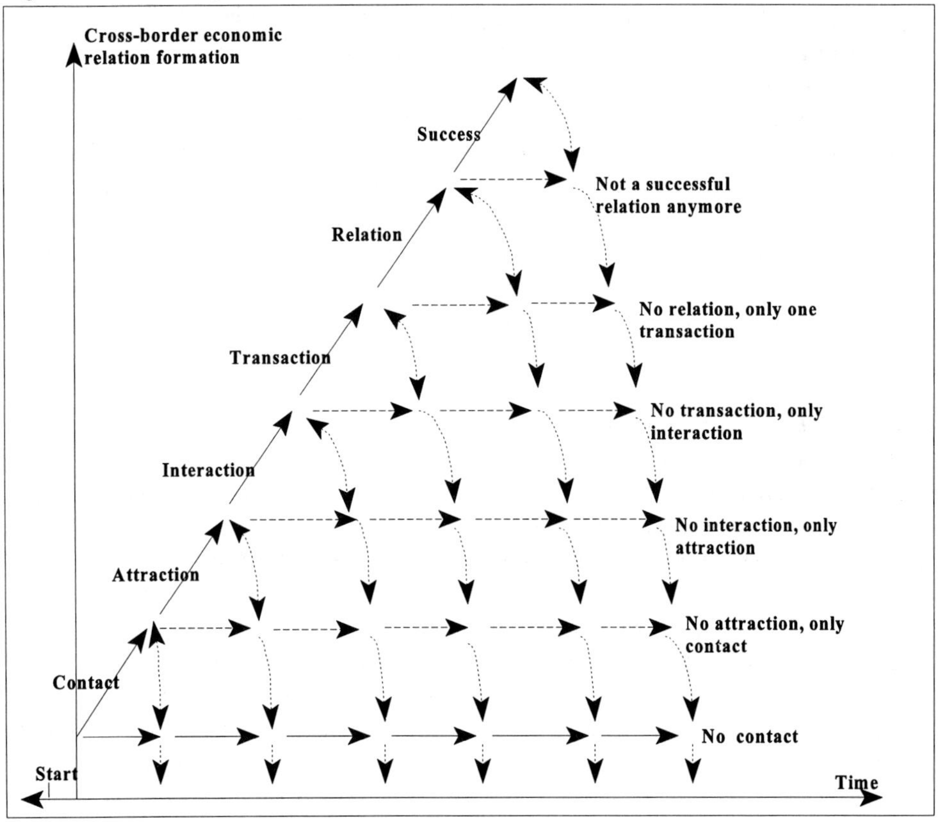

Over time there are several opportunities to retry entering a higher level of relation formation. I should note here that a reversal to a lower level in the scale, followed by a restart, implies another content than an initial start at that level. The distinction is the difference in experience (for a further explanation on retrogressive transitions in relationships, see, e.g. Levinger and

Snoek, 1972; Nooteboom, 1995). The different stages of the model, *i.e* contact, attraction, interaction, transaction, relation, and success, will be dealt with extensively in this chapter. The final stage of the INTERFACE model, success, is to be interpreted as the growth in intensity and the perception of the merit of the relationship.
It is important to note that the economic theories concerning the formation of international economic relationships - the transaction costs theory, the psychic distance theory, and the network theory - that were discussed have not been incorporated *in extenso* in the above model. It is based in part on the lessons from these theories, but does not articulate them *in toto*. This would be impossible, as the theories overlap in some places and are opposed in others. I would rather say that elements of these theories have been *used* as handles to arrive at a more integral approach to the development of cross-border economic relationships. The INTERFACE model, as presented here, offers the surrounding framework. This chapter describes the construction of the model, and how it can be used to gain insight into the explanation of the economic interweaving of companies in the neighbouring country.

However, it would go too far to test the entire model, in all its aspects, for its relevance in one single study. This is an impossibility. In the present study, the following delimitations have been adhered to. Only those enterprises who, in the path of their development, have factually entered into a successful relationship are analysed. This choice makes it possible to gain a first important insight into the meaning and content of the various stages of the model. None of the other possible developmental paths is analysed. Whenever, in the remainder of this study, reference is made to the INTERFACE model, this may be taken to imply the linear developmental process from contact to attraction, to interaction, to transaction, to relation, and success (figure 4.2).

Figure 4.2 - The INTERFACE model in this study

Contact* ➤ *Attraction* ➤ *Interaction* ➤ *Transaction* ➤ *Relation* ➤ *Success

The formation process of a successful cross-border economic relationship, from the quantitative point of view, much resembles a Russian doll made from wood and hollowed out to hide another doll, which in turn hides another, and so on. For one may assume that, from all existing enterprises, but few come into contact on the international level, intending a certain degree of business with an enterprise in the neighbouring country. An even fewer number actually develop mutual attraction. Still fewer succeed in coming to mutually optimised business agreements. For fewer of those, still, the transaction develops into a relationship. And finally: the relationship proves successful, eventually, for an even smaller number of enterprises.

I should remark here that the INTERFACE model is not a causal scheme. Moreover, it is not a deterministic scheme either. Divergences and overlaps may occur. The possible variations are not, however, submitted to closer examination in this study. The INTERFACE model is a stage model, indicating the most likely course the development of a bilateral cross-border economic relationship will follow. By means of the INTERFACE model this study focuses primarily on the examination of the *formation* and the eventual success of *cross-border relationships between firms.* The examination of these topics coincides with the three components of the problem central to this dissertation (see chapter 1), being:

1. The detection of the characteristics of attitude, behaviour and structure of the enterprise/entrepreneur that determine why some enterprises *do* and why others *do not* have one (or more) economic relations
2. The detection, for the companies that do have economic relations, of the factors that determine *the number of cross-border economic relationships*
3. Finally, this study examines one relationship in particular, for example a highly important one, more closely for each company with economic relations in the neighbouring country. The determinants in the INTERFACE model enable the researcher to determine, for this one existing economic relationship, how it has been able to become *successful.*

In short, the proposed model should lead to the establishment of an insight into the importance of the determinants in the process of the formation of cross-border economic relationships, by explaining why enterprises do/do not have economic relations, how many relations they have, and how the success of the most important economic relationship in the neighbouring country is to be explained. In section 4.3 the hypotheses upon which the investigation is founded are discussed. Below, the determinants for the various stages of the INTERFACE model are explained more clearly.

4.2.1 Contact

The contact stage is of great importance in the INTERFACE model. Without contact, no relationship can be developed. The contact stage determines where and how two entrepreneurs of different nationalities meet. Furthermore, it determines whether the contact is pursued or stops at the meeting of the two entrepreneurs. If the meeting has a sequel, the development process of a relationship between the two entrepreneurs is also given direction and content during the contact stage.

Kamann (1989, after Goddard, 1973) makes a useful distinction between exploratory contacts, planning contacts, and routine contacts. *Routine contacts* are most numerous. These determine the communication between two actors to an important extent, and most often consist of simple exchanges of information directed at standardised activities. *Planning contacts* are purposely sought contacts with strategic objectives, such as the organisation of R&D activities (cf. Kamann, 1989). Information is sought consciously and specifically.

Exploratory contacts are directed towards the longer term and principally involve a 'scanning' of the possibilities in the environment (*idem*, 1989). The exploratory contact will most often be face-to-face, but may also be organised through telecommunications (telephone, telefax, e-mail, teleconference, Internet). It is not so much programmatic or routine, but is sought (un)consciously.

Just a contact, however, does not suffice to start an economic transaction/relationship. At least one of the parties involved must have the intention, latently or obviously, to develop economic relationships in the neighbouring country. An encounter without (latent) *intentions* (cf. Fishbein and Azjen, 1975) in at least one of the entrepreneurs will not lead to an economic relationship, but remains a mere encounter, which may at most influence or strengthen the image of the entrepreneurs concerning entrepreneurs in the neighbouring country. The contact I am speaking of, however, is an encounter between two entrepreneurs in which, at least one of whom is aware, or thinks, that there are business opportunities in the other country. It may occur anywhere, in principle, but the most obvious location is in one of the regions in which the entrepreneurs are established. In the establishment of cross-border relationships, *routine* contacts are less adequate. The contacts are new in many cases and cannot, in most cases, be called routine. I am concerned, therefore, to study the beginning of those contacts that have emerged because they were more or less 'consciously sought after': the *exploratory* and *planning* contacts.

There are several ways in which exploratory and planning contacts may occur. The encounters may be spontaneous, that is, occur in places that have little or nothing to do with business: one may think of parties, festivities, and vacations. The encounter may also be staged. There are typical places for planning and exploratory contacts, for example the trade meeting days organised by the Chambers of Commerce in border regions, which occur on a reasonably regular basis. The introduction of a contact or business associate in the neighbouring country provides another opportunity to meet a potential business partner from the neighbouring country. Such a meeting could be called an 'indirect' meeting, to which colleagues in one's own company, business acquaintances, formal 'contact bureaus', and family members may all contribute.

Figure 4.3 represents schematically which factors are important in determining the chance that two entrepreneurs from different countries will meet, in which at least one intends further contact. An important insight provided by chapter 2 is that actors (and groups of actors) have several kinds of borders, namely 'functional' borders on the one hand, indicating the concrete political borders of, for example, a state, and the socially constructed 'affective', 'cognitive' and open/closed (or 'action') borders on the other hand. This distinction coincides with the distinction generally made in the study of attitudes in social psychology: 'affective', 'cognitive' and what is called 'conative' or 'behavioural' attitudes (see amongst others, Rosenberg and Hovland (1960); Fishbein and Azjen, 1975; Werlen, 1993).
As was shown in chapter 2, these three dimensions of human borders in space are only rarely identical in permeability or territorial impact (see, e.g. Golledge and Stimson, 1987; Riedel,

1994). On the basis of the different types of borders, a distinction is made in the contact-phase of the INTERFACE model between **'action space'**, **'cognition space'**, and **'affection space'**. **'Action space'** is the space defined by the deeds, the acts and the striving of people. One may think of, for example, the geographical sales distribution of a firm or the information-seeking behaviour of an entrepreneur. In the above, the borders of the action-space were referred to as open versus closed borders. By **'cognition space'** I mean the knowledge an individual has about his environment (see chapter 2). '**Affection space**' is understood to mean the valuation of a space (see chapter 2). This aspect of space relates to the feelings and emotions people have about a certain space, which are motivated by desires and values that are embodied in images of the environment (cf. Golledge and Stimson, 1987).

In order to determine the 'readiness and preparedness' of individual actors for cross-border contact with a possible economic partner, figure 4.3 distinguishes these three spatial dimensions: the actor's actions in cross-border space, the actor's cognition of cross-border space, and the actor's affection towards cross-border space. Within these three dimensions, the most important determinants are summed up. These will be analysed here.

Figure 4.3 - Contact determinants

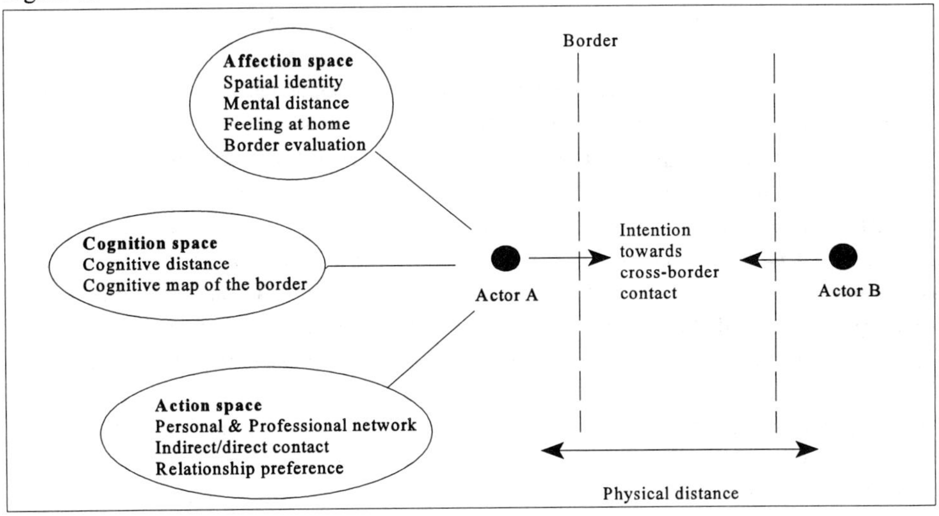

I Action-space

1. The strength and relative size of the informal network pattern in the neighbouring country

It is important to the analysis of the formation of cross-border economic relationships to recognise that economic interactions between two entrepreneurs are embedded in their mutual social and professional circle of acquaintances. By social and professional acquaintances, I mean the informal contacts with which no exchange agreement has been established (see also Raap, 1995). The network theory that regards enterprises as embedded in a network of relationships, which was treated in chapter 3, combined with the transaction costs theory, which regards enterprises as structures for transactions, provides an image of an enterprise that is socially embedded in a great number of contacts and socially embedded in a great number of economic relationships, in which it ideally seeks to achieve those relationships that will produce the necessary transactions in as reliable, good and economical a manner as possible. The establishment of such economic relationships then leads to possible contact points with other networks. Moreover, the (new) contacts and relationships direct the image of the action space in question and embed future actions. In the words of two network theorists, Knoke and Kuklinski (1991): 'the nature of the relationships a given actor has with other system members thus may affect that focal actor's perceptions, belief and actions.' (p.173) (see also Knoke and Kuklinski, 1986). The insight provided by the psychic distance theory is that the new contact or relationship may lead to a positive learning effect, implying an experience that may be useful in a new step in the internationalisation process of the company.

Thus, where it concerns cross-border contacts for small and medium-sized companies, regionally closed network structures offer little solace. The border, in such cases, divides the regional networks. It is important to link the regions, so that new information and resources can be obtained (see also Giaoutzi, Suarez-Villa, and Stratigea, 1993b). In addition to the network theory, Granovetter's metaphor of 'weak ties' is important in this respect (1982). His concept departs from the thought that people in every society live in groups, which causes strong ties to develop between those people: the networks. The stream of information and resources circulates rapidly in the network of associated individuals. New information and resources however do not so much originate within the network, but are provided by actors outside of the group with whom weaker ties exist, the so-called 'weak ties'. Typical weak ties therefore fill bridging functions between two distinct networks (see also Kamann, 1989). According to Granovetter, it is important to maintain the links with these weak ties. They may be of less importance to everyday business activities, but can be of crucial importance to activate new activities or strategies.

Burt, too, stresses the importance of such weak ties (1992). He associates them with so-called 'non-redundant contacts' (p. 17). He regards these contacts as highly important to obtain new information or resources. He describes redundant contacts as contacts leading to the same information or resources, while non-redundant contacts are separated by 'structural holes' (Burt, 1992, p. 18). When two networks are separated, a structural hole comes into existence between them. One single weak tie between actor A in one network and actor B in the other can link the two networks, thereby closing the structural hole for actors A and B. The position of A and B in their own networks may be strengthened considerably by this link.

According to Burt, the strength of a relationship means two things: frequent contact and emotional closeness. Typical examples of relationships without structural holes are man and wife, father and son, mother and daughter. These direct contacts are characterised by a strong degree of cohesion. The contacts may also be indirect. In this context, Burt speaks of redundancy due to structural equivalence. In such close-knit or closed networks, the chance of entering into contact with an actor outside of one's circle, which may provide new information or resources, is small. New contacts, with the intention of establishing an economic relationship, are typically formed in a network that knows many contact points and has a highly diversified character. In these cases, the chance of developing weak ties or non-redundant contacts is greater. In line with Burt's theory (1992), entrepreneurial opportunity in a network is therefore dependent on the existence of numerous structural holes around your contacts, and none attached to yourself.

The geographical distribution of the informal network provides a useful indication of the stream of information and resources between actors in different regions (see Boissevain, 1974). A number of investigations have already established that there are a smaller number of contacts between people from different countries, even for people that are active at short distances from each other (see, e.g. Passchier *et al.*, 1981; Cramer *et al.*, 1984; Dagevos *et al.*, 1992, Steiner *et al.*, 1993; Ratti, 1993b; Van den Tillaart *et al.*, 1994; Corvers *et al.*, 1994, Van der Velde *et al.*, 1995, 1996, 1997).

Two different types of networks are distinguished in this study:

a. The personal network in the home country versus that in the neighbouring country

This refers to the *number* of personal acquaintances of an entrepreneur in a certain region. This can be friends, family members, or other personal acquaintances. They are, in any case, acquaintances that are not professionally involved in the enterprise. A social network that crosses the border may be considered advantageous to the development of economic relationships.

b. The professional network in the home country versus that in the neighbouring country

What applies to personal acquaintances also applies to professional acquaintances. Professional acquaintances are persons that are associated with the company of an entrepreneur due to their profession. Under this category fall, for example, clients, colleagues, suppliers and informal investors.

The *strength* of the direct personal and professional ties will be measured in terms of intensity, that is to say, in terms of 'visiting frequency' (Granovetter, 1982).

2. Direct versus indirect contact

As stated above, where it concerns the formation of the contact between two entrepreneurs of different nationalities in different countries, an important function is reserved for the existence of 'weak ties' between the regional networks. These may be social or professional relations. These relations may be located in one's own country or in the country of the partner.

Besides, these relations may also be professional mediators. In border regions, numerous intermediary organisations struggle to establish cross-border networks. One may think of Euregions and Chambers of Commerce. It is interesting, in this respect, to analyse the role such mediators may play in linking two diverging networks. It is expected that a cross-border economic relationship that is established indirectly through a trusted or known person or organisation will be more successful than an economic relationship that is established directly.

3. The entrepreneur's relationship preference

In all possible examples of types of encounters, the chance to come into contact with other actors is strongly dependent on the actor him or herself. One may suppose that some actors are more open to contacts and/or more active in seeking out contacts than others. This is a matter concerning the strategic preference of the entrepreneur/enterprise. The *entrepreneur's relationship preference* is therefore an important determinant in the contact stage.

In the first place, it appears to be highly dependent on the personal characteristics with regard to affiliation/contact. Some entrepreneurs have a relationship preference that strongly resembles a chronic need for affiliation (Atkinson, 1958). They may, for instance, be searching for projects with high profits and are prepared to live with the higher risks. Others are characterised by a transient arousal of an affiliation desire (Schachter, 1959). In both cases, there exists, however, a certain readiness or openness to enter into new contacts. Their sight is not only directed towards their own tasks, but also to others and to new experiences. For others, durability and security in the economic relationship are of the utmost importance. These, therefore, prepare themselves thoroughly and weigh alternatives against each other very carefully. Another context is provided if contact is experienced as a threat or potential competitor, or if the entrepreneur's orientation is mostly restricted to the company, region or country. One may imagine, therefore, various types of preferences with regard to relationships. In chapter 7 it will be examined wether preferences can indeed be distilled from the various possibilities, and which.

II Affection-space

1. Mental distance

At the surface level, the image both entrepreneurs have of each other is an important element (Duck, 1977; Levinger and Snoek, 1972, Levinger, 1980). The image is based upon their own experience, the experience of other entrepreneurs, and other sources of direct communication and information. It determines to a great extent the estimation by individuals of the characteristics of other countries and/or cultures. To see what the distance between two regions is, it is not sufficient to measure (estimations of) road distance or travel time; one must also measure the mental distance between them. Two people who live at a mutual distance of 20 metres may be at a mental remove that is greater than that between two people who live at a distance of 20 kilometres. This may influence the interaction pattern between the two.

Usually, the notion 'cultural distance', introduced by Hofstede (1980), is most often used in economic literature to indicate how far removed cultures are. The cultural distance between countries A and B then means: the objectivated difference in culture between two countries. The concept of cultural distance and especially the cultural distance index have proved very useful in cross-cultural comparisons (see, e.g. Kogut and Singh, 1988).

However, for the purposes of this investigation I have selected a different principle. If one wishes to have a measure by which one may explain why entrepreneurs will start a cross-border contact with the intention of establishing a bilateral economic relationship, it is not so much the cultural distance between the two countries that matters, but insight into what I define here as the *mental distance* between the actors from those two countries. There are three fundamental differences between the notion of cultural distance and the notion of mental distance that is formulated here. In the first place, the concept mental distance does not merely deal with the culture of a country, but with *the entire range of formal and informal conventions* in a country that matter to a company. Michael Storper most notably uses the term conventions in his analyses of co-operating enterprises in technological districts, meaning the taken-for-granted mutually coherent expectations, practices, routines and agreements, and their associated informal or institutional forms (Storper, 1993, 1997). Storper defined this set of conventions, which are of crucial importance in the creation of community feeling, as a (local) world of production. Concretely, then, this involves the socio-economic conditions for doing business, socio-cultural conditions (including language), and legal-administrative preconditions.

The second important difference is that cultural distance is not individually and relatively experienced, whereas mental distance is. In the cultural distance index, *objectivated* differences between countries are involved. The concept mental distance, to the contrary, expresses an entrepreneur's *individual, subjective estimation* of the similarity to another country. In other words, the cultural distance index considers it from the top-down, and is calculated through the sum of individual values, which then provide the average for all individuals in a country. It is therefore a means to measure differences between countries. Mental distance is individual, may eventually be calculated for groups, but regards the matter from the bottom-up. The cultural distance index is symmetrical by definition; the distance between countries A and B equals the distance between B and A. The mental distance between those countries will be the same only by chance. The mental distance between countries A and B as perceived by entrepreneur X in country A does not have to equal the mental distance between them as perceived by entrepreneur Y in country B.

The third difference between these two types of distance is that, in the case of mental distance, an estimation is also provided regarding the consequences of the differences. The entrepreneur estimates the consequences of the differences in formal and informal conventions to the success of the relationship. Mental distance thereby also *evaluates* the conventions of another country, while cultural distance does not.

In chapter 3, I discussed the concept of 'psychic distance', which was defined as 'factors preventing or disturbing firms' learning about and understanding a foreign environment' (Nordstrom and Vahlne, 1992, p. 3). Contrary to the concept of mental distance, the definition of psychic distance does not, however, express the individual *perceptions* of differences. Especially in the most recent update of the notion as provided by Nordstrom and Vahlne (1992), it becomes clear that it is not the individual perceptions that are considered, but the cultural distances. They regarded cultural distance as a component of psychic distance. The notion of mental distance proposed here has a fundamentally different connotation, which concerns the *estimation* of differences in formal and informal conventions with regard to business in a foreign country and of their consequences. The concept mental distance embraces not so much the knowledge as its interpretation and application, as well as the unfounded estimations concerning the differences in characteristics and their consequences for doing business. In short, mental distance is here defined as:

The estimation by entrepreneurs of the differences and the consequences of these differences in formal and informal business conventions between a foreign country and the home country

INTERMEZZO: THE INTERPRETATION OF THE CONCEPT OF DISTANCE

In this study, four kinds of distance are distinguished: *physical, cultural, mental and cognitive*. The difference between these four types is explained schematically.

Figure 4.4 - Types of distances

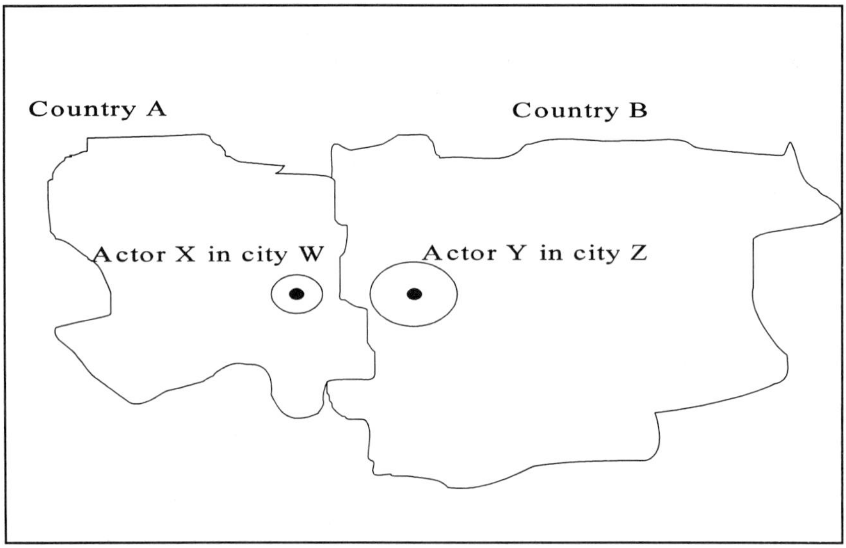

In the above figure, two cities W and Z in two different countries A and B are represented. In these cities are two actors X and Y.

The *physical* distance between actors X and Y is calculated by determining the travelling distance or time from city W to city Z. The distance from W to Z equals that from Z to W; the distance index is symmetrical.

The *cognitive* distance between X and Y is the knowledge- and experience-based estimated distance. It is calculated here by asking X and Y to estimate the physical distance to Z, respectively to W. This estimation is subjective and not necessarily symmetrical.

The *cultural* distance between countries A and B is the difference between the cultural values for all Xs and Ys in both countries. The cultural distance is symmetrical.

The *mental* distance between actors X and Y is determined by the estimation by actor X in country A of the differences with the conventions used by actor Y in country B when doing business and their consequences, and the other way around. This index is not necessarily symmetrical.

The notion of estimation refers to the *thinking and feeling* about a certain thing from the perspective of a certain pattern of expectations and/or a certain experience and knowledge. It can be considered as a construct that can be used to link ideas, knowledge and emotions on the one hand, and behaviour on the other. Personal ideas are important to the input for estimations. An individual's ideas are influenced by the personal or indirect interaction with the environment and the groups of reference within which he or she functions.

In indirect interaction, involving learning from the experience of others, I believe four processes play an important role simultaneously: *negation, innovation, socialisation,* and *imitation.* To begin with the last factor, *imitation*, one can say that the individual partly imitates the desired ideas and opinions of other actors in the environment, such as parents, colleagues, or friends. This form of imitation generates a place in the environment for the individual. His environment, in this case, is the group to which he belongs and/or wishes to belong. This may be an association, but also a city, a region, or even a country. With regard to *socialisation*: the individual entrepreneur is a social component of society, that is to say of a group of people that have the tendency to protect their group from influences from the outside. That protection is what keeps a society together, while at the same time it creates mental borders. The region, the country in which the entrepreneur grows up and in which he learns about the *mores* of colleague entrepreneurs and other inhabitants, usually becomes his 'home country', the territory with which he identifies. He experiences a certain degree of security, a 'feeling of being at home', with regard to his direct living and working environment, which he tends to miss upon entering an alien living and working environment that 'belongs' to another. The individual, nevertheless, will also wish to escape from an overly strict straitjacket of socialisation and imitation. For the sake of the creation and/or strengthening of his personal identity he may deny (*negation*) existing thinking patterns and/or norms, or may wish to create new combinations on the basis of existing thinking patterns and may select new paths (*innovation*).

From the perspective of entering into cross-border contacts, what determines his perception will be the degree to which the entrepreneur is attached, on the one hand, to the security created by a certain form of socialisation and as a result of imitation, and on the other hand to breaking certain patterns and generating innovations in his production process and/or market orientation. It is expected that this trade-off between security and insecurity determines, to a great extent, the perception towards entering into and developing economic relationships in the neighbouring country. The greater he perceives the differences in having relationships with entrepreneurs in the home country and neighbouring countries, and the more negative his evaluation of these differences, the greater is the mental distance with regard to having such relations in the neighbouring country. The expectation, then, is that the perception of great differences leads to refraining from establishing contacts (and relationships) with entrepreneurs in the neighbouring country. The reasoning behind this expectation is that great differences lead to greater adaptations and efforts to make the relationship in the neighbouring country to a comparable success. Formulated differently, a greater investment is required, costing more mental effort, money, and time. As a consequence of differences, there exists greater uncertainty with regard to economic relationships in the neighbouring country. Entrepreneurs will wish to safeguard against this uncertainty, which leads to higher transaction costs and greater pressure upon the trust in one another that is required for the success of the economic relationship.

Furthermore, it is expected that experience will diminish the effect of mental distance. Experience was brought forward as an important factor in the internationalisation process most notably in the psychic distance approach. Having experience in entering into/having economic relationships in the neighbouring country, whether it be positive or negative, matures an entrepreneur/enterprise. The learning effect with regard to matters such as how one should/should not react and which entrance should/should not be taken, renders the entrepreneur/enterprise more experienced (see also Barkema *et al.*, 1996). Moreover, experience often takes away a part of the insecurity or initial hesitation in entering into and having economic relationships in the neighbouring country, which facilitates beginning contacts and benefits the development of relationships with entrepreneurs in the neighbouring country. The experience will be measured in terms of the number of economic relations in the neighbouring country.

I should remark here that the dissimilarities between business conventions may, to the contrary, also be exaggerated *cognitively*, which may lead to stereotyping of the behaviour of the entrepreneurs in the neighbouring country. Since virtually no verification against reality is made when stereotyping occurs, these simplified beliefs tend to be persistent (cf. Paasi, 1996). Moreover, a group usually sees advantages in de-personifying another group. This makes one's own group more cohesive. A preference for the familiar and the 'like me' argument underlies this identification with and attraction to members of the in-group, the 'us' (Hogg, 1992; Pilkington and Lydon, 1997; Ray and Hall, 1995). As stated in chapter 2, the similarities may also be exaggerated *affectively*. In that case, the attraction to 'equals' leads to 'prejudiced opinions' with regard to 'others'. Stereotyping and prejudice enforce the faith in and security with regard to members of one's own group, for example in a region, but do not necessarily repose on economic reality.

Therefore it must be stressed here that the factor that matters is the *estimations* with regard to the differences and their consequences. These do not necessarily correspond to the actual differences. In this case, therefore, the impact upon the establishment of cross-border contacts (and relationships) exerted by the estimation of the differences in, and the economic consequences of, having economic relationships in the home country as opposed to the neighbouring country must be established from the perspective of the behaviour and decisions of entrepreneurs.

2. The degree of 'feeling at home' in the culture of the neighbouring country

Foreign cultures begin where national borders end. For an individual entrepreneur, however, a cultural difference does not necessarily lead to xenophobia. It is important in this context to examine what the entrepreneur's emotional, affective involvement is with the culture of the neighbouring country (cf. Riedel, 1994). Following Harris, culture is now defined as '...the total socially acquired life-style of a group of people including patterned, repetitive ways of thinking, feeling, and acting.' (Harris, 1993, p. 104). It is important to establish the degree to which an individual actor is capable of empathising and feeling affinity with the culture prevailing in the neighbouring country. It is a matter of individual affection vis-à-vis the overall culture of the neighbouring country.

I shall distinguish between the culture of the neighbouring country as perceived by the entrepreneur as private individual and the entrepreneur as business person. This implies that 'feeling at home' is differentiated into culture of living on the one hand, and business culture on the other. According to my expectations, a strong emotion of feeling at home in the neighbouring country will benefit economic involvement as well as the success of cross-border economic relationships in that country.

3. Spatial identity

In chapter 2, I also discussed the importance of an actor's social identity as determining the appreciation of other actors. Spatial identity reflects the spatial group (village, city, region, country, continent, world) with which the actor identifies, and the degree to which he does so. It was indicated that a typification in terms of 'we' and 'the other' also operates in individual actors. For that reason, spatial identity is here included as a condition for establishing contact with individual actors from the neighbouring country. The degree of identification with a space is inversely proportional to its size. The smaller the area, the greater the possibilities for active socialisation, and the stronger the feelings of identification with that space will be. Thus, the ties with space are stronger at the local level than at the regional level and the ties at the national level are stronger than at the European level.

The assumption is that there exists a positive connection between the 'preparedness to establish contacts' and the number of economic relations in the neighbouring country on the one hand, and the psychological connection with the neighbouring country on the other. In the same way, entrepreneurs identifying exclusively with (actors from) the direct regional living and working environment are expected to display less preparedness to establish international economic contacts, and will have fewer economic relationships than entrepreneurs who apply a wider horizon in their world of social identification. The gradual decline of the power of spatial identity, in the remainder of this study, will be called the *distance effect* of spatial identity.

However, another effect enters into consideration. Most people will be more attracted by the idea of feeling European or 'citizen of the world' than by having the neighbours' identity. The degree of identification, the degree of solidarity with a certain space also depends upon the size of the 'threat' emanating from other geographical unities. During international sporting competitions, for example, one may notice quite clearly that the proximity of the competitors enhances the mutual relationships of competition. The inhabitants of a region therefore often identify themselves less with their neighbours than would be expected on the basis of their proximity. This is defined here as the *neighbours' effect*. In that case, the supposition is that the solidarity with the space of the neighbours is smaller than the solidarity with general, international space.

4. Border evaluation

A border is not a neutral phenomenon. It is evaluated by the actors who have to deal with it. Still, that evaluation is seldom measured. And that while this, *a priori* less obvious, influence of the border may certainly play a role in spatial activities across that border. In economics and geographical economics, the state border is usually incorporated into the analytical model as a *barrier* to (spatial) activity. The role played by the actor's attitude towards the border as a barrier is often considered less extensively. We are then talking not of the function, but of the symbolical value of the border. In a time in which people generally speak of a 'de-functionalisation' of the borders and of a 're-symbolisation' of (national and regional) borders consequential upon the movements towards internationalisation and globalisation in economics, it is worthwhile to examine the degree to which the border is evaluated as a barrier.

In addition, environmental psychologists and socio-geographers (e.g. Leimgruber, 1987; Paasi, 1996; Riedel, 1994) generally point to the *relevance* of the border. People consider the border more or less important or valuable to their occupations. The powers that be, for instance, have an interest in maintaining state borders; entrepreneurs, far less. The population may derive feelings of identity and self-esteem from state borders.

In the present analysis, both the aspect of the border as *barrier* and its *relevance* will be considered. A suitable method to render this symbolism and the value attached to the concept and phenomenon of borders analytically operational is to measure them through attitudes that express the evaluation of the border (cf. Reynolds and Mc Nulty, 1968; Leimgruber, 1987; Riedel, 1994). It is possible to investigate the degree to which the evaluation of the border is associated with spatial activity, that is to say, with having economic relations in the neighbouring country and their number. The expectation is that entrepreneurs who regard the state border as irrelevant and not as a barrier will have more economic relationships.

III Cognition-space

1. Cognitive distance

In chapter 2 (§2.5), I have indicated that one can distinguish between things as they really are and things as they appear to us (Koffka, 1935). People have a cognitive representation of reality. That representation is knowledge and experience-based. There are many methods to measure cognitive distance. The principle of each of these methods is that they concern the analysis of the range of the cognition of the actors involved. In the present study, the method applied is restricted to estimated distances and drawing the border on a map (see point 11). See, for example, Riedel (1994) for other measurements. Cognitive distance will be measured by means of the estimated physical distance between two real locations on a map, in this case, two cities. While the distances between the own village and village A in the homeland, and between the own village and village B across the border may be equivalent in reality, the estimations may diverge (see §2.5). It is important that this divergence between the cognitive and real distance is explained. The accuracy of the estimate of physical distance, in kilometres on the road, to a city across the border is expected to express the personal experience and knowledge of the culture and space involved (cf. Evans, 1980; Riedel, 1994). The expectation is that the distance to cities across the border will be estimated higher than the distance to cities within the homeland. An overestimation of the distance indicates a low degree of personal experience and knowledge with regard to the distances to those cities. The city in the neighbouring country is far away. An underestimation, on the other hand, indicates that the city is close by in the subject's perception.

2. Physical distance

The cognitive distance is the estimation of the physical distance. The actual distance between two actors is in itself an important condition for the establishment of contact. If the distance between two entrepreneurs increases, it will render their coming into contact more difficult (Festinger *et al.*, 1950; Levinger *et al.*, 1972, Kahn *et al.*, 1977). The reason is that entrepreneurs between whom a great physical distance lies simply have less opportunity of meeting. Furthermore, the possibility to control and to have contact is rendered more difficult and costly when the physical distance is great, which is expected to hinder the intensity of the relationship. This will lower the intention to enter a cross-border economic relationship.

There are various methods by which the concrete, physical distance can be measured. One may look at the distance in kilometres as the crow flies, but this is inaccurate for the factual analysis of cross-border traffic to the neighbouring country, which occurs mostly through roads. One may also measure the distance in kilometres on the road, which is far more accurate. The flaw of this method is that it does not account for delays on the road, for example traffic-jams, waiting times for ferries, or mountain passes. Manshanden (1996) has recently demonstrated in his dissertation that the accessibility index of cities in the Netherlands changes drastically if the distance is measured not in kilometres, but in actual travelling time - that is, including delays caused by traffic-jams. Cities that are centrally located and therefore scored high on the national accessibility index, are far less centrally located when account is taken of traffic-jams. For the purposes of this study, I will measure physical distance in actual travelling time. Note that for the cognitive distance, I have chosen to measure the distance in kilometres on the road, for traffic-jams may determine part of the under- and overestimations, which obscures the image of the estimation of the distance.

3. A cognitive map of the border

People place the border in space more or less accurately. That is the assumption underlying the last factor that is of importance in the context of the contact stage of economic relationships. An idea about the location of the border can be represented in a cognitive map of the border; this subject has been discussed in chapter 2 (§2.5). Actors, then, have an idea of the factual location of the state border on the map. This question pertains to their spatial knowledge or cognition. The greater the spatial cognition with regard to a neighbouring country, the greater the chances of and points of departure for an actual step into the neighbouring country (see chapter 2). The expectation, conformable to the line of reasoning proposed for the factor of cognitive distance, is that that which is more familiar will be estimated more accurately (in this case, will be drawn more accurately). The purpose is to establish the nature of the divergence with regard to the factual border.

4.2.2 Attraction

An encounter between two entrepreneurs remains a one-off encounter if both do not have the idea that an economic relationship with the other will be profitable. The question then is what is (are) the reason(s) are for establishing the relationship with that partner out of all others. Put differently, what factors make it so that one can speak of a certain degree of attraction, a 'click' between these two actors causing them to decide to do business together? As Ring and Van de Ven (1994) put it, entering into bilateral business transactions is 'a meeting of the minds'.

Only little attention, however, is devoted, in economic theories on transactions, to this phase. So as to verify the importance of the attraction stage in the development of cross-border economic relationships, an appeal must be made to the socio-psychological theories concerning interpersonal attraction that elucidate the (determinant factors of the) process of attraction[1].

In addition, an extensive search for the determinants of the arising of attraction is made. From

---

1 When applying non-economic theories to economic behaviour, the problem usually called 'the ecological fallacy' enters into play. The question at hand is: Do the assumptions with regard to socio-psychological behaviour also hold true for entrepreneurial behaviour? (see, for instance, Iacobucci and Ostrom, 1996). When discussing the assumptions, I will indicate how the socio-psychological theory should be applied to the situation of entrepreneurs or how entrepreneurial behaviour differs from 'normal' socio-psychological behaviour).

the relevant literature, the following determinants of attraction have been distilled (Baron and Byrne, 1997; Meertens and Grumbkow, 1988/1992,Veen and Wilke, 1986):

1. Similarity
2. Complementation
3. External or physical attraction
4. Spatial proximity

1. Similarity as factor of attraction

In a first encounter between entrepreneurs, mutual feelings - whether positive or negative - for or about the other, arise that are not necessarily economic in nature at the first instance, but may have an economic impact. These feelings for the other often arise intuitively and spontaneously. What is recognised in the other is often regarded as attractive. This is the similarity effect. When an actor compares himself to another, he feels more attracted as the similarities (or positive results of the comparison) are greater and the dissimilarities (or negative results) smaller (Baron and Byrne, 1997; Byrne and Clore, 1970; Byrne, 1971; Newcomb, 1961; Sharma and Kaur, 1996; Singh and Tan, 1992; Snyder, 1979;Turner *et al.* 1987). The entrepreneur himself evaluates the professional opinions, ideas, habits, or behaviour of the potential partner. The results, therefore, are arranged differently from the cognitive point of view by different entrepreneurs. Recognition leads to a more positive estimation of the benefits of the economic relationship, which is expected to be an advantage for the development of the relationship. Discovering similarities in the other reduces the insecurity issuing from the unfamiliarity with that other (Byrne, 1971; Festinger, 1954). In some economic studies on similarity, subsumed under terms like 'shared norms' or 'compatibility', the relationship between similarity and success of the relationship has been tested (see, e.g. Bucklin and Senguta, 1993; McAllister, 1995; Sarkar, Cavusgil and Evirgen, 1996). These studies indicate that there is a strong direct link between partner match and the success of the relationship.

2. Complementation as a factor of attraction

'Opposites attract' is a maxim that applies to the second reason for the emergence of interpersonal attraction. A certain degree of inequality in skills and character traits can be attractive (Byrne, 1971; Rijsman, 1981). The idea here is that personal identity and mutual appreciation may provide benefits if the other does not have exactly the same notions, behaviour or skills (Baron and Byrne, 1997). Especially in relationships between enterprises, joining unequal information or resources may be desirable. One might think of the contacts or relationships of the other entrepreneur, the access he may provide to a certain market, and diverging professional ideas. For strategic reasons, complementation may be preferable to similarity between partners (Van Oudenhoven and De Boer, 1995). A synergetic effect might be the result, which will affect the success of the economic relationship in a positive manner (Contractor and Lorange, 1988; Harrigan, 1988; Bleeke and Ernst, 1991). Nevertheless, it is generally assumed that the effects of complementation plays a smaller role in the emergence of attraction than the effects of similarity (Drigotas, 1993). Too great a difference increases insecurity; additional trust and/or additional safeguards are then necessary in the agreement between the parties.

3. External or physical attraction as factor of attraction

The theories on interpersonal attraction ascribe an important role to the factor of physical attraction. In the first meeting especially, the other's looks, or in other words his/her physical characteristics, are important determinants (Berscheid and Walster, 1974; Berscheid, 1985). It would be difficult for it to be otherwise, as a person's looks are often the first source of information allowing an immediate judgement. In relationships of friendship and especially romance, someone's looks are often an important factor of attraction. What is considered attractive is often even overestimated: 'What is beautiful is good' (Dion, Berscheid and Walster, 1972; Dion and Dion 1987). External attractiveness is then superimposed onto other personal characteristics. The opposite also often holds true. Positive information concerning other than physical characteristics often enhances a person's physical attractiveness: 'What is good is beautiful' (Gross and Crofton, 1977). The question is how this dimension of attraction should be interpreted when the attraction occurs not in a social, but in an economic context. How do two entrepreneurs/enterprises evaluate one another where it concerns external attractiveness? One should think most notably of matters such as the price and the quality of the products sold or supplied by the other. These external characteristics may be strategically influenced by means of marketing and image-building.

4. Spatial proximity as factor of attraction

A last factor which is of importance to the emergence of attraction between entrepreneurs is spatial proximity. The simple fact that two individuals live and/or work at a short distance of one another is in many cases decisive to the arising of attraction. Marriage and friendship often bring together people living or working in the same municipality, the same street, or even on the same floor (Festinger, Schachter and Back, 1950). Proximity by itself, however, does not explain attraction. Proximity is not a cause. It must be determined why attraction emerges between people that live and/or work in close proximity.
The scientific discipline that has made an important place for the study of the financial aspect of spatial proximity as an economic explanation for attraction between companies, is regional economics or economic geography.

In view of the importance attached to spatial proximity in (regional) economics, according to some partly due to the trend of globalisation (see, e.g. Porter, 1990), I shall delve deeper into this dimension of attraction. I will discuss the theoretical developments in the explanation of the relationship between spatial agglomeration and distance in regional economics. Finally, I will examine in how far this development concurs with present ideas in the attraction theories proposed by social psychology.

4a. Distance and spatial attraction in regional economic science

In the traditional regional economic theory of Lösch (1940/1954), spatial proximity was the central element in the explanation of the company's process of choosing a location. Attention was turned especially towards the minimisation of transport costs to optimise profits. It was assumed that a linear connection existed between distance and transport costs. In later, neo-classical explanations of the agglomeration of companies, the element of the expectations of consumers and manufacturers with regard to costs and benefits was included. Thereafter, the nature of the rationality of economic behaviour became an important phenomenon in those explanations (Lambooy, 1992). Hotteling's theory (1929) provides an example of a neo-classical theory of attraction between entrepreneurs. In his now celebrated example, two independent ice-cream vendors each start at one end of the beach, ending in a sort of establishment game at the middle of the beach, where each has the same share of the market: the point of stability in competition. In their explanations of the agglomeration of companies Stewart (1947) and later Harris (1954) stressed that theoretical attention should be focused on the potential of the market. In their opinion, entrepreneurs mainly focus on the market. Entrepreneurs will establish their businesses in close proximity to each other if the greatest sales are expected at that location.

This line of thinking has set through mainly in gravity models and accessibility indices, which attempt primarily to analyse the connection between physical distance and the growth of economic accommodations on a mathematical basis (see, amongst others, Clark *et al.*, 1969; Keeble *et al.*, 1982; Dieperink and Nijkamp, 1986; Bruinsma, 1994; Manshanden, 1996).
A popular idea in the theme of accessibility, disputed in writing even today, is the 'urban field concept' of Friedman and Miller (1965). Looking ahead at the next generation, these authors foresaw, in the United States, 'a new scale of urban living that will extend far beyond existing metropolitan cores and penetrate deeply into the periphery. Relations of dominance and dependency will be transcended' (1965, p. 313). The city ought not to be regarded as a physical, delimited political and geographical entity, but as an 'urban field'. The authors argued that the urban field should be regarded as an 'enlargement of the space for urban living that extends beyond the boundaries of existing metropolitan areas into the open landscape of the periphery' (p. 314). Thus, it would become impossible to distinguish between 'properly urban' and properly rural'. According to them, two forces would contribute to realise this prediction. In the first place, the centripetal pull to the inner cities would be weakened due to changing living preferences (more quiet, nature and space). And in the second place, substantial centrifugal forces would drive the settlement of the population and the location of activities from the city towards the periphery. The impact of these forces would be strengthened due to the increase in leisure time, income and transport opportunities. The result would be a stronger degree of interdependency between the centre and the periphery. The urban field, according to Friedman and Miller, occupies a zone of core areas of at least 300,000 people and the region beyond covered by two hours travelling distance (ground transport). The urban field concept, after its introduction, became popular in smaller European countries. In the Netherlands for instance, Wever uses the concept quite regularly, but more to express the similarities between various regions in a country

(Wever, 1987, 1991; Atzema and Wever, 1994). In general terms, one might even say that the notion 'urban field' in the Netherlands has been used mainly to describe the pattern of urban elements in a country that displays a reasonably uniform spread of agglomeration advantages (cf. Manshanden, 1988).

The concept of agglomeration advantages was the point of departure for a current of neo-classical regional economists who emphasised that these cost advantages of the agglomeration, the so-called 'agglomeration economies', should be regarded as a reason for the spatial clustering of enterprise. This current has also gone through a strong development, and remains popular today. Agglomeration advantages are regarded as external advantages. A growing agglomeration enables enterprises to increase their production efficiency. Up to a certain critical value of population size in the agglomeration, these external advantages are net positive, above that, they are net negative (Manshanden, 1996). Above this level, strongly negative external effects, such as congestion and environmental pollution, arise. The economies of agglomeration are now distinguished according to four categories of cost (*idem*). In the first place, transportation and communication costs are reduced when enterprises are located in close proximity to each other (transfer economies). Moreover, management, research and/or production costs can be shared when several subsidiaries/branch offices of a company are localised in the same area (internal economies of scale). The costs of individual companies are diminished when the number of companies in an agglomeration increases (localisation economies). Finally, the marketing and production costs incurred by individual companies are reduced as the agglomeration grows in size (urbanisation economies).

During the mid-fifties, French economic geographical scientists focused attention especially on the factors relating to dependency and polarisation in explaining the spatial attraction of enterprise. Central to the analysis of Chardonnet (1953), for example, is the 'key firm', a large enterprise with different kinds of dependency relationships in a certain region. A few years later, Perroux presented his 'growth pool concept', which incorporated Chardonnet's notion of key firms (Perroux, 1955). Perroux referred to the various relationships with supplier industries as 'economic space'. Towards the end of that decade, regional economist Myrdal's developed the principle of 'cumulative causation' (Myrdal, 1957), through which he tried to clarify the effects that are to be expected on a (regional) economy when a key firm is established at a certain location. According to the above-mentioned three French theorists, the force of attraction between companies can have technical, economic, geographical, and historical causes, but also psychological ones. In fact, they drew attention to the aspect of business relationships as a reason for spatial clustering. In comparison with the traditional and until then popular neo-classical theories, this was a new element. These theorists laid the foundation for the modern theories on network formation and industrial districts. The cost aspect alone no longer sufficed in the explanation, which was confirmed again by Pred, who some years later posited his ideas on the rationality of the process of selecting a location for establishment (Pred, 1967). He departed from the view that entrepreneurs could not make an entirely rational choice, but only a restrictedly rational one. This behaviourist approach created space for subjective factors in the choice for a business location as well as subjective interpretations of information concerning (cost aspects of) business locations.

In modern-day and newly arising theories, too, it appears that it is exactly this space in the explanation, which remains if one does not depart from the full rationality of entrepreneurs, that is elaborated further. In the flexible specialisation approach, subject of much discussion nowadays, this development in the theory of regional economics is clearly visible.

Originally, flexible specialisation was a spatial interpretation, made by Scott, of Williamson's transaction costs theory (Scott, 1988). Scott argued that companies that enter into economic relationships with each other (most notably in the case of vertical disintegration), will be located, or established, at small distances from each other. The reason, according to him, was the reduction of transaction costs, *i.e.* the transfer costs of information, commodities and services. The intensive interaction required in economic interaction would be very costly if its partners were spatially dispersed. Thus, to the extent that transactions have geographically sensitive cost structures, the increased level of external transaction in a production system will lead to a clustering of producers in order to minimise the resources, of both money and time, necessary to the transaction. Scott's argumentation regarding the reasons of regional (re-)agglomeration is actually built upon the neo-classical approach to agglomeration economies. In such a situation, a reduction of the transaction costs provides a financial argument for businesses to agglomerate in space.

Still later, however, several authors sharply criticised the explicitness of the transaction costs theory by arguing that there might be other reasons causing companies to cluster in space (e.g. Gertler, 1988; Sayer, 1989; Amin and Robins, 1990; Henry, 1992; Amin, 1992). They argued, although spatial concentration may result from the move towards flexible specialisation, it is not a deterministic process. Henry, in particular, has argued that there is no 'logic of agglomeration' if one bases one's arguments solely and simply upon the transaction costs approach (Henry, 1992). The process of agglomeration, he argues, should not be defined simply in terms of an efficient combination of factors, but more as a logic of interaction. Agglomerative tendencies, then, may result from the point of view of the transaction costs approach, but are certainly not a necessary, mechanistically determined consequence. Different mechanisms may produce the same result (see also Ernste *et al.*, 1992; James and Bhalla, 1993). As Henry puts it: 'To adduce that the agglomeration is the result of the transaction costs mechanism of agglomeration is merely to infer causality on the basis of a pre-theorised logic [...] The mere existence of linkages between (spatially close) establishments says nothing about the process of their creation' (1992, pp. 384-5).

Other theorists, such as Storper, Walker, and Schoenberger, have further elaborated the assumed positive relationship between the existence of networks and the geographical agglomeration of important components of the production system. They contend that the relationship exists especially in technologically dynamic industries. Storper calls the kind of agglomerations that evolves 'technological districts' (Storper, 1992, 1993). He argues that flexible production and agglomerative tendencies are to be considered as two of a kind. In other words, flexible production is not based on 'flexible space'. On the contrary, in order to be adequately informed concerning new insights and innovations in the technology used, the contracted suppliers of a company would have to specialise on an industry-wide level and be physically close to each other. Receiving information from customers, suppliers and their institutional context enables businesses to evolve a technological learning process. This consultative behaviour of firms in the production chain is essential to the principle of flexible specialisation. Whilst full dependency of one core company does have the short-term positive impact of reducing uncertainty, the long-term negative impact will be to reduce the stimuli to innovation, resulting in a 'lock-in' to a given technology (Miles and Snow, 1992; Krugman, 1991). In order for information to flow freely, it may be clear that within such a district a special link must exist between the nature of co-operation and competition on the one hand, and the path-dependent cultural background of its location on the other. We have discussed this, what we have called, CCC model - Co-operation, Competition and Community - of industrial districts elsewhere (Van Houtum and Boekema, 1995). Factors such as trust, commitment, mutual involvement, and common history between the critical agents in the production system are considered to be vital, for they are able to lead to technological learning (Storper, 1993, 1997). Proximity and face-to-face contacts are essential to this process (see also Gottmann, 1961; Manshanden, 1996). Establishing a spatially bounded group strategy, which builds and acts back upon the individual enterprise, is, within the 'flex-spec model', perhaps the most characteristic way to explain the assumed paradox between competition, co-operation, community, and economic growth (Best, 1990; Van Houtum and Boekema, 1995; Van Houtum, 1996).

The proponents of the flexible specialisation approach have proposed a concept that is said to be especially evident in industries like electronics, designer clothing, craft products, and other light industrial consumer products (Amin and Thrift, 1992). These industries, in their niche markets, have had to face pronounced volatility and production innovations, resulting in reduced product life cycles. Although quite a few differences can be noticed between examples, Western spatial examples most commonly given are Third Italy, the US Sunbelt region (including Orange County, Silicon Valley, Dallas, and Fort Worth), Boston's Route 128, the M4 Corridor in England, the Jura region in Switzerland, and Baden-Württemberg in Germany (e.g. Scott, 1988; Amin and Thrift, 1992).

It is now widely acknowledged that qualitative factors such as the personal preferences of the manager, an area's business climate, education facilities, historical precedent, the attitude of the local work force, the cultural attributes of an area, or government co-operation, cannot be overlooked when one is analysing the reasons for the spatial economic attraction between businesses. Krugman, for example, in his explanation regarding economic clusters, posits that non-economic factors may often encourage initial activities in an area, thus giving rise to the spatial clustering of firms as local firms and consumers both come to prefer more substantial markets (1991).

Porter (1990), too, developed an influential theory on economic clustering in space (see also chapter 2). Porter argues that successful economic activities are clustered and embedded in space. It is the embeddedness of the activities, or, as he calls it, the 'diamond' that shapes the international competitive performance of companies over time. Since firms mostly develop their market within the domestic, short-distance environment prior to international expansion, the specific configuration of the 'home base' plays a key role in determining the character of the human capital, the resources, and the identity of the firm. Porter said, 'What I am really exploring here is the way in which a firm's approximate "environment" shapes its competitive success over time' (*idem*, p. 29). As he sees it, the typical national or regional diamond characteristics that determine the local environment of the company are a vital factor in the success of the firm and thereby in the growth pattern of the region: 'Competitive advantage is created and sustained through a highly localised process' (*idem*, p. 19). Thus, 'geographical concentration of firms in internationally successful industries often occurs because the influence of the individual determinants in the "diamond" and their mutual reinforcement are heightened by close geographic proximity within a nation' (*idem*, p. 156-7), '[...] the leaders in particular industries and segments of industries tend to be concentrated in a few nations and often within a few regions in those nations' (*idem*, p. 158).
Thus, according to Porter, regional competition and the nature of regional demand can serve as testing fields for the initial development of enterprise in a region. To the extent that they are flexible, existing and evolving links in the region are important in that they can permit efficient and rapid access to the necessary goods and services, information and insights. Hence, interaction between the firm and its subcontractors becomes profitable and self-enforcing. The production factors, divided into basic and advanced factors, must be upgraded continuously. It is not the stock itself that is important, but rather the rate at, and efficiency with which they are created, upgraded and deployed in particular industries. Historical and cultural values of a region are not mentioned separately, but do play a vital role in influencing the characteristics of the factors mentioned above. Governments should only play an indirect, not a direct, role as they are not believed to be capable of creating competitive industries; only firms can do that.

Porter, therefore, contends that economic development does not occur accidentally in a certain area. With this view, he protests against the comparative cost advantage theories in international trade. These theories, he argues, neglect the process through which the competitive advantage of firms and countries is created. Although Porter's theory is far from sound still (see, amongst others, Van Houtum, 1991; Beije and Nuys, 1995), his approach and that proposed by the flexible specialisation model do make clear that proximity and face-to-face contacts are considered important elements in modern regional economics.

To summarise the above, it can be said that the entrepreneur's economic rationality, where it concerns the minimisation of costs and maximisation of profits, is no longer taken to be the only point of departure in economic geographical theories. Firms are no longer seen as 'black boxes'. Instead, theories focus more and more on the internal organisation of the firm as well as on the individual entrepreneurial level. Profound theoretical developments focusing on the forces of these 'internal mechanisms' of both firms and entrepreneurs in relation to spatial proximity have barely started in regional economics/economic geography. To the individual entrepreneurial behaviour, perceptions, cognitions, the barriers to face-to-face contacts, and the latter's merits are gradually being taken into account. In my view, these are promising developments. It is gradually recognised that the social and institutional context within which entrepreneurs function feeds the rationale underlying their economic behaviour to an important extent. Entrepreneurs sometimes opt for clustering with certain companies in certain locations, which cannot be explained by a rational economic costs/benefits analysis. The reverse also holds true. Entrepreneurs sometimes clearly refuse clustering with certain companies in certain locations where this would be economically and rationally feasible or even desirable. In modern regional economics, geographic proximity is not merely the mathematical reverse of distance (Lambooy, 1992).

4b. Distance and attraction in socio-psychology

The analogy between the evolution of economic geographical and regional economic theories on the attraction between firms on the one hand, and socio-psychological theories on factors of attraction between entrepreneurs on the other, is remarkable. In socio-psychology, too, the argument that the costs aspect of spatial proximity is not the only determinant is voiced clearly (Schutte and Light, 1978).

In this respect, Meertens and Grumbkow (1992) point out another influence that is thought equally essential in explaining the importance of spatial proximity at the international level. The *repeated contact effect* or *mere exposure effect* especially is regarded as the most important alternative explanation (Zajonc, 1968; Moreland and Zajonc, 1982). The first impression of another cannot be more than a limited, often stereotypical impression of his factual personality. Nevertheless, even a single contact may sometimes suffice to engender a positive/more positive emotion. If the contact becomes more frequent, his/her personal characteristics become more familiar, which generally also increases the attraction towards him/her. This in turn benefits the development of the bilateral economic relationship. A good reputation may also reduce insecurity about that person, and have a similar effect on attraction and the relationship's development. In economic literature on the establishment of economic relationships, the psychic distance theory most notably has drawn attention to the learning and reputation aspect of repeated contact.

The repeated contact effect is in line with the argument of the proponents of 'the contact hypothesis' (see, Allport, 1954; Cooke, 1985), who argue that direct personal contact between individuals from different social groups might have a harmonious effect on the intergroup relations. It might lead individuals to perceive the in-group and out-group as more similar to each other, and it results in more favourable evaluations of the out-group (Gaertner *et al.* 1994; Kosmitzki, 1996).

Thus, face-to-face contact, and therefore physical distance, should still be seen as an important factor in establishing cross-border contacts. Modern communication means, such as the telephone, telefax, or the Internet, which might in principle be used to establish business contacts at a distance, offer insufficient replacement for the personal certainty concerning the other that may be obtained through face-to-face contact (cf. Gottmann, 1961). Telecommunications and face-to-face contact are complementary. Even if complete security can never be obtained about the person with whom one will do business, the personal experience of how that person looks and behaves does usually inspire confidence (*idem*).

It should be noted, that in a context of direct contact, the positive effect will not hold, or at least to a lesser extent, if the initial reaction to a first exposure is negative. Repeated contact in this case may have the opposite effect. People who experience intergroup contacts in such cases focus even more strongly on the differences between groups, and stereotyping is enhanced (Turner *et al.*, 1987; Krueger, 1992; Kosmitzki, 1996). It has been argued in psychological literature that the condition of interpersonal attraction in particular and co-operative interaction between the actors, an equal status of the actors in question, and supportive norms within and outside of the contact, are to be marked as important stimuli to reduce this negative bias in direct personal contact. These conditions alter the actors's cognitive representations of the memberships from 'us' and 'them' to a more inclusive 'we' (Gaertner *et al.*, 1994).

4.2.3 Interaction

After the first *contact* and the emergence of *attraction* between two entrepreneurs, a new stage begins: the *interaction*. This is a phase during which deliberations are undertaken concerning the benefits each of the entrepreneurs wishes to obtain from the relationship. It determines whether the contact between the two entrepreneurs will actually grow into an economic relationship. In the interaction stage, the transaction stage is prepared, during which the decision whether or not to commit the final agreements to paper (the contract) is made.

Two entrepreneurs will enter into an economic relationship if it provides an attractive alternative, if the benefits for both are greater than the costs (Blau, 1964; Homans, 1958). The behaviour strategy in the interaction stage depends upon the motivation and behaviour of the other. The other's behaviour is, to a certain extent, uncertain. This means that both entrepreneurs must make an *estimation* of the outcome of the interaction. Thus, each must be convinced that doing business with the other confidently must be possible, in such a way that it may be expected that the relationship will actually deliver the desired benefits (Veen and Wilke, 1986; Ligthart, 1995). Personal trust reduces the uncertainty. In the interaction stage, therefore, the actors' norms, including their notions of equality and fairness, become important.

The economic theory specifically focused on this interaction stage is, as discussed in chapter 3, the transaction costs theory. This theory, which is influential in organisation literature, offers handles for selecting the most efficient governance structure for transactions. In other words, the theory deals with the decision moment whether or not to do something oneself. Williamson and other theorists advocating the transaction costs theory have expanded the options, later on, with the possibility of choosing intermediate governance structures (Richardson, 1972; Williamson, 1985). As indicated in chapter 3, the transaction costs theory presupposes entrepreneurs to be boundedly rational and opportunist. These are the pillars upon which the theory is built. There would be no transaction costs in Williamson's model if complete rationality and/or no opportunism were assumed. The presuppositions of bounded rationality and opportunism, in combination with the assumptions concerning the atmosphere within which the transaction occurs, the uncertainty involved in the transaction, the frequency of the transaction, and the specificity of the human and material assets of the firm, ensure that a measured decision scheme is created. Via a process of 'private ordening', a balance is achieved in the mutual dependency associated with the transaction. In the end, the governance structure that is most efficient is chosen for an international transaction, given the frequency of the transaction, the uncertainty involved, and the degree to which the investments are relation-specific. The measure of efficiency is the height of the costs involved in organising and managing the transaction - the transaction costs. Thus, TCE provides a forceful instrument to analyse the nature and risks of economic transactions, and how to reduce the risks of transactions.
In chapter 3, I already indicated what criticism could be made on the theory. The theory is clear and powerful, but at the same time only partially realistic. It wields a very narrowly-defined image of human behaviour in economic traffic. Moreover, the static character of the transaction costs model does no justice to the complexity of the dynamic reality of learning and experience. It is therefore doubtful whether the existence of the enterprise, economic relationships, or other governance structures can be explained entirely and solely by the transaction costs theory. However, in spite of these shortcomings, the concept of transaction costs remains valid. The notion of transaction costs is a useful one when seen as a point of departure and indicator for deliberations that may be of an opportunist nature, thus rendering necessary investment costs and/or modification costs. It forcefully summarises part of the behaviour that plays a role in the deliberation process during the interaction stage.

The international network approach of Johanson and Mattsson (1987, 1988), also discussed in chapter 3, posit the argument of mutual dependency (reciprocity) in international economic relations. They reserve an important role for the learning effect and interactions between entrepreneurs. Entrepreneurs learn from each other's behaviour and attempt to achieve a relationship optimal for both through an iterative process (see also Larson, 1992; Raap, 1995). These network theorists furthermore argue that the exchange of money against goods or information is central in a transaction, but that the social element of trust plays a more important role than that assigned it by the transaction costs model (see also Lorenz, 1991). The assumption of the learning effect also applies to trust; the creation of trust is a process of development. The entrepreneurs involved must have had several meetings so that a memory of former experiences may emerge. In economic literature trust is generally seen as the extent to which an entrepreneur expects or believes that its exchange partner is benevolent and honest, and will not take advantage of the other even when the opportunity is available (cf. Axelrod, 1984; Dwyer, Schurr, and Oh, 1987; Bromily and Cummings, 1992; Geyskens and Steenkamp, 1995; Morgan and Hunt, 1994; Ring and Van de Ven, 1992; Scheer and Stern, 1992).

Williamson, in shrill contrast to this, argues that there is no such thing as trust (Williamson, 1991, 1993). 'Trust is redundant at best' (Williamson, 1993, p.453). He asserts that there are merely varying degrees of credibility in commitments. Trust is such a degree of credibility. Credibility, he argues, may be regarded as a calculative assessment of the efficacy of the effect of reputation. Reference to trust therefore adds nothing (*idem*). It is thus that Williamson attempts to fit the concept of trust into the scheme of his transaction costs model.

In short, whereas the transaction costs theory focuses mainly to reduce risk and uncertainty by means of contracts (the safeguards), the main assumption in the international network theory is that trust functions as the central factor in economic relationships. The proponents of this theory have a point there. Williamson's argumentation does not do justice to the notion of trust, which is not a calculated assessment of credibility. Trust is a social term, an interpersonal phenomenon that has an important role to play in trying to explain the characteristics and development of negotiation processes and patterns (Zucker, 1986; Gulati, 1995). For, economic relationships are constructed socially and process-wise. A(n) (economic) society is a network of interacting individuals, a series of social relationships (Harcourt and De Waal, 1992). In these professional relationships, institutionalised patterns and expectations with regard to the other's professional conventions, behaviour and opportunism are important.

Trust alters the assessments of the uncertainty and counteracts fear of opportunism in the interaction between firms, thereby possibly reducing the transaction costs. As for the process of negotiations in the interaction stage, which in the INTERFACE model leads to the transaction stage, I subscribe to Gulati's conclusion in his interesting article dealing with the development of trust and contractual choice in alliances (1995):

> The most basic conclusion that follows from this study is that contracts chosen in alliances do not depend wholly upon the activities included within the partnership and their associated transaction costs. Rather, such choices depend on the trust that emerges between organizations over time through repeated ties. My findings suggest that neither transaction costs nor social factors should dominate discussion of alliances and that in the final analysis, any explanation should encompass both (p.108)

In order to examine the exact role of trust in the interaction between firms, the concept or trust has to be specified more clearly. Trust has two, closely related dimensions. First of all, trust is the *perception and interpretation* of the other's expected 'dependability'. Expected dependability, in my opinion, is the inverse of deviations in one's expectation of the reaction of the other to one's actions. When the other reacts in an unexpected and unpleasant way, the perceived dependability decreases. Consequently, trust is based upon the expectation that one will find what is expected rather than what is feared (Deutsch, 1973). Opportunism can only come into existence if both businesses are dependable from the start. Without dependability as a basis within a relation, there can be no deviation, that is, opportunism. And without dependability, there can be no relationship. The emergence of trust therefore occurs at the beginning of the relationship as an expectation of dependability. One might even say that the element of trust, in the form of similarity between the partners - which is, as stated above, often related to 'in-group' membership -, already plays a role in the attraction stage of the relationship's development.

Secondly, the expected trust is tested during the interaction stage. During the interaction process, expectations about the other's behaviour are confirmed or denied, and entrepreneurs learn from each other's behaviour. Next to the cognition-oriented 'expected dependability', which Zucker in 1986 called 'character-based trust', trust therefore also refers to the factual behaviour of the two entrepreneurs. Trust is therefore as much an expectation as a result. The perception of trust is an ongoing process. Firms learn about each other and develop expectations around mutual habits and conventions. As Shapiro *et al.* (1992) put it, trust is also 'knowledge-based', or in the words of Zucker (1986) 'process-based'. For this reason, the ratification of the working agreements is not a static decision. The degree of trust in the factual bilateral interaction will be discerned in practice through the degree of openness and informality of the contact with the other and the suppleness of communication betwixt the partners (Smith and Barclay, 1997).

The argument used in the paper on trust in collaborative ventures by Sarkar *et al.* (1996) wraps up the above reasoning in an appealing manner:

> '...trust seems to be fostered by a commonality of cultures and a mutual feeling of suitability while it is maintained by open two-way communications between partners.' (p. 23).

Some authors separate trust operationally in the two dimensions - one referring to the cognitive expectation of the partner, and the second a behavioural dimension (see, e.g. Zucker, 1986; Knorringa, 1995; Mc Allister, 1995; Smith and Barclay, 1997). Together with Morgan and Hunt (1994) however, I believe that combining these conceptions of trust is more meaningful. The two dimensions together make up trust. For behavioural intent is implied in the perception and expectation of trust (*idem*). Trust as expected dependability and the trust displayed in the interaction, must therefore be combined.

Furthermore, it is postulated here that trust in the interaction is a precondition for the eventual success of the cross-border relationship. This postulate coincides with recent findings in economic literature (Aulakh, Kotabe, and Sahay, 1996; Bleeke and Ernst, 1991; Morgan and Hunt, 1994; Nooteboom *et al.* 1995; Parkhe, 1993; Ring and Van de Ven, 1994; Wilkins and Ouchi, 1983). The gradual building of an economic relationship between two people could be seen as the formation of a small group, a bilateral community. Trust is an essential element in the gradual growth of the feeling of 'we-ness' in an economic relationship. Especially when the relationship has evolved, interdependence and normative regulation, which are both unique to the relationship, become noticeable. As mutuality grows during the building of a relationship, the partners show increasing concern for each other's outcomes as well as pride and possessiveness regarding their joint 'we-ness' (Levinger and Snoek, 1972). Behaviour aiming at the enhancement of the other's satisfaction and self-esteem is common to each relationship (*idem*). The 'we-feeling', the feeling of belonging together, which causes the cohesion of the relationship, is graduated. One-off or short relationships will have less 'we-ness' than long-term relationships. Besides, love bonds will therefore be based more soundly upon trust than upon calculation. Yet this does not mean that economic relationships are entirely or even principally based upon mutual calculation and that there is no trust other than calculative credibility. In economic relationships too, a certain degree of 'we-ness' emerges and in a relationship of friendship or love, too, there is a critical limit to the acceptance of opportunist behaviour (see Nooteboom, 1993). It is important that the trust shown by the partners reduces the insecurity, thereby increasing the chances for the economic success of the relationship.
At the same time, increasing attachment in the relationship reduces the independence of the partners. This can be disadvantageous; it might cause a certain 'lock-up' leading to rigidity. Stability may lead to staleness (see chapter 3). Trust is 'a building factor' for the 'we-ness' in a relationship, thereby stimulating the success of the relationship, but might at the same be a 'constraint'. It is to be verified empirically to which extent success can be explained through the existence of trust between the partners.

In short, trust is expected to be both a condition for and a result of interaction, as well as a precondition for the success of the relationship. The correlation between the dimensions of the attraction stage, as a condition for the start-up of the interaction phase, and the dimensions of the interaction stage will be examined in chapter 7. The correlation between trust and success will be verified through a multivariate analysis (see chapter 7).

To summarise this section, in the interaction stage, the factors of importance are: (1) *the height of the transaction costs*, and (2) *the degree of trust in the interaction between the partners*. The height of the transaction costs shall be measured by means of the specificity of the investments in the product or production process; the resources, the knowledge and the manpower required to enter into the transaction; and the degree of uncertainty concerning the behaviour of the other (see Williamson, 1975, 1985; Rindfleisch and Heide, 1997). The degree of trust in the bilateral interaction will be measured through the degree of expected faithfulness, the degree of openness and informality of the contact with the other, and the suppleness of communication betwixt the partners.

4.2.4 Transaction

When the international interaction proceeds according to the expectations of both parties and the conditions have been agreed upon, the decision to ratify the intention to exchange resources or information may be taken: this is the moment of transaction. It may be decided to put the agreements down in writing or not. One may speak of an international transaction when two legally autonomous, separately constituted business organisations enter into an economic relationship, whether or not in writing, across the national borders (cf. Tallman and Shenkar, 1994). It seems reasonable to suppose that those agreements whose transaction costs are elevated (due to high asset specificity) and whose trust is low will be committed to paper. Because of higher transaction costs and lower trust, it is expected that *formal* agreements are less successful than *informal* agreements. It must be determined, therefore, under which circumstances the parties will decide to commit the agreements to paper, and under which circumstances they will deem it unnecessary to do so.
The term contract is reserved, in this study, for an 'agreement in writing'. Whether on paper or not, it is crucial that the agreement is recorded in a mutual settlement indicating the temporary or sustained action both actors commit themselves to perform, in which what is an obligation for one actor is the other's right. The right can be enforced if the commitments are not fulfilled. A full discussion of the legal details of the agreements in this transaction stage is beyond the scope of this investigation.

4.2.5 Relationship

When a transaction has materialised, it may be a step towards a relationship. Then, it is crucial that *continuity* is maintained in the exchange traffic between the enterprises (Duck, 1995). A relationship is a repeated transaction between two enterprises. More precisely, a border-crossing economic relationship has been defined as (see chapter 1): *an agreement, whether or not in writing, between two autonomous, separately constituted enterprises from two neighbouring countries and of a different nationality, which provides in the regular occurrence of a business activity or transaction, or that the business activity or transaction has been placed under a certain division of joint management.*

The type of relationship
Economic relationships are distinguished according to types, of which the following are defined:
1. Control relationships
2. Production process relationships

3. Service relationships
4. Sales market relationships

Control relationships are such economic relationships between enterprises that one may speak in fact of a new (part of a) firm. A (partially) joint financial administration is kept.
Production process relationships involve economic relationships between companies, whether in writing or not, concerning activities and goods that the one delivers or outsources to the other.
Service relationships are economic relationships, whether in writing or not, concerning services that the responding company outsources to a person outside the company/to another company.
Sales market relationships are regarded as economic relationships, whether or not in writing, between the responding company and a person outside the company/another company concerning the stimulation of the sales of the commodities in question.

In scheme 4.1 a number of possible types is indicated for the four categories. The scheme of examples is not exhaustive. I have listed important types that may occur in practice.

Scheme 4.1 - Types of cross-border economic relationships

1. Sales market relationships
- Agent / representative
- Transport, storage and distribution
- Market research bureau
- Advertising / promotion bureau

2. Service relationships
- Cleaning, security, catering
- Business / financial services

3. Production process relationships

3a Supply of
- Research and development
- Design and work preparation
- Base materials / (semi)manufactured goods / waste products / residues
- Maintenance / repair / quality control

3b Outsourcing of
- Research and development
- Design and work preparation
- Base materials / (semi)manufactured goods / waste products / residues
- Maintenance / repair / quality control

4. Control relationships
- Joint venture
- Participation in other company
- Participation in your company
- Merger with another company

To have or not to have a relationship; the number of cross-border economic relations
The matter at hand is to establish which factors determine that a contact between two enterprises will evolve into a relationship or not, and how many and which type of relationships are developed across the border. This will provide a good impression of the size and the cross-border economic interweaving of regions.

4.2.6 Success

The last stage in the INTERFACE model is the degree to which a border-crossing relationship is successful. Often, the basis of the relationship's success is already laid during earlier stages of the relationship's evolution process. Factors such as the degree of attraction, the degree of trust in the interaction, and the compulsion of the contract are expected to play a role in the degree to which the established relationship will be successful. In other words, the success of border-crossing economic relationships is expected to be heavily *path-dependent.*
This study will not investigate how actors interact on the longer term in the course of an established relationship; it will assess the degree to which the factors determining the establishment of the relationship actually contribute to its success. The entrepreneurs will be asked to indicate how they (1) themselves assess the success of the relationship (see Emerson, 1981; Sarkar, Cavusgil, and Evirgen, 1996), and (2) in how far the *intensity* of the relationship has altered since the moment of transaction.

4.2.7 Overview of the determinants in the INTERFACE model

In the preceding section, I have examined the factors that should be considered important in the various stages of the development process of cross-border economic relationships. In scheme 4.2 below, the determinants in the INTERFACE model distinguished in section 1 are summarised (in appendix 2 an overview of the indicators (and their measurement level) of these determinants is presented).

Scheme 4.2 - Determinants in the development stages of the INTERFACE model

I. Contact

Action space

a. Social & Professional network; number of personal and professional acquaintances
b. Visiting frequency of the personal and professional acquaintances.
c. Direct or indirect contact
d. Relationship preference

Affection space

e. Mental distance
f. 'Feeling at home in the neighbouring country's culture'
g. Spatial identity
h. Evaluation of state border

Cognition space

i. Cognitive distance versus physical distance
j. Cognitive map of the border

II. Attraction

a. Spatial proximity
b. Similarity
c. Complementation in business contact and relationships
d. External or physical attraction: price/quality of the goods

III. Interaction

a. Height of transaction costs
b. Degree of trust

IV. Transaction

Formal versus informal relationship

V. Relationship

a. Yes or no
b. Number of relations

VI. Success

a. Growth in intensity of the economic relationships since the moment of transaction
b. Perception of success

Characteristics of the enterprise

In addition to the above-mentioned factors, the most important characteristics of a (growing) enterprise are incorporated in the analysis as control variables. The following manifest variables will be included in the analyses:

1. The enterprise's age
2. The size of the enterprise (in number of active persons)
3. The number of economic relations in the home country
4. The percentage of cross-border workers
5. The export percentage
6. The sector to which the enterprise belongs

These more traditional explanatory variables have been incorporated to demonstrate their relative importance in comparison with the variables in the INTERFACE model. They are the so-called control variables.

Sub 1. *The enterprise's age* indicates its settlement within the direct environment. It may not only be expected that an older enterprise has succeeded in partly endogenising its direct environment, such as employees, inhabitants in the vicinity, and the local government, but also that it has been able to create direct or indirect ties with markets beyond the local environment, such as in the neighbouring country.

Sub 2. *The enterprise's size.* An enterprise that becomes larger, in terms of the number of active persons, generally has buying, selling and economic relationships spread over a larger area.

Sub 3. *The number of economic relations in the home country* may also indicate in how far the enterprise is integrated into the national environment. The expectation is that a firm with a large national network has a greater chance of developing a 'weak tie' in neighbouring countries. The selection of this variable was partly inspired by the psychic distance theory. Assuming that the internationalisation of businesses is a gradual, step-wise process, an enterprise begins building and experiencing economic relationships and gradually expanding the area of activity on a national level. When a company has many relations nationally, a certain learning effect has already come into being with regard to having economic relationships beyond its own regional area of activity, which makes the step to having relations in the neighbouring country more easy.

Sub 4. Economic involvement also becomes evident from the *number of employees in the enterprise coming from the neighbouring country, the cross-border workers.* Their presence may provide valuable lessons for entering into and developing economic relationships with entrepreneurs in the neighbouring country. The number of cross-border employees in a company is the first indication of its international orientation.

Sub 5. A very different measure for typifying a company's position is its *export percentage*. Companies with high export rates may be expected to enter into economic relationships with companies in the neighbouring country in order to sell their products on the market. One might think in the first place of representatives, but also of economic relationships with enterprises offering financial services or transport companies. In the psychic distance model, the export rate is an important step in the internationalisation process (see chapter 3). The idea here is that export causes a certain degree of habituation, a certain learning effect that reduces the psychic distance vis-à-vis the neighbouring (business) conventions, thus rendering subsequent steps more easy.

Sub 6. The last variable included is the *sector type of the company*. The degree to which this sector influences the extent of international economic interweaving is examined. In the course of the empirical research, three sectors will be considered: construction, wholetrade and industry (see chapter 5). Construction firms are generally more restricted by national regulations than wholesale or industrial companies. This is why the former kind of company may be expected to be less active on the international level. Wholetrade and especially industry are traditionally expected to have more cross-border economic relationships than construction.

4.3 Formulating the research hypotheses

This section presents the research hypotheses as they will be tested in the empirical research, comprising part II of this study.

On the basis of the INTERFACE model three research models, applying to all respondents included in the survey, regardless of regional provenance, will be utilised. These models aim at explaining the last two stages in the INTERFACE model, stage 5 - relationships, and stage 6 - success:

1. Having an economic relationship or not
2. The number of cross-border economic relations
3. The success of one cross-border economic relationship

These three variables in the INTERFACE model may be tested for relevance following various empirical methods. It is possible to conduct a quantitative investigation on a one-off basis and among all respondents concerning the importance of the determinants in the development of cross-border economic relationships. One then asks the respondents to provide an overview of their economic relations. The advantage of this approach is that all respondents are reached; its disadvantage is that one will obtain no notion as to the developmental process of the relationships.

An alternative method is the 'snowball method' (see Knoke and Kuklinski, 1986; Marsden, 1990). In this method, case-based research examines who has entered into economic relationships with whom, and how this was done. Its advantage is its great depth. The method, moreover, most strongly considers the process-based character of the development of an economic relationship. Nevertheless, the benefits provided by depth go at the expense of the insight into the relative importance of the separate factors, due to the restricted scale on which such research can be done. Such an investigation, moreover, is expensive both in time and in money. Another disadvantage is that this kind of research does not provide a proper idea of the quantitative influence of the state border.

In the present study, I have chosen to work according to an approach attempting to combine the best of two worlds. In the first place, this means a large-scale survey of individual enterprises. The general part of this survey investigates the quantitative interest of factors that have not, or barely, been investigated in the literature of the theories on the development of international economic relations: the cognition and attitude of economic actors in cross-border economic relationships with regard to the border and doing business in the neighbouring country. These factors are expected to contribute considerably to present insights. In the questionnaire, the companies with economic relations in the neighbouring country are requested to indicate and typify the separate stages in the process, by reference to their most important economic relation. The respondents select this relation themselves (see chapter 5).

This demarcation of the model to be tested and the choice of this method has several major consequences. The questionnaire to be developed has to be submitted to the greatest possible number of enterprises in the regions concerned, because the number of respondents needed to be as large as possible to guarantee the external validity and interest of the analysis. Since an effort is made to predict which factors influence or do not influence the three points above, multivariate analytical techniques will be employed.

The comprehensive character of this study limits the possibilities for detailed and transaction-specific data collection on firms and their relationships. Disentangling the different transactions in more specific components than what will be done here would require more detailed, case-study like information on the transactions and partners themselves (cf. Gulati, 1995).
Furthermore, a dividing line was thus created between those respondents having cross-border relations and those without them. That is an important limitation of the model's demarcation, which has consequences principally for the analysis of the presence or absence of economic relations in the neighbouring country. For this reason, including the bilateral process variables of the INTERFACE model in the explanation of the development path of the firms who *do not have* cross-border economic relations is impossible. For such an analysis longitudinal case-studies would be the proper research method.

Moreover, because of this limitation of the research method, studying all the development processes of all the possible cross-border economic relations is impossible. The research would grow too large in size. This implies that no bilateral process variables of the INTERFACE model (attraction, interaction, transaction) either can be used for the explanation of the *number* of economic relations.

Furthermore, it is impossible to include all variables that are important during the *contact* stage in the multivariate analysis 'whether or not having an economic relationship in the neighbouring country'. The same holds true for the multivariate analysis of 'the number of economic relations in the neighbouring country'. The variables 'physical distance', 'cognitive distance', 'cognitive map of the border', and 'spatial identity' are excluded from the general multivariate analysis, since they are expected to be largely determined on a regional level. Moreover, the variables of 'cognitive map' and 'spatial identity' especially contain too many items. The multivariate analyses would thereby contain too many independent variables. However, the variables in question will be investigated, in the bivariate correlation analysis, for their connection with the variable 'number of economic relations in the neighbouring country' (see chapter 7).

The companies who do have one or more cross-border economic relationships however, can indicate *how and why* they have these relationships, and how and why these relationships have become *successful*. These latter questions are addressed by means of the INTERFACE model. Regarding the first and second analyses, the explanation of the quantitative influence of borders is the subject of study, *i.e.* the frequency and number of cross-border economic relations. What matters then is to explain the frequency and number of economic relations that cross the 'function space', the state border. This 'function space' is physical, visible, and artificial. With the elaboration now given, it may be said that the spatial economic influence of borders on the development of economic relations across borders, from the analytical point of view, means that a part of a firm's action space, *i.e.* the economic relations across the functional, national borders, has to be explained through the firm's affection space, cognition space and other parts of its action space.

The expected influences of the independent variables in the three models are outlined below.

1. To have or not to have an economic relationship in the neighbouring country

This is the first variable that I will attempt to elucidate by using the INTERFACE model.

The research question is as follows:

Which factors can cause a significant distinction between the group of companies with (an) economic relationship(s) in the neighbouring country and the companies without economic relationships in the neighbouring country?

The distinction between having or not having economic relationships in the neighbouring country, is made on the basis of variables belonging to *affective space* (*i.e.* mental distance and evaluation of the state border) and *control variables* (*i.e.* age, size, cross-border workers, export rate, number of economic relations in the home country, sector type). Inclusion of variables belonging to the first category, affective space, in the analysis provides insight into the relative importance of the affective variables in the determination of the reasons for firms to enter into a cross-border economic relationship. The variables of the second category, the control variables, are indications of the 'maturity' and growth of the firm.

Below, in the hypotheses, the factors important to the determination of the decision whether or not to have relationships in the neighbouring country are discussed by reference to their expected impact.

Contact

Mental distance

The greater the entrepreneur's perception that the co-operation with economic relations in the neighbouring country differs from economic co-operation in the home country, and that the differences have negative consequences for the success of cross-border co-operation, the less likely it will be that the enterprise has an economic relationship in the neighbouring country.

Border evaluation

The more the entrepreneur regards the border as a barrier, the less likely it is that the enterprise will have an economic relation in the neighbouring country; the less relevant the entrepreneur considers the border, the more likely it is that the enterprise has an economic relationship in the neighbouring country.

Control variables

The number of economic relations in the home country

The greater the number of economic relations in the home country, the greater the likelihood that the enterprise will have an economic relation in the neighbouring country.

Percentage of cross-border workers employed

The higher the percentage of cross-border workers employed by an enterprise, the greater the likelihood that the enterprise will have an economic relationship in the neighbouring country.

Export percentage to the neighbouring country

The higher the export percentage to the neighbouring country, the greater the likelihood that the enterprise will have an economic relationship in the neighbouring country.

Age of the enterprise

The 'older' the enterprise, the more likely it is that the enterprise will have an economic relationship in the neighbouring country.

Size of the enterprise

The greater the size of the company, the greater the likelihood that it will have an economic relation in the neighbouring country.

Importance of the sector
If the company is industrial, it probably does have an economic relationship in the neighbouring country; if it is a construction company, it probably does not have such a relationship.

2. The number of cross-border economic relationships

The number of cross-border economic relationships provides a good indication of the degree to which the enterprise is economically involved in the neighbouring country.

The research question is:

Which factors determine the number of a company's cross-border economic relationships with companies in the neighbouring country?

The determinants of the contact stage will be considered most notably as explanatory variables to the total number of relations. These variables determine, in the first instance, the intention to get into contact and the contact pattern. As not all relationships were followed on the longer term as mentioned above, no bilateral process variables have been included as explanatory variables in the explanation of the total number of relations. In the multivariate analysis described here, the control variables have however been incorporated. The hypotheses are given below.

Contact

- ***Action space:***

Type of relationship preference
The more the entrepreneur's prefers an active search for relations and contacts in the neighbouring country, the more economic relationships the enterprise will have in that country.
Network of acquaintances
The more personal and professional acquaintances the entrepreneur has in the neighbouring country, the more economic relationships the enterprise will have in that country.

- ***Affection space:***

Border evaluation
The more the entrepreneur regards the border as a barrier, the smaller the number of economic relationships he will have in that country; and the less relevant the entrepreneur regards the border to be, the more economic relationships the enterprise will have in that country.
Mental distance
The greater the entrepreneur perceives the mental distance between the home and neighbouring countries to be, the smaller the number of economic relationships the enterprise will have in that country.

Feeling at home culturally
The more the entrepreneur feels at home in the living and working environment of the neighbouring country, the more economic relationships his company will have in that country.

Control variables
Age of the enterprise
The older the enterprise, the more economic relationships it will have in the neighbouring country.
The number of active persons
The greater the size of the company, the more economic relationships it will have in the neighbouring countries.
The percentage of cross-border workers employed
The higher the percentage of cross-border workers employed by the enterprise, the more economic relationships it will have in the neighbouring country.
Export percentage in the neighbouring country
The higher the export percentage to the neighbouring country, the more economic relationships the enterprise will have in that country.
The number of economic relationships in the home country
The more economic relations in the home country, the greater the number of economic relationships in the neighbouring country.
Importance of the sector
If the company is industrial, it will have more economic relationships in neighbouring countries; a construction company will have a smaller number of economic relations.

3. The success of a cross-border economic relationship

The third analysis, regarding the success of cross-border economic relations, involves a study of the formation of a particular bilateral cross-border economic relationship, given the fact that an initial contact has been established.

The research question is:

What determines the success of a cross-border economic relationship?

This third dependent variable will be elucidated through a multivariate analysis as well. By means of the process model that will be used in this study, it is possible to demonstrate which factors are of great explanatory value to the eventual degree of success of cross-border economic relationships, once the contact has been established. The aim is to analyse the relation between the different formative stages of the cross-border economic relation and its eventual success.

The expectation is that, besides the more general or structural variables, the determinants in the bilateral process of the cross-border relationship can explain its success. Below, in the hypotheses, the explanatory values whose contents were discussed in section 4.1, are listed. Here I will shortly indicate their expected influence:

Attraction

Similarity
The greater the attraction due to the similarity factor, the greater the relationship's success.

Complementation
The greater the attraction due to the factor complementation, the greater the success of the economic relationship.

Spatial proximity
The greater the attraction due to spatial proximity, the greater the success of the cross-border economic relationship.

Price/quality ratio
The greater the attraction due to price/quality ratio, the greater the success of the cross-border economic relationship.

Interaction

Trust
The greater the trust between the two parties involved, the greater the success of the cross-border economic relationship.

Transaction costs
The lower the transaction costs, the greater the success of the relationship.

Transaction

An informal agreement leads to a more successful relationship than a formal agreement.

Control variable

Importance of the sector
If the company is industrial, the success of the cross-border relationship is greater than when it is a construction company.

4.4 Summary and conclusion

For the sake of clarity, the hypotheses regarding the last two stages of the INTERFACE model are here summarised in a separate chart. In table 4.1 below, the expected influence of the explanatory variables is summarised for the dependent variables relationship yes/no, the number of relationships and the success of a cross-border economic relationship.

Table 4.1 - The hypotheses of the multivariate analyses for the relationship and success stages.

			Expected influence: +/-		
			Cross-border relation yes/no	Number of cross-border relations	Success of cross-border relation
Contact	1. Feeling at home in the culture of the neighbouring country		n/a	+	n/a
	2. Mental distance		-	-	n/a
	3. Border evaluation	Barrier	-	-	n/a
		Irrelevance	+	+	n/a
	4. Spatial identity, per region		n/a	n/a	n/a
	5a1. Social network: number of personal acquaintances		n/a	+	n/a
	5a2. Social network: visiting frequency of personal acquaintances		n/a	n/a	n/a
	5b1. Professional network: number of professional acquaintances		n/a	+	n/a
	5b2. Professional network: visiting frequency of professional acquaintances		n/a	n/a	n/a
	6. Direct (+) or indirect (-) contact		n/a	n/a	n/a
	7. Relationship preference		n/a	+	n/a
	8. Cognitive distance, per region		n/a	n/a	n/a
	9. Cognitive map of the border		n/a	n/a	n/a
Attraction	1. Spatial proximity		n/a	n/a	+
	2. Similarity		n/a	n/a	+
	3. Complementation		n/a	n/a	+
	4. Price/quality of the products		n/a	n/a	+
Interaction	1. Height of the transaction costs		n/a	n/a	-
	2. Degree of trust		n/a	n/a	+
Transaction	Formality		n/a	n/a	-
Control variables	Age of the firm		+	+	n/a
	Size of the firm		+	+	n/a

	Export percentage	+	+	n/a
	Number of cross-border workers employed	+	+	n/a
	Number of economic relationships in home country	+	+	n/a
	Sector: Industry	+	+	+
	Sector: Construction	-	-	-

* n/a stands for 'not applicable', meaning that it is impossible to make a (meaningful) theoretical prediction on the basis of the research design used.

Conclusion

In this chapter, I have proposed a new conceptual model to explain the establishment of cross-border economic relationships. From a survey of economic and economic geographical literature on the internationalisation process of enterprises, it emerged that a hiatus existed regarding the description of the development dynamics in the formation of relationships between two entrepreneurs. The new model was presented under the name of *INTERnational Formation of Autonomous Co-operation between Enterprises* (INTERFACE), and distinguishes six stages: *contact, attraction, interaction, transaction, relationship*, and *success*. On the basis of the various theoretical insights in economics, economic geography, and socio-psychology, a search has been made to establish the determining factors decisive to the outcome of each stage. The model, therefore, provides a description of the process of the formation of cross-border relationships. By means of this model, I will endeavour to explain why companies enter/do not enter into economic relationships, how many cross-border economic relations they have, and how the most important relationship came to be successful.

With this model and the ensuing hypotheses, the objective of part II of this study is to analyse the spatial-economic influence of the state border between the Netherlands and Belgium on the development of cross-border economic relationships between companies in the border regions. In the subsequent part, 'Empiricism', the research conducted in the border regions Zeeland in the Netherlands and Gent/Eeklo in Belgium, based upon the INTERFACE model, will be described.

Part 2

Empirical research

Chapter 5

Characterisation of the research in Zeeland & Gent/Eeklo

5.1 Introduction

After the theoretical reflections on the influence of borders and the development of cross-border economic relationships, and the presentation of the analytical frame of reference in part I of this dissertation, part II proceeds to the empirical verification of the obtained insights. This part of the dissertation consists of three chapters in total. In the present chapter, the construction of the empirical research that was conducted is described. Chapter 6 indicates the spatial scope of the economic actions and relations of the companies included in the survey. Chapter 7 describes the results of the INTERFACE model in stages for the most important cross-border economic relationship of the respondents in the surveyed regions. Furthermore, in chapter 7, the results of the verification of the explanatory model will be presented.

The present chapter is subdivided as follows: I will begin by discussing recent investigations in northwest Europe aimed at studying cross-border economic relationships (section 5.2). In section 5.3, the localisation of the investigation central to the present study will be established. My research methods will be presented in section 5.4, followed by the design of the questionnaire in section 5.5. The general characteristics of the research population will be discussed in section 5.6, followed by the responses to the questionnaire in 5.7 and the general characteristics of the response population in section 5.8.

5.2 Previous investigations in northwest Europe on the influence of the (opening of the) border on cross-border economic activities

The research as executed in 1996 and 1997 in Zeeland and Gent/Eeklo has three concrete precedents, which are comparable in objective. Research has been conducted in three Euregions by three different Dutch research bureaus, which aimed at studying the influence of the (opening of the) border on economic relationships between companies in border regions. These investigations were done during the first half of the Nineties, which has everything to do with the commencement of the internal market on the European continent. Moreover, the researches were inspired by the policy of the European Commission with regard to the Euregions, which became truly operational during this period. In 1990, the Community's Initiative INTERREG was initiated, with the intention of encouraging the integration of the internal border regions within the framework of the completion of the internal market. This programme, involving 1,034 million ECUs in total, has strongly stimulated interest in the problems faced by border regions, thus encouraging expansion of the Euregions' activity programmes. This first INTERREG programme was concluded in 1993, followed by the launching of INTERREG II in 1994. This sequel, running until 1999 and involving 2,4 billion ECUs, aims at the further integration of border regions within the framework of the realisation of the Economic and Monetary Union.

The first scientific investigation discussed here concerns an inventory of the cross-border economic relationships between companies in the regions Midden Brabant (NL) and the Turnhout district in Belgium (Dagevos *et al.*, 1992). This investigation was executed by a team of researchers, including myself, of the 'Economisch Instituut Tilburg' (EIT, Economic Institute of Tilburg). The second investigation, conducted in the Euregion Maas-Rhine (Corvers *et al.*, 1994), was done by the Maastricht Institute for Research and Innovation (MERIT). Another investigation, comparable in design and objective, concerned a study of the cross-border economic relationships between companies on either side of the Dutch-German border, *i.e.* the Euregion Rhine-Waal (Van den Tillaart *et al.*, 1994), and was executed by the 'Instituut voor Toegepaste Sociale Wetenschappen' (Institute for Applied Social Science) in Nijmegen.

5.2.1 Midden-Brabant (NL) and the Turnhout district (B)

The research question approached in 1992 was in how far concrete economic relationships existed at that moment between companies in the region Midden-Brabant and the Turnhout district, and what bottlenecks and problems the companies were facing in establishing relationships across the border.
We conducted this research according to two methods. In the first place, a large-scale and extensive questionnaire was sent out in March 1992 to approximately 3,700 enterprises in Midden-Brabant and the Turnhout district. In Midden-Brabant, 459 enterprises (= 24.1%) responded; in the Turnhout district, 250 enterprises (13.8%) returned the questionnaire. Secondly, a number of (in-depth) interviews was done with entrepreneurs in both areas.

The questionnaire was sent to companies in the sectors manufacturing industry, building and construction, wholesale trade, transport, banking and insurance, and business servicing. Companies in the primary sector, retail trade, and governmental institutions/organisations were excluded. In the first instance, all enterprises in the selected sectors with at least ten active persons were approached. In wholesale trade and transport, all enterprises with between four and ten active persons were also approached.

The most important part of our questionnaire consisted of questions relating to the extent of cross-border economic relationships between enterprises in the border regions concerned. In total, the survey distinguished approximately thirteen different relationships, ranging from relationships relating to transport, storage and/or distribution, outsourcing (or sharing) production, and outsourcing research and development activities to financial and professional servicing.
Besides this emphasis upon the existence of factual economic relationships, the questionnaire also touched upon possible bottlenecks experienced by entrepreneurs in developing economic relationships across the national border, especially with enterprises located in the neighbouring region.

In addition to the written survey, information gathering was also done by means of discussions with twenty entrepreneurs in Midden-Brabant and twenty entrepreneurs in the Turnhout district. During these interviews, emphasis lay most notably on gaining more insight into the problems experienced by entrepreneurs when entering into relationships with other companies across the border, and how they tried to solve these problems, whether or not with the aid of a third party.

The most important conclusions of our research were (cf. Dagevos *et al.*, 1992; Boekema and Van Houtum, 1994; Van Houtum, *et al.,* 1994a, 1996):

●51.4% of the enterprises in Midden-Brabant that responded said they were exporting; for Turnhout, this was 62.8%. The relative importance of the export was measured by means of the share export occupies in the total turnover. The majority of the responding companies in both regions sell more nationally than directly across the border (75.4 and 64.9% of the turnover). From exporting companies, the somewhat larger transport and industrial enterprises export most. Companies in both regions export most to the neighbouring country, that is to say Belgium and the Netherlands, followed by Germany and France. When asked to evaluate their business return and turnover evolution, neither were very positive regarding their own export performance.

●Economic relationships between companies in the regions Midden-Brabant and the Turnhout district focus especially on transport, storage, and distribution. In view of the trade relationships existing between both countries, this is what was expected. In addition, relationships also relate to production and processing of components.

●Companies in Midden-Brabant with economic relationships in the Turnhout region are distinguished from companies without relationships on the following points:
- Companies with relations are larger on the average
- Companies with relations export more often
- Companies with relations have a higher export percentage
- Companies with relations have a lower national sales percentage

•Companies in Turnhout with economic relationships in the Midden-Brabant region are distinguished from companies without relationships on the following points:
- Companies with relations grow slightly faster
- Companies with relations export more often
- Companies with relations have a higher export percentage
- Companies with relations have lower national sales percentage

•A positive attitude via-à-vis co-operation with other enterprises (co-operation leads to market/sales advantages) in most cases leads to a greater number of economic relationships with other companies, whilst the opposite holds true for a negative attitude (co-operation leads to executional problems, a lack of clarity, and uncertainty).

•Companies in Midden-Brabant and the Turnhout district were found not to differ, or to differ very little, where it concerns the problems experienced in expanding their cross-border trade and economic relationships. The availability of information concerning potential (co-operative) partners and subsidy schemes, or rather the lack of it, was said to be one of the major problems experienced. Furthermore, it was found that the (differences in) social and fiscal legislation and the (procedures surrounding) the obtention of licences is problematic. Entrepreneurs from both regions did not consider language, educational differences, the recognition of diploma's, and telecommunications and business accommodation structures as overly problematic.

•The preparedness to enter into new economic relationships with companies in the neighbouring border region was a little greater amongst enterprises in the Turnhout district as compared to those in Midden-Brabant. Around 14% of the former were considering doing so on the short or very short term, against 8% in Midden-Brabant.
Future economic relationships for Midden-Brabant principally relate to the production of components and business servicing. In Turnhout, entrepreneurs mentioned transport, storage, distribution and business services especially.

In short, for all kinds of economic relationships that were distinguished, the national border forms an important barrier for both populations. This applies most for business-supporting economic relationships, least for those forms concerning the primary business process.

5.2.2 The Euregion Maas-Rhine

The research institute MERIT, by order of the 'Commissie Ontwikkeling Bedrijven '(COB, Commission for the Development of Enterprises) of the 'Sociaal-Economische Raad' (SER, Socio-Economic Council), has investigated the question in how far the opening of the European internal borders will lead to better use of the supply of technological knowledge by companies in the border region Maas-Rhine (Corvers *et al.* 1994). The subregions in these so-called

Euregions, that is to say South Limburg (NL), Limburg (B), the province of Liège (B), and the Aachen region (D), are characterised by a re-structuring process of traditional industries, proceeding in various stages. The production environment for technologically oriented companies is advantageous most notably in Aachen, due to this region's enormous supply of knowledge infrastructures.

So as to map the formation of cross-border technical and economic networks in the region Maas-Rhine, all industrial companies with more than ten employees (2,163 in total) were surveyed in the period from September 1992 to April 1993 (response 22.3%). The most important partners for discussion concerning the development or introduction of technically improved or new products or procedures were said to be clients and suppliers. Of the respondents, 90.4% regards the first group and 88.5% regards the second group as useful or necessary. Geographically speaking, these discussion partners were found to be located mostly in the home region or country.
Approximately 14% of the companies in question have an important customer or supplier in one of the foreign parts of the Euregion. Of all respondents having attracted technological knowledge from research institutes and universities, 6% indicates that an institution located in one of the foreign parts of the Euregion was involved. The survey demonstrates that the border is still a reality in the transfer of knowledge and ideas. This applies slightly more for German companies than for Belgian and Dutch companies. The obstacles to cross-border contacts and relations have been analysed in a qualitative study, through in-depth interviews with a total of 30 entrepreneurs. Problems with the road infrastructure, cultural differences, language differences, and differences in legislation were singled out as major obstructions.

These conclusions are all the more remarkable since the Euregion Maas-Rhine, in comparison with other Dutch Euregions, has a dense and solid network of cross-border contacts between authorities and intermediary organisations. The purpose of this co-operation is, amongst others, to help enterprises in their cross-border activities by providing information. The entrepreneurs themselves, however, indicate having no connection with the administrative concept of, and the agencies concerned with, the Euregions. The information considered necessary to organise their entrepreneurial activities is mostly obtained through informal channels. But as stated above, these informal information channels are not internationalised extensively as yet.

5.2.3 The Euregion Rhine-Waal

The third study I wish to discuss in this context comprises a survey of the awareness process of individual entrepreneurs with regard to the changes that set in with the opening of the internal borders. The question was whether they regard these changes as threats or simply as new opportunities. Attention was thereby devoted to the question in how far the information requirements of entrepreneurs are answered by the established supportive infrastructure in the regions. This research project was executed by order of DG XXIII of the European Union by the 'Instituut voor Toegepaste Sociale Wetenschappen' (ITS) and the 'Sozialforschungsstelle' (SFS) Dortmund, in the Euregion Rhine-Waal (Van den Tillaart and Busse, 1994). In the Netherlands, this mainly concerns the regions Arnhem, Nijmegen and northeast Brabant. On the German side, this concerns the Kreise Kleve and Wesel and the city of Duisburg.

A total of 20 interviews has been done with persons providing information, advice or guidance to entrepreneurs that are active across the border, or intend to become so. In addition, a questionnaire was submitted to small companies in building and construction and in business servicing. In total, the questionnaires were sent to 900 Dutch and German enterprises; well over 25% completed and returned it. Approximately 95% of these employed less than 50 active persons. With twenty of these companies, additional discussions were held. The most important queries concerned the percentage of companies with contacts with a foreign partner, the area in which this partner is located, and since when the entrepreneur has cross-border contacts.

It was found that, from the entrepreneurs in construction and business servicing engaged in cross-border activities, the greater number is Dutch. About 25% of the firms indicate having cross-border contacts. The findings further made clear that the cross-border activities, in half the cases, contribute less than 10% to the total turnover, which indicates that cross-border economic co-operation is not, for the time being, an important source of income for most small entrepreneurs in the region.

The ITS also analysed pressure points and hindrances, distinguishing between companies with relations in the neighbouring countries and companies who do not have such relations. The former were asked to clarify the reasons for which they have not become active across the border as yet. Thus, the factors deterring entrepreneurs from entering into transnational activities were examined.
Both for Dutch and German entrepreneurs, four factors were shown to be of relatively great importance: the expected growth opportunities in the national market, a lack of knowledge concerning the foreign market, a lack of time and energy, and the size of the company. The fact that the national market offers sufficient opportunities for growth indirectly indicates that entrepreneurs concentrate on the internal market initially; transnational activities are therefore developed only if the national market provides insufficient opportunity for growth.

The second group of companies distinguished, those with relations, were asked to recount their experience regarding a great number of potential bottlenecks. Frequently mentioned problems have to do with obtaining the required licences, signing contracts, agreeing upon terms of payment, complying with the new VAT regulations, and dealing with diverging product requirements and technical standards. Each of these problems was mentioned by one third to half of the entrepreneurs that were questioned. Less than half finds a way to solve such problems. Dutch entrepreneurs, however, are more successful on this point than German entrepreneurs, which undoubtedly has to do with their being able to speak the language of the neighbouring country better. For German entrepreneurs, this is a greater hindrance then for Dutch entrepreneurs. There is very little difference, however, between Dutch and German entrepreneurs with regard to the most important problem, that is to say, gaining insight into and access to the market on the other side of the border. More than half of the entrepreneurs experience this as a great problem, adding almost always that they see no immediate solution.

Summarised, three independently organised but comparable investigations for areas in the Netherlands, Belgium, and Germany that are confronted to the presence of the border on a daily basis, have established as a fact that the border has functioned as a barrier until now, or as the case may be, still functions as a barrier, in the internationalisation process of small and medium-sized companies. This research shows that the imaginary 'market circle' of the companies in border regions generally has the form of a half rather than an entire circle due to the presence of the border (Van Houtum, 1993, 1994). It is not self-evident for these companies to establish trade and economic relationships, or to search for sources of knowledge, across the border. Economic co-operation between small and medium-sized companies across the border, in comparison with national patterns, is even relatively rare.
The three researches are valuable as far as a first inventory of the border effect in cross-border contacts and relations is concerned (see also Donkers, 1995; Van Geenhuizen *et al.*, 1996;Van 't Veer, 1996). The question remains what the exact causes of the observed pattern are, as these investigations did not have an explanatory character and did not put theoretical hypotheses with regard to the formation and success of cross-border economic relations, to the test (Van Houtum *et al.,* 1996).

5.3 Localisation of the survey in Zeeland-Gent/Eeklo

In this dissertation, I have chosen to examine the province of Zeeland in the Netherlands and the region Gent/Eeklo in Belgium, which are both part of the Euregion Scheldemond. This part of the Dutch-Belgian border has not yet been investigated on *the influence of the border* on cross-border economic interweaving. However, during an economic inventory concerning a part of the Euregion, the Channel zone Gent-Terneuzen, it had been established that there was sufficient reason to justify a better, well-founded insight into the contacts and relationships between companies on either side of the border in the Euregion as a whole (Allaert *et al.,*1991). An important discovery was that the Channel Zone appeared to have formed a cross-border economic 'conglomeration' unique to border regions. In 1990, Kamann *et al.*, in their research on the present and future spatial characteristics of the Channel Zone, drew a similar conclusion: 'A conglomeration that should not be underestimated, stretching to the Belgian Channel zone and the axis Kortrijk-Antwerpen, emerges from the strong mutual economic relationships between the companies in the Channel zone Zeeland Flanders. In fact, the Channel zone Zeeland Flanders and Belgian Flanders form one economic region' (Kamann *et al.,* 1990, p. II, my translation). The connections, deliveries, outsourcing, and information links were found to be present to a great extent.

These findings of Allaert *et al.* (1991) and Kamann et al. (1990) on the network *structure* in this part of the Dutch-Belgian border are appealing. They have opened up the way for theoretical propositions and empirical research so as to delve deeper into *the process of the formation and reasons for the success* of cross-border economic relationships. In this dissertation the attention is directed towards such an explanation of the process and the success. Besides, in this study the attention is not so much focused upon the analysis of the network structure, but on the measurement of the magnitude of the *influence of the border* in the development process of cross-border economic relations. The results obtained will be compared to the theoretically expected influence of the state border. The INTERFACE model, as described in chapter 4, will serve as the theoretical handle for this goal.
The investigations of Allaert *et al.* (1991) and Kamann *et al.* (1990) focused upon the mutual relationships between the offices/subsidiaries of the most important firms in a specific area of the Euregion as a whole. The firms surveyed were all relatively large, measured according to the number of working persons. Kamann *et al.*, for instance, focused upon a total of seventeen companies.
The present dissertation, in principle, examines the cross-border interweaving pattern of all companies in the region. Besides, in this investigation, the area covering Zeeland and the district Gent/Eeklo will be examined as a whole. Not only the companies within the Channel zone, but also companies in the remainder of Zeeland Flanders, Zeeland, and the remainder of Gent/Eeklo will be included in the analysis.

5.4 Research approach

The investigated area embraces Gent/Eeklo, Zeeland Flanders, and Central and North Zeeland. These research areas are typified below.

Gent/Eeklo
The Gent/Eeklo district is the capital and economic pool of the province of East Flanders in Belgium. Two other economic centres in the area are the axis Eeklo-Maldegem and the axis Deinze-Zulte in the west. The city of Gent lies on a junction of motorways, the E17 and E40. It also touches a junction of waterways, the harbour on the Westerschelde via the channel Gent-Terneuzen and the Leie and Schelde. The international harbour of Gent presents itself as a distribution harbour, focusing on the diversification of the circulation of goods.

The district of Gent/Eeklo covers an area of 1,277 km^2 and has 571,216 inhabitants (NIS 1995/1996). Its most important municipalities are Gent, Zelzate, Eeklo, and Deinze.

In total, 188,251 persons are working in the region. Besides agriculture and horticulture (including the cultivation of ornamental plants) and construction, the sectors servicing and industrial manufacture are strongly represented in the district. Approximately 67% of the working population are active in servicing, namely 125,529 individuals in 10,393 institutions. Educational institutions employ the greatest number of people. In the city of Gent alone, 44,104 individuals work in educational organisations. The most important branches of industry are the automotive industry and metallurgy; other important branches in the district include steel, textile, foodstuffs, chemistry, the petroleum industry, wood and furniture, the printing business, and paper. The harbour district employs a total of 24,428 individuals.

The district of Gent/Eeklo accommodates 12,317 companies in all, of which 68.8% has less than five employees. Of all companies, 96.2% are small and medium-sized enterprises with less than 50 employees. This division tallies with the general picture of Flanders and Belgium as a whole. The 47 large enterprises (employing more than 500 persons) are concentrated mainly in the industrial area of the harbour and to the south of the city of Gent.

Zeeland[1]

On the other side of the state border with Gent/Eeklo lies the Dutch province of Zeeland, at the southwest extremity of the Netherlands. The province's surface is transected by the Ooster- and Westerschelde. Approximately one third of Zeeland's surface consists of water. The present number of inhabitants in Zeeland is approximately 365,500. Of these, approximately 257,000 live to the north of the Westerschelde (Central and North Zeeland). To the south of the Westerschelde lies Zeeland Flanders (approximately 107,500 inhabitants). The mean population density (inhabitants/km^2) in Central and North Zeeland is 217, in Zeeland Flanders it is 143.

Zeeland Flanders is the only Zeeland area not yet opened up by Dutch infrastructure. Two provincial ferry lines serve the Westerschelde: Vlissingen-Breskens and Kruiningen Perkpolder. Plans for a permanent cross-channel connection replacing the ferries have now been approved by the national government. The completion of the Westerschelde tunnel is scheduled for November 2002. It will join the N61 in the south, the east-west connection in Zeeland Flanders, and the N254, direction Middelburg and Goes, in the north (see also Lambooy and Verburg, 1992). Several roads, however, connect Zeeland Flanders to its neighbour Belgium. Zeeland Flanders is 'connected' to Belgium, but institutionally it belongs to the Netherlands. Nationally, the area is peripheral, but internationally, its position is more favourable.

The four largest Zeeland cities, in order of size, are Vlissingen, Middelburg, Goes (Central and North Zeeland), and Terneuzen (Zeeland Flanders).

The most important east-west connection in Zeeland, at present, is the national trunk road A58, which runs from Bergen-op-Zoom to Vlissingen. From north to south, there are the 'Zeeland route' (via the Zeeland bridge built by the province) and the 'Dammen route' (via the storm surge

---

1 The general data for Zeeland are derived from http://www.zeelandnet.nl/provincie

barrier Oosterschelde). There is one train connection for travellers (Roosendaal-Vlissingen) with a branch for the transportation of goods towards the industrial area of Vlissingen-Oost and a train connection for transportation of goods exclusively, running from Terneuzen to Sas van Gent and on to Gent in Belgium.

The Westerschelde is an important international waterway, providing access to the harbours of Antwerp, Vlissingen, Terneuzen, and Gent (see also Drewe, 1993). Four channels complete the 'watery' infrastructure in the region: the channel through South Beveland, the channel through Walcheren, the channel running from Gent to Terneuzen, and the Schelde-Rhine Channel (which provides the direct connection between Antwerp and Rotterdam for inland navigation).

The four principal sectors in Zeeland's economy are industry, agriculture, fishery, and tourism. The large industrial enterprises have established themselves mainly in the harbour regions in Vlissingen and Terneuzen. In total, approximately 14,000 workers are directly employed here. The principal activities are chemistry/petrochemistry, heavy industry, shipbuilding, offshore, storage and transfer, and energy production.
Approximately 8,500 people (including family members) are directly active in agriculture. Crops derive mainly from arable farming, but other types are under development.
Fishery embraces two main groups: fish (sole, flounder, codfish, etc.) and shellfish (mussels, oysters, cockles, shrimp and lobsters). Fishery directly employs approximately 1,500 people.
Recreation and tourism-related organisations in Zeeland directly provide work for approximately 8,000 people. The North Sea beaches and various waterways, such as the Veerse Meer, the Oosterschelde and Grevelingen, attract the greatest number of tourists.

The composition of the business community in Zeeland Flanders does not differ much from that in Central and North Zeeland. In both regions, the sectors building and construction, wholesale, and industry account for approximately 22% of all business activity. The number of enterprises, however, diverges considerably. In Zeeland Flanders, there are 6,308 companies; in Central and North Zeeland, the number is 2.25 times as large, adding up to 14,751 (Chambers of Commerce Zeeland, 1996/1997). In table 5.1, the most important data concerning the research area are summarised.

Table 5.1 - Facts and figures concerning the research area (1996/1997)

	Zeeland Flanders	Central and North Zeeland	Gent/Eeklo
Population	107.500	257.000	380.000
Population density (persons/km^2)	143	217	520
Number of companies	6.308	14.751	12.317
Total employment	41.000	84.000	188.251
Export share in turnover	51%	21%	46.24%

N.B. The figures represent round, indicative figures
Source: Van Houtum, 1997a,b, p. 9

So as to be able to evaluate the relative volume and intensity of cross-border economic traffic, neighbouring regions (*i.e.* reference areas) in the home and foreign countries are included in the research area. In Belgium, the regions Antwerpen/St. Niklaas and Brugge have been included. In the Netherlands, the research area embraces the Corop area Rotterdam/Rijnmond (see figure 5.1). Table 5.2 below outlines the general data relating to the reference areas.

Table 5.2 - Facts and figures reference areas (1996)

	Rotterdam/ Rijnmond	District Antwerp	District St. Niklaas	District Brugge
Population	1,13 milj.	933.000	230.000	268.000
Population density (persons/km^2)	1.140	933	464	405
Number of enterprises	63.000	24.300	5.267	7.700
Total employment	392.000	356.300	70.283	86.400
Export share in turnover	(1)	54.8%	41.60%	30.37 %

(1) No data available
N.B. These are round, indicative figures. Employment figures for Flanders include independent workers.
Source: Van Houtum, 1997a,b, p.10

Figure 5.1 - Map of the research area

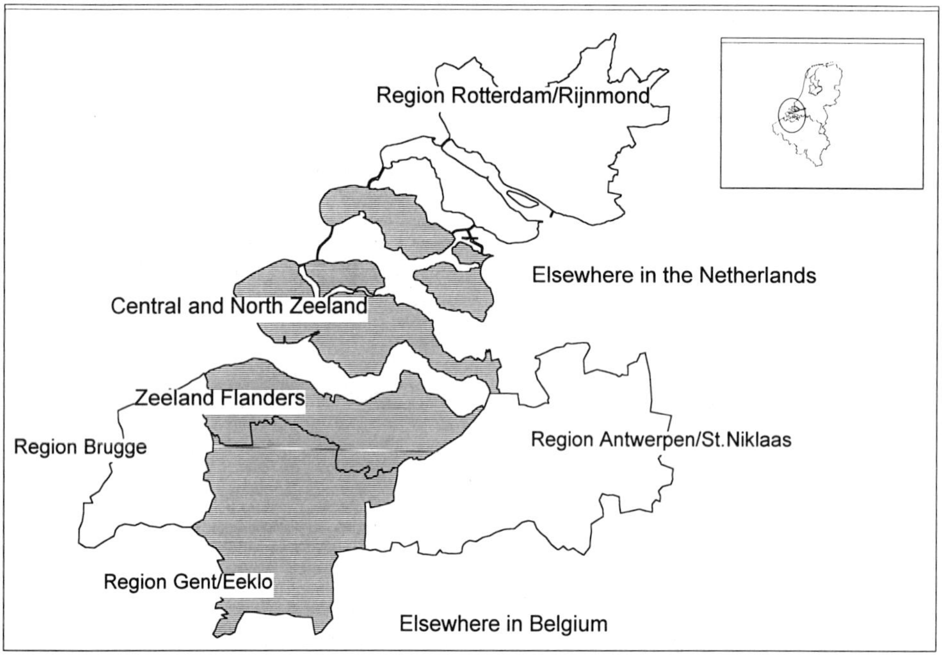

Approach

The approach to the research area's investigation is micro-economic, *i.e.* focuses on the level of individual companies. The respondent is taken to be the representative of the entire enterprise. To ensure, in as far as possible, a correct image of the individual enterprise, the enterprises were requested to treat the questionnaire at management level.

A last general remark concerns the force of the connections tested. There are boundaries within which the observed connections are assumed not to be coincidental. This is indicated with the term 'significance'. There are different levels of significance, noted as exact values or with asterisks: *** means that the chance that the result is founded upon coincidence is less than 1% - the connection is very strong. ** stands for a level of significance smaller than 5%, * for a level of significance smaller than 10%. At this lower level, the connection is only relatively indicative. The chance of that it is coincidental is ten times greater than at the 1% level. No difference is made between <1% and <5%, except where this is mentioned explicitly. Both these levels are 'significant'. Levels above 5% are not significant. If the level of significance is higher, but the result is important nonetheless, the level will be mentioned.

5.5 The questionnaire

The questionnaire was entitled: 'Inventory of cross-border relationships: Relationships between enterprises in the regions Central and North Zeeland (Netherlands), Zeeland Flanders (Netherlands), and Gent/Eeklo (Belgium).'

Before the questionnaire was sent out, a considerable number of scientists and business persons evaluated its validity and consistency. The final questionnaire comprised 51 questions, yielding a total of 338 variables (see appendix 1). A letter of recommendation from the Chamber of Commerce was joined to the questionnaire, explaining the significance of the investigation for the entrepreneurs and assuring them that the data would be treated confidentially. The companies were requested, furthermore, to treat the questionnaire at management level.

Introductory questions inventoried, per region, the factual spatial division of all types of economic relationships: the active space (see chapter 2). This inventory was intended to provide a clear image of the state border's influence upon, or, to put it differently, to establish the extent of the discontinuity at the border in the frequency and number of economic relationships maintained by the companies in the research area.

A detailed analysis of the most intensive kind of co-operation between companies in neighbouring countries followed. Since it proved impossible to follow so many companies longitudinally, the following method has been used. Respondents were asked to think of their most important relation in the neighbouring country and to answer the questions relating to this subject with that relation in mind. This retrospect enabled me to follow *the process* of the formation of relationships over time. Questions were asked relating to the identity of the respondents, their evaluation of the state border, and their perception of the differences experienced in entering into relationships in their home country and the neighbouring country. To obtain a greater uniformity of responses and ease of data processing, many questions required the respondent to score on 7-points Likert-type scales, most of them ranging from 'very .. to very...' (Babbie, 1990). For the statistical analyses, the statistical programme SPSS 6.1 for windows 3.11 was used.

Overall, the questionnaire contained the following clusters of questions (see appendix 1):

- General characteristics of the company
- Economic relations in the Netherlands and Belgium
- The most important relation in the neighbouring country
- The differences experienced between relationships in the Netherlands and in Belgium
- State border and identity
- Concluding questions

Figure 5.2 summarises the design of the research: its objective is to study the effect of the state border upon the development of cross-border economic relationships. A, B, C, and D are enterprises active in construction, wholesale, or industry in the regions.

Figure 5.2 - Design of the research

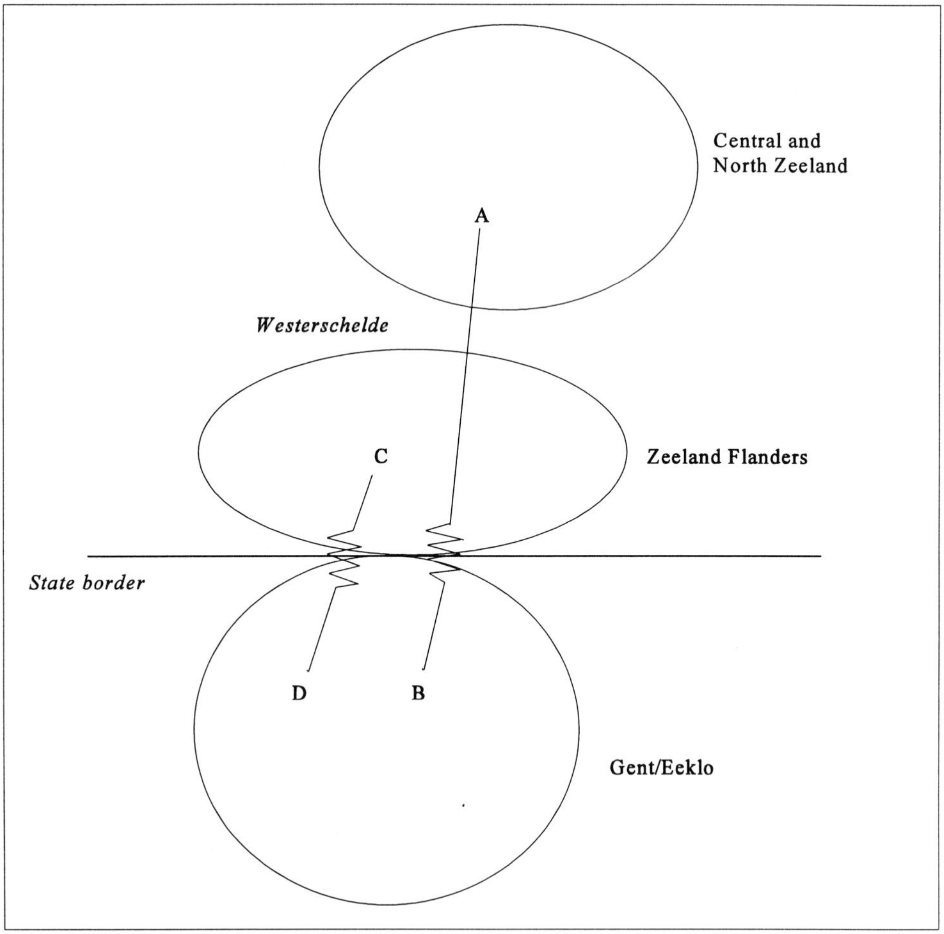

Research organisation

The investigation was executed by order of the Chambers of Commerce of Gent/Eeklo, Central and North Zeeland, and Zeeland Flanders. The investigation was organised on a collaborative basis. The Chambers of Commerce executed the logistic tasks in the research, *i.e.* announcements by media, sending out the questionnaire, mailing the follow-up and giving a reminder by telephone, an important part of the data entry related to responses, and printing the final report. I myself was responsible for the activities relating to the analysis, *i.e.* writing the questionnaire, part of the data entry, further processing, dissecting and interpreting the data, reporting, and formulating recommendations with regard to policy-making (see Van Houtum, 1997a,b).

5.6 Research population

The approach of the investigation is the analysis of the transfer of commodities and/or control between different companies from neighbouring countries. The research was restricted to three important sectors - industry, construction and wholesale - which are highly suitable for the analysis of such streams. Moreover, construction, wholesale and industry comprise an important part of the business composition in the entire research area.

For all three regions, I have tried to select a sample survey providing the best reflection of the composition of enterprise in the area. In Zeeland Flanders, all companies in the sectors construction, wholesale and industry of more than two active persons were approached. A draw from companies with more than five active persons was preferred as these may be expected to have positioned themselves in the market in such a manner as to have developed a number of economic relationships. Moreover, much 'noise' generally occurs in companies of one to five persons, especially those employing one person or less. Many of the very small companies are not even active and others have only been active for a short while. However, such a draw would have meant a strong restriction and distortion of the total number of companies in the region Zeeland Flanders, there being a relatively great number of small companies. A total number of 623 companies were approached, each employing more than two persons.

In Central and North Zeeland, an integral draw was made from amongst similar companies, this time of more than five active persons, however. In total, 817 companies were approached in this region.

The Belgian Chambers of Commerce, in comparison with Dutch ones, have a rather special function. They are non-compulsory membership associations, meaning that not all relevant companies in the district Gent/Eeklo could be selected, only members and prospective members being listed. An analysis of non-members in Gent/Eeklo was found to be impossible due to the lack of accessible data bases. As the data base of the Chamber of Commerce for the district Gent/Eeklo could not select firms according to sector or number of active persons, it became necessary to approach all members and prospective members, a total of 1,428 companies.

It appeared however, that the files containing the research populations were not completely pure. The file for Gent/Eeklo was greatly contaminated. The eventual automation of this file by the Chamber of Commerce, several months after the draw, made clear how many relevant companies were present amongst the members: the relatively low total of 344.

For a number of companies in Zeeland it was unclear whether they still existed; their names and telephone numbers were found to be incorrect. These companies were a source of 'noise' in the files and were therefore excluded from further processing. The corrected research population for Zeeland Flanders thus embraced 558 companies, for Central and North Zeeland, 795 companies.

Sector distribution of the research population

In table 5.3 the distribution of the research population, *i.e.* all companies approached, over the sectors industry, construction and wholesale is indicated.

In Zeeland Flanders and Central and North Zeeland, the sector distribution of companies is fairly uniform. In the district of Gent/Eeklo, the construction sector rises below, and wholesale declines above the level of the two Dutch regions.

Table 5.3 - Sector distribution of the research population

	Zeeland Flanders (n=588)	Central and North Zeeland (n=795)	Gent/Eeklo (n=344)
Construction	35.4%	36.4%	12.8%
Wholesale	40.1%	34.7%	51.7%
Industry	24.3%	28.9%	35.5%

5.7 Response

So as to encourage potential response, a number of public announcements were made in addition to the letter of recommendation that was joined to the questionnaire. These included an article in the *Kamerkrant* (Chamber Journal) in Zeeland Flanders and news reports in De Stem, Provinciale Zeeuwse Courant, Omroep Zeeland, and Omroep Oost Vlaanderen. Moreover, the opportunity to announce the questionnaire and research was used at each conference or seminar of the Chambers of Commerce in the three regions.

The usual reminder was unnecessary for Zeeland Flanders and Central and North Zeeland, as the response had attained the desired level at the closing date. Response problems, however, were experienced for Gent/Eeklo, where only 53 questionnaires were returned before the closing date. The number finally increased to 94 after a telephone reminder.

Response population

The first response from the research population amounted to 167 for Zeeland Flanders, 231 for Central and North Zeeland, and 94 for the Gent/Eeklo district. Some of the forms were filled so badly that they could not be included in the analysis. The final research population comprises 470 companies, as represented in table 5.4.

Table 5.4 - Final response quotas per region

	Response % (Usable response/'clean' research population)
Zeeland Flanders	161/588= 27.4%
Central and North Zeeland	219/795= 27.5%
Gent/Eeklo	90/344= 26.2%
Average	470/1727= 27.2%

The final response quotas for the regions are virtually equal. These response percentages are sufficiently accurate to provide a dependable and representative image of the real number of companies in the said sectors in the three regions involved.

Sector distribution of the response population

Table 5.5 indicates how the response populations are distributed over the three sectors. The Zeeland Flanders and Central and North Zeeland business composition, in the response population, is fairly evenly distributed over the sectors and tallies reasonably well with the research population. In the Gent/Eeklo district, industry is over-represented and wholesale under-represented in comparison with the research population. By means of a non-response analysis it has been checked whether a weight coefficient was necessary to correct this bias. The independent variables have been tested for differences between the sectors wholesale and industry. No significant differences were found, implying that no correction was necessary on this point.

Table 5.5 - Sector distribution of the response population

	Zeeland Flanders (n=161)	Central and North Zeeland (n=219)	Gent/Eeklo (n=90)
Construction	32.9%	42.9%	14.4%
Wholesale	37.9%	28.3%	30.0%
Industry	29.2%	28.8%	55.6%

5.8 Characteristics of the response population

Size of the enterprises

To complement the first inventory of the companies in the response population, the size of the enterprises and the percentage of cross-border workers employed were analysed. An often used and reliable indication of the size of companies in a population is the number of persons employed. A working person has been described in the questionnaire as a person working at least fifteen paid hours per week for the company involved. Two definitions can be used to divide the companies into two classes. The first is that used by the Chambers of Commerce. The Chambers categorise companies on the basis of various classes of the number of working persons. When this definition is applied, it can be found that 67% of the companies in the three regions employ less than twenty persons. 85.7% falls in the category of companies with less than fifty active persons; 92.6% employ less than 100 persons.

To prevent divergences in definitions regarding enterprises in the European Community, the European Commission has framed an unambiguous guideline on February 17th, 1996. The European Commission uses the following categorisation according to the standards for the number of active persons: Enterprises employing more than 250 active persons are defined as large. To belong to the category of small and medium-sized enterprises (SMEs), a company may not employ more than 250 persons. A company is defined as medium-sized if it employs between 50 and 250 persons. The companies employing more than 10 but less than 50 persons are considered small; those with less than 10 employees are considered very small. Figure 5.3 reflects this categorisation for the companies in this study.

Figure 5.3 - The number of persons employed, categorisation according to the EC

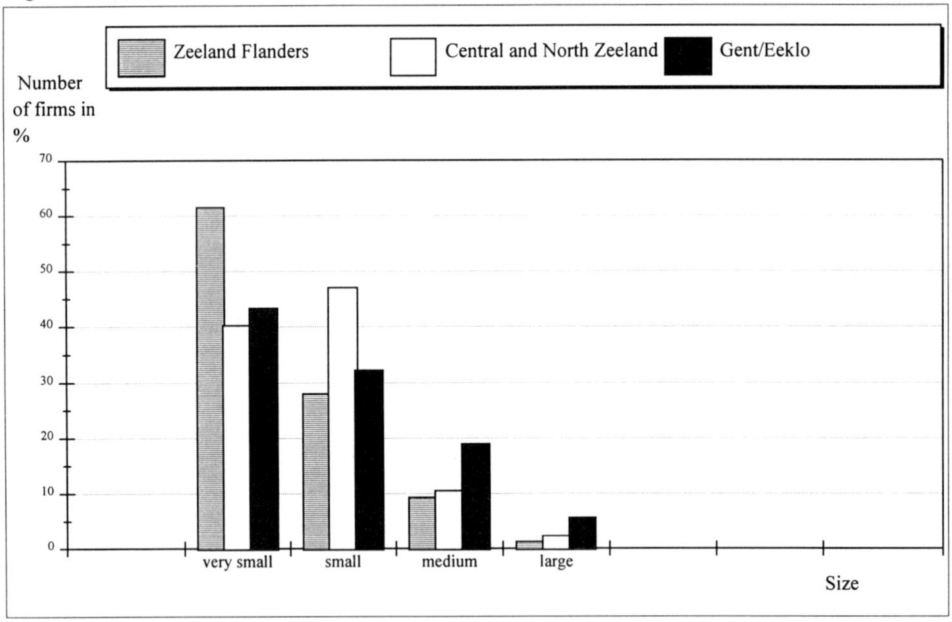

According to the definition of the European Commission, 97.4% of the business community in the response population are very small to medium-sized companies.

Figure 5.4 demonstrates that the average company in the population is small to very small, which tallies with the national picture of both Belgium and the Netherlands. In the regions Central and North Zeeland and Gent/Eeklo, the average company size is significantly larger than in Zeeland Flanders. In Zeeland Flanders, all relevant companies with more than two persons have been approached; in Central and North Zeeland all relevant companies with more than five persons were asked to complete the questionnaire, but in Gent/Eeklo, all members of the Chamber of Commerce in the district were approached - these are generally the somewhat larger companies in the region. This explains why, on the average, the largest companies of the total response population appear here. In the analyses of contacts and economic relationships in the neighbouring country, I have examined in how far the size of the company influences the result.

Number of cross-border workers employed by the companies

One does expect a certain number of cross-border workers to be employed in companies located in border regions. The number of cross-border workers, in terms of the percentage of the total number of people employed, provides a first indication to the degree of economic interweaving between regions. Table 5.6 represents the number of cross-border workers in % of the total response population. In Zeeland Flanders, this covers more than 9% of the total number of working persons in the response population. In Central and North Zeeland, this figure is lower than 1%, *i.e.* 0.43%. The number of people living in Belgium and working in the Netherlands, over the past few years, has fluctuated around 14,000 (CBS, 1997). This represents approximately 0.40% of the working population in Belgium. The percentage of cross-border workers employed by the investigated companies in Zeeland Flanders is thus significantly higher. The percentage of cross-border workers living in the Netherlands and working in Gent/Eeklo is around 0.72%, the total number of people living in the Netherlands and working in Belgium fluctuating around 4,500 over the past few years. This represents approximately 0.07% of the working population in the Netherlands (CBS, 1997). For all three regions, therefore, it may be affirmed that the average number of cross-border employees per company is greater than the national average.

In short, the greatest average number of cross-border workers, *i.e.* Belgians, is employed in Zeeland Flanders. The difference between Zeeland Flanders on the one hand, and Central and North Zeeland and Gent/Eeklo on the other, is significant. As expected, the region Central and North Zeeland employs a smaller number of cross-border workers due to the fact that the border with Belgium is farther away. The district Gent/Eeklo does a little better with regard to the number of cross-border workers.

Table 5.6 - Cross-border workers in the regions, in % of the response population

	Total number of employed persons in the regions (1)	Absolute number of cross-border workers (2)	Proportion (in %) of cross-border workers in the regions (3)
Zeeland Flanders (n=161)	4252	388	9.13%
Central and North Zeeland (n=219)	7228	31	0.43%
Gent/Eeklo (n=90)	5379	39	0.72%

(1) (The total number of responding companies in the region) * (the number of persons employed in these companies)

(2) (The percentage of cross-border employees in the responding companies) * (the number of employed persons in these companies)

(3) (Absolute number of cross-border workers) / (Total number of working persons in the region) *100

5.9 Conclusion

In this chapter, the research approach has been explained. The survey aims at inventorying and analysing the number and characteristics of cross-border economic relationships between companies in the regions Gent/Eeklo, Zeeland Flanders, and Central and North Zeeland.

The obtained response to the questionnaire is representative of the research population. 470 companies in total, all from the sectors construction, wholesale and industry, were analysed, of which 161 are established in the region Zeeland Flanders, 219 in Central and North Zeeland, and 90 in the district Gent/Eeklo.

Furthermore, this chapter touched upon the number of working persons in the companies and the percentage of cross-border workers in the research population. The following results were most noteworthy. The companies in the region Gent/Eeklo are, on the average and in keeping with the values for the research population, larger. The region Zeeland Flanders, in keeping with the research population, has a relatively large number of small companies. Moreover, this region is most receptive to workers from the neighbouring country; companies in Zeeland Flanders, on the average, employ the greatest number of people of Belgian nationality. This average is far higher than the Belgian average. The region Central and North Zeeland was found to have the lowest average number of cross-border employees. In the next chapter, the influence of the border on the action space of the firms in the response population, i.e. their sales and economic relations across the border, is analysed.

Chapter 6

Sales and economic relationships of the companies in Zeeland & Gent/Eeklo

6.1 Introduction

This chapter factually ascertains the degree to which the border acts as a dividing or contact line between companies in border regions. The border's impact will be analysed by means of the action space - the action radius of the *economic relations* of the respondents in the research areas Zeeland & Gent/Eeklo. To this end, I will examine the number of companies with and without economic relations, and the total number of economic relationships actually involved. Thus, this chapter provides insight into the factual economic interweaving across the border.

So as to render the picture of economic interweaving complete, the present chapter will not be limited to a presentation of the frequency and distribution of economic relationships alone. The *sales pattern* of the respondents is also examined. 'Sales' should here be understood as referring to the one-off sale of commodities and/or products to a person or company. An economic relationship was earlier defined as 'an agreement between two different companies, whether in writing or not, that a commercial activity or transaction will regularly occur, or that a commercial activity or transaction has been placed under joint administration or management'.

Chapter 6 consists of two parts. The first three sections discuss the sales distribution; the final sections are devoted to the distribution of economic relations. Section 6.2 treats the average number of customers for the companies in the three regions. The second section compares how sales are distributed nationally and internationally. Section 6.3 then examines whether it is possible to discern connections between the various sales areas. Is an orientation towards one region or country associated with an orientation towards other regions or countries? This section also presents the sales distribution on maps. In section 6.4, conclusions are drawn concerning the sales distribution for the firms.

The remainder of this chapter analyses the distribution of the economic relations of the surveyed companies over the Netherlands and Belgium. In section 6.5 the frequency and the spatial distribution of economic relationships over the two countries as a whole will be presented. In section 6.6, this pattern is further refined by distinguishing several subregions in the Netherlands and Belgium. The last section of this chapter, 6.7, summarises the total economic interweaving between the companies in the three research regions Zeeland Flanders, Central and North Zeeland, and Gent/Eeklo.

6.2 Whether or not to export to the neighbouring country

In the questionnaire, the enterprises were asked to specify, in terms of percentages, the division of their sales between the home country and foreign countries. This division can provide insight into their spatial market range. In figure 6.1 below, the categorisation of the companies according to national sales percentages are represented.

Figure 6.1 - National sales in categories, per region

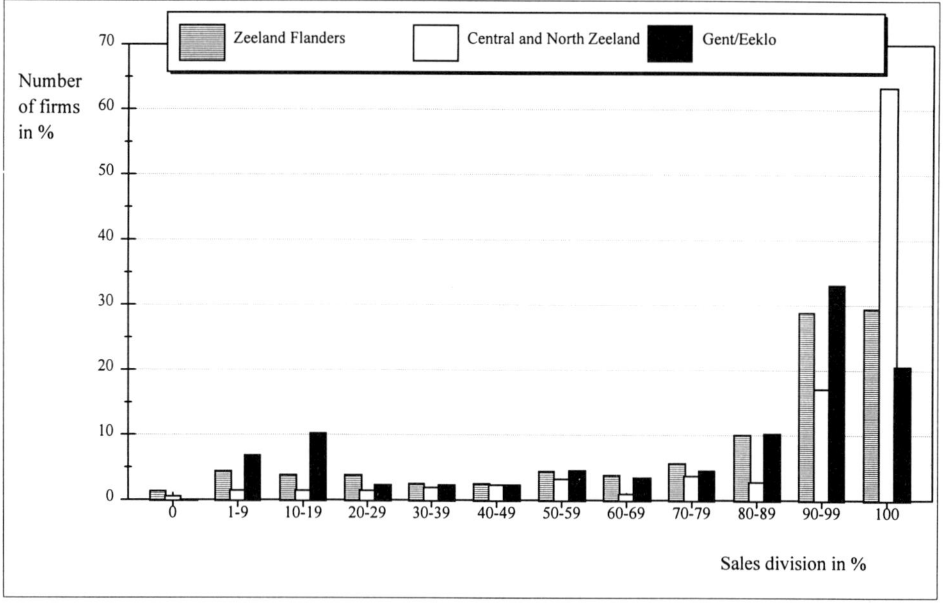

Among the three regions, the companies in Central and North Zeeland are most obviously oriented towards the home country. Well over 60% of all companies in Central and North Zeeland sell their products on a national scale exclusively. In Zeeland Flanders, this proportion is significantly lower (less than 30%); in Gent/Eeklo, only 20% of the companies sell their products on a national scale exclusively.

With regard to the export frequency to the neighbouring country, a reasonable number of companies, on average, were found to export to the neighbouring country. An average of three quarters of the companies in Gent/Eeklo export to the Netherlands, just a little more than the companies exporting from Zeeland Flanders to Belgium (table 6.1). The difference with companies in Central and North Zeeland is far greater. The percentage of companies in this region that exports to the neighbouring country lags far behind Zeeland Flanders and Gent/Eeklo.

Table 6.1 - Export to the neighbouring country?

	Zeeland Flanders	Central and North Zeeland	Gent/Eeklo	Total
No export to the neighbouring country	n=52 k%=32.5	n=144 k%=66.7	n=24 k%=27.0	n=220 k%=47.3
Export to the neighbouring country	n=108 k%=67.5	n=72 k%=33.3	n=65 k%=73.0	n=245 k%=52.7
Total	n=160	n=216	n=89	n=465

n=absolute number, k%=column percentage (from top to bottom)

Furthermore, it was found that construction firms lag far behind wholesale and industry where it concerns export to the neighbouring country. The reason for this might be that construction is often more restricted by national regulations than the other two sectors. One might think of licences to establish a business and social legislation.

The export frequency, however, tells us nothing about the export volume. Figure 6.2 reflects the share of the export volume of the companies to the neighbouring country. The various categories of export percentages are listed horizontally. The percentage of companies per region is represented vertically.

Figure 6.2 - Export volume to the neighbouring country, in categories and per region

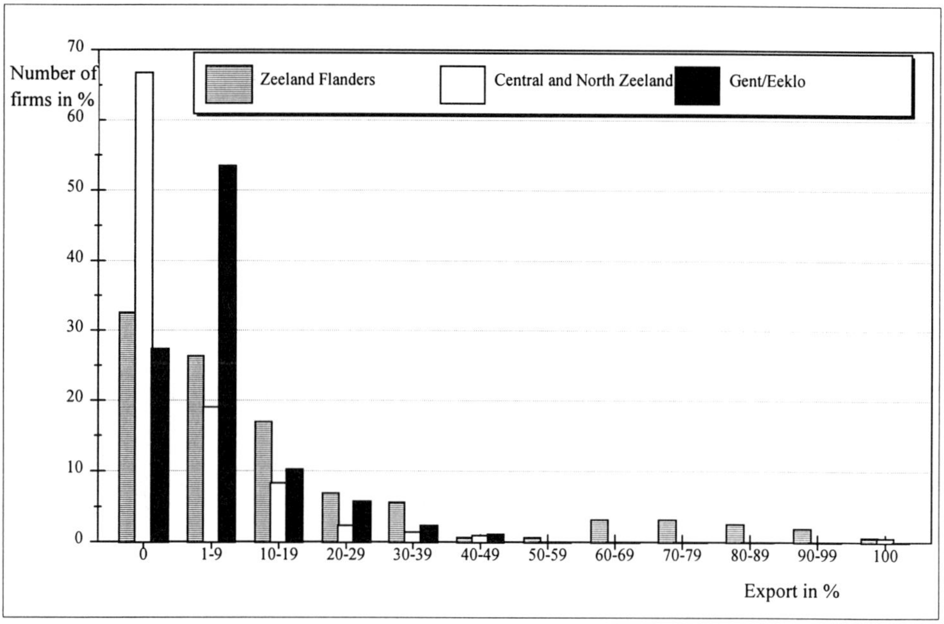

The figure clearly shows that the division is unequal. Few of the companies export more than 50% of their turnover to the neighbouring country. Most of them export less than 10%. Furthermore it can be seen that the companies in Gent/Eeklo export relatively often to the Netherlands, but that the export volume covers no more than a relatively small percentage of their total turnover. While companies in Zeeland Flanders export less often than the companies in Gent/Eeklo, the volume covers a higher percentage of their total turnover.

Export frequency to the rest of Europe and the world

An analysis of the export frequency to other countries shows that companies in the district Gent/Eeklo tend to be more international in outlook than the companies in Zeeland Flanders and Central and North Zeeland (table 6.2).

Table 6.2 - Export frequency to Europe and the world

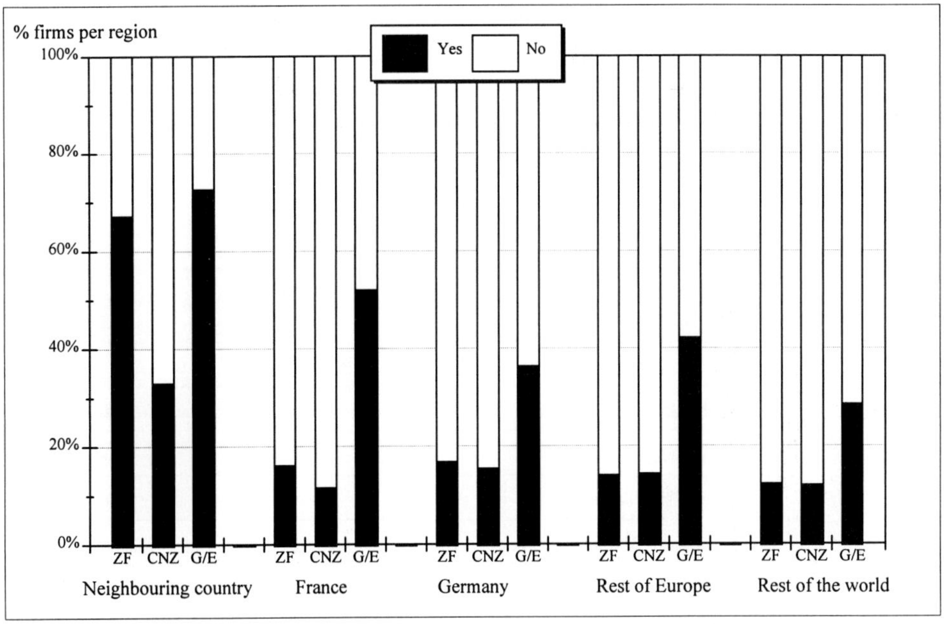

(ZF=Zeeland Flanders, CNZ=Central and North Zeeland, G/E=Gent/Eeklo)

The firms in Gent/Eeklo do not only export more, but also more often to France and Germany, to the rest of Europe, and to the rest of the world. The firms in the two Dutch regions, compared among themselves, have similar export frequencies and volumes to these countries. The fact that companies in Gent/Eeklo are more often internationally oriented is an important observation, as the physical distance to the neighbouring country (the Netherlands/Belgium), or to France, Germany, and the rest of Europe and the world barely differs for companies in the three regions. The companies in Gent/Eeklo in this response population are, on average, slightly larger than their counterparts in the Dutch border regions, most notably in comparison with Zeeland Flanders, but that does not quite explain the significant difference. The attraction and stimuli provided by the international harbour of Gent seem another explanation for the observed difference. A last possibility is that the Belgian companies in question are simply more willing/able to find the way to foreign outlets than the Dutch companies in the other two regions.

6.3 Spatial order and coherence in the firms' sales

The question arises whether a certain spatial order may be discerned in the sales volume of the companies in the three separate regions. The export sales average of the respondents in the three regions has been compared to answer this question. The comparison is reproduced in table 6.3.

Table 6.3 - Spatial division of average sales in %, per research region

		Zeeland Flanders	Central and North Zeeland	Gent/Eeklo
Home country	Zeeland Flanders	63.47	6.30	
	Central and North Zeeland	5.01	61.15	
	Rotterdam/Rijnmond	2.50	7.30	
	North Brabant	3.06	6.89	
	Elsewhere in the Netherlands	4.97	9.41	
	Total the Netherlands	76.57	89.06	
	Gent/Eeklo			31.86
	Region Brugge			10.04
	Antwerp/St. Niklaas			11.97
	Elsewhere in Belgium			20.26
	Total Belgium			72.03
Neighbouring country (Belgium/the Netherlands)		14.23	3.85	5.72
France		2.64	1.17	5.45
Germany		2.91	1.46	5.60
Rest of Europe		1.73	2.52	6.82
Rest of the world		1.93	1.90	4.64
Total		100%	100%	100%

A clear pattern emerges, which can be explained quite adequately. The firms in each of the three regions focus principally on their home country, and within that, principally on the home region. That is the most important outlet for all companies. It is noteworthy, however, that companies in Gent/Eeklo sell relatively more in other regions in the home country than the companies in Zeeland Flanders and Central and North Zeeland. An important explanation for this phenomenon is the national distributive function of Gent's harbour.

The second area is found to be of major importance to provide insight into the sales orientation of the firms. The firms in Zeeland Flanders, in comparison with the other regions, focus most on Belgium; the firms in Central and North Zeeland look 'elsewhere in the Netherlands', and the firms in Gent/Eeklo look 'elsewhere in Belgium'.

The following significant conclusions are to be drawn from the table:

1. The average company in Zeeland Flanders, of all regions, is oriented most towards the market in the neighbouring country.

2. The companies in Central and North Zeeland, of all regions, focus most on the home country.

3. The companies in the Gent/Eeklo district, of all regions, focus most on France, Germany, and the rest of Europe. Thus, these companies are more internationally inclined. The Netherlands appear to be regarded as a 'foreign country' like any other.

The sales pattern charted

Figures 6.3 to 6.5 render the national and international sales pattern surveyable, illustrating the average distribution of the companies' sales volumes over the various subregions.

Figure 6.3 - Sales pattern of the companies of Zeeland Flanders, in %

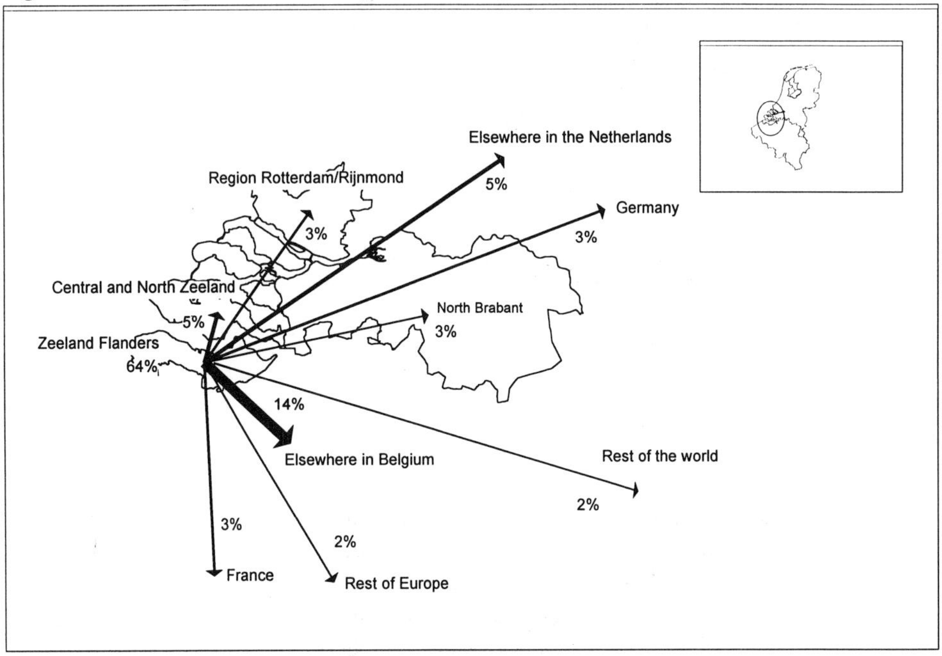

Figure 6.4 - Sales pattern of the companies of Central and North Zeeland, in %

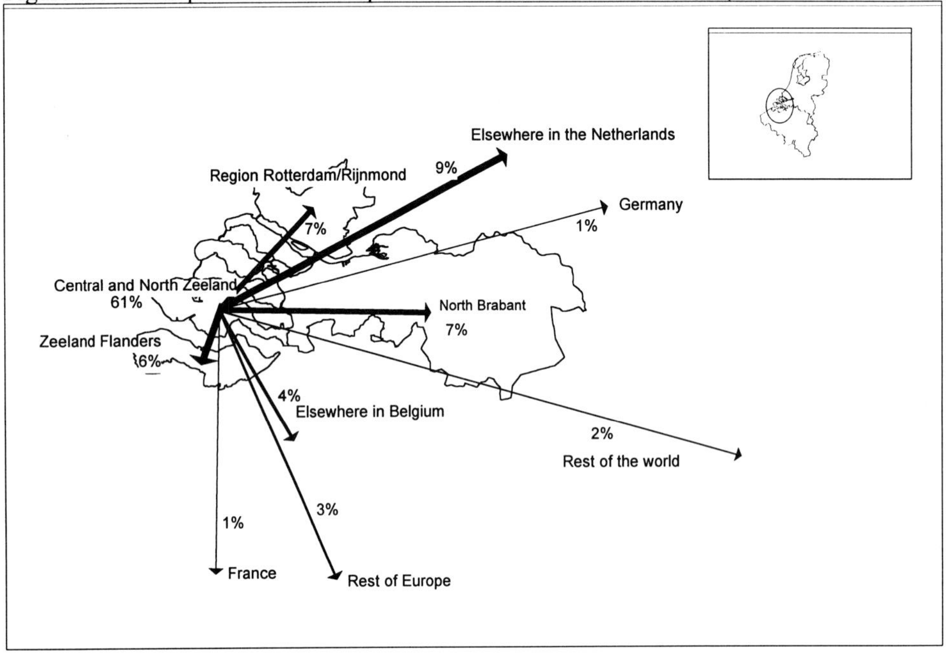

Figure 6.5 - Sales pattern of the companies of Gent/Eeklo, in %

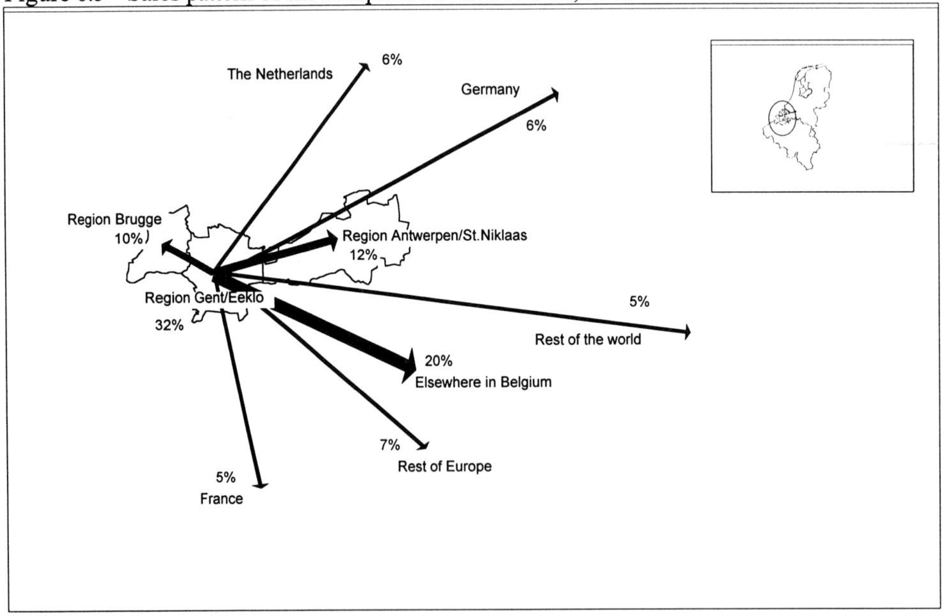

Correlations in the sales areas

The above analysis shows that there are clear differences in the sales distributions of the companies in the research area. This, however, does not clarify whether a link can be discovered between the sales areas. Companies deploying activities beyond their own region often display a spatially coherent sales pattern. The step-wise model proposed by the psychic distance approach predicts that the expansion into new areas and the penetration into new markets evolve along with the knowledge and experience concerning those markets and areas. One could apply this idea to the national market, with the regional market acting as home base, the national market as a second step, and the international market as the next.

It can therefore be tested whether a certain trend exists in the supra-regional sales pattern. For example, is it true that companies geared to France also focus their sales efforts on Germany? And does an orientation towards North Brabant coincide with an orientation towards the region of Rotterdam?

A suitable measure for valuing connections is the correlation coefficient, which indicates whether a connection is positive or negative and establishes its importance. The fact that a link exists between sales areas, it should be noted here, does not mean that the one area of necessity entails the other, but that the two sales areas move in the same or the opposite direction. Correlation does not imply causality. If two sales orientations are positively correlated, the coefficient is positive; if they are opposed, the coefficient is negative. The strength of the connection relates to the height of the value, 1.0 representing complete correlation, 0 none. The degree of significance is indicated by means of asterisks: *** meaning that there is less than a 1% chance that the observed result is based on coincidence, ** stands for a level of significance smaller than 5%, and * for a level smaller than 10%, which means that a certain degree of correlation exists, but only indicatively.

In tables 6.4 to 6.6, the correlation values between the sales areas are given for the responding companies in each of the three regions. The three tables for the separate regions should be read from left to right, thus: 'Companies in Zeeland Flanders selling in ... correlates with sales in ...'

As an example, the second row reads as follows: Companies in Zeeland Flanders selling in Central and North Zeeland (CNZ) also sell in North Brabant (indicative positive correlation). The third row reads as follows: Companies in Zeeland Flanders selling in the region Rotterdam/Rijnmond also sell in North Brabant (indicative positive correlation), in the rest of Europe (indicative positive correlation) and in the rest of the world (indicative positive correlation).

Table 6.4 - Correlation matrix sales areas for companies in Zeeland Flanders

	Zeeland Flanders	CNZ	Rotterdam/ Rijnmond	North Brabant	Elsewhere in NL	Belgium	France	Germany	Rest of Europe	Rest of the world
Zeeland Flanders	1.0000	-0.4152***	-0.5028***	-0.5038***	-0.6167***	-0.1637**	-0.1572**	-0.1753**	-0.1601**	-0.2286**
CNZ		1.0000	0.0220	0.1289*	0.0097	-0.0639	-0.0153	-0.0798	-0.0765	-0.0765
Rott../Rijnm.			1.0000	0.1086*	0.1208	0.0184	0.0119	0.0260	0.1293*	0.1869*
North Brab.				1.0000	0.0568	0.1754**	-0.0328	-0.0320	0.0624	-0.0269
Elsewhere in NL					1.0000	0.0711	0.3212***	0.0660	0.2172**	0.3611***
Belgium						1.0000	0.0210	-0.0689	-0.0485	-0.0824
France							1.0000	0.1511**	0.2524**	0.1780**
Germany								1.0000	0.1776**	0.1899**
Rest of Europe									1.0000	0.3205***
Rest of the world										1.0000

*** significance level <1%, ** significance level <5% , * significance level <10%

Table 6.4 for companies in Zeeland Flanders allows the following significant connections to be made:

-Companies selling their products in Central and North Zeeland are also likely to sell in North Brabant.

-Companies specifically oriented towards the region of Rotterdam also attempt to realise sales in North Brabant as well as European and global sales.

-An orientation towards North Brabant runs parallel to an orientation towards Belgium.

-Companies selling their commodities in the rest of the Netherlands (in addition, of course, to the home region) are also likely to direct their sales efforts towards France, other European countries and the rest of the world.

-Companies who focus upon foreign countries beyond Belgium turn their attention to the whole of Europe and to the rest of the world.

Table 6.5 - Correlation matrix sales areas for the companies in Central and North Zeeland

	Zeeland Flanders	CNZ	Rotterdam/ Rijnmond	North Brabant	Elsewhere in NL	Belgium	France	Germany	Rest of Europe	Rest of the world
Zeeland Flanders	1.0000	-0.2708***	-0.0718	-0.0505	-0.0631	0.0355	-0.0059	-0.0230	-0.0354	-0.0055
CNZ		1.0000	-0.5109***	-0.4461***	-0.6862***	-0.3707***	-0.2719***	-0.3461***	-0.3339***	-0.3144***
Rott../Rijnm.			1.0000	0.0603	0.0598	0.0506	0.0231	0.2043**	0.1153*	0.3558***
North Brab.				1.0000	0.0708	0.1118*	0.0388	0.0763	0.1486**	0.0195
Elsewhere in NL					1.0000	0.2278**	0.3800***	0.3477***	0.3581***	0.2134***
Belgium						1.0000	0.2423***	0.1440**	0.1028*	0.0272
France							1.0000	0.4449***	0.5624***	0.1328**
Germany								1.0000	0.3702***	0.2965***
Rest of Europe									1.0000	0.2369***
Rest of the world										1.0000

*** significance level <1%, ** significance level <5%, * significance level <10%

The following correlations are significant for the companies in Central and North Zeeland:

-Companies strongly oriented towards the region of Rotterdam do not necessarily focus upon France and Belgium, but tend to direct their sales efforts towards Germany, the rest of Europe, and the rest of the world.

-An orientation towards North Brabant means that a company in Central and North Zeeland will also be oriented towards Belgium and to European countries other than Germany and France.

-Companies focusing on the rest of the Netherlands are likely to sell their products in the rest of Europe and the world as well.

-Companies strongly focused upon foreign countries (including Belgium) include in their sales efforts all of Europe. The companies in Central and North Zeeland apparently consider Belgium as 'farther away', that is, 'more foreign', than companies in Zeeland Flanders.

Table 6.6 - Correlation matrix sales areas for the companies in Gent/Eeklo.

	Gent/ Eeklo	Region Brugge	Region Antwerp	Elsewhere Belgium	The Netherlands	France	Germany	Rest of Europe	Rest of the world
Gent/Eeklo	1.0000	-0.1653*	-0.3564**	-0.6376***	-0.2974***	-0.3381***	-0.619	-0.2817***	-0.2532**
Region Brugge		1.0000	0.0782	-0.3218**	-0.077	-0.2376**	-0.2417**	-0.3100**	-0.2116**
Region Antwerp			1.0000	-0.2642**	0.1945**	-0.0219	0.0149	-0.1362	-0.0913
Elsewhere Belgium				1.0000	0.2061**	0.4611***	0.1856*	0.4996***	0.1401
The Netherlands					1.0000	0.0417	0.1341	0.0585	0.0052
France						1.0000	0.2146**	0.5530***	0.2259**
Germany.							1.0000	0.4330***	0.2608**
Rest of Europe								1.0000	0.3308**
Rest of the world									1.0000

*** significance level <1%, ** significance level <5%, * significance level <10%

The following can be said about the sales orientation of the companies in Gent/Eeklo:

-An orientation towards Antwerp is likely to entrain an orientation towards the Netherlands. This does not apply for an orientation towards Brugge.

-A sales orientation towards the rest of Belgium goes together with an orientation towards European countries (including the Netherlands).

-A sales effort focusing on areas beyond the Netherlands is oriented towards several countries at the same time.

Especially noteworthy in the three matrices are the values for the category 'the rest of the home country' (distinguished as the 'rest of the Netherlands' and the 'rest of Belgium'). These sales markets are located outside the home region and beyond the directly neighbouring regions. The physical distance to those national markets is therefore relatively great. For all three regions, it appears that when countries direct their efforts towards the rest of the home land, the sales orientation towards the foreign market likewise increases.

Furthermore, the values for the various sales areas outside the home country also appear to be positively connected. This means that the companies that have decided to sell their commodities outside the home country as well, are likely to do so in several countries simultaneously.

6.4 Conclusions concerning the sales distribution for the companies in question

Three conclusions can be drawn from the sales analyses presented in the previous two sections of this chapter:

1. The companies in Central and North Zeeland are mostly nationally oriented, more so than the companies in Zeeland Flanders. The companies in Central and North Zeeland tend to sell a lot, proportionately, to North Brabant and Rotterdam. Companies in Zeeland Flanders sell most to the neighbouring country. These companies, moreover, have a more internationally-based turnover than the companies in Central and North Zeeland.
2. It is a fact that the Gent/Eeklo district is not an economically peripheral region within Belgium, but a vigorous economic centre. This was confirmed by its companies' sales distribution. The responding companies in the Gent/Eeklo district tend to be more multi-national and bi-national in their sales market orientation.
3. A general development pattern can be distinguished in the order of sales areas for the companies in the three regions. Sales in directly neighbouring regions are often coupled with sales in the rest of the home country; widely spread sales in the home country correlate with sales in the directly neighbouring country; and sales in the directly neighbouring country are often coupled with sales in other countries. This tallies with the fundamental idea within the step-wise model proposed by the psychic distance approach. Penetration and expansion into markets beyond the home region are gradual, also on the national scale.

6.5 Cross-border economic relations: Yes or No

After having gained some insight into the spatial distribution of entrepreneurial behaviour in terms of sales orientations and correlations, the analysis will be continued in the study of the spatial distribution of economic relationships. I have, for the three research areas selected, determined whether the respondents have cross-border economic relations, how many, and how the economic relations of the companies in these regions are distributed nationally and internationally. This will make clear which companies have interregional and/or international relations, and what impact the regional and country borders factually have.

The first element of study concerned the frequency of cross-border economic relations. It was found that on average two out of three respondents in the three research areas has no economic relationship whatsoever in the neighbouring country (table 6.7).

Table 6.7 - An economic relation in the neighbouring country: Yes or No?

	Zeeland Flanders	Central and North Zeeland	Gent/Eeklo	Total
No economic relation in the neighbouring country	n=93 k%=57.8	n=173 k%=79.0	n=50 k%=55.6	n=316 k%=67.2
Economic relation in the neighbouring country	n=68 k%=42.2	n=46 k%=21.0	n=40 k%=44.4	n=154 k%=32.8
Total	n=161	n=219	n=90	n=470

n = absolute number, k% = column percentage (from the top down)

Both in Zeeland Flanders and in Gent/Eeklo, almost half of all surveyed enterprises have one ore more economic relationships with a company in the neighbouring country. The average is pulled down mainly by entrepreneurs in Central and North Zeeland, of which one out of five on average has one or more cross-border economic relations in Belgium.

6.6 The number of economic relations

The next element of study concerned the average number of relationships in the neighbouring country. For all tables and figures relating to the number of economic relations, the mutually differing types of relationships have been inventoried for each region. A company may have several connections of the same type with various companies in the neighbouring countries, but these data have not been included in the analyses. The number of companies that have indicated having more than one relation of the same type in a region was found to be negligible. It follows that I have only examined the distribution of the number of differing relationships in the different regions in the Netherlands and Belgium. Figure 6.6 shows how the companies can be categorised on the basis of the number of relations in the neighbouring country.

Figure 6.6 - The absolute number of economic relations in the neighbouring country, per region

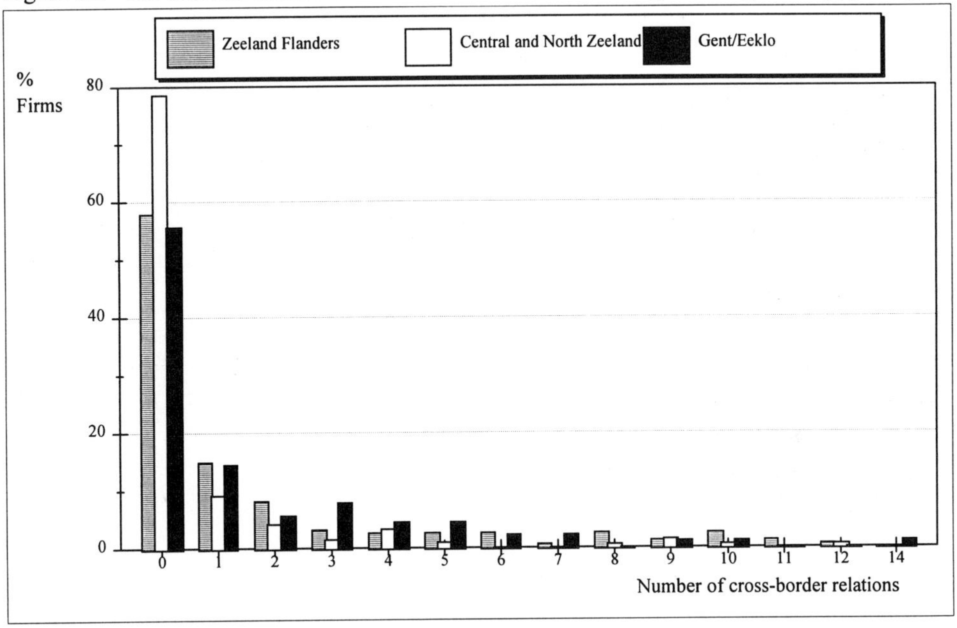

Above it was found that an average of 67% of the companies said that they have no economic relationship at all in the neighbouring country. In figure 6.6, it is shown that of the companies who do have economic connections in the neighbouring country, the majority have only one. The average number of cross-border relationships for all companies taken together is 1.14. The companies in Zeeland Flanders have an average of 4.57 economic relations in their home country and 1.59 economic relations in the neighbouring countries. This gives a ratio of 2.9:1. For the companies in Central and North Zeeland, that ratio amounts to 7.4:1 (4.81 against 0.65), and for Gent the ratio is 4.9:1 (7.57 against 1.54). It was found that the companies in the three regions on average have 4.6 times as many economic relations in their home country as in the neighbouring country.

A first important conclusion must be drawn here. One cannot speak significantly of an assumed sizeable international co-operation between the companies in the three research areas in the vicinity of the national border. Such a typification would go too far and does not describe the existing situation adequately. There is clearly a divisive effect in the geographical distribution of economic relationships at the state border. The next subsections will specify this finding further into regional differences.

6.6.1 Regional differences in the number of relations in the Netherlands and Belgium

Each company has its own network of various types of relationships. It is therefore not only interesting to know how many relations the respondents have, but also what kind of cross-border economic relationships they have, and how these are geographically distributed. To this end, I have first ordered the four types of relationships in table 6.8 in such a manner as to distinguish the regional differences in the number of relations for the Netherlands on the one hand and Belgium on the other. The table contains values representing the average number of relationships of a certain type for the companies in the region. The bracketed figures indicate the order of the types of relationships.

Table 6.8 - Average number of relations per company in the Netherlands (NL) and Belgium (B)

	Zeeland Flanders	Central and North Zeeland	Gent/Eeklo
Sales market relationships	0.47 (5)	0.46 (4)	0.50 (5)
Sales market relationships	0.20 (8)	0.21 (6)	0.74 (4)
Service relationships NL	0.80 (3)	0.88 (3)	0.12 (10)
Service relationships B	0.21 (7)	0.06 (9)	1.00 (3)
Supply relationships NL	2.07 (1)	2.28 (1)	0.47 (6)
Supply relationships B	0.73 (4)	0.23 (5)	3.78 (1)
Outsourcing relationships NL	1.08 (2)	1.01 (2)	0.31 (7)
Outsourcing relationships B	0.34 (6)	0.12 (8)	1.80 (2)
Control relationships NL	0.15 (9)	0.18 (7)	0.14 (9)
Control relationships B	0.11 (10)	0.03 (10)	0.24 (8)

For all regions it was found that national economic relationships most often relate to supply and outsourcing. The service relationships rank in third/fourth place for the companies in the three research areas. Matters such as cleaning, catering and security, counselling and financial services are part of everyday occurrences in business life. These services are most often sought regionally or eventually somewhere else in the home country. The number of control relationships is low for all regions. The probable reason for this phenomenon is that the relationship goes far beyond an exchange of commodities for money; it involves extensive co-operation with another company. Such a step is taken warily and relatively rarely.

Furthermore, it can be ascertained that the average number of relations per company in the home country and in the neighbouring country is unevenly distributed. This applies for the companies in all three regions, albeit not to the same degree. The orientation is primarily national, and expands to the international level afterwards. International relationships most often relate to supply.

The companies in Zeeland Flanders have the highest relative degree of economic interweaving with the neighbouring country. They not only have significantly more supply and outsourcing relationships in Belgium than the companies in Central and North Zeeland, but also more supply and outsourcing relationships in Belgium than the companies in Gent/Eeklo have in the Netherlands.

Differences between Zeeland Flanders and Central and North Zeeland

It is interesting to examine the specific differences in the relationship pattern of companies in Zeeland Flanders on the one hand, and Central and North Zeeland on the other, more closely. Both these regions are close to the border, but where Central and North Zeeland disposes of excellent connections with Breda, Rotterdam and Antwerpen, the Dutch region of Zeeland Flanders is separated from the rest of the Netherlands by the Westerschelde; it has not (yet) been opened up by any infrastructure on Dutch territory. Analysis shows that there are indeed significant differences in the relationship pattern between companies in both regions where it concerns the spatial distribution of economic relations in Belgium and in the home country. Companies in Zeeland Flanders are found to have significantly more administrative, outsourcing, supply and service relationships in Belgium than companies in Central and North Zeeland. The companies in Zeeland Flanders are quite literally 'closer' to the neighbouring country.

6.6.2 Regional differences in the number of relationships in subregions in the Netherlands and Belgium

A more detailed analysis of the number of different relationships yields a subdivision according to the various subregions in the Netherlands and Belgium (table 6.9).

Table 6.9 - Ranking order of the average number of relationships in subregions, per region

	Zeeland Flanders	Central and North Zeeland	Gent/Eeklo
Zeeland Flanders	2.73 (1)	0.36 (4)	0.43 (6)
Central and North Zeeland	0.64 (4)	1.46 (1)	0.20 (8)
Region Rotterdam / Rijnmond	0.53 (5)	0.70 (3)	0.37 (7)
Elsewhere in the Netherlands	0.98 (2)	0.79 (2)	0.56 (5)
Gent/Eeklo	0.71 (3)	0.16 (7)	3.62 (1)
Region Brugge	0.19 (8)	0.08 (8)	1.01 (4)
Region Antwerp / St. Niklaas	0.33 (7)	0.18 (5)	1.30 (3)
Elsewhere in Belgium	0.35 (6)	0.17 (6)	1.63 (2)

A number of important conclusions can be drawn from this table. It is clear that the companies in Zeeland Flanders are oriented, after their home region and country, more clearly towards the region Gent/Eeklo than towards Central and North Zeeland. The 'water border' - the Westerschelde separating Zeeland Flanders and Central and North Zeeland - has an important dividing effect. Furthermore, it is noteworthy that the companies in Zeeland Flanders have but little economic interaction with the region of Brugge, while the physical distance between Zeeland Flanders and Brugge is equal to that between Zeeland Flanders and Gent/Eeklo. Apparently, the (functional) affinity with the region of Brugge is smaller. The important channel linking Gent and Terneuzen, allowing passage to many ships and neutralising the barrier effect of the border, plays an important role in the explanation of the economic interaction between firms in Gent and Terneuzen.

Belgium is less important for companies in Central and North Zeeland; they consider the travelling time too long or are more reluctant to enter into economic relationships in Belgium. The average number of relationships in the neighbouring country for the companies in the region is relatively low. Here, the dividing line between the Netherlands and Belgium is clearly discernable. Companies in Central and North Zeeland clearly enter more often into relationships in the region Rotterdam/Rijnmond than in Zeeland Flanders or Belgium.

The dividing line is also present for companies in Gent/Eeklo, but it is less abrupt. The companies in this region are oriented more towards the rest of the Netherlands than towards Zeeland Flanders or Central and North Zeeland. Where companies in Zeeland Flanders seem to turn naturally towards Gent/Eeklo when entering into economic relationships in the neighbouring country, companies in Gent/Eeklo appear less eager to enter into economic relationships in Zeeland Flanders. Figure 6.7 lists the number of relationships per subregion for the three research areas.

Figure 6.7 - Number of economic relationships in the Netherlands and Belgium

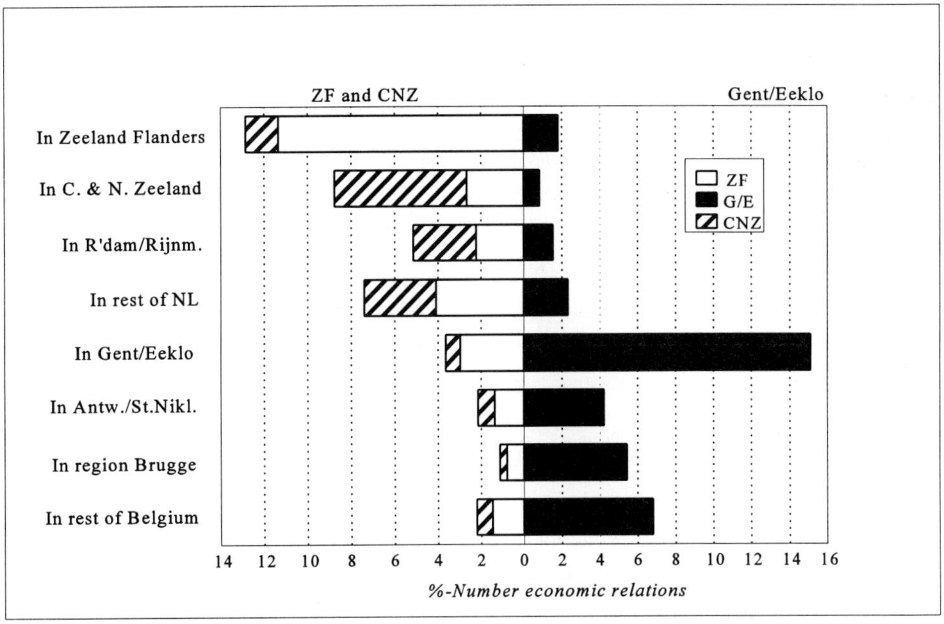

The figure should be read as follows. Three regions have been distinguished: Zeeland Flanders (ZF), Central and North Zeeland (CNZ), and Gent/Eeklo (G/E). There are eight subregions, four in the Netherlands and four in Belgium. These are listed vertically. To the left of the zero line, the two Dutch regions ZF and CNZ have been placed next to one another. The zero line should therefore be regarded as the border line between the Netherlands and Belgium. De horizontal axis represents the percentage of economic relationships in the different regions[1]. The figure shows the distribution of the economic relationships in the three research areas over the eight subregions in the Netherlands and Belgium. It should be noted that the figure concerns the total of the regional orientation differences for sales market relationships, service relationships, production process relationships, and control relationships.

The most important conclusions to be drawn from this figure are as follows:

1. The greater majority of the economic relationships concern the home region.
2. The proportion of national relationships clearly stands no comparison with the number of international economic relationships.

---

[1] $\frac{\text{Total number of relationships in sub-region X from region CNZ or G/E or ZF}}{\text{Total number of potential relationships in X from region CNZ or G/E or ZF}} * 100\%$

3. In addition to the effect of the national border, the effect of the 'water border' (the Westerschelde) is also visible. This physiographic border (see chapter 2) between Zeeland Flanders and Central and North Zeeland constitutes a clear dividing line for companies in both regions. Taken relatively, companies in Zeeland Flanders have more relationships in Gent/Eeklo than in Central and North Zeeland, and the companies in Central and North Zeeland have more relationships in the region Rotterdam/Rijnland and the rest of the Netherlands than in Zeeland Flanders or in Belgium. Nevertheless, this effect should not be overestimated. In total, the effect of the state border on the geographical distribution of economic relationship is far greater than that of the 'water border'.

4. The companies in the district Gent/Eeklo have economic relations throughout the Netherlands.

5. Companies in Zeeland Flanders, relatively taken, have the greatest number of economic relationships in the neighbouring country (*i.e.* Belgium).

6.6.3 The geographical distribution of the various types of economic relationships charted

Finally, I have examined the geographical distribution of the various types of economic relationships over the subregions in the Netherlands and Belgium. This reflects the total picture of the number of cross-border economic relationships, their types and distribution. The data obtained was charted (see figures 6.8 to 6.12). The frequency distributions over the subregion that were distinguished earlier are represented, in other words: what percentage of the companies in the research areas has one or more relations of a certain type in a certain area?

Figure 6.8a - Sales market relationships of the companies in Zeeland Flanders

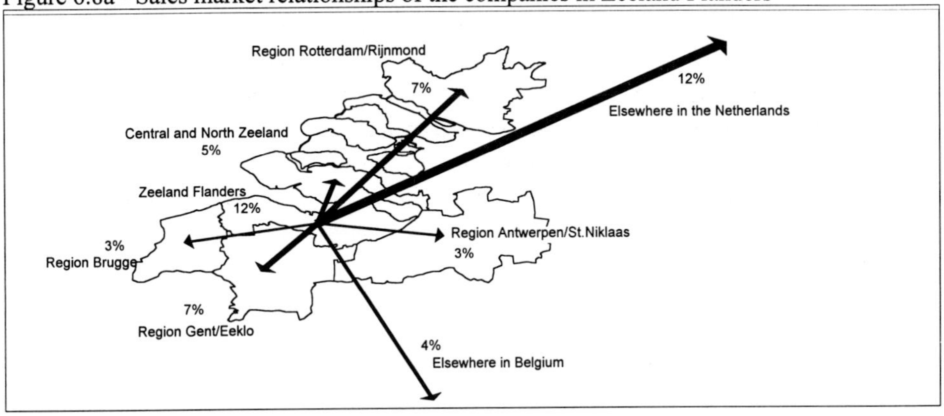

Figure 6.8b - Sales market relationships of the companies in Central and North Zeeland

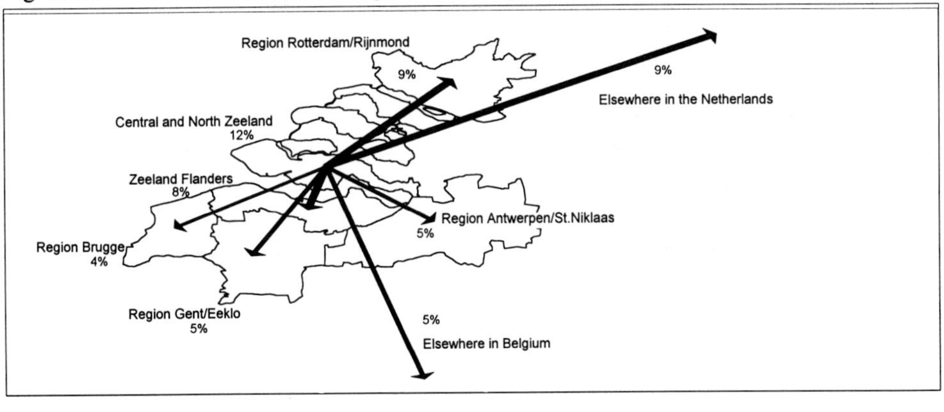

Figure 6.8c - Sales market relationships of the companies in Gent/Eeklo

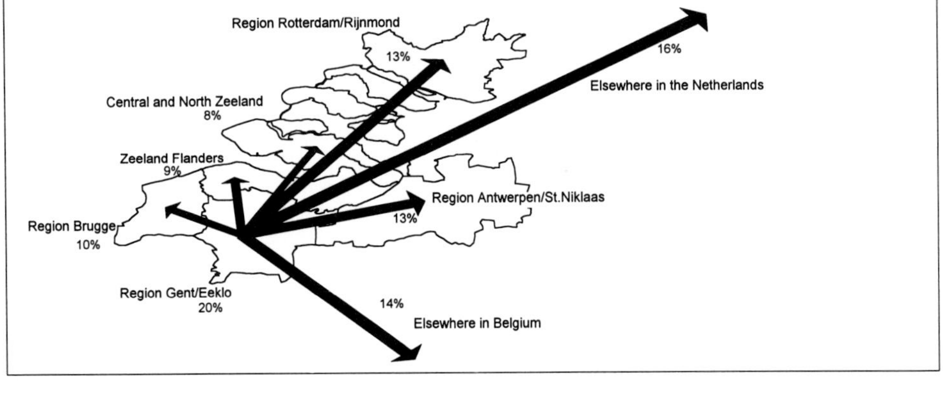

Figure 6.9a - Service relationships of the companies in Zeeland Flanders

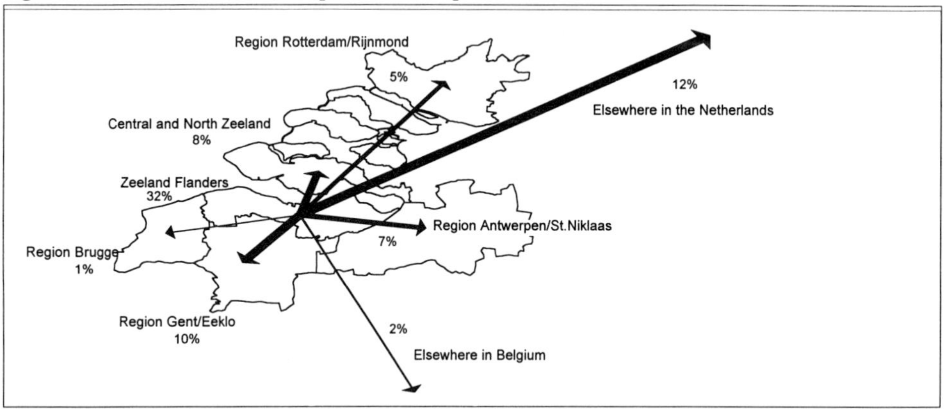

Figure 6.9b - Service relationships of the companies in Central and North Zeeland

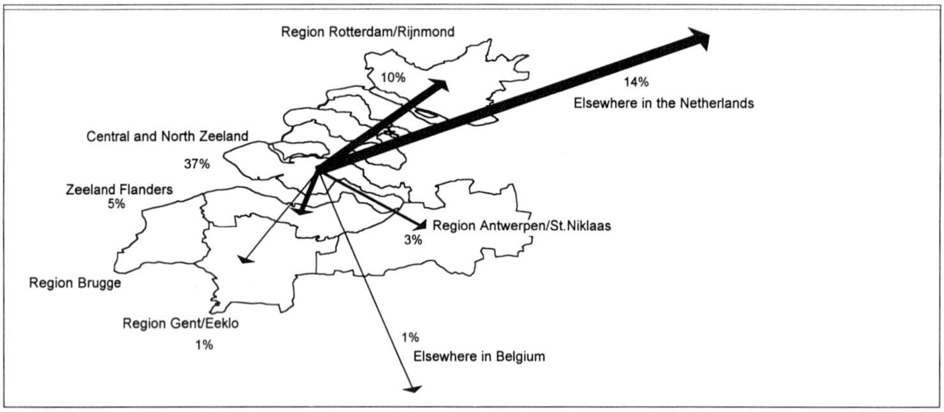

Figure 6.9c - Service relationships of the companies in Gent/Eeklo

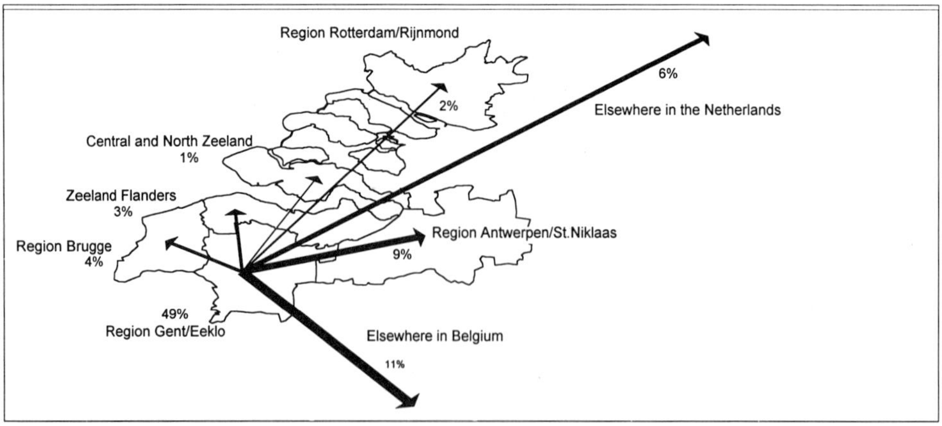

Figure 6.10a - Supply relationships of the companies in Zeeland Flanders

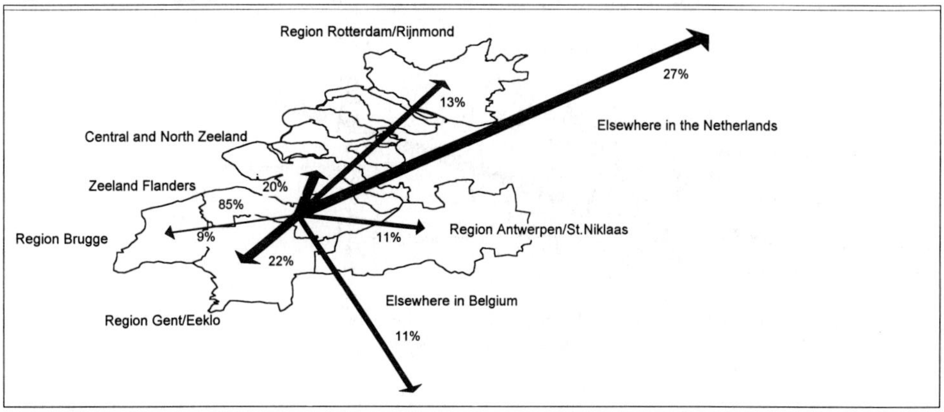

Figure 6.10b - Supply relationships of the companies in Central and North Zeeland

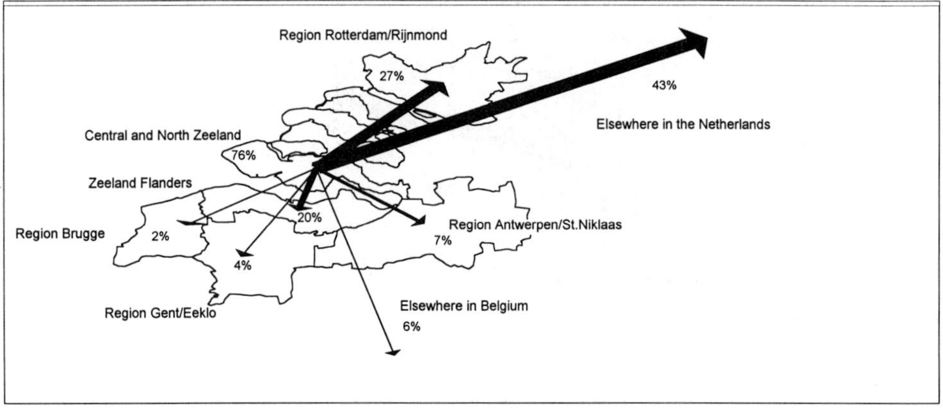

Figure 6.10c - Supply relationships of the companies in Gent/Eeklo

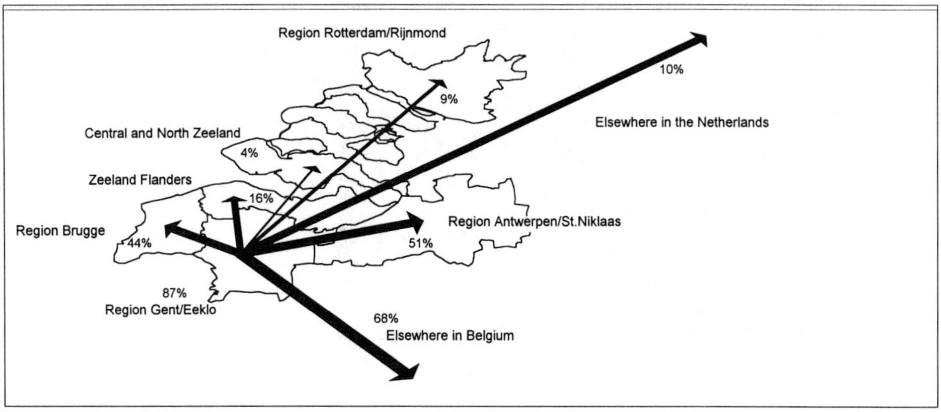

Figure 6.11a - Outsourcing relationships of the companies in Zeeland Flanders

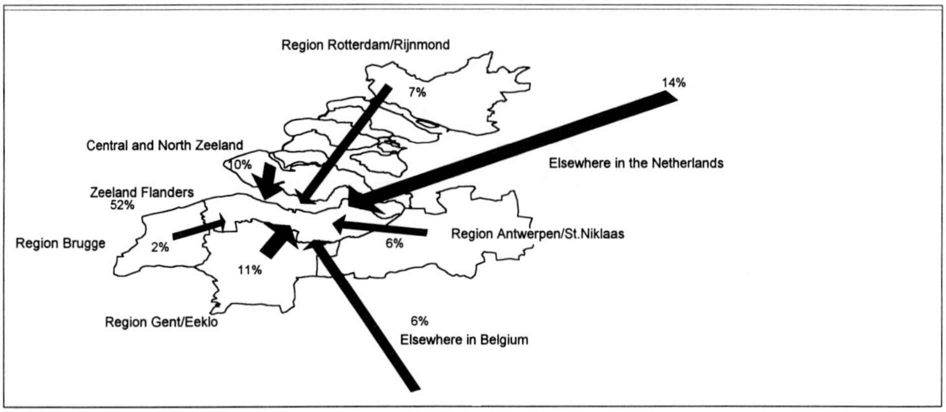

Figure 6.11b - Outsourcing relationships of the companies in Central and North Zeeland

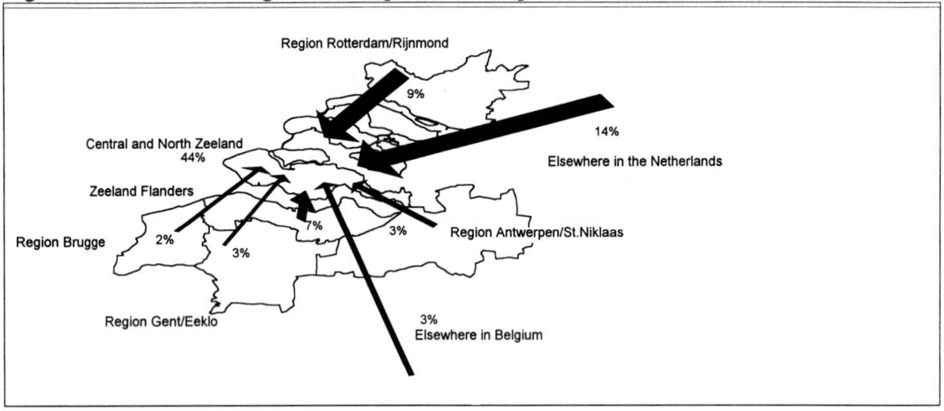

Figure 6.11c - Outsourcing relationships of the companies in Gent/Eeklo

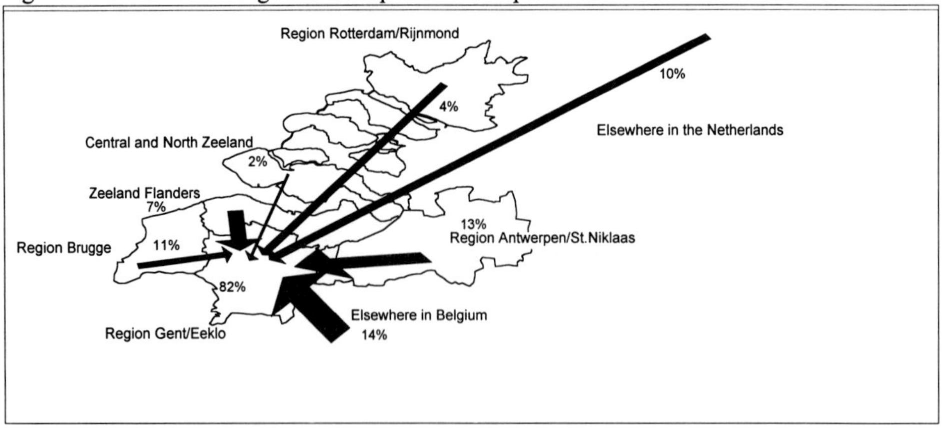

Figure 6.12a - Control relationships of the companies in Zeeland Flanders

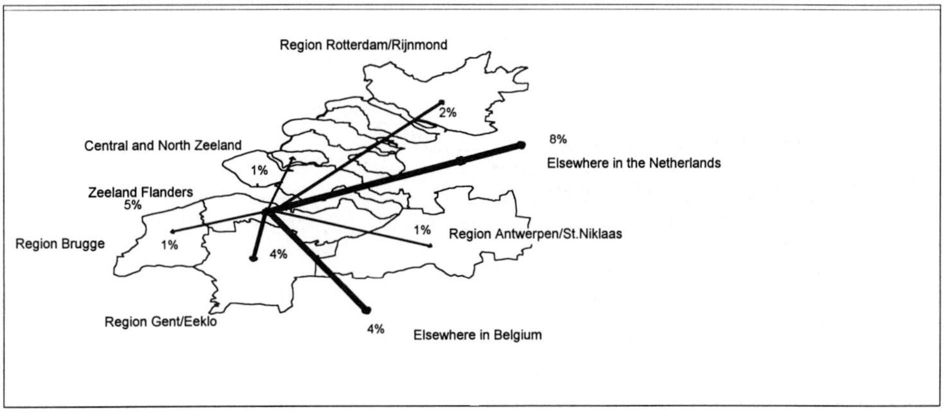

Figure 6.12b - Control relationships of the companies in Central and North Zeeland

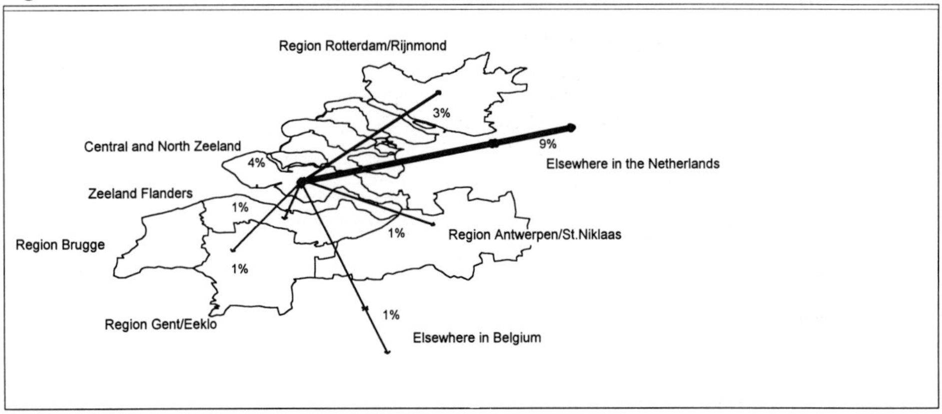

Figure 6.12c - Control relationships of the companies in Gent/Eeklo

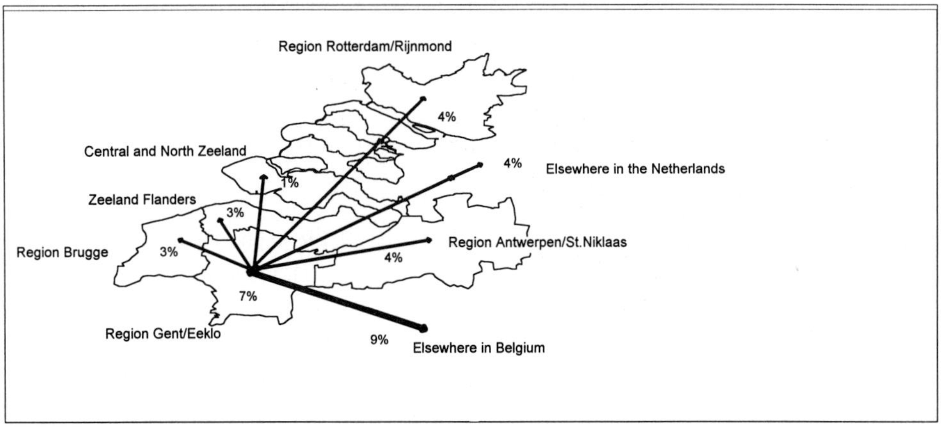

6.7 Summary cross-border economic interweaving

The chart below provides a summary of the economic interweaving between the companies in the three research areas that were analysed in chapters 5 and 6:

Table 6.10 - Economic interweaving of the three regions

		Zeeland Flanders	Central and North Zeeland	Gent/Eeklo
Average percentage of cross-border workers in the region		9.13%	0.43%	0.72%
Export to neighbouring country?		67.5% Yes	33.33% Yes	73.0% Yes
Economic relation(s) in neighbouring country?		42.2% Yes	21.0% Yes	44.4% Yes
Mutual average sales, in %	From Zeeland Flanders to:	64%	5.01%	14.23% (average export to Belgium)
	From Central and North Zeeland to:	6.3%	61%	3.85% (average export to Belgium)
	From Gent/Eeklo to:	5.72% (average export to the Netherlands)		32%
Average number of economic relations per company in neighbouring regions	Zeeland Flanders companies in:	2.73	0.64	0.71
	Central and North Zeeland companies in:	0.36	1.46	0.16
	Gent/Eeklo companies in:	0.43	0.20	3.62
Average number of economic relations per company in neighbouring country		1.59	0.65	1.54
Average number of economic relations per company in neighbouring country		4.57	4.81	7.57

As the preceding analyses already showed, the companies in the region Zeeland Flanders have interweaved most successfully with the neighbouring country. This is affirmed most obviously by the categories 'percentage of cross-border workers', 'export to the neighbouring country', 'Economic relation(s) in neighbouring country' (in both categories, twice as many 'Yes' in Zeeland Flanders as in Central and North Zeeland), as well as by the average number of relationships per company in the neighbouring country. Most of the cross-border economic relationships of the companies in Zeeland Flanders are located in the region Gent/Eeklo. The ratio between the number of economic relationships in the home country and those in the directly neighbouring region of the neighbouring country, *i.e.* Gent/Eeklo, is 6.4:1. The ratio of the number of economic relationships in the home country to those in the neighbouring country is 2.9:1 for Zeeland Flanders.

Companies in the region Central and North Zeeland are mostly focused upon the home region and country, much less upon the neighbouring country. Where it concerns the Belgian market, they are actually interested only in export, whether or not through a steady sales market relationship. The greater distance and reluctance to enter into economic relationships in Belgium appear to play a role in the explanation of the difference with the companies in the other two regions. The ratio between the number of economic relationships in the home country and those in Gent/Eeklo is 30.1:1. The ratio of the number of economic relations in the home country to the neighbouring country for the companies in Central and North Zeeland is 7.4:1.

Although the companies in Gent/Eeklo are active on the international level relatively often, they are oriented less towards their directly neighbouring region Zeeland Flanders. Apparently, Zeeland Flanders is a less interesting region for Gent/Eeklo than the other way around. The ratio between the number of economic relationships in the home country and the directly neighbouring region in the Netherlands, *i.e.* Zeeland Flanders, is 17.6:1. The ratio between the number of economic relationships in the home country and those in Central and North Zeeland, is even higher, 37.9:1. The ratio of the number of economic relations in the home country to the neighbouring country is 4.9:1 for companies in Gent/Eeklo.

6.8 Conclusion

The factual spatial distribution of *the action space*, measured in terms of direct sales of products and economic relationships, of the companies in the border regions under consideration was established in this chapter. This action space was found to be bounded quite literally by the state border. The border was found to be a dividing line not so much for exporting or having economic relationships, but it restricts the volume of the export and the number of economic relations. Most enterprises export less than 10% of their total turnover to the neighbouring country. The number of economic relationships in the neighbouring country is, on average, 4.6 times lower than in the home country. The number of economic relationships in the directly neighbouring region in the neighbouring country is, on average, about 23 times lower than the number of economic relationships in the home country.

However, these results varied strongly per region. The economic interweaving in national and international space is strongly being influenced by the origin of the companies, their regional context. Companies in the region Zeeland Flanders, the most peripheral in the home country, were found to be directed most strongly towards the neighbouring country, especially towards the directly neighbouring region Gent/Eeklo. The respondents in Central and North Zeeland clearly have a different space of action for economic relationships than the entrepreneurs in Gent/Eeklo and Zeeland Flanders. They have economic relationships in the neighbouring country less often, the relations are also fewer in number and are mostly nationally oriented. Chapter 7 will attempt to provide an explanation for the patterns that were found in this chapter regarding the having, or not having, and the number of cross-border economic relationships.

Chapter 7

Results yielded by the INTERFACE model

7.1 Introduction

This chapter examines and elucidates the establishment and evolution process of economic relationships between Dutch and Belgian companies in the three research areas through the INTERFACE model. The outcome culled from the various stages of the INTERFACE model are first *described.* This will be done in section 7.2. Then the hypotheses as formulated in chapter 4 will be put to the test in section 7.3. In this section therefore an *explanation* of the results will be given. Finally, section 7.4 presents the most important conclusions drawn with regard to the development of cross-border economic relationships between Dutch and Belgian enterprises.

7.2 Description of the results of the INTERFACE model

So as to be able to explain the establishment and development of cross-border economic relationships, the present section describes the values found for the determinants in the various stages of the INTERFACE model (see appendix 2 for the extended definition of the indicators of the different determinants)

Thus, before offering an explanation of the action patterns established in chapter 6 and of the success of economic relationships, the facts concerning the formation process of cross-border economic relationships will be examined, each time considering whether these can be differentiated according to region, sector, or type of relationship, and mentioning only significant differences. In scheme 7.1, the determinants of the development stages in chapter 4 are recapitulated.

Scheme 7.1 - Determinants in the development stages of the INTERFACE model

I. Contact

Action space

a. Social & Professional network; number of personal and professional acquaintances
b. Visiting frequency of the personal and professional acquaintances.
c. Direct or indirect contact
d. Relationship preference

Affection space

e. Mental distance
f. 'Feeling at home in the neighbouring country's culture'
g. Spatial identity
h. Evaluation of state border

Cognition space

i. Cognitive distance versus physical distance
j. Cognitive map of the border

II. Attraction

a. Spatial proximity
b. Similarity
c. Complementation in business contact and relationships
d. External or physical attraction: price/quality of the goods

III. Interaction

a. Height of transaction costs
b. Degree of trust

IV. Transaction

Formal versus informal relationship

V. Relationship

a. Yes or no
b. Number of relations

VI. Success

a. Growth in intensity of the economic relationships
b. Perception of success

Stage I: Contact

The first stage in the development process of cross-border economic relationships is the contact stage. The outcome for the determinants of the contact stage is examined for the three research areas. Conform chapter 4, a distinction is made between three categories: action space, affective space and cognitive space.

Action space

I.-a Number of personal and professional contacts and relationships in the neighbouring country

In the first place, the informal contact pattern of the companies with one or more economic relations was examined. It was established clearly, for all three regions and for all types of relationships, that the respondents have far more professional and personal acquaintances/ relations in the home country than in the neighbouring country. This was measured by means of seven-point Likert scales. The value 7 means that a higher number of personal or professional acquaintances was reported in the neighbouring country, value 1 means that a higher number of these acquaintances was reported in the home country. The scale has been interpreted as an interval scale to enable a comparison of average values. The average values for the number of professional and personal acquaintances in the neighbouring country were established at 2.05 and 1.99, respectively.

Results were found to differ on the regional level. The respondents in Zeeland Flanders have significantly more personal acquaintances in the neighbouring country than the companies in Central and North Zeeland and Gent/Eeklo. The results also differ according to sector, not according to the type of relationship. Companies in the wholesale sector have significantly more personal acquaintances in the neighbouring country than industrial or construction companies. Thus, wholesale trade tends to be more 'informally embedded' in the neighbouring country's society.

I-b. Visiting frequency

The visiting frequency of the personal and professional acquaintances in the neighbouring country is a measure for the active participation in its society and the 'strength of ties' with the acquaintances in that society. It may be assumed that a high visiting frequency stimulates a sense of familiarity, of feeling at home in the culture of the neighbouring country. The point of gravity in this ordinal scale of the visiting frequency (the median) is the category 'every few months' for both personal and professional acquaintances. The types of relationships do not display significant differences on this point. A significant regional difference in visiting frequencies, however, has been observed. The companies in Zeeland Flanders visit their personal and professional acquaintances in the neighbouring country Belgium most often, while the companies in Central and North Zeeland, in turn, visit their acquaintances in the neighbouring country more often than those in Gent/Eeklo.

I-c. Direct or indirect contact

It may be assumed that personal and professional contacts are directly useful in generating new contacts, which may lead to new economic relationships. The network theory on this subject (see chapter 3) indicates that contacts and relationships are most often initiated through other contacts and relationships. The chances in a certain 'market' are, according to this theory, determined by the quantity and quality of the contacts and relationships one has in that 'market'.

This factor thus establishes the degree to which others have helped in bringing about the contact/relationship. For all respondents with one or more relations in the neighbouring country, regardless of the type of relationship, it was found that 47.1% of all relationships were brought about with the aid of others (indirect contact). A small majority of the respondents (52.9%) did not call in the help of others in developing the contact or relationship with their most important partner (direct contact). The difference is therefore not large, it is almost 'fifty-fifty'. No significant differences were found as regards region, sector, or the type of relationship. The respondents in Zeeland Flanders used their contacts and relations more in bringing about (the contact with) their most important relation than those in Central and North Zeeland or Gent/Eeklo. Table 7.1 reflects these matters.

Table 7.1 - Direct/Indirect contact

	Zeeland Flanders	Central and North Zeeland	Gent/Eeklo	Total
Indirect	54.9%	37.8%	45.5%	47.1%
Direct	45.1%	62.2%	54.5%	52.9%
Total	n=51	n=37	n=33	n=121

n=absolute number

I examined, furthermore, *who* gave help or advice in bringing about the new contact/relationship in the neighbouring country, and found that most entrepreneurs consult their professional relations - such as suppliers, customers or counsellors. In as much as 49% of the cases, aid or advice was proffered by an existing professional relationship in the home country (35%) or neighbouring country (14%). The percentage of companies that consulted the Chambers of Commerce was very low. Of all companies that indicated having been helped by others, only 1.7% said to have gone to a Dutch Chamber of Commerce; 3.5% had sought advice from a Chamber of Commerce in Belgium. It may be said, therefore, that the Chambers of Commerce did not play any important role in the establishment of the most important economic relationships of the companies in the research population. The links between the regional economic networks on either side of the border thus tend to be existing professional relations in the home country.

I-d. Relationship preference

The relationship preference of the companies with one or more relations in the neighbouring country was examined through seven questions. Their answers were measured against a seven-point Likert scale. The scale was interpreted as an interval scale, allowing comparison of average values. Table 7.2 shows the ranking order of the items in the relationship preference of the entrepreneurs in the three research regions. The average values are followed by their ranking order according to importance (in brackets).

Table 7.2 - Ranking order of relationship preference items, per region

	ZF	CNZ	G/E	Total
Preference for projects with high profits despite higher risk	2.23(7)	2.12(6)	1.66(7)	2.02(7)
Preference for steady, long-term relationships	5.69(1)	5.86(1)	5.94(1)	5.81(1)
Preference for relations with a large network of business contacts	3.58(5)	4.22(3)	4.44(2)	4.02(3)
Business contacts and relations are consciously sought after in the neighbouring country	4.23(3)	3.54(4)	3.59(3)	3.85(4)
Preference for relations at short distances	4.30(2)	3.07(5)	3.09(6)	3.60(5)
Preference for knowledge concerning price/quality ratio of alternative partners	4.19(4)	4.62(2)	3.58(4)	4.13(2)
Preference for relations in the home country	2.71(6)	2.11(7)	3.39(5)	2.75(6)

It appears that, on average, respondents tend to prefer steady, long-term relationships, which indicates a risk-avoiding behaviour in relationships. This is confirmed by the relatively strong disapproval of projects with high profits incorporating greater risks. Generally, entrepreneurs prefer having the choice between various price/quality alternatives. The companies favoured as relations do not have to be located in the home country. Entrepreneurs seek fairly actively for contacts and relations in the neighbouring country, displaying a slight preference for contacts and relations with a large network of business contacts. A significant regional dissimilarity exists for the item 'preference for relations at short distances', which is clearly preferred by companies in Zeeland Flanders as compared to companies in the other two regions. This confirms its strong inclination towards the region Gent/Eeklo, which is the nearest region for most of the companies in Zeeland Flanders.

No significant difference was found for the type of relationship, but a significant difference exists between sectors, showing that construction companies have a significantly stronger preference for relations in the home country as compared to industrial and wholesale enterprise. This has much to do with the project-based character of building activities and the fact that the construction industry is often more restricted by national regulations. Wholesale, to the contrary, has a significant preference for business contacts and relations across the border with a large network of business contacts. This is, of course, logically connected with their main activity, trade. Respondents in the wholesale sector are also significantly more interested in projects with high profits than respondents from the other two sectors, thereby accepting a higher risk.

Affection space

I-e. Mental distance

In order to determine the mental distance (for the definition of mental distance see chapter 4, section 4.2.1) between Dutch and Belgian respondents, I measured their perceptions and evaluations of the differences in working with an entrepreneur from their home country and an entrepreneur from the neighbouring country, and the consequences of these differences for the success of the co-operation. In general, it was found that the respondents perceive great differences, and evaluate these as having major consequences. First of all, this means that the border is perceived as a dividing line by entrepreneurs of both nationalities, which in itself is an important observation. In chapter 6, we have already seen that the action space, with regard to the frequency and number of cross-border economic relationships, is effectively divided by the border. The outcome here demonstrates that an effective dividing line exists between the Netherlands and Belgium in perception as well. The economic space in the research area can therefore not be characterised as 'borderless'.

A relationship with an entrepreneur in the neighbouring country appears to be perceived, in the majority of cases, as a relationship involving more mental uncertainty, greater adaptation, and higher costs than a relationship with an entrepreneur in the home country. It is characteristic, however, that foreign relationships are considered by the respondents as being of greater business interest than a relationship in the home country. It would seem that a compensation effect is involved. The entrepreneur in the neighbouring country is expected to compensate for the additional costs and insecurity of the relationship by his better market position. The entrepreneur therefore wants the foreign entrepreneur to have a better market position compared to economic relations in the home country.

The type of relationship the respondents have with an entrepreneur in the neighbouring country does not seem to affect the mental distance items significantly. The picture that emerges from the analysis of the regional differences is that the respondents in Central and North Zeeland expect to encounter greater difficulties in getting to know and communicating with the partners in the neighbouring country, and therefore underestimate the intensity and efficiency of the co-operation with partners in the neighbouring country. The Zeeland Flanders respondents gave the most positive estimate of the chance of success of a cross-border relationship.

When analysing sectoral differences, it clearly emerges that the construction sector, in comparison to industry and wholesale, perceives higher barriers and greater difficulties in cross-border economic relationships on many points.

Personal experience of pressure points and problems

An open question requested all respondents to describe the pressure points and problems they experienced personally, thus providing them with the opportunity to voice their estimation of the differences in their own words. In total, 25.7%, answered the open question: 'Please indicate which problems and pressure points you experienced personally in doing business with Belgian (Dutch, respectively) entrepreneurs'. Many companies said that they did not have any experience doing business with entrepreneurs in the neighbouring country. The answers below are therefore no more than indications to the bottlenecks that were experienced. These have been brought back to some three categories, *business conventions, market and government*, which are listed below.

Table 7.3 - The problems experienced in doing business in the neighbouring country

Business conventions	ZF (%)	CNZ (%)	G/E (%)
Not keeping appointments, bad 'paying morals'	20.5	12.2	12.5
Belgians are untrustworthy in business	2.7		
Belgian business life is corrupt, and that is what they call personal contact	1.4	6.1	
The Dutch have no scruples about false complaints, fraud, and financial unreliability			12.5
Belgians are too easy-going / lazy	1.4	4.1	
Belgians do not come to the point	1.4	2	
As Dutchman, they do not want you to be straightforward		2	
I notice distrust via-à-vis Dutch entrepreneurs	2.7	2	
Privately, a Belgian is pleasant, not so in business		2	
Dutchmen think themselves superior, they look down on Belgians, they are conceited			25
The Dutch are good at communicating, the results are not always in keeping with that			16.6
Difference in business mentality and culture	5.5	4.1	8.3
Belgians tend to choose Belgian companies for doing business	4.1		
Belgians always think the price is too high		6.1	
It is difficult to agree about prices	1.4		

Continuously changing people in business relationships	1.4		
Belgians are too indirect	1.4		
A Belgian says 'yes' but means 'no'	1.4		
Belgians are too sensitive to the informal aspect of doing business	1.4		
One first has to win the trust of Belgians, then it is pleasant business	1.4		
The Dutch are very price-conscious			4.2
The Dutch are less flexible, but more punctual			4.2
Total	48.1	40.6	83.3

Market	ZF (%)	CNZ (%)	G/E (%)
High costs (including time) of financial traffic	8.2	10.2	4.2
It is difficult to gain insight into rapidly changing market conditions	1.4	2	4.2
Heavy competition on the Belgian market		4.1	
The great distance		2	
Language problems	4.1	6.1	
Disparities in taste	1.4	2	
Total	15.1	26.4	8.4

Government	ZF (%)	CNZ (%)	G/E (%)
Tax laws are different and it is difficult to claim back VAT	5.5	4.1	
Social laws are different	4.1	4.1	
Product standards are different			4.2
The paperwork associated with doing business abroad	12.3	10.2	
Belgians themselves could not care less about regulations but they are severe in their dealings with Dutch and other foreign entrepreneurs	5.5	2	
Unfair competition, the Belgian government tries to exclude Dutch enterprise through regulations	8.2	4.1	
The Belgian market is more difficult to penetrate for Dutch entrepreneurs than the German or English market	1.4	2	
The Dutch government is less flexible and serviceable			4.2
Total	37	26.8	8.4

The answers, such as reproduced here, can be quite harsh, reflecting much frustration at times. A number of stereotypes and prejudices are prominent. Quite clearly, a 'We-Them' relationship is voiced between Belgians and Dutchmen.

Entrepreneurs from Zeeland Flanders have difficulties especially with the fact that Belgians do not respect their agreements, with what they call the 'bad payment morals', and with the barriers they feel the Belgian government is raising. Entrepreneurs from Central and North Zeeland tend to agree with the last two criticisms. The Dutch also often complain about the protective constructions of the Belgian government. More than entrepreneurs from Zeeland Flanders, the respondents in Central and North Zeeland are irritated by what they call the 'lazy professional attitude' displayed by the Belgian entrepreneur. They consider that business is hindered by the indirect, overly informal manner of Belgians.

Belgian entrepreneurs complain mainly about Dutch arrogance. They furthermore think that the Dutch are effective in communication, but add that the results are not always in keeping with their promises.

These perceptions of entrepreneurs coincide with the 'objective' cultural distance between the Netherlands and Belgium as a whole, as measured by Hofstede (1980, 1991). As argued in chapter 3, Hofstede measured the differences in a set of cultural dimensions between a number of countries (see section 3.7). Based on this work, Kogut and Singh introduced a cultural distance index. It appears that the cultural distance for the neighbouring countries of the Netherlands and Belgium is very large. According to Hofstede's analysis Belgians are much more sensitive to power and hierarchy than the Dutch, Belgians are much more keen on the avoidance of uncertainty than the Dutch, and finally Belgians are much more focused on 'masculinity' in society, meaning that in Belgian society assertivity and materialism are prominent values , and that society's members in Belgium are less caring and serviceable towards each other. As Hofstede put it:

> The cultural gap between the Netherlands and Dutch-speaking Belgium is somewhat smaller than between the Netherlands and French-speaking Belgium, but it is still very wide. In fact, no two countries in the HERMES data with a common border and a common language are so far culturally apart, according to the HERMES indices, as Belgium and the Netherlands. The gap occurs in Power Distance, Uncertainty Avoidance, and Masculinity; only in Individualism do Belgium and the Netherlands come together. (Hofstede, 1980, p. 335)

Below, the cultural distance index of Kogut and Singh for the countries of the European Union is used to determine the cultural distance between the Netherlands and Belgium[1]. This distance is symmetrical for two countries, as explained in chapter 4 (see Intermezzo). The cultural distance from country A to B is the same as the distance from B to A. The value for the distance between the Netherlands and Belgium is therefore the same (i.e. '1.93'). But the cultural distances from country A to other European countries differs from the cultural distances from country B. Based on Hofstede's data a ranking then arises, showing the cultural distances from Belgium, and the Netherlands, respectively, towards the different European countries (table 7.4)

Table 7.4 - Cultural distance index for the European Union, from Belgium and the Netherlands

Ranking of the EU (α), cultural distance from Belgium (β)	Ranking of the EU, cultural distance from the Netherlands
1. France (0.10)	1. Sweden (0.34)
2. Italy (0.42)	2. Finland (0.36)
3. Spain (0.67)	3. Denmark (0.66)
4. Germany (1.14)	4. Great Britain (1.47)
5. Greece (1.59)	5. Germany (1.49)
6. Finland (1.74)	6. France (1.56)
7. The Netherlands (1.93)	7. Ireland (1.66)
8. Great Britain (2.13)	8. Italy (1.78)
9. Portugal (2.38)	9. Spain (1.79)
10. Ireland (2.38)	10. Belgium (1.93)
11. Austria (3.22)	11. Austria (3.26)
12. Sweden (3.49)	12. Portugal (4.06)
13. Denmark (4.14)	13. Greece (4.26)

(α) Luxembourg was not available in the data of Hofstede.

(β) Cultural distance index value between brackets

The ranking shows a clear division in the cultural distance index of the European Union, seen from the Netherlands and Belgium. Belgium is culturally close to countries which are mostly

---

1 As explained in chapter 3, mathematically, the cultural distance index of Kogut and Singh has the following form: $Cd_j = \sum\{(I_{ij} - I_{iN})^2/V_i\}/4 \quad i = 1$, in which Cdj = the cultural distance between the home country and the host country/countries, Iij= the index value for cultural dimension i of country j, Vi = the variance of the index of dimension i, N= home country

South European. The Netherlands, on the contrary, is culturally more connected to Nordic countries of the European Union. The subjective perceptions and stereotypes of each other, as mentioned in table 7.3, are well in line with the objective cultural distance between the two countries. Belgian entrepreneurs are more like South European entrepreneurs to the Dutch, whereas Dutch entrepreneurs are more Nordic-like to the Belgians. To summarise this subsection, measured objectively and perceptively the cultural difference between the Dutch and the Belgians is considerable.

I-f. Feeling at home in the neighbouring country's culture

The next aspect that came under consideration was to what extent respondents 'feel at home in the neighbouring country'. I have examined in how far the respondents with one or more economic relations feel at home in the living culture and in the business culture of the neighbouring country. The factor 'feeling at home' is an important indication of the affective boundary in the common space shared by Dutchmen and Belgians. Table 7.5 list the average values registered for the companies in the three regions.

Table 7.5 - Feeling at home in the neighbouring country's culture

	ZF	CNZ	G/E	Total
Feeling at home in the living culture	4.61	2.75	2.25	3.38
Feeling at home in the business culture	3.86	2.89	2.78	3.26

Generally, the respondents do not really feel at home in the neighbouring culture. The neighbouring country has a culture that is regarded as 'not their own', as foreign. At the border, a new culture truly begins. Of all three regions, the respondents from Zeeland Flanders were found to feel significantly more at home in the neighbouring culture than the respondents from the other two regions. This coincides with the generally prevailing image of Zeeland Flanders, being that Zeeland Flemings have a strong affinity with Belgium. The results that the respondents in Zeeland Flanders have significantly more personal acquaintances in the neighbouring country than the respondents in the other regions and that they visit these acquaintances most often, add further to this image.

An analysis of sectoral differences showed that wholesale companies feel significantly more at home in both the living and the business cultures of the neighbouring country. This corresponds with the fact that respondents in the wholesale sector have more personal contacts in the neighbouring country than respondents in the other two sectors (see I-a). There are no differences according to the type of relationship.

I-g. Spatial identity

Entrepreneurs were expected to have a strong spatial affective bond, a spatial identity. All entrepreneurs were asked to indicate how strongly they felt related to their own region, province and country, and to other regions and countries. This connectedness is a good indicator for geographical identity. The assumption was that the identification with an area decreases as the area gets larger, the so-called *distance effect* of spatial identity (see chapter 2, section 2.4.6 and chapter 4, II-3). In addition to the distance effect, the *neighbour effect* (*idem*) is distinguished. It assumes that the spatial identification with the neighbouring country/region is smaller than the identification with international space in general.

In chapter 2 (section 2.4.6), the theoretical hierarchy within the human shell-like 'spatial identity' was discussed. In the survey the following levels were distinguished (see figure 7.1): (1) Regional: Zeeland Fleming/Zeelander; (2) Inhabitant of border region; (3) National: Dutchman/Fleming/Belgian; (4) European; (5) World citizen.

Figure 7.1 - The hierarchy of spatial identity

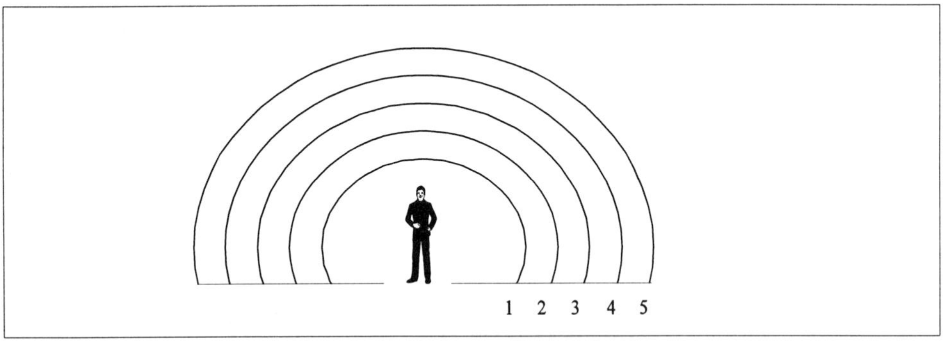

In the survey, the ranking order of these levels was determined for the respondents through the question: 'I feel that I am ... (see the questionnaire, appendix 1). The table below indicates how the diagram should be interpreted for the respondents in the three regions (the average values on the scale range from 1 = 'strongly connected with' to 7 = 'very little connected with', and are bracketed). The scale was interpreted as an interval scale, allowing for comparison of average values (table 7.6).

Table 7.6 - Spatial identity for the respondents in the three research areas

Level	Zeeland Flanders	Central and North Zeeland	Gent/Eeklo
1.	Zeeland Fleming (6.11)	Dutchman (6.52)	Fleming (6.26)
2.	Dutchman (5.38)	Zeelander (5.72)	Belgian (5.79)
3.	Zeelander (5.03)	European (4.52)	European (5.40)
4.	Border region inhabitant (4.44)	World citizen (4.18)	World citizen (4.68)
5.	European (4.43)	Zeeland Fleming (1.94)	Border region inhabitant (2.96)
6.	World citizen (3.78)	Border region inhabitant (1.79)	Zeeland Fleming (1.87)
7.	Fleming (3.58)	Fleming (1.66)	Zeelander (1.69)
8.	Belgian (2.17)	Belgian (1.40)	Dutchman (1.67)

In general, it was found that there are very strong regional differences for identity. Spatial identity is, as expected, a theme about which entrepreneurs think differently according to the region in which they work.

Furthermore, a hierarchical scale can indeed be constructed according to the assumptions, reflecting a gradation of spatial identity, which ranges from regional via national and European to global. *The distance effect* does apply for spatial identity. The hierarchy ranges from regional, via national, to international.

But at the same time, as expected, *the neighbour effect* also operates. Moreover, it was found that entrepreneurs, in the transition from national to international, regard themselves as Europeans or world citizens rather than as connected with the neighbouring country. And this holds true for all entrepreneurs, regardless of their regional background. It must be assumed that a unity of several foreign countries is perceived as less of a threat to the individual's nationality, and is therefore more attractive in terms of identification than the 'neighbouring country'. Note, that for the respondents in Central and North Zeeland, the neighbour effect operates even on a national level. Entrepreneurs in Central and North Zeeland feel more connected to the European or global level, than to Zeeland Flanders.

Moreover, all entrepreneurs have a higher level of identification with the border region than with the neighbouring country. The border-regional identity therefore stands exactly at the midpoint between the identification with the home country and the identification with the neighbouring country, as expected (see chapter 2). This effect is strongest for Zeeland Flanders. Of all respondents, they feel the strongest connection with the classification 'inhabitant of a border region', even over and above the feeling that they are Europeans or world citizens. This contrasts with Central and North Zeeland and Gent/Eeklo, whose respondents feel more connected with Europe or the world than with the border region in which they live.

It is likely that the connotation 'border region inhabitant' involves two aspects: one feels that one is an inhabitant of the border region because of the direct proximity of the border on the one hand, and because of the nationally peripheral situation of the region on the other. For this reason, the respondents from Zeeland Flanders feel more connected with the denomination 'inhabitant of the border region'; the region is nationally peripheral and lies in close proximity of the border.

The respondents in Central and North Zeeland feel less strongly connected with the border region than those in Gent/Eeklo, which is probably caused by the immediate proximity of the border in the case of Gent/Eeklo.

This could also explain why entrepreneurs in Central and North Zeeland feel more like Dutchmen than like Zeelanders in comparison with the entrepreneurs in Zeeland Flanders. Reversely, entrepreneurs in Zeeland Flanders feel a stronger relation with the term 'Fleming' and 'Belgian' than their Central and North Zeeland neighbours.

Entrepreneurs in Gent/Eeklo do not associate themselves with a peripheral region, which is confirmed by their association with the European and global identity. They feel significantly more European than the respondents in the Dutch regions and more like world citizens than the entrepreneurs in Zeeland Flanders.

I-h. The 'national border evaluation' between the Netherlands and Belgium

The next analysis concerns how the entrepreneurs regard the state border itself (cf. Leimgruber, 1987, 1991; Brücher and Riedel, 1992; Riedel, 1994). A total of ten properties have been included in the questionnaire (see appendix 1), varying from the state border is 'useless' as against 'useful' to 'the state border acts as a division' as against 'the state border acts as a link'. All respondents could indicate their opinion on seven-point Likert scales. Their evaluations were found to diverge significantly from the point of complete indifference, the scales 'cost-increasing', 'restrictive' and 'noticeable' excluded. Thus, entrepreneurs are certainly not indifferent to the state border's existence. Figure 7.2 indicates whether any regional differences were observed. The empty spaces between the curves in the figure reflect the divergences in the opinions of the respondents of the three regions.

Figure 7.2 - Border evaluations

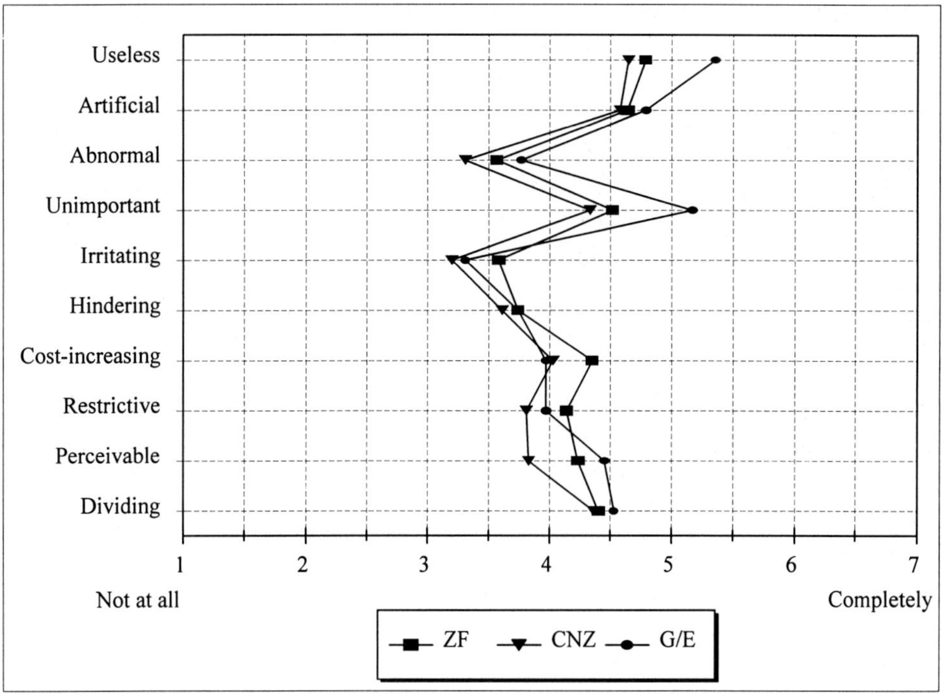

The respondents appear to agree considerably in their evaluations. The significant regional differences concern the judgements 'useless', 'unimportant', and 'noticeable'. Entrepreneurs in Gent/Eeklo regard the border as significantly more useless, unimportant, and at the same time more 'noticeable' than the entrepreneurs in Central and North Zeeland, and significantly more useless than those in Zeeland Flanders. This would seem to indicate that the respondents in Gent/Eeklo are more desirous to broaden their identification than the respondents in the two Dutch regions, who wish to limit their identification to the national level. The result tallies with the earlier observation that the respondents in Gent/Eeklo feel significantly more solidarity with the European and global level than the Dutch regions.

Cognition space

I-i. Physical distance versus cognitive distance

The factual *travelling distance* in minutes at the outset of the relationship between the two partners was also analysed. Analysis of the evolution process of the most important economic relation in the neighbouring country shows that the average travelling time to that relation was approximately 40 minutes for companies in Zeeland Flanders, 69 minutes for companies in Central and North Zeeland, and 105 minutes for companies in Gent/Eeklo. Companies in Zeeland

Flanders therefore have the shortest travelling times to the office/company of their most important relation in the neighbouring country. In comparison with Central and North Zeeland, this is not surprising, as companies in Zeeland Flanders tend to be closer to the border in the first place. It is more remarkable that the companies in Gent/Eeklo, on average, have significant longer travelling times than the companies in Zeeland Flanders. These findings confirm earlier assumptions that the companies in Zeeland Flanders, in their connections with the neighbouring country, focus on relationships in Gent/Eeklo. The companies in Gent/Eeklo, to the contrary, have relations in the rest of the Netherlands as well as relations in Zeeland Flanders. Companies in Gent/Eeklo also tend to search significantly further away than Central and North Zeeland. A reasonably long travelling time is apparently no hindrance for the companies in Gent/Eeklo to develop important economic relationships in the Netherlands.

Next, the *estimation* of physical distance is analysed. If the distance is overestimated, the city is perceived, by the respondents, as farther away than it really is. If it is underestimated, the city is perceived as closer than it really is (see chapter 2 and 4). The idea was that, if a situation of a closely interwoven international economy exists, estimates of the distance to cities in the neighbouring country will not be overestimated, but will rather be estimated accurately or even underestimated. The question was put to all respondents. Table 7.7 reflects the average estimates by respondents in the research areas of the distance to various cities in Belgium and the Netherlands.

Table 7.7 - Over- or underestimation of distances in kilometres

Distance to:	Zeeland Flanders	Central and North Zeeland	Gent/Eeklo
Rotterdam	++	+	+++
Breda	+	0	-
Terneuzen	n/a	++++	- - - - -
Middelburg	++++	n/a	+++++
Gent	++	++++	n/a
Brugge	+	+++++	+
Antwerp	++	-	- -

n/a stands for ‘not applicable’

Legend:

++++++	Overestimation > 100%	- - - - - -	Underestimation >100%
+++++	Overestimation > 50%	- - - - -	Underestimation > 50%
++++	Overestimation > 25%	- - - -	Underestimation > 25%
+++	Overestimation >10%	- - -	Underestimation >10%
++	Overestimation >5%	- -	Underestimation >5%
+	Overestimation > 0%	-	Underestimation >0%
0	Correct estimation		

The table allows for the following deductions. On average, respondents in Zeeland Flanders overestimate the distance to cities in the home and foreign countries. Both the home and foreign countries are perceived as 'far away'. The distance to Middelburg is overestimated most of all (average +37.7%). Middelburg is, in the perception of the respondents in Zeeland Flanders, farther away than it really is. This is characteristic. A likely explanation seems to be the isolated position of Zeeland Flanders in comparison to Central and North Zeeland. The region is situated at the southwest extremity of the Netherlands, and moreover lacks a permanent connection with the rest of Zeeland. Overland transport to the Netherlands can only be done through Belgium. The directly neighbouring region can only be reached per boat, or one must take a roundabout route through Belgium. This strengthens the perception of distance.

Respondents in Central and North Zeeland also overestimate the distance to Terneuzen, although slightly less. Apparently, Terneuzen and Middelburg were found to be far apart from a cognitive point of view. Respondents in Central and North Zeeland also overestimate the distance to Gent and Brugge. The distance to Brugge is, significantly, estimated least correctly by the respondents in this region. This clearly links up with their average number of economic relations with Gent/Eeklo, which, as we have seen earlier, is relatively low. The estimates of the distance to Antwerp, Breda and Rotterdam, however, are very accurate on average. Apparently, the respondents in Central and North Zeeland are more familiar with these cities.

The respondents in Gent/Eeklo largely underestimated the distance to Terneuzen. Terneuzen is perceived as nearby. It is remarkable that the respondents in Central and North Zeeland tend to overestimate the distance to Terneuzen more than those in Gent/Eeklo. Furthermore, the respondents in Gent/Eeklo overestimate the distance to cities such as Rotterdam and Middelburg. Of all three regions, the estimation to these cities of respondents in Gent/Eeklo is the highest. They perceive Rotterdam and Middelburg as being far away. They perceive Antwerp to be closer by than it really is; the distance to Brugge they estimate fairly accurately. Their estimation of the distance to Breda, which they underestimate slightly, is equally characteristic. This appears to indicate familiarity with the geographical position of Breda.

I-j. Cognitive map of the border

A question in the survey asked the respondents to sketch the state border between the Netherlands and Belgium on a blind map of the two countries. So as to ensure that the map gave a perfectly true picture of reality, a graphics programme containing satellite photographs of countries was used (Mapinfo 4.1 for Windows 3.11). The respondents had to draw the border on the blind map (cf. Riedel, 1994). Despite the unusual character of the question, it was answered relatively often. In total, 380 of the 470 respondents drew a border of some sorts.

In the subsequent analysis, the line was divided into various points indicating the direction of the Dutch-Belgian state border. The average values for the border points were then compared with the objective values, which enabled a statistic analysis of the deviations for the most important points on the border. It was found that for all points, the deviation between the estimations of the three regions and the real values diverged significantly from the zero point. Respondents in all three regions therefore drew a border line that deviates significantly from the real border. It is interesting to examine the course of these deviations. Figure 7.3 represents the average border lines as drawn by the respondents in each of the three research regions (ZF=Zeeland Flanders, CNZ=Central and North Zeeland, G/E=Gent/Eeklo).

It is noteworthy that the border lines drawn by the respondents in the two Dutch regions and the border drawn by the Belgian respondents in Gent/Eeklo are significantly different.

Respondents in Gent/Eeklo estimate the border in the region Zeeland Flanders far away. To their perception, therefore, Zeeland Flanders is, geographically, a part of Belgium. The average Zeeland entrepreneur is more accurate in drawing the border here. The border of the rest of the south of the Netherlands and Flanders in Belgium is drawn beneath the factual border by entrepreneurs in Gent/Eeklo; they think it is part of the Netherlands. They are generally unfamiliar with the extra protuberance in the border line caused by Limburg, while the Dutch respondents tend to draw some sort of protuberance representing Limburg. Thus, while the Dutch respondents of Zeeland include Limburg (however inaccurately) in their cognitive map of the borderline between the Netherlands and Belgium, it is absent in the map as drawn by the Belgian respondents. A remarkable result, of which the cause is not quite clear. It might be considered characteristic that the two Dutch regions that had rather strong anti-Dutch feelings when they became part of the Netherlands at the split up between the Netherlands and Belgium in 1839 and are generally assumed to still have a strong affinity with Belgium, i.e. Limburg and Zeeland Flanders, are annexed to Belgium in the maps drawn by Belgian entrepreneurs.

Figure 7.3 - The cognitive map of the border

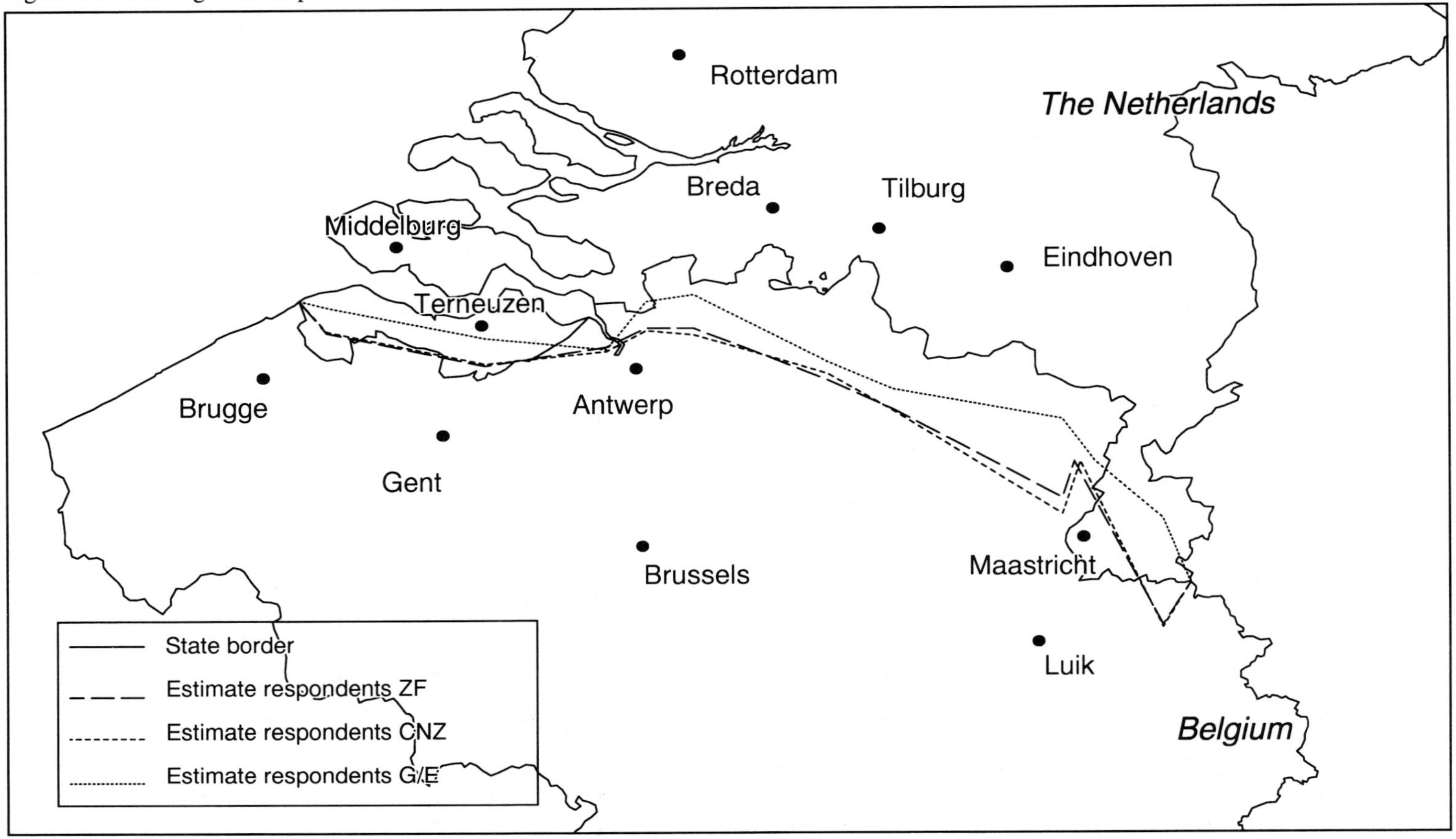

Entrepreneurs from Zeeland Flanders and Central and North Zeeland differ significantly on many points in their estimations. The respondents from both these regions draw the border between Zeeland and Belgium similarly, but the line between the remainder of the south of the Netherlands and Belgium displays strong differences. The respondents from Zeeland Flanders estimate it more accurately than respondents from Central and North Zeeland. The respondents from Central and North Zeeland estimate the line farther away than the respondents from Zeeland Flanders. Apparently, the respondents from Central and North Zeeland think that the Netherlands are bigger and Belgium is smaller than the respondents from Zeeland Flanders.

II Attraction

I will now discuss the results of the determinants in the next stage of the INTERFACE model, the attraction stage. The first acquaintance and meetings often determine whether or not the contact evolves to an economic relationship. In the attraction stage, the point is to analyse why two entrepreneurs decide to enter into an economic relationship. The respondents with one or more cross-border economic relationships were asked to explain the reasons for the attraction of their partner in the neighbouring country. A ranking order of factors involved can be made, which is indicated in table 7.8 through the bracketed figures.

Table 7.8 - Ranking order of attraction factors, per region

	ZF	CNZ	G/E	Total
His business contacts and relations	3.77(9)	3.70(9)	4.48(3)	3.95(8)
You got along well	4.31(6)	4.47(4)	4.00(8)	4.27(5)
His company already had relationships with other companies	3.64(10)	4.06(7)	4.07(7)	3.89(9)
He seemed someone to count on	4.53(4)	4.79(2)	4.23(4)	4.53(3)
Short travelling distance	4.76(2)	3.88(8)	3.00(10)	4.00(7)
Recognition of business notions	4.66(3)	4.36(5)	4.07(6)	4.40(4)
The relation provided a better market position	4.86(1)	4.87(1)	5.10(1)	4.93(1)
The low price	2.93(12)	2.97(11)	2.93(11)	2.94(11)
The high quality	4.48(5)	4.53(3)	4.62(2)	4.54(2)
His specific material resources	3.83(8)	3.27(10)	3.38(9)	3.53(10)
He had differing and interesting business notions	3.25(11)	2.57(12)	2.38(12)	2.79(12)
He provided access to the market	4.05(7)	4.28(6)	4.16(5)	4.15(6)

The most important attraction factor for all respondents was an improvement in their market position, which indicates a fundamental characteristic of all enterprise: the search for profits. The attraction of another is determined principally by a potential improvement of the market position through the transaction with the other. Another meaningful point is that the quality of resources and personal 'guarantee' (dependability) are mentioned as very important factors of attraction. The price and specificity of resources on the other hand, are of relatively small importance, as well as the factor involving 'differing but interesting business notions'. The recognition of the other's ideas is apparently considered more important.

The only significant regional difference concerned the short travelling distance. Respondents in Zeeland Flanders regarded this factor as significantly more important than the respondents in the other two regions. The only significant difference associated with the type of relationship was that companies with a control relationship in the neighbouring country, more than companies with a supply relationship, consider it important that the partner entertains relationships with other companies. The analysis of sectoral differences indicated that the wholesale sector was more concerned about the reputation and dependability of the partner than the industrial sector.

III Interaction

If, in the stage of acquaintance, a certain degree of positive attraction between the two entrepreneurs emerged and the intention to begin an economic relationship still exists, the interaction stage begins. Interaction may lead to working agreements, which may or may not be officially enforced by means of a written contract. The questionnaire contained some six questions concerning the interaction process, which have been put to all companies with one or more economic relations in the neighbouring country.

It was found that the respondents considered that the interaction process is characterised by smooth communication and an informal and open atmosphere. One knows fairly well what to expect from the other. Few or no investments in knowledge or human and material resources or adaptations to the product/production process were required of them to realise the relationship. Disadvantageous proposals were, in fact, practically not made, although this point was characterised by a significant difference according to the type of relationship. In comparison to outsourcing relationships, control relationships were more often attended by disadvantageous proposals from the other party. This, of course, seems logical, as this type of relationship more often involves the question of the balance of power than the outsourcing relationship, in which the question of power is usually more evident.

Furthermore, the wholesale and industry sectors described the atmosphere surrounding the interaction process significantly more often as informal and open, and as involving smooth communication, than construction companies. In the latter sector, cross-border interaction was more difficult. In comparison to industrial companies, construction companies also stated more often that the working agreements required them to make investments in manpower / resources / knowledge, a fact also reported by respondents with a control relationship in the neighbouring country. They clearly stated that they had to invest more, on average, in their own company to bring about the transaction. This is quite adequately explained by the fact that control relationships always have a more profound impact upon the essence of a company than the other types of relationships distinguished in the survey. Regional differences were not found here.

IV Transaction

Almost 63% of the agreements with the important economic relations in the neighbouring country are not ratified by means of a contract, meaning that the agreements are most often verbal. No regional or sectoral differences were found in this respect, although the type of relationship did cause some difference. As control relationships are the most far-reaching type of relationship, it is logical that this type is ratified more often through a contract.

V Relationship

The next stage in the INTERFACE model is the actual entering into a bilateral cross-border economic relationship. In chapter 6, I have already discussed the frequency, number, and regional and typical spread of economic relationships extensively. The most important results are recapitulated here. With regard to the having or not having of one or more relationships in the neighbouring country, it was found that in the region of Zeeland Flanders, 42.2% of the responding companies have one or more relations in the neighbouring country. In Central and North Zeeland, this percentage totals 21%, and the regions Gent/Eeklo top the list with an average of 44.4% of companies with one or more economic relations in the neighbouring country. In total, an absolute number of 316 companies (67.2%) in the response population have no relationship whatsoever in the neighbouring country as against 154 (32.8%) with a relationship. The industrial sector has by far the most frequent 'one or more economic relations in the neighbouring country' (44.4%), against 36.7% of the wholesale companies and 17.5% of the construction firms.

The number of relationships in the home country is, on average, 4.6 times higher than in the neighbouring country and, on average, 23 times higher than in the directly neighbouring region of the neighbouring country. Companies in Zeeland Flanders and Gent/Eeklo, on average, have significantly more relations in the neighbouring country than those in Central and North Zeeland. The industrial sector was found to have significantly more relationships than the wholesale sector, which in turn has more than the construction sector.

Finally, the companies with control relationships in the neighbouring country have significantly more relations in the neighbouring country than the companies with production process, service, or sales market relationships. This means that companies with control relationships are more closely interwoven economically than companies with other types of relationships.

VI Success

As indicated in chapter 4, it is impossible to examine the development process of all relationships the responding companies may have. This is why I chose to let the companies select that relationship which they considered most important. The questionnaire indicated what exactly should be considered important. The importance of the relationship was measured in terms of the intensity of the relationship, that is to say, the degree to which it involves the essence of the company. A joint venture has a more profound impact than a relationship with a cleaning company. The import of the relationship is not necessarily reflected in its influence upon the company's turnover. The choice of this definition was determined by the delimitation of the research (see chapter 1): the study of the development process and success factors of economic relationships between two *different* companies in two *different* countries. It is not sought, therefore, to establish which economic relationships have the greatest economic interest for a company. A control relationship, such as a joint venture or a merger, is the most far-reaching form of co-operation because it is the most intensive form of co-operation. Next in line is the production process relationship, which involves a physical exchange in terms of commodities to complete the product. Then comes the service relationship, involving consultancy or the outsourcing of a certain supportive service, and finally the sales relationship, which involves the representation or promotion of the products by another company. In short, the following ranking order was maintained (see the questionnaire, appendix 1):

1. Control relationship
2. Production process relationship
3. Service relationship
4. Sales market relationship

In total, the respondents selected 75 production process relationships (53 supply and 22 outsourcing relationships), 7 service relationships, and 30 sales market relationships in the neighbouring country.

Furthermore, 31 control relationships were selected. As this study concerns two *different* enterprises entering into a relationship, 'daughters' (0% control) and 'mothers' (100% control) have not been included in the analysis of the success of the relationships. After deduction of these cases and the cases in which the degree of control was unclear ('missing values'), 21 control relationships were included in the analysis.

Most often selected form of cross-border relationships

The most often selected type of the most important cross border economic relationship of the company barely differs for the three regions. Most of the companies in Zeeland Flanders with an economic relation in the neighbouring country were found to have entered into a supply relationship - especially the supply of waste and raw materials or (semi)manufactures to another company. Companies in Central and North Zeeland and Gent/Eeklo also relatively often selected a representative - a person acting as intermediary in the delivery of goods - as their most important economic relation in the neighbouring country. Thus, the economic transaction most often selected as a company's most important relationship is characterised as a more than one-off delivery of commodities, with or without the intervention of an agent, to a partner in the neighbouring country.

Sector of the most important cross-border relationship

Another aspect that was examined touched upon the sector in which the economic partner functioned. This involved a comparison of the sectors to which the responding company and the partner's company in the neighbouring country belong. Table 7.9 outlines the results.

Table 7.9 - Sector types

	Sector type of the respondent			
Sector type of partner	Industry	Construction	Wholesale	Total
Industry	44.8%	27.3%	25.5%	34.6%
Construction	10.3%	36.4%	6.4%	13.4%
Trade, hotel and catering industry	22.4%	9.1%	42.6%	27.6%
Transport, storage, and communication	5.2%	0%	4.3%	3.9%
Banking, insurance, professional servicing	6.9%	22.7%	10.6%	11.0%
Other	10.3%	4.5%	10.6%	9.4%
Total	n=58	n=22	n=47	n=127 (100%)

n=absolute number

It was found that companies entering into an economic relationship often belong to the same sector. The most important economic relation industrial companies have in the neighbouring country is most often an industrial company, construction companies often team up with industrial or construction companies, and wholesale companies often associate with trade companies.

Region of the most important economic relation

Regional analysis shows that companies in Zeeland Flanders have most of their most important economic relations in Gent/Eeklo. Most of the companies in Central and North Zeeland have their most important cross-border economic relation in Gent/Eeklo as well, but the Antwerp district also figures high in the list. Companies in Gent/Eeklo do not seem to have a preferred region in the Netherlands, Central and North Zeeland being the only region they hardly ever mention.

Success of the most important economic relationship

On average, the success of the most important cross-border economic relationship is described by the respondents as reasonable to very reasonable. Furthermore, the intensity of the co-operation has increased slightly since the transactions were initiated. This holds true for all regions and all types of relationships, but does not apply for all sectors evenly. Construction firms are the great exception, as they judge the success of their most important economic relationship significantly lower than the industrial and wholesale companies. The co-operation's intensity has increased but little. It appears once again that the companies in the construction sector experience more problems in developing their cross-border economic relationships.

7.3 Towards a verification of the hypotheses and an explanation of the results

In the previous section, I have *described* the development process of cross-border economic relationships for companies in the three research regions, thus providing an inventory of facts in the formation process of cross-border economic relationships for enterprises in border regions. In the precedent chapter, I already demonstrated the regional differences with regard to the factual sales and economic relationship pattern across the state border between Belgium and the Netherlands. In the present section, I will seek to *explain* the observed patterns of the *frequency* and *number* of economic cross-border relationships, and to elucidate the *success* of the economic cross-border relationships that were formed. To this end, the hypotheses formulated for the multi-variate models in chapter 4 will be verified (see section 4.3). Appendix 3 contains the model's determinants that were analysed by means of factor analyses. The items that emerged from these factor analyses will be used in the three multivariate analyses that follow (Hair *et al.*, 1995). All the analyses have been checked on multicollinearity.

7.3.1 An economic relationship in the neighbouring country: Yes or No

In the first place, I have sought to answer the following question:

> *Which factors may allow for a significant distinction to be made between the groups of companies with and the group of companies without one or more economic relations in the neighbouring country?*

To solve this question, the methodology of discriminant analysis was used. This method explicitly distinguishes between the possession or lack of a group characteristic. The discriminant analysis was executed with the aid of an additive dummy regression approach (ENTER method) (see Tacq, 1992). As indicated in chapter 4 (see section 4.3), the distinction between having or not having economic relationships in the neighbouring country, is made on the basis of variables belonging to *affective space* (*i.e.* mental distance and evaluation of the state border) and *control variables* (*i.e.* age, size, cross-border workers, export rate, number of economic relations in the home country, sector type).

In the first place, I verified whether it was possible to construct the distinction between the groups of companies with and without cross-border economic relations in a significant manner by means of this proposed global model. I found that this was possible ($F(12,436) = 15.68$, $p < 0.01$, adjusted R square $= 0.28$).

Subsequently, the contributions of the separate characteristics were weighted by means of univariate tests. Such tests verify whether there is a significant difference in the average level of the variable between the companies with and without economic relationships in the neighbouring country.

The table below presents the results. The symbol before the column 'Coefficients' shows whether the contribution is positive or negative (see table 7.10). The column 'Significance' in the table below shows whether the characteristic contributes significantly to the distinction of having or not having one or more economic relationships in the neighbouring country.

Table 7.10 - The determinants of the difference between having and not having one or more economic relationships in the neighbouring country

Independent variables:	Dependent variable: Having or not having one or more economic relations in the neighbouring country	
	Coefficients (1)	Significance (2)
Mental distance (3): The expected negative effect of the relationship	-0.20	0.00***
Mental distance: The expected discrepancy in business conventions in the relationship	-0.22	0.00***
Mental distance: The stringency of the financial-economic conditions of the relationship	-0.08	0.00***
Evaluation of the state border (4): The state border is a barrier	-0.03	0.47 n/s
Evaluation of the state border: The state border is irrelevant	0.13	0.01**
Age of the enterprise in years	-0.04	0.44 n/s
Number of employees	0.09	0.06*
Proportion of cross-border workers in %	0.09	0.06*
Proportion of sales in neighbouring country in %	0.35	0.00***
The number of economic relationships in the home country	0.30	0.00***
Dummy Industrial sector	0.16	0.01**
Dummy Construction sector	-0.22	0.00***

(1) This expresses the direction (positive/negative) and the force of the impact (Beta)
(2) *** level of significance < 1%; ** level of significance < 5%; * level of significance < 10%; N/S=Not significant
(3) See appendix 3 for the three dimensions of mental distance
(4) Idem for the two dimensions of state border evaluation

The model is valid for all companies, regardless of their regional background. The table shows on the basis of which characteristics a significant distinction can be made between the companies with and the companies without one or more economic relationships in the neighbouring country. The typical company with one or more cross-border economic relationships:
- is larger
- has, on average, a greater number of cross-border employees
- on average exports more to the neighbouring country
- on average has a greater number of economic relationships in the home country
- is more often an industrial company
- is less often a construction company

The typical entrepreneur of the company with one or more economic relations in the neighbouring country:
- expects a more positive effect to emerge from the relationship with the company in the neighbouring country than the entrepreneur without cross-border economic relationship(s)
- expects a smaller discrepancy in business conventions than the company without relation(s)
- is less stringent in his/her financial-economic conditions than the company without relation(s)
- regards the state border more often as irrelevant than the entrepreneur of the company without relation(s) in the neighbouring country

The analysis shows clearly that the typical company *with* one or more cross-border economic relations is, on average, further developed than the typical company *without* cross-border economic relations. This result coincides with our previous findings (Dagevos *et al.*, 1992). The present study demonstrates yet another important aspect. The typical entrepreneur belonging to a firm with one or more cross-border relations has a smaller *mental distance* to the neighbouring country. This last result demonstrates that the perception and attitude of entrepreneurs play a crucial role in the internationalisation process. That is an important observation, suggesting that companies without relations in the neighbouring country are more reluctant to initiate them, that they tend to hang back.

7.3.2 Determinants of the number of economic relationships in the neighbouring country

The second analysis involves an investigation of the factors that play a crucial role in determining the *number* of economic relationships in the neighbouring country. The question is therefore:

> *What determines, for the typical enterprise in one of the three regions, the number of cross-border economic relationships?*

This allows a prediction of the degree to which what types of companies will be economically interwoven with companies in the neighbouring country.

So as to gain a first insight into the connection between the number of economic relations in the neighbouring country and the independent variables, first the bivariate correlations will be inventoried and analysed before attempting to answer the question. Table 7.11 sums up the correlations.

Table 7.11 - The bivariate correlations between the independent variables and the number of economic relations in the neighbouring country(3)

Independent variables:	Dependent variable: The number of cross-border economic relations in the neighbouring country	
	Coefficient (1)	Significance (2)
Number of professional acquaintances in the neighbouring country	0.19	0.02 **
Number of personal acquaintances in the neighbouring country	0.19	0.02 **
Type of relationship preference: networking	0.05	0.17 n/s
Type of relationship preference: bold and well-informed	0.01	0.38 n/s
Type of relationship preference: regionally/nationally bounded	-0.05	0.16 n/s
Feeling at home in the culture of the neighbouring country	0.08	0.05*
Mental distance: The expected negative effect of the relationship	-0.12	0.01**
Mental distance: The expected discrepancy in business conventions in the relationship	-0.14	0.00***
Mental distance: The stringency of the financial-economic conditions of the relationship	-0.08	0.05*
Evaluation of the state border (4): The state border is a barrier	0.00	0.50 n/s
Evaluation of the state border: The state border is irrelevant	0.12	0.00***
Zeeland Flanders: Identification(4) with the own periphery and with the neighbouring region and country	0.08	0.15 n/s
Zeeland Flanders: International/national identity	0.01	0.46 n/s
Zeeland Flanders: Zeeland identity	-0.30	0.00***
Central and North Zeeland: Identification with the own periphery and with the neighbouring region and country	-0.05	0.26 n/s
Central and North Zeeland: International identity	0.21	0.00***
Central and North Zeeland: National identity	-0.23	0.00***
Gent/Eeklo: Identification with the own periphery and with the neighbouring region and country	0.10	0.18 n/s
Gent/Eeklo: International identity	-0.12	0.24 n/s
Gent/Eeklo: National identity	-0.12	0.24 n/s

(1) This expresses the direction (positive/negative) and the force of the influence (Beta)
(2) *** level of significance < 1%; ** level of significance < 5%; * level of significance < 10%; N/S= not significant
(3) As the variables 'cognitive distance' and 'cognitive map of the border' demand a lot of space - which would have affected the clarity of the table - these have not been incorporated in the table. The results will be discussed below
(4) See appendix 3 for the dimensions of regional identity for the three regions

It was found that a great number of the variables involved in the analysis correlate significantly with the variable 'number of economic relations in the neighbouring country'. In general, however, correlation does not imply causality. The correlation analysis makes it possible to determine the direction and force of the connection between a pair of variables. The various results of the correlation analyses are discussed below.

The number of economic relations in the home country, informal contact pattern, and feeling at home in the culture of the neighbouring country

In section 7.2 (I-a), I have shown that the average respondent has fewer business and personal acquaintances in the directly neighbouring country than in the home country. The spatial distribution of the entrepreneurs' informal embeddedness was found to be strongly discontinuous along the state border. The matter at hand then is: Is it possible to state that the entrepreneurs with more contacts in the neighbouring country also have more relations in the neighbouring country?

In the analyses a strong positive, significant connection was found to exist between the number of professional acquaintances and the number of economic relations in the neighbouring country (see table 7.11). In addition, a positive and significant connection was discovered between the number of personal acquaintances and the number of economic relations in the neighbouring country. These analyses indeed lead one to conclude that a great number of personal and professional contacts goes together with a great number of economic relations.

In section 7.2 (I-c), it has been ascertained that approximately half of the entrepreneurs use their personal and professional acquaintances to enter into a cross-border economic contact/ relationship. But it may also be assumed that the contacts, especially those in the neighbouring country, can be important indirectly. The idea is that a great number of contacts is likely to stimulate the entrepreneur's familiarity with the foreign environment and culture, causing the neighbouring country to be 'less far away' in perception. Thus, the expectation is that having social and business contacts in the neighbouring country runs parallel to a greater feeling of being at home in the neighbouring country and a greater number of economic relations in the neighbouring country.

Analysis confirms this expectation. Entrepreneurs with many personal contacts in the neighbouring country also feel more at home there. The same connection exists between the visiting frequency of personal and business contacts and feeling at home in the neighbouring country. Finally, a significant positive correlation was found between feeling at home in the culture of the neighbouring country and the number of economic relationships in the neighbouring country. These are important results. I have already mentioned the observation that respondents in Zeeland Flanders feel most at home in the neighbouring country. These correlation analyses have provided greater clarity with regard to a possible explanation of this observation. It has now become plausible that, partly because Zeeland Flemings have the greatest number of personal and professional acquaintances in the neighbouring country, visit these most often, and feel most at home in the neighbouring country, they have the greatest number of economic relationships in the neighbouring country (most notably in Gent/Eeklo). The reverse may also occur, as correlation does not imply causality - it is because the respondents have, on average, many economic relations in the neighbouring country that they also have relatively more informal contacts, which makes them feel at home there. The three variables 'feeling at home in the neighbouring country's culture', 'informal embeddedness in the neighbouring country', and 'the number of economic relations in the neighbouring country' are mutually highly influential.

The number of economic relations and relationship preference

The results of the correlation analysis, as shown in table 7.11, demonstrate that the strategic variable 'relationship preference' does not influence the number of economic relations in the neighbouring country directly. It may be said that the relationship preference is relatively unimportant. It has no significant impact upon the number of economic relationships in the neighbouring country. Other explanatory factors should be regarded as far more important.
Further analysis demonstrated that a significantly positive correlation was found to exist between 'searching boldly and in a well-informed manner' and the number of professional and personal contacts in the neighbouring country. Moreover, the respondents displaying this kind of relationship preference and the respondents characterising themselves as 'networkers' feel significantly better at home in the neighbouring country. Thus, any connection between the relationship preference and the number of economic relationships appears to be no more than indirect.

The number of economic relations in the neighbouring country and mental distance

Estimates with regard to the differences in having economic relationships in the home country and the neighbouring country do not mean that these differences are pressure points or problems in reality. In order to analyse whether they are, it is necessary to examine how companies react or act in the face of the differences they perceive. The consequences these perceived differences have can be found in the maintenance or absence of economic relationships. The companies who have economic relationships will perceive the differences as less acute, and assign less value to them, than those who do not have economic relationships. The analysis of companies with and without relationships did indeed justify this assumption (see section 7.3.1). In looking at the correlation with the number of relations in the neighbouring country, as shown in table 7.11, the above observations were confirmed. It was found that:

- there exists a significant negative correlation between the expected discrepancy in business conventions and the number of economic relations in the neighbouring country. Thus, the greater the number of economic relations in the neighbouring country, the smaller the expected discrepancy, and vice versa.
- there exists a significant negative correlation between the expected negative effect of an economic relationship in the neighbouring country and the number of economic relationships in the neighbouring country. Companies with more relations have greater trust in the success of their relationships, and the other way around.

• there exists a significant negative correlation between the stringency of the financial-economic conditions set on the relationship in the neighbouring country and the number of economic relationships in the neighbouring country.

In short, the *mental distance* with regard to initiating economic relationships in the neighbouring country displays a negative correlation with having economic relationships in the neighbouring country and their number.

The number of economic relations and the evaluation of the state border

The expectation voiced in chapter 4 was that entrepreneurs who do not see the state border as a barrier and regard it as irrelevant, are more likely to enter into economic relationships. Above, I already observed that companies with economic relations regard the border as significantly more irrelevant than companies without them. The same holds true for the number of economic relations. A strong positive correlation was discovered between the number of economic relations in the neighbouring country and the perceived irrelevance of the border. The perception of the border as a barrier matters little or not at all in this context.

Both analyses therefore showed that companies who are strongly oriented towards foreign countries tend to look differently at an abstract phenomenon such as the state border. They regard the border not more or less as a barrier, but as more irrelevant than companies who are not internationally oriented. The companies without economic relations clearly assigned greater value to the border. This seems to be related to the idea that the border represents an identity value. The perception of the border seems to be expressed mainly through the protective value that is assigned to it, a value that can be linked back to the 'We-Them' relationship between the two countries. On the micro level, this seems to express itself mainly through the mental distance factor as described above.

A more detailed analysis of the connection between mental distance and the perception of the border showed that such a connection does indeed exist. A strong degree of mental distance to the neighbouring country was found to go together with the border's perception as a barrier, but especially with the border's relevance. Thus, respondents without cross-border economic relations attach great importance to the border. It would seem that the border, on the one hand, is accused of being a barrier, but on the other hand offers protection against undesired influences from the outside, which is considered important. This paradoxical combination is characteristic of the respondents with a great mental distance to economic relationships in the neighbouring country.

The number of economic relationships in the neighbouring country and spatial identity

In general, it may be said that all companies in the three regions whose entrepreneurs experience a great spatial affinity with the neighbouring country have more cross-border economic relationships. Companies whose entrepreneurs feel strongly connected with the home region or country have fewer cross-border economic relationships. A strong geographical affinity with an area thus goes together with a great number of economic relationships in that area. For the most part, these general conclusions are based on indicative correlations (significance level < 10%). The following significant results (significance level < 5%) have been found. There exists a significant negative correlation between the respondents in Zeeland Flanders with a strong Zeeland identity and the number of economic relations in the neighbouring country. A significant positive correlation exists moreover between the respondents in Central and North Zeeland with a more strongly international identity and the number of economic relations in the neighbouring country, and a significant negative correlation emerged between the respondents in Central and North Zeeland with a strong national identity and the number of economic relations in the neighbouring country.

The number of economic relations in the neighbouring country and cognitive distance
To ensure the clarity of table 7.11, the results for the correlations between regional estimates by the respondents and the number of economic relationships have not been included. There are too many answer categories. The hypothesis as formulated above (see chapter 4), stating that respondents with relations in the neighbouring country made more accurate estimates, has however been put to the test. The results are discussed here. First, the deviation - being the respondent's estimation minus the factual distance in kilometres - was rendered absolute. This method made it possible to discover whether the deviation value for the estimation of the distance to a certain region in the neighbouring country displayed a negative correlation with the number of economic relations in that region. It was found not to be so to any significant extent, nor did the correlation between the relationships in a certain region in the neighbouring country with the accuracy of the distance estimation yield any convincing results.

Only for the respondents of Gent/Eeklo was it possible to demonstrate that the deviation of the estimates of the distance to Terneuzen correlated significantly with the number of economic relations in Zeeland Flanders. The correlation was found to be negative. A more detailed analysis of this outcome yielded the expected result that the respondents who overestimated the distance to Terneuzen have fewer economic relations in Zeeland Flanders than those who underestimate the distance or estimate it correctly.

In general, it seems possible to justify the conclusion that there is no strong connection between cognitive distance on the one hand, and the number of economic relations on the other.

The number of economic relations and the cognitive map of the border
Also due to the sheer volume of answer categories, the correlation between the number of economic relations and the cognitive map of the border has not been included in table 7.11. The cognitive deviation - being the estimation of the location of the border minus the factual location of the border - was rendered absolute before being compared with the number of economic relations in the neighbouring country. The hypothesis that a greater number of economic relations in the neighbouring country goes together with a smaller deviation (greater precision) and vice

versa could not be ratified. It was not possible either to confirm the correlation between having or not having economic relations in the neighbouring countries and the accuracy of the drawn border.

The borders drawn by the respondents yielded interesting systematic deviations as shown in figure 7.3, but it appears that an explanation should not so much be sought in having or not having cross-border economic relations and their number. Again, as with cognitive distance, it appears that the effect on the widening of the cognition of having (a number of) cross-border economic relations should not be overestimated. The precision and deviations in the cognitive map of the border are most likely caused by other factors, such as the topographical education in a country and/or region, the use of / familiarity with maps, and the knowledge of the regions as gleaned from newspapers, television and magazines. Such factors may make a more lasting impression to influence the cognitive image of a country than the entrepreneur's effective action space.

7.3.2.1 Multivariate analysis of the number of economic relations in the neighbouring country

After this inventory of bivariate correlations, which provided a first insight into the mutual connections between the variables, a multiple regression analysis was executed for the number of economic relations in the neighbouring country. The scheme representing this analysis can be found in figure 7.4.

Figure 7.4 - Analysis of the number of cross-border economic relations

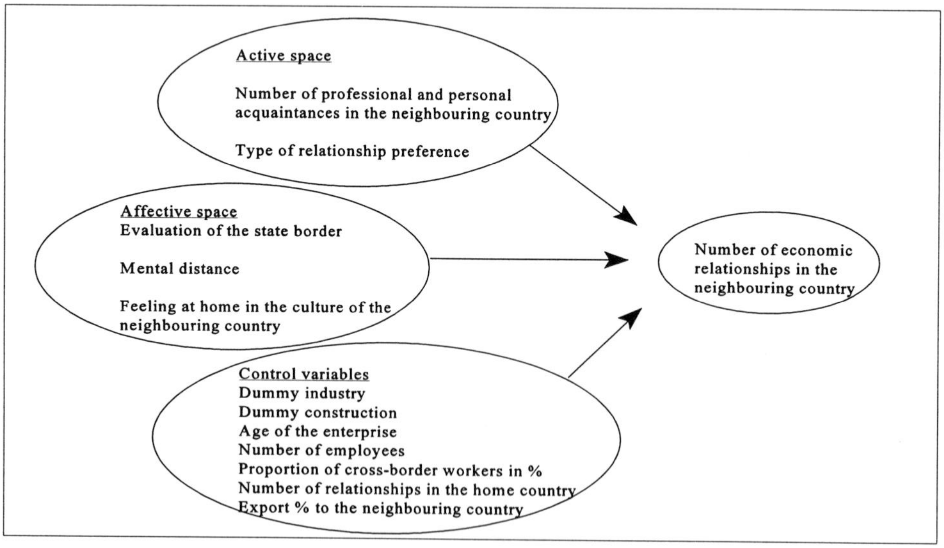

The table below presents all the independent variables of the analysis and their explanatory value. The complete model applies for the companies in all regions and was found to explain the number of economic relations of the companies significantly ($F(18/430)=13.21$, $p< 0.01$, adjusted R Square =0.33).

Table 7.12 - Multiple regression analysis of the number of economic relations in the neighbouring country

Independent variables:	Dependent variable: The number of cross-border economic relations in the neighbouring country	
	Coefficient (1)	Significance (2)
Number of professional acquaintances in the neighbouring country	0.01	0.92 n/s
Number of personal acquaintances in the neighbouring country	0.15	0.01 ***
Type of relationship preference: networking	0.08	0.05 *
Type of relationship preference: bold and well-informed	-0.06	0.16 n/s
Type of relationship preference: regionally/nationally bounded	0.02	0.73 n/s
Feeling at home in the culture of the neighbouring country	-0.01	0.73 n/s
Mental distance: The expected negative effect of the relationship	-0.08	0.08 *
Mental distance: The expected discrepancy in business conventions in the relationship	-0.09	0.04 **
Mental distance: The stringency of the financial-economic conditions of the relationship	-0.09	0.03 **
Evaluation of the state border: The state border is a barrier	0.05	0.22 n/s
Evaluation of the state border: The state border is irrelevant	0.07	0.08 *
Age of the enterprise in years	-0.01	0.81 n/s
Number of employees	-0.04	0.31 n/s
Proportion of cross-border workers in %	-0.02	0.67 n/s
Proportion of sales in neighbouring country in %	0.31	0.00 ***
The number of economic relationships in the home country	0.45	0.00 ***
Dummy industrial sector	0.10	0.03 **
Dummy construction sector	-0.01	0.91 n/s

(1) This expresses the direction (positive/negative) and the force of the influence (Beta)
(2) *** level of significance < 1%; ** level of significance < 5%; * level of significance < 10%; N/S= not significant

It can be said that the number of economic relations in the neighbouring country is significant dependent from:
- the industrial character of the company
- the number of personal acquaintances in the neighbouring country
- the export volume to the neighbouring country (in %)
- the number of economic relations in the home country
- 'networking' as a type of relationship preference
- the positive expectation relating to the effect of the relationship in the neighbouring country
- the expectation of a small discrepancy with regard to the business conventions of the relation in the neighbouring country
- a small degree of stringency in setting financial-economic conditions to the relation in the neighbouring country
- the degree to which the entrepreneur regards the state border as irrelevant

In short, the number of economic relations in the home country, the export volume to the neighbouring country, and a relatively small mental distance to the neighbouring country, are decisive factors in determining the size of the network of economic relations of a company in the neighbouring country.
Again, as in the analysis of the distinction between companies with and companies without economic relations in the neighbouring country, we find that the development path of the company on the one hand, and the entrepreneur's perception and attitude on the other, are crucial factors in the explanation of the internationalisation pattern.
The importance of the first aspect, the development phase, connects quite specifically with the ideas contained in the phase model of the psychic distance approach.
The second aspect, the importance of the evaluation of the differences in doing business in the neighbouring country and their consequences, is an innovative element in the explanation of the internationalisation pattern. On the one hand, it indicates that the rationality of the economic actors is overestimated in the transaction costs theory and should be modified in favour of the role of perception and attitude; on the other hand it emphasises, as it were, the body of ideas upon which the psychic distance approach is founded - with as fundamental distinction the fact that it is not so much the absolute knowledge with regard to the neighbouring country or the absolute difference in culture between countries that is important in entering into cross-border economic relationships, but the entrepreneur's perception of and attitude vis-à-vis enterprise in the neighbouring country, which, as has been discussed, may be strongly coloured affectively.

7.3.3 Determinants in the success of cross-border co-operation

Some economic relationships are more successful than others. A vast array of factors may be at the bottom of that success. The question is whether it is possible to predict what will be a successful relationship on the basis of the factors of the INTERFACE model, once the contact between the partners has been established. This is what will be examined in the course of this section. The central question here is:

What determines the success of a cross-border economic relationship?

Before tackling this question through multivariate analysis, I will first indicate the bivariate correlations between the various stages of the INTERFACE model preceding the actual start of the relationship when the contact has been initiated. Thus, I am concerned here with the connection between the stages of attraction, interaction, and transaction.

The correlation between attraction and interaction

In the first place, there appears to exist a strong and meaningful connection between the variables of attraction and the variables of interaction. Table 7.13 reflects the correlation coefficients between these two phases.

Table 7.13 - The correlation between the dimensions of attraction and interaction

	Trust	Transaction costs
Similarity	0.46***	-0.01
Complementation	0.16**	0.31***
Price/quality ratio	0.13*	0.00
Spatial proximity	-0.06	-0.15**

*** level of significance < 1%; ** level of significance < 5%; * level of significance < 10%

The degree of correlation between the dimensions of attraction and interaction are represented here. The strongest link between attraction and interaction is doubtless the degree of similarity. It would seem that a high degree of trust in the interaction goes together with a high degree of similarity in the attraction stage. Similarity between the partners and trust therefore go hand in hand. This is an important finding and is in line with the expectations (see chapter 4, section 4.2.3).

The effect of other attraction dimensions is clearly more restricted. A negative correlation might *a priori* be expected between complementation and trust, since complementation implies a certain degree of uncertainty, which may be attractive. Opposite attracts. It may stimulate a fruitful interchange of ideas and processes. In a way, attraction as a result of the complementation of the other therefore implies, for the entrepreneur's own company, the *capitalisation of uncertainty*. The attraction due to complementation, however, does not necessarily inspire confidence. It was therefore expected that a negative correlation between trust and complementation would exist. A possible explanation of the positive relation between complementation and trust is that the dimension of complementation also implies that the other has a strong market and network position. If an actor has contacts and relationships with many other companies, this will strengthen the trust in that actor. And apparently, this positive 'market and network position effect' is stronger than the negative 'uncertainty effect'.

The strength of the 'uncertainty effect' of attraction because of complementation however, is clearly visible in the transaction costs. It was found that transaction costs are strongly and positively correlated with the evaluation of the degree of complementation with the other. This is in line with the expectations. If the other is considered highly attractive because of a high degree of complementation, this implies that the diverging ideas of the other and his many contacts and relations are valued, but that they generate, at the same time, extra uncertainty and/or additional investments and adaptations to make the relationship possible. This uncertainty and/or the investments and adaptations drive up the transaction costs.

In sum, the attraction dimension of complementation has two possible effects operating at the same time. On the one hand, it may generate a 'market and network position effect' which increases the trust in the partner, on the other, and more strongly so, it may create an uncertainty effect, which increases the transaction costs.

Furthermore, it was found that a good price/quality ratio and trust are positively and indicatively connected. A high product quality against a good price implies that there exists a high degree of trust in the other.

No significant correlation was found between trust and spatial proximity. That is a meaningful result. It leads one to conclude that a short physical distance between partners is not enough to create a sense of trust. Between spatial proximity and transaction costs, however, a negative correlation exists (see table 7.13). This negative correlation cannot be explained as a reverse effect of the correlation between trust and spatial proximity. For it is not the increase of trust between physically close working partners, that reduces the transaction costs. The possible threat of malfeasance, causing uncertainty, is not lessened in a situation of spatial proximity. Considering the indicators of transaction costs I included (see section 4.2.3 and appendix 2), the explanation must then be that spatial proximity reduces the investment and/or adjustment costs that are a consequence of the initiation of the transaction. Apparently, on a short distance across the border those transactions take place, that do not request major investments in knowledge and resources, and major adjustments in the product and production process of the firm. Vice versa, when the physical distance between the partners increases, the transaction costs rise.

The connection between interaction and transaction

Between the two dimensions of the interaction stage, trust and transaction costs on the one hand and the variable of the transaction stage (contract Yes/No) on the other, a strong and meaningful connection exists. It was found that a significant negative connection exists between the formality of the transaction and the degree of trust, and a significant positive connection between the formality of the transaction and transaction costs. These results coincide with the theoretical perspectives as set out in chapter 4 (section 4.2.3 and 4.2.4). The conclusion that mutual trust goes together with informality of the transaction tallies with the body of ideas central to the network theory (see chapter 3) The conclusion that high transaction costs go together with formality of the transaction tallies with the body of ideas central to the transaction costs theory (see chapter 3). The formalisation of the agreement, in short, happens especially in cases of high transaction costs and low trust, which require extra security in the form of a contract. These findings confirm that there is space for two dimensions side by side in the interaction stage: trust and transaction costs. Each dimension fills its own role in the interaction process.

7.3.3.1 Multivariate analysis of the success of the most important cross-border economic relationship

Next, the multivariate analysis has been conducted. The scheme representing this analysis can be found in figure 7.5.

Figure 7.5 - The analysis of the success of a cross-border economic relation

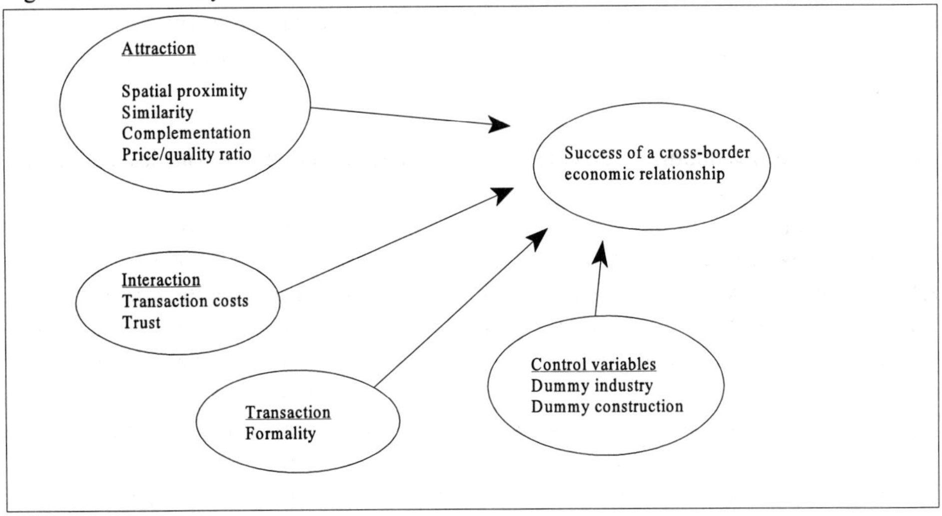

Table 7.14 outlines the influence of the independent variables as obtained through a multiple regression analysis for the success of a cross-border relationship. The complete model applies for all companies in all regions, and was found to explain the number of economic relationships of the companies in a significant manner ($F(9/121) = 5.85$, $p < 0.01$, adjusted R square = 0.25).

Table 7.14 - Determinants for the success of the cross-border economic relationship

Independent variables		Dependent variable: Success of the economic relation: Coefficient (1)	Significance (2)
Attraction	Spatial proximity	-0.10	-0.20 n/s
	Similarity	0.16	0.07 *
	Complementation	0.04	0.96 n/s
	Price/quality ratio of the resources	0.14	0.37 n/s
Interaction	Transaction costs	-0.05	0.51 n/s
	Trust	0.37	0.00 ***
Transaction	Formal: yes or no	0.13	0.11 n/s
Control variables	Dummy: Industry	0.06	0.48 n/s
	Dummy: Construction	-0.13	0.12 n/s

(1) this expresses the direction (positive/negative) of the influence (Beta)
(2) *** level of significance < 1%; ** level of significance < 5%; * level of significance < 10%, N/S= not significant

The success of economic relationships in the neighbouring country was found to depend of only two factors.

The first important determinant of the success of a cross-border economic relationship is the degree of similarity between the partners. This attraction factor expresses the equality of ideas and the trust that the partners have in each other at the outset of the contact. This is in line with the expectations as formulated in chapter 4. This aspect of similarity, which plays a role at the outset of the contact, was found to be of positive importance in determining the eventual success of the economic relationship.

The second and most important determinant of the success of a cross-border economic relationship is the effective mutual trust between the partners. This effect is by far the most important one of the two (coefficient 0.37). This result too, is in line with expectations (see chapter 4). A greater success of the relationship will result if there is a strong degree of trust during the deliberations concerning working agreements.
It should be noted in this context that the reverse effect cannot be excluded. Just because the economic relationship is successful, the partners look back upon the degree of trust that existed during the deliberations more positively. This possibility is not entirely imaginary in a study looking retrospectively at the initiation and development process of economic relationships. Still, the importance of trust between the partners with regard to the success of the relationship is

convincing. Attraction factors other than similarity might, from the perspective of a more positive evaluation of successful relationships afterwards, also have a significant influence. The fact that these effects are of little or even no importance to the degree of success is expressive, therefore, with regard to the importance attached to similarity and trust in the relationship.
Note that the factor transaction costs was found to be especially important in the interaction stage, which decides whether or not a contract should be compiled to ensure compliance with the working agreements. The factor trust was also found to be important in this respect. Trust, however, is the most important determinant for the eventual future success of the cross-border economic relationship.

7.4 Overview of the results

In this chapter, the actual evolutionary process of cross-border economic relationships for companies in the research areas Zeeland Flanders, Central and North Zeeland, and Gent/Eeklo has been described with the aid of the INTERFACE model. Furthermore, three multivariate analyses were executed with the purpose of discovering the determinant factors in having or not having economic relationships in the neighbouring country, their number, and their eventual success. The results of these analyses are summarised below.

Table 7.15 - The results(1)

			Observed result: +/-		
			Cross-border relation: Yes/ No	Number of cross-border economic relations	Success of a cross-border economic relation
Contact	1. Feeling at home in the culture of neighbouring country		n/a	-0.01 (0.73)	n/a
	2. Mental distance	Expected negative effect of the relationship	-0.20 (0.00)***	-0.08 (0.08)*	n/a
		Expected discrepancy with regard to business conventions	-0.22 (0.00)***	-0.09 (0.04)**	n/a
		Stringency in financial-economic conditions	-0.08 (0.00)***	-0.09 (0.03)**	n/a
	3.Border evaluation	Barrier	-0.03(0.47)	0.05(0.22)	n/a
		Irrelevance	0.13(0.01)**	0.07(0.08)*	n/a
	4. Spatial identity, per region		n/a	n/a	n/a
	5a1. Social network: number of personal acquaintances		n/a	0.15 (0.01)***	n/a
	5a2. Social network: visiting frequency of personal acquaintances		n/a	n/a	n/a
	5b1. Professional network: number of professional acquaintances		n/a	0.01(0.92)	n/a
	5b2. Professional network: visiting frequency of professional acquaintances		n/a	n/a	n/a
	6. Direct (+) or indirect (-) contact		n/a	n/a	n/a
	7. Relationship preference:		n/a		n/a
	Networking			0.08 (0.05)*	
	Bold and well-informed search			-0.06 (0.16)	
	Regionally/nationally bound			0.02 (0.73)	
	8. Cognitive distance, per region		n/a	n/a	n/a

	9. Cognitive map of the border	n/a	n/a	n/a
Attraction	1. Spatial proximity	n/a	n/a	-0.10 (-0.20)
	2. Similarity	n/a	n/a	0.16 (0.07)*
	3. Complementation	n/a	n/a	0.04 (0.96)
	4. Price/quality of the resources	n/a	n/a	0.14 (0.37)
Interaction	1. Height of the transaction costs	n/a	n/a	-0.05 (0.51)
	2. Degree of trust	n/a	n/a	0.37 (0.00)***
Transaction	Formal (+) or informal (-) relationship	n/a	n/a	0.13 (0.11)
Control variables	Age of the company	-0.04 (0.44)	-0.01 (0.81)	n/a
	Size of the company	0.09 (0.06)*	-0.04 (0.31)	(n/a)
	Export rate	0.35 (0.00)***	0.31 (0.00)***	n/a
	Number of cross-border employees	0.09 (0.06)*	-0.02 (0.67)	n/a
	Number of economic relations in the home country	0.30 (0.00)***	0.45 (0.00)***	n/a
	Sector: Industry Yes or No	0.16 (0.01)**	0.10 (0.03)**	0.06 (0.48)
	Sector: Construction Yes or No	-0.22 (0.00)***	-0.01 (0.91)	-0.13 (0.12)

(1) Indicated are the standardized coefficients, between brackets the significance level, n/a stands for 'not applicable', meaning that it is impossible to make a (meaningful) theoretical prediction on the basis of the research design used.

This table concludes chapter 7. In the following and last part of this dissertation, the results of the empirical research are confronted with the theoretical assumptions, which confrontation will lead to the final conclusions.

Part 3

Confrontation between theory and empirical research

Chapter 8

Confrontation and conclusions

In this concluding chapter, the hypotheses proposed at the theoretical outset of the present study in chapters 2, 3, and 4, will be set against the findings that emerged from the empirical research, as presented in chapters 5, 6, and 7. This confrontation will be described in section 8.1. The results of the study will then be summarised and the most important conclusions will be discussed in section 8.2.

8.1 Confrontation between hypotheses and results

In chapter 4, table 4.1 outlined the expected influence of the variables in the INTERFACE model. In chapter 7, the outcome of three multivariate analyses was presented. Now, the theoretical predictions, as shown in table 4.1, and the empirical results, as shown in table 7.15, will be compared, as represented in table 8.1.

Table 8.1 - The hypotheses versus the results

			Economic relations in the neighbouring country yes or no		Number of economic cross-border relations		Success of an economic cross-border relation	
			Hypotheses	Results	Hypotheses	Results	Hypotheses	Results
Contact	1. Feeling at home in the culture of the neighbouring country		n/a	n/a	+	-(n/s)	n/a	n/a
	2. Mental distance:	Expected negative effect of the relationship	-	-(s)	-	-(s)	n/a	n/a
		Expected discrepancy with regard to business conventions	-	-(s)	-	-(s)	n/a	n/a
		Stringency in financial-economic conditions	-	-(s)	-	-(s)	n/a	n/a
	3. Evaluation of the border	Barrier	-	-(n/s)	-	+(n/s)	n/a	n/a
		Irrelevance	+	+(s)	+	+(s)	n/a	n/a
	4. Spatial identity, per region		n/a	n/a	n/a	n/a	n/a	n/a
	5a. Social network: number of personal acquaintances		n/a	n/a	+	+(s)	n/a	n/a
	5b. Professional network: number of professional acquaintances		n/a	n/a	+	+(n/s)	n/a	n/a
	6. Indirect (+) or direct (-) contact		n/a	n/a	n/a	n/a	n/a	n/a
	7. Relationship preference Networking Bold and well-informed search Regionally/nationally bound		n/a	n/a	 + + -	 +(s) -(n/s) +(n/s)	n/a	n/a

	8. Cognitive distance, per region	n/a	n/a	n/a	n/a	n/a	n/a
	9. Cognitive map of the border	n/a	n/a	n/a	n/a	n/a	n/a
Attraction	1. Spatial proximity	n/a	n/a	n/a	n/a	+	-(n/s)
	2. Similarity	n/a	n/a	n/a	n/a	+	+(s)
	3. Complementation	n/a	n/a	n/a	n/a	+	+(n/s)
	4. Price/quality of the resources	n/a	n/a	n/a	n/a	+	+(n/s)
Interaction	1. Height of the transaction costs	n/a	n/a	n/a	n/a	-	-(n/s)
	2. Degree of trust	n/a	n/a	n/a	n/a	+	+(s)
Transaction	Formal(+) or informal(-) relation/ship	n/a	n/a	n/a	n/a	-	+(n/s)
Control variables	Age of the enterprise	+	-(n/s)	+	-(n/s)	n/a	n/a
	Size of the enterprise	+	+(s)	+	-(n/s)	n/a	n/a
	Export rate	+	+(s)	+	+(s)	n/a	n/a
	Number of cross-border employees	+	+(s)	+	-(n/s)	n/a	n/a
	Number of economic relations in the home country	+	+(s)	+	+(s)	n/a	n/a
	Sector: Industry Yes or No	+	+(s)	+	+(s)	+	+(n/s)
	Sector: Construction Yes or No	-	-(s)	-	-(n/s)	-	-(n/s)

* n/a stands for 'not applicable', meaning that it is impossible to make a (meaningful) theoretical prediction on the basis of the research design used.

Model 1

Table 8.1 indicates in how far the theoretically expected influences have actually materialised in the course of the empirical research. In the first model - the analysis of 'having or not having one or more economic relations in the neighbouring country' - the control variables, the variables 'export rate' and 'number of economic relations in the home country' especially were found to play a significant, strongly positive role. This indicates that the internationalisation is a gradual process. The internationalisation of business starts with the nationalisation of it. This finding is most in line with the stage theory of the psychic distance model. The greater the number of economic relations in the home country, and the greater the export volume to the neighbouring country, the greater the likelihood that an economic relationship will be initiated in the neighbouring country.

Furthermore, the dimension *of mental distance* was found to exert a strong influence upon the distinction between having and not having an economic relationship in the neighbouring country. The greater the mental distance, the smaller the likelihood that an economic relationship in the neighbouring country will be initiated. This result confirms the hypothesis that mental distance plays an important role in the initiation of cross-border economic relationships.

Model 2

In the second model - the analysis of the number of cross-border economic relations - a diversified picture emerges from the confrontation of theory and empiricism. The direction (positive and negative) of the significant variables conformed to my expectations. However, not all variables that were expected to play a crucial role appeared to be significant in the explanation of the number of cross-border economic relations.
The variable 'the border as a barrier' is not significantly important in determining the number of cross-border economic relations. Whether the border is regarded as a barrier does not, does not play a significant role in having or not having cross-border economic relations, nor does it exert any significant influence upon their number. The perceived relevance of the border does however, as was expected, play a significant role, both in the frequency as in the number of cross-border economic relations. Those firms who regard the border as relevant, have less often and fewer cross-border economic relations.

Another remarkable observation is that the variable 'number of professional acquaintances in the neighbouring country' is not significant, while the variable 'number of personal acquaintances' is. *Personal* informal embeddedness in the society of the neighbouring country is apparently more important in explaining the number of cross-border economic relations than *professional* informal embeddedness.

The dimensions of mental distance, in accordance with expectations, were significant and negative. Mental distance was therefore found to be of significant importance in the distinction between the companies with and without economic relationships, and in determining the number of economic relationships in the neighbouring country. The present study demonstrates that the perception and attitude of entrepreneurs vis-à-vis the border and the neighbouring country, as represented through mental distance, has a significant influence upon the frequency and number of cross-border economic relationships.

Furthermore, it was observed that the variable of 'relationship preference' could be subdivided into three categories. Relationship preference characterised as 'networking' appears to play a significant role in determining the number of cross-border economic relationships, which was according to expectations. Contrary to expectations, however, the other two types of relationship preference, 'bold and well-informed' and 'national/regional', were not found to be of significant importance. Among the control variables, 'export rate', 'the number of economic relations in the home country', and the dummy sector 'industry' were found again to be strongly positive and significant, thereby confirming the stage concept of internationalisation.

Model 3

The third model that was analysed - the success of an economic relationship in the neighbouring country - led to the following findings.

The attraction dimension 'similarity' lived up to the expectations in playing a significant role. This dimension has a positive influence upon the success of the relationship. It is of much more importance, so it would seem, to have a great deal in common, in character and in (business) conventions, than to complement each other, in order to have a successful, long-term relationship. This conclusion coincides with important findings in the empirical tests of the 'similarity' versus 'complementation' hypothesis in social psychology (see Meertens and Grumbkow, 1988/1992). The other attraction dimensions appeared, contrary to expectations, not to exert any significant influence.

The effect of the factor 'height of transaction costs' on success was found not to be significant, while it was expected to be negatively significant. Transaction costs were found to be of great importance in determining the formality of the relationship, but were not found to be of any direct relevance in determining its eventual success. One might argue, however, that transaction costs do play an important role, indirectly, in the eventual success of the relationship by determining its formality. But this is not the only determinant of the formality of a transaction. In the interaction stage there is yet another important determinant of the transaction's formality: trust. Moreover, it is this second dimension of interaction that has a strong positive effect on the success of a cross-border economic relationship. This important result is in line with my expectations as set out in section 4.2.3.

In short, the third model indicates that there is a strong link between similarity in the attraction and trust between the partners in the interaction, and the degree of success of the relationship. At the same time there seems to be a second link, beginning with complementation in the attraction stage, the height of the transaction costs in the interaction stage, and the degree of the transaction's formality. The empirical results in this research do not allow for further theoretical statements on this point, but the findings as described do suggest that these two lines do not stand by themselves. There might well be a pattern. But for that to be established, further research into this intriguing relationship between attraction, interaction, transaction and success would be necessary.

8.2 Summary and conclusions

In this dissertation, the central question concerned the influence of the state border, within an economic union, upon the development of economic relationships between two companies in regions on either side of that border. For the purposes of this study, development involved the frequency, number, and success of cross-border economic relationships between companies in the border regions of the Netherlands and Belgium, to wit, Zeeland Flanders and Central and North Zeeland on the Dutch side of the border, and Gent/Eeklo on the Belgian side.

The state border in relation to *active* space, *affective* space and *cognitive* space
In order to be able to answer the research question, I have first examined what kind of possible influences of the functional state borders on actors and groups of actors can be distinguished. I found that there are three kinds of space, each with its own borders: active space, affective space, and cognitive space, that may strongly be influenced by state borders.

Active space is the space constructed through the actual actions of actors, in this case the factual spread of the economic activities of the entrepreneurs in the research areas. One might think here of the sale of products, the contact pattern, of having or not having economic relationships and their number. The expectation was that actions in space follow a discontinuous pattern at the border between two countries.

Affective space is space determined by man's affections, his emotional connectedness with space. Affective space is concretised through the perception of mental distance, the feeling of being at home in the culture of a foreign country, one's spatial identity, and one's evaluation of the phenomenon of the state border *per se*. The assumption was that the national border (still) is strongly present in an affective sense.

Actors divide space not only according to action and affection, but also through cognition. *Cognitive* space is that space about which knowledge exists, originating in personal experience, information or study. This knowledge was tested during the research through the estimation of physical distances and through drawing the border on a blind map. Both indicators are part of a cognitive map that an actor forms about space. The assumption in relation to both measurements was that the accuracy of the estimate/drawing would increase proportionally to an increase in the knowledge about real distances/the real location of the state border (cf. Riedel, 1994).

These three kinds of space (affective, active, and cognitive) can be distinguished with regard to the state border, which is *artificial, concrete, and functional*. The deviation, the discontinuity in the spatial course of action with regard to the state border can be called *the effect of the border*. In this study this influence of the border on the *active space* of firms in border regions was the centre of interest. Cross-border action space, with regard to the frequency and the number of cross-border economic relationships, was expected to be strongly related to (1) the deviations in the *other variables of active space*, such as the informal contact pattern in the neighbouring country and the preference for a certain type of relationship; (2) deviations in *affective space*, such as spatial identity and feeling at home in the culture of the neighbouring country, and (3) *cognitive space*, measured through the cognitive distance towards cities in the neighbouring country and the respondents' cognitive map of the border.

Economic theories on the formation of international economic relationships
With the aid of the dominant economic theories on international economic relationships, to wit the transaction costs theory (TCE), the international network approach (INA), and the psychic distance approach (PDA), I have subsequently indicated which elements should be considered important in the process of the formation of economic relationships across a border. It was found that the three dominant theories differ most strongly from one another in their assumptions on *human nature* in (inter)actions.

The *transaction costs theory,* in its views, departs from 'contractual man'. The economic actor, according to TCE, is capable in principle of opportunist behaviour. The insecurity this creates for other actors, in addition to an assumed restricted possibility of gaining information about the economic partner and the circumstances, leads to contracts intended to reduce the risk involved in mutual transactions.
In the face of this postulate, the *international network theory* sets up the assumption of trust. In the interaction between actors, so this theory states, the economic actor does not aim so much at improving himself at the cost of the other, but first and foremost to give the relationship form and content. Economic society is a network of relationships between actors. The economic relationships in that society differ as to content and depth. In the eyes of network theorists, trust is an important factor in the determination of the content and depth of the economic relationship. Trust is built according to an iterative process; it is not static. Economic actors learn.

The learning effect is also central to the third theory that was discussed in this study to position the notion of international economic relationships in economic literature - the *psychic distance theory*. In this theory, it is not so much the interaction between two actors that is central, as the actor's knowledge of the environment in which he is situated. The actor is reluctant to enter economically into the environment of the other actor because he does not have sufficient knowledge about it. In order to be able to analyse the differences between two or more societies, the theory often uses the cultural distance index based on Hofstede's research in its functionalisation. As the actor gathers more knowledge and experience concerning the foreign environment, the degree and depth of internationalisation will increase. The psychic distance theory uses a stage model, in which internationalisation begins with direct export, continues as a sales relationship (*e.g.* through a representative), and is completed with the organisation of a branch office (foreign direct investment).

None of these three theories was found, on its own, to be able to answer the question I asked concerning the influence of the border upon the development of bilateral cross-border economic relationships. The overview of economic theories, nonetheless, did yield the insight that the opposition between transaction costs and trust on the one hand, and the opposition between the dynamics in the internationalisation process according to the psychic distance theory especially and the predominantly static approach of the transaction costs theory on the other, is blocking a more integrated view on the process of cross-border economic relationships. Furthermore, the examination of economic theories has shown (1) that economics leaves little space for a micro-economic analysis of the meaning and influence of the state border on international actions and interactions, (2) that the inclusion of individual perceptions and attitudes is rarely practised, although it is more and more regarded as a way potentially capable of deepening our insights into the formation of international economic relationships, and (3) that the study of the process of the formation of economic relationships does not generally concern the entire process from bilateral initial contact and attraction to transaction/relationship, but always begins in the interaction stage, the moment at which actors deliberate about working agreements. These voids in the theories under consideration are remarkable, at the very least, in view of the decreasing importance of great distances and borders in modern economy on the one hand, and the value that is increasingly attached to proximity and personal face-to-face contacts in the development of economic relationships on the other. This finding led me to formulate the postulate that a study on the economy of borders should be regarded as a study that has much to do with the borders of economics.

The INTERFACE model

Next, on the basis of the theories that were investigated and evaluated, a model was developed that purposed to describe the development of cross-border economic relationships between two companies accurately and could be used to answer the research question. This model is called the INTERFACE model, which is an acronym for *INTERnational Formation of Autonomous Co-operation between Enterprises*. The model comprises six stages:

- *Contact* (the encounter),
- *Attraction* (the choice of the partner),
- *Interaction* (the negotiation concerning the conditions),
- *Transaction* (the realisation of the agreement/contract),
- *Relationship* (continuity in transactions), and
- *Success* (intensity and evaluation).

The six stages were functionalised through factors that play an important role in each separate stage. The model assumes that actors are driven by what is called *context rationality*. Thus, economic rationality does not merely embrace strategic rationality, but also the weighing of affective and cognitive elements of the context within which the action occurs. On the basis of the INTERFACE model research hypotheses were formulated to explain the frequency and the number of economic relationships as well as their success.

Empirical research

In 1992, during the course of our investigation in the border regions of Central Brabant (the Netherlands) and Kempen (Belgium), I gained the insight that the border acts as a dividing line (Dagevos *et al.*, 1992). This first exploration of the role of the border in international economic interweaving strengthened the idea that a need existed to elucidate the functioning and consequences of the border. The research done on border regions and on the influence of the border on cross-border economic relations seldom focused on developing and testing theories.

In this study, I have tried to make a start in filling this gap. As a consequence, the measurement methodology and the development of a theoretical model both became important and innovative dimensions of this study. The research hypotheses, which were formulated on the basis of the INTERFACE model, have been put to the test. An extensive questionnaire was sent to 1,727 companies in three regions on either side of the border between the Netherlands and Belgium, to wit Zeeland Flanders and Central and North Zeeland in the Netherlands and the district of Gent/Eeklo in Belgium. All companies that were approached belonged to the construction, industrial, and wholesale sectors. In all, 27.2% of the companies completed and returned the questionnaire in time.

The questionnaire began by inventorying the distribution in the *sales*, the *number* and the *type* of the economic relationships maintained by the companies. This analysis served to factually determine the effect of the state border upon action space - the spatial activities of the enterprises in the research areas in the Netherlands and Belgium.

The sales and economic relations were found to be distributed unequally, the great majority of relationships being located in the home region and country. However, I observed a great disparity between the number of economic relationships in the home country and those in the neighbouring country; the three regions average one economic relation in the neighbouring country against 4.6 national ones.

The results, however, differed per region. This study has made clear that entrepreneurs' activities, perceptions and attitudes cannot be viewed independently of the region in which the entrepreneurs function. Their activities have an effect upon the region, but at the same time their regional context affects their cross-border action and affective space. It matters significantly where (in which region) a company is located. This influence emerged clearly from the regional analysis of the number of economic relations in the neighbouring country. To illustrate the regional differences in this part of the dissertation, the influence of the border upon the distribution of economic relationships was shown on maps.

The companies in Central and North Zeeland have the smallest number of economic relationships in the neighbouring country. The ratio of their economic relationships in the neighbouring country against those in the home country is 1:7.4. These companies are oriented principally towards the Netherlands, upward rather than downward. Concretely, they are focused more towards the region Rijnmond/Rotterdam than towards the Belgian regions. Belgium, to these companies, is truly a 'foreign' country. In fact, to enter Belgium they have to contend with a double border: the water border of the Westerschelde and the state border between the Netherlands and Belgium. The latter causes the most important disruption in the spatial activity as well as in the affective space of the entrepreneurs.

The companies in Zeeland Flanders focus, outside their own region, upon the rest of their home country and upon the Flemish market. It became clear that the companies in this region, of all three regions, have the most international outlook. The region of Gent/Eeklo draws them most strongly; the number of relations there even surpasses the number of relationships they have in Central and North Zeeland. The most important reason for their relatively strong orientation towards Gent/Eeklo is the functional link between Gent and Terneuzen, the Channel Zone. For the enterprises in Zeeland Flanders this highly industrialized Channel Zone literally shortens the distance to a relatively large market in Gent/Eeklo. The number of relationships in the neighbouring and home country is disproportionate here too (1:2.9), but it is more evenly distributed than for the other two regions.
Yet the relativity of this orientation towards the neighbouring country should not be lost from sight. In spite of the relatively strong orientation towards Gent/Eeklo, it was found that the companies in Zeeland Flanders are clearly more directed towards the Netherlands, compared to the sales and the number of economic relations they have in Belgium. Moreover, the companies in Zeeland Flanders sell and deliver their products mostly in their own home region. They are more active on the regional level than companies in Central and North Zeeland, and even twice as much as companies in Gent/Eeklo. The companies in Zeeland Flanders focus more upon their own region, with respect to sales and economic relations, than the companies in the other two regions.

The region Gent/Eeklo was found to have a truly international business community. The companies in Gent/Eeklo sell their products most often to consumers and to other companies outside their own region. As much as 73% of the companies, for example, are engaged in export to the Netherlands. That is almost 6% more than the companies in Zeeland Flanders and almost twice as much as the companies in Central and North Zeeland. Since the companies also export relatively more often and more to other countries, the export volume to the Netherlands remains, in general, small nonetheless. Also, it was found that the companies tend to have more economic relations in their home country than the companies in the two Dutch regions. The average number of economic relationships in the neighbouring country, as compared to the home country, is 1:4.9. The number of cross-border economic relationships of these companies is therefore greater than in Central and North Zeeland. At the same time, their economic relationships appear to be more evenly distributed in space than those in Zeeland Flanders. They are not concentrated in one region, but cover all of the neighbouring country. As with the companies in the two Dutch regions, the cross-border economic relationships maintained by companies in Gent/Eeklo are mostly sales market and supply relationships.

Regarding the sectoral distribution, the following can be said. Construction companies lag behind wholesale and industrial companies where it concerns international economic interweaving. The contrast is greatest with industrial companies, which most notably enter into cross-border economic relationships.

The influence of the state border

I have sought to explain the observed patterns in the cross-border action space of the enterprises. On the basis of the INTERFACE approach, three analytical models have been put forward, which investigate the development of cross-border economic relationships. The first model attempts to explain the 'having or not having' of economic relationships; the second model tries to explain the number of cross-border economic relationships; and the third model tries to find the most important determinants of the success of a cross-border economic relationship.

The most important conclusion of the first two models is that the immediate proximity of the border is a major problem in the development of cross-border economic relationships by firms in border regions. To answer the central question in this investigation: the state border is present mainly *mentally*. The spatial economic behaviour of entrepreneurs appears to be guided quite clearly by the abstract administrative borders of provinces and countries. The distance to the region on the other side of the border is generally quite small, but the *mental distance* is often far greater. The market is thereby divided not just in a spatial, but also in a mental sense. The state border is rooted in the minds of people.

Concretely, the mental impact of the border was found to emerge from the fact that specific differences are perceived in the manner and success of economic co-operation with companies in the neighbouring country as compared to economic co-operation with companies in the home country. Such perception was not independent - it was found to affect entrepreneurial behaviour. Companies without economic relations across the border look at cross-border co-operation with significantly less confidence, are more reluctant to enter into such co-operation. They experience a greater mental distance. Moreover, the size of the mental distance has a proportionately negative effect on the frequency and the number of cross-border economic relationships. The fact that companies without economic relations, which generally have a larger mental distance, do not regard the border so much as a barrier, but as relevant, is significant in this respect.

I have attempted to explain the frequency and number of cross-border economic relationships through the effect of the border on the cognitive space of the entrepreneurs. Cognitive space was first of all measured through the accuracy of the estimation of distances to cities in the home country and in the neighbouring country. I expected the accuracy of the estimates of distances to cities across the border to be closely related to low cross-border activity. The less accurate the

estimate, the fewer relationships would exist. This expectation could not be confirmed conclusively, the hypothesis applying in only two cases.
The cognitive map of the state border was used as the second measurement method of cognitive space. This method was constructed to test whether the distortions of the sketches of the state border made by the respondents are related to the existence and number of cross-border economic relationships. However, the map could not add a convincing dimension to an explanation of the observed distribution of economic relationships. Still, the cognitive map showed that the Belgian respondents systematically believed their country to be smaller - except for the Dutch regions Zeeland Flanders and Limburg, which Belgian respondents believed to be Belgian - and that Dutch respondents systematically believed their home country to be bigger than it really is. There is cause for centering attention, in a subsequent study, on the analysis of the impact of other cognitive space indicators upon cross-border action space. Closer study of the meaning of the over- and underestimations of the size of the home countries on a cognitive map is equally recommended.

In this study, it is found that a strong contrast exists as to the perception and experience of mutual business connections between Dutch and Belgian entrepreneurs. On some points, irritation clearly exists. The image that emerged from this analysis coincides with the general stereotypes of, and prejudices towards, each other. The Belgians consider the Dutch arrogant; the Dutch perceive the Belgians in some respects as untrustworthy and their government as overly opaque, too closed up. The 'mental gap' between the entrepreneurs from the two countries is wide, a result coinciding with Hofstede's analysis on the general cultural distance between the two countries (1980, 1991). The analysis of the cultural distance between the Netherlands and Belgium made clear that the Netherlands is culturally closely connected to countries in Northern Europe, whereas Belgium is more closely related to the countries in Southern Europe.

Seen from this perspective, 'Euregionalisation', or in general, internationalisation through the formation of cross-border economic relationships means a process involving 'an expansion of the circles of space', that is to say, the circles of *action space* and *affection space*. Internationalisation is a process. The international orientation of the decision-maker, is for a large part, a learning process. The entrepreneur 'matures' in doing business on an international scale. Experience in cross-border economic co-operation in many cases modifies the negative perception of the other or of the idea of cross-border co-operation. Having professional and especially personal contacts in the neighbouring country certainly helps to initiate economic relationships, but it is not an absolute condition. Other conditions are involved, such as feeling at home in the other culture and being familiar with its rules and conventions. Yet the entrepreneur's perception with regard to entering into cross-border economic relationships, that is, whether he believes that there are great differences in doing business, is therefore of much greater importance. Economic actors do not always appear fully capable or willing to gather the relevant objective information; they seem to draw their own subjective borders and build their own behavioural patterns, possessing certain 'belief sets' that do not necessarily align with what is economically realistic or desirable. In general, international co-operation on a large scale is associated with relatively far-reaching national economic interweaving and a 'border-crossing' perception. Internationalisation is a process that starts in the home country. When a decision is made to initiate relationships with companies in other regions or even further away, the first step towards the neighbouring country has been made.

An open, non-prejudiced attitude is all the more important as the success of the cross-border economic relationship, once established, is strongly dependent of the mutual trust between the partners. This was confirmed in the third analytical model used in this study. The third model, which investigates the reasons for success of cross-border economic developments, furthermore established that similarity between partners, measured in the recognition of each other's business notions, the expected dependency and the mutual sympathy, is an important determinant in the success of a cross-border economic relationship as well. These important findings of the INTERFACE model lead to the conclusion that the development of a successful cross-border economic relationship in fact asks for the 'crossing of two borders'. Not only does the development of a cross-border relationship presuppose that the entrepreneur crosses the border of the own state into a foreign country - which may involve mental distance -, but it also assumes that the entrepreneur crosses 'a bilateral border', meaning that a successful relationship presupposes the presence of similarity and trust between the two partners.

The entrepreneurial horizon

Economic interweaving between regions in neighbouring countries renders the society in the regions involved more complex and turbulent. As may be expected, this renders individual companies and administrative instances insecure. Insecurity often restrains dynamics. The regional networks of companies on either side of the border in such areas appear rather isolated and reluctant to become interactive. Because of this, it is not easy to create a borderless economic zone in Zeeland and Gent/Eeklo, which is what is attempted on a Euregional basis.

The three regions in the research area seen as a whole do not seem to use their economic potential to the full. The most important reason is that as yet unused opportunities for the division of labour leave space for growth through interdependence and competition in the border regions.
A network making numerous contacts possible could lead to a breakthrough in now often limited action and affection patterns. A slowly emerging network can be observed in Zeeland and Gent/Eeklo, which however is neither fully cross-border nor structurally sound as yet. This finding, as presented here, does not stand on its own. Other empirical researches on the depth and strength of networks between (inhabitants and entrepreneurs of) border regions in Europe tends to point in the same direction. There is great optimism about the potential of the co-operation between border regions, but factual progress seems to lag behind.

If the objective is to decrease the (mentally) restraining effect of the state border upon the establishment of economic relationships across the border, the question as to how a horizon should be shifted must be answered. Reasoning from a theoretical perspective, the simulation of the formation of cross-border economic relationships may mean breaking through a pattern or vicious circle. The entrepreneur estimates that cross-border economic relationships cost more, *i.e.* that they require more mental effort and increase insecurity. The threshold, the mental distance with regard to entering into economic relationships is, in this case, higher, which contributes to the entrepreneur's reluctant attitude. He exaggerates differences in conventions and rules in comparison to what they really are. The chances of success are estimated slimmer and financial-economic conditions for partnership are perceived as more strict for cross-border economic relationships. What commenced as fear of the threshold then becomes a true threshold itself. A similar line of reasoning, but then the other way around, applies for the entrepreneur who, little by little, experiences and learns that cross-border economic relationships can add value to his company.

In short, the shifting of the horizon involves a reduction of the costs of the formation of economic relationships and an improvement of clarity and the mutual familiarity with formalities and conventions. In an *inter*national relationship, higher costs and a more restricted degree of clarity and familiarity are involved than in a national economic relationship. Costs may arise from, for example, seeking out contacts, attending international exhibitions, travelling expenses, gathering information about potential partners and locations, deliberation costs, and contract costs.
For a lasting, profound co-operation to develop, trust is the keyword. In terms of economic behaviour this means that the horizon of the economic subjects must be widened; their mental borders must be removed. Cross-border economic communication and co-operation are important first steps towards this goal.

The link between macro and micro

The present study leads to the conclusion that the mental influence of the state border, cannot and should not be undervalued in theories on cross-border economic relationships. The state border must still be considered as a significant delimitator of space in this respect, despite the existence of the economic union. It is not possible to speak of a '*de*-limitation' such as that hoped for and maybe expected at the instauration of the Benelux and European Union; nor it is possible to speak of a unified, 'borderless' economic zone in the border regions of the Netherlands and Belgium. Such a typification does no justice to the great differences in regional economic orientations between the companies in the area under consideration. Moreover, it underestimates the significance that the state border still has for the attitude and perception with regard to, and the true development of, cross-border economic relationships. For the same reason, the 'objective' measure cultural distance alone, which is often used in economic studies to emphasise the importance of cultural differences between countries in the internationalisation of economic organisations, is not satisfactory. It is not the 'objective' difference between cultures that is crucial to the initiation and further development of bilateral economic relationships, but the *perceived divergence* of business formalities and conventions between (the actors of) the countries involved and the *perception of its consequences* for the success of an economic co-operation between companies in those countries.

The state border that exists between the partners lays down an important link between the macro- and the micro-levels, at which the study of cross-border economic relationships moves. At the macro-level (the level of countries), national identity plays an important role in the cohesive force of the demarcated society. Nationalism is the ideology belonging to a territory demarcated by state borders. The national tie that separates economic actors at the border, fed by the cohesive action emanating from a demarcated society, is expressed on the one hand through the perceivedly continued relevance of the border's presence, and on the other hand through de-personified impressions of the people on the other side of the border. The relationships between countries were described in this respect in terms of the emergence of a 'We-Them' relationship. Nationalism, at bottom, is a normatively charged concept (cf. Paasi, 1996), which results in interaction through a We-Them relationship, which is also strongly evaluative.

This national identity also affects the micro-level of economic activities: the individual entrepreneurs in a country. At the outset, the fact that affective space is divided is a theoretical issue; it only becomes a subject of practical relevance when the question emerges as to how it translates into action space - how it influences people's actions. In this study, I have demonstrated that the We-Them relationship, at the micro-economic level for the relationships between actors in Belgian and Dutch border regions, is actively expressed through the amount of insecurity, mental distance, and trust in the success of cross-border economic relationships. In other words, the force of the We-Them effect 'feeds' the mental distance and reduces the trust between entrepreneurs of different nationalities in cross-border economic relationships.

Within the European Union and the Benelux Union, which embrace the research area, a unity of countries without trade obstructions for commodities, services, labour and capital formally exists. That is, formally the borders are indeed open in this sense; in practice however, for the case of the border between the Netherlands and Belgium, it has now been demonstrated that more is needed to ensure that the formal removal of the borders achieves a practical depth and content.

References

Aharoni, Y. (1966). *The Foreign Investment Decision Process*. Harvard Business School: Boston.

Akerlof, G.A. (1983). Loyalty Filters. *American Economic Review, 73 (1)*, 54-63.

Allaert, G. *et al.* (1991). Een Economische Inventarisatie van de Kanaalzone Gent-Terneuzen. *Een Aanzet tot Grensoverschrijdende Samenwerking op Economisch Gebied*. Gent/Terneuzen.

Allport, G.W. (1954). *The Nature of Prejudice*. Addison-Wesley: Reading, MA.

Amin, A., and Thrift, N. (1992). Neo-Marshallian Nodes in a Global Network. *International Journal of Urban and Regional Research, 16(4)*, 571-587.

Amin, A., and Robins, K. (1990). The Re-Emergence of Regional Economies? The Mythical Geography of Flexible Accumulation. *Environment and Planning D: Society and Space, 8*, 7-34.

Amin, A. (1992). The Potential for Turning Informal Economies into Marshallian Industrial Districts. *Paper Presented at the UNCTAD/GTZ Symposium on the Role of Industrial Districts in the Application, Adaptation and Diffusion of Technology*. UNCTAD: Geneve.

Anderson, J.C., Håkansson, H., and Johanson, J. (1994). Dyadic Business Relationships Within a Business Network Context. *Journal of Marketing, 58*, 1-15.

Anderson, B. (1983 (1991)). *Imagined Communities*. Verso: London.

Anderson, E., and Gatignon, H. (1986). Modes of Foreign Entry: A Transaction Cost Analysis and Proportions. *Journal of International Business Studies, Fall 1986*, 1-26.

Arrow, K. (1974). *The limits of organization*. Norton: New York.

Atkinson, J.W. (Ed.) (1958). *Motives in Fantasy, Action, and Society*. Van Nostrand.

Atzema, O., and Wever, E. (1994). *De Nederlandse Industrie: Ontwikkeling, Spreiding en Uitdaging*. Van Gorcum: Assen.

Augelli, J.P. (1980). Nationalization of Dominican Borderlands. *Geographical Review, 70*, 19-35.

Aulakh, P.S., Kotabe, M., and Sahay, A. (1996). Trust and Performance in Cross Border Marketing Partnership: A Behavioral Approach. *Journal of International Business Studies, 27(5)*, 1005-1032.

Axelrod, R. (1984). *The Evolution of Cooperation*. Basic Books: New York.

Babbie, J.S. (1990). *Survey Research Methods, 2nd. ed.* Wadsworth Publishing Company: Belmont, CA.

Balassa, B. (1961). *The Theory of Economic Integration*. Richard Irwin: New York.

Barkema, H.G., Bell, J.H.J., and Pennings, J.H. (1996). Foreign entry, Cultural Barriers, and Learning. *Strategic Management Journal, 17(2)*, 151.

Baron, R.A. and Byrne, D. (1997). *Social psychology, 8 ed.* Allyn and Bacon: Boston.

Bartlett, C.A., and Ghoshal, S. (1989). *Managing Across Borders: The Transnational Solution*. Harvard Business School Press: Boston, Massachusetts.

Beek, J. van (1996). *Samenwerking? Er Zijn Grenzen!: Onderzoek naar de Invloed van de Culturele factor op het Proces van Economische en Politiek-Bestuurlijke Integratie in de Euregio Maas-Rijn*. Syntax Publishers: Tilburg.

Beije, P.R., and Nuys, H.O. (Eds.) (1995). *The Dutch Diamond. The Usefulness of Porter in Analyzing Small Countries*. Garant/SISWO: Apeldoorn/Leuven.

Bell, J.H.J. (1996). *Joint or Single venturing?: An Eclectic Approach to Foreign Entry Mode Choice*. Wibro Dissertatie Drukkerij: Helmond.

Benito, G.R.G., and Gripsrud, G. (1992). The Expansion of Foreign Direct Investments: Discrete Rational Location Choices or a Cultural Learning Process? *Journal of International Business studies, Third Quarter, 461-476.*

Benschop, A. (1996). Transactiekosten in de Economische Sociologie. *Http:// www.pscw.uva.nl / sociosite / ORGANIZATION / tk / tk.html, 1-56.*

Berger, J., Noorderhaven, N.G., and Nooteboom, B. (1995). The Determinants of Supplier dependence: An Empirical Study. In: J. Groenewegen, C. Pitelis, and S.E. Sjöstrand (Eds.), *On Economic Institutions; Theory and Applications*. Edward Elgar: Aldershot, 195-212.

Berscheid, E. (1985). Interpersonal Attraction. In: G. Lindzey, and E. Aronson (Eds.), *Handbook of Social Psychology, 3rd ed., Vol.2.* Random House: New York.

Berscheid, E., and Walster, E. (1974). Physical Attractiveness. In: L. Berkowitz (Ed.), *Advances in Experimental and Social Psychology, Vol.7.* New York *158-215*, Academic Press.

Best, M.H. (1990). *The New Competition: Institutions of Industrial Restructuring*. Polity Press: Cambridge.

Bilkey, W.J., and Tesar, G. (1977). The Export Behavior of Smaller-Sized Wisconsin Manufacturing Firms. *Journal of International Business Studies*, *8*, 93-101.

Blau, P.M. (1964). *Exchange and Power in Social Life*. Wiley: New York.

Bleeke, J., and Ernst, D. (1991). The Way to Win in Cross-Border Alliances. *Harvard Business Review*, *69(6)*, 127-135.

Blois, K.J. (1990). Transaction Costs and Networks. *Strategic Management Journal*, *11*, 493-496.

Boekema, F. and Kamann, D. (1989). Netwerken: een introductie. In: Boekema, F. and Kamann, D., *Sociaal-economische Netwerken*. Wolters-Noordhoff: Groningen, 1-8.

Boekema F., and Houtum, H.J. van (1994). Grensoverschrijdende samenwerking in de Benelux, het voorbeeld van de grensregio Tilburg-Turnhout (Coopération transfrontalière dans le Benelux, l'exemple de la region frontalière Tilburg-Turnhout). *Benelux in de kijker (Regards sur le Benelux)*. Benelux: Brussel (Bruxelles), 299-312.

Boekema, F. (1996). *Geografie en Economie: De Complexe en Ondergewaardeerde Rol van de Ruimtelijke Dimensie in de Economie*. KUN: Nijmegen.

Boerman, W.E. (1923). *Grenzen*. P. Noordhoff: Groningen, 3-27.

Boesch, E.E. (1963). Raum und Zeit als Valenzsysteme. In: Hiltmann, H. and F. Vonessen (Eds.), *Dialektik und Dynamik der Person*. Köln, 135-154.

Boissevain, J. (1974). *Friends of Friends, Networks, Manipulations and Coalitions*. Basil Blackwell: Oxford.

Boogaard, R. van den (1997). *Nationalisme Onder een Nieuwe Loep*. In: NRC Handelsblad, p.37.

Brass, P.R. (1979). Elite Groups, Symbol Manipulation and Ethnic Identity among the Muslim of South Asia. In: Taylor, D. and M. Yapp (eds.), *Political Identity in South Asia*. Curzon Press: London, 35-43.

Bröcker, J. (1984). How Do International Trade Barriers Affect Interregional Trade? In: A.E. Andersson, W. Isard, and T. Puu (Eds.), *Regional and Industrial Theories*. Elsevier Science Publishers: North-Holland, 219-239.

Broek, J.O.M. (1941). The Problem of 'Natural Frontiers'. *Frontiers of the Future*. University of California, Committee on International Relations: Berkeley, 2-20.

Bromily, P., and Cummings, L.L. (1992). *Transaction Costs in Organizations with Trust. Working paper No.28*. Strategic Management Research Center: University of Minnesota.

Brücher, W., and Riedel, H. (1992). L'espace frontalier sarro-lorrain: ses structures socio-demographiques et sa perception. *Espace, Populations, Sociétés, 2*, 153-165.

Bruinsma, F. (1994). *De Invloed van Transportinfrastructuur op Ruimtelijke Patronen van Economische Activiteiten*. Nederlandse Geografische Studies: Utrecht/Amsterdam.

Buckley, P.J., and Casson, M. (1988). A Theory of Cooperation in International Business. In: F.J. Contractor, and P. Lorange (Eds.), *Cooperative Strategies in International Business*. Lexington Books: Lexington, MA, 31-55.

Buckley, P.J., and Casson, M. (1976). *The Future of the Multinational Enterprise*. MacMillan: London.

Buckley, P.J., and Casson, M. (Eds.) (1985). *The Economic Theory of the Multinational Enterprise*. St. Martin's Press: New York.

Buckley, P.J. (1989). Foreign Direct Investment by Small and Medium Size Enterprises: The Theoretical Background. *Small Business Economics, 1*, 89-100.

Bucklin, L.P., and Senguta, S. (1993). Organizing Succesful Co-Marketing Alliances. *Journal of Marketing, 57(april)*, 32-46.

Burt, R.S. (1992). *Strucural Holes: The Social Structure of Competition*. Harvard University Press: Cambridge, Massachusetts.

Buursink, J. (1987). Regionale Geografie: nieuw of opnieuw? *Geografisch Tijdschrift, XXI*, 198-211.

Byrne, D. (1971). *The Attraction Paradigm*. Academic Press: New York.

Byrne, D. and Clore, G.L. (1970). A reinforcement-affect model of evaluative responses. *Personality: An International Journal, 1*, 103-128.

Caves, R.E. (1982). *Multinational Enterprise and Economic Analyis*. Cambridge University Press: Cambridge, MA.

Cavusgil, S T. (1980). On the Internationalisation Process of Firms. *European Research, 273-281*.

CBS (1997). *Several publications*.

Chambers of Commerce Zeeland (1995/1996). *Zeeland in Cijfers*. Terneuzen/Middelburg.

Chardonnet, J. (1953). *Les grands types de complexes industriels*. Libairie Cliffs: Paris.

Christaller, W. (1933 (1966)). *Central Places in Southern Germany*. Englewood Cliffs.

Christensen, P.R., and Lindmark, L. (1993). Location and Internationalization of Small Firms. In: L. Lundqvist, and L.O. Persson (Eds.), *Visions and Strategies in European Integration*. Springer-Verlag: Berlin, Heidelberg, 131-151.

Church, A., and Reid, P. (1995). Transfrontier Co-operation, Spatial Development Strategies and the Emergence of a New Scale of Regulation: the Anglo-French Border. *Regional Studies*, *29(3)*, 297-316.

Clark, C., F. Wilson, J. Bradley (1969). Industrial Location and Economic Potential in Western Europe. *Regional Studies*, *3*, 197-212.

Clark, T. (1994). National Boundaries, Border Zones, and Marketing Strategy: A Conceptual Framework and Theoretical Model of Secondary Boundary Effects. *Journal of Marketing*, *58*, 67-80.

Coase, R.H. (1937). The Nature of the Firm. *Economica*, *4(November)*, 386-405.

Coase, R.H. (1988). The nature of the firms: Influence. *Journal of Law, Economics and Organization*, *4*, 33-47.

Cohen, S.B. (1982). A New Map of Global Geopolitical Equilibrium: A Development Approach. *Political Geography Quarterly*, *1*, 223-41.

Commandeur, H.R., en Hartog, G.J. den (1991). Voor- en Nadelen van Strategische Samenwerking. *Economische Statistische Berichten*, *773-775*.

Connor, W. (1978). A Nation is a Nation, is a State, is an Ethnic Group..., *Ethnic and Racial Studies*, *1(4)*, 379-88.

Contractor, F.J., and Lorange, P. (1988). Why Should Firms Cooperate? The Strategy and Economics Basis for Cooperative Ventures. In: F.J. Contractor, and P. Lorange (Eds.), *Cooperative Strategies in International Business*. Lexington Books: Lexington, Mass, 3-30.

Cooke, P. (1985). Radical Regions. In: G. Rees (Ed.), *Political Action and Social Identity*. MacMillan: London.

Corvers, F., Dankbaar, B., en Hassink, R. (1994b). *Eén, Twee, Drie naar het Buitenland: Actiepunten voor Bedrijven en Grensregio's*. COB/SER: Den Haag.

Corvers, F., Dankbaar, B., en Hassink, R. (1994a). *Nieuwe kansen voor Bedrijven in Grensregio's. Eindrapport*. COB/SER: Den Haag.

Couwenberg, S.W. (1994). *Nationaliteit en Nationalisme, Bron van Integratie en Desintegratie*. SDU Uitgeverij: Den Haag.

Cramer, N., Logie, F., and Mergaerts. B. (1984). Grens en Sociale Relaties. *K.N.A.G. Geografisch Tijdschrift* , *XVIII(3)* , 190-198.

Crush, J.S. (1980). On Theorizing Frontier Underdevelopment. *Tijdschrift voor Economische en Sociale Geografie*, *71(6)*, 343-350.

Cyert, R.M., and March, J.G. (1963). *A Behavioral Theory of the Firm*. Prentice Hall: Engelwood Cliffs, New Jersey.

Dagevos, J., Oerlemans, L., Hulsinck, P., Houtum, H. van, and Boekema, F. (1992). *Grensoverschrijdend Perspectief: Een Kennismaking Tussen en Met het Midden-Brabantse- en Kempense Bedrijfsleven*. EIT, Economisch Instituut Tilburg: Tilburg.

De Swaan, A. (1992). Identiteit. VUGS-congres, *Stuck in the Region, changing scales for regional identity*. Utrecht.

Delwaide, J. (1996). De Imagined Community en Wij: Vlaanderen, Nederland en Europa. In: Koch, K, en Scheffer, P. (Eds.), *Het Nut van Nederland: Opstellen over Soevereiniteit en Identiteit*. Uitgeverij Bert Bakker: Amsterdam, 239-271.

Deutsch, M. (1973). *The Resolution of Conflict: Constructive and Destructive Processes*. Yale University Press: New Haven.

Dicken, P. (1992). *Global Shift: The Internationalization of Economic Activity*. Paul Chapman Publishing Ltd: London.

Dieperink, H., en Nijkamp, P. (1986). De Agglomeratie-Index: Een Ruimtelijke Indeling op grond van Agglomeratieverschijnselen. *Planning, Methodiek en Toepassing*, *27*, 2-8.

Dijck, J. van (1992). Transnationalization of Economic and Social Life in Europe. In: J.J.J. van Dijck, and A.A.L.G. Wentink (Eds.), *Transnational Business in Europe: Economic and Social Perspectives*. Tilburg University: Tilburg, iv-xiii.

Dijck, J. van and Groenewegen, J. (1994). An Institutional Framework for Studying International(izing) Business Systems. In: J. van Dijck, and J. Groenewegen (Eds.), *Changing Business Systems in Europe*. VUBPRESS: Brussels, 13-40.

Dion, K.L, and Dion, K.K. (1987). Belief in a just world and physical attractiveness stereotyping. *Journal of Personality and Social Psychology*, *52*, 775-780.

Dion, K., Berscheid, E., and Walster, E. (1972). What is Beautiful is Good. *Journal of Personality and Social Psychology*, *24*, 1-10.

Donkers, M.M.H.M. (1995). *Transnationale Strategische Samenwerking in Theoretisch en Empirisch Perspectief*. Katholieke Universiteit Brabant: Tilburg.

Dosi, G., Freeman, R., Nelson, G, Silverberg, L., Soete (Eds.) (1988). *Technical Change and Economic Theory*. Printer Publishers: London.

Douma, S., and Schreuder, H. (1991). *Economic Approaches to Organizations*. Prentice Hall International (UK) Ltd: Hemel Hempstead.

Drewe, P., (1993). Infrastructure Barriers, Cooperation and Innovative Policies in a Frontier Region: The Scheldt Estuary. In: R. Ratti and S. Reichman, *Theory and Practice of Transborder Cooperation*. Helbing and Lichtenbahn: Basel und Frankfurt am Main, 303-315.

Drigotas, S.M. (1993). Similarity Revisited: A Comparison of Similarity-Attraction Versus Dissimilarity-Repulsion. *British Journal of Social Psychology*, *32*, 365-377.

Dubini, P., and Aldrich, H. (1991). Personal and Extended Networks are Central to the Entrepreneurial Process. *Journal of Business Venturing*, *6*, 305-313.

Duck, S. (1977). *The study of Acquaintance*. Saxon House: Farnborough, England.

Duck, S. (1995). Talking Relationships into Being. *Journal of Social and Personal Psychology*, *12(4)*, 535-540.

Dunning, J.H. (1977). Trade, Location of Economic Activity and the MNE: A Search for an Eclectic Approach. In: B. Ohlin, P.O. Hesselborn, and P.M. Wijkman (Eds.), *The International Allocation of Economic Activity*. MacMillan: London, chapter 12.

Dunning, J.H. (1979). Explaining Changing Patterns of International Production: In Defence of the Eclectic Theory. *Oxford Bulletin of Economics and Statistics*, *41*, 269-296.

Dunning, J.H. (1981). *International Production and the Multinational Enterprise*. Allen and Unwin.

Dunning, J.H. (1988a). *Explaining International Production*. Unwin Hyman: London.

Dunning, J.H. (1988b). The Eclectic Paradigm of International Production: A Restatement and Some Possible Extensions. *Journal of International Business Studies*, *19(Spring)*, 1-31.

Dunning, J.H. (1989). The Study of International Business: A Plea for a More Interdisciplinary Approach. *Journal of International Business Studies*, *Fall*, 411-436.

Durkheim, E. (1893 (1933)). *The Division of Labour in Society*. Free Press: Glencoe, Illinois.

Dwyer, F.R., Schurr, P.H., and Oh, S. (1987). Developing Buyer-Seller Relationships. *Journal of Marketing*, *51(April)*, 11-28.

Eggertson, T. (1990). *Economic Behaviour and Institutions*. Cambridge University Press: Cambridge.

Emerson, R.M. (1981). Social Exchange Theory. In: M. Rosenberg, and R.H. Turner (Eds.), *Social Psychology, Sociological Perspectives*. Basic Books Inc. Publishers: New York, 30-65.

Enright, M. (1992). The Geographic Scope of Competitive Advantage. VUGS-congres, *Stuck in the Region, changing scales for regional identity*: Utrecht.

Ernste H. and V. Meier (Eds.) (1992). *Regional development and contemporary industrial response : extending flexible specialisation*. Belhaven Press: London.

Eskelinen, H. (1994). *Milieus or Clusters as Seedbeds for Internationalization? Lessons From a Comparative Study of Nordic SMEs*. Paper presented at the 34th European Congress of the Regional Science Association: Groningen.

Etzioni, A. (1988). *The Moral Dimension: Towards a New Economics*. The Free Press: New York.

European Commission (1990). INTERREG. *Publikatieblad van de Europese Gemeenschappen*. European Commission: Brussels *Nr. C 215/4, 30.9.90*.

Evans, G.W. (1980). Environmental Cognition. *Psychological Bulletin*, *88*, 259-287.

Evans, G.W. and Pezdek, K. (1980). Cognitive Mapping: Knowledge of Real-World Distance and Location Information. *Journal of Experimental Psychology: Human Learning and Memory*, *6*, 13-24.

Ewing, G.O. (1981). On the Sensitivity of Conclusions about the Bases of Cognitive Distance. *Professional Geographer*, *33*, 311-314.

Falk, A. (1983). Border Symbolism Revisited. In: Stein, H.F. and W.G. Niederland (Eds.), *Maps from Mind - Readings in psychogeography*. London, 1989, Reprint from: International Review of Psychoanalysis, 10, pp.215-220 *151-160*.

Festinger, L. (1954). A Theory of Social Comparison Processes. *Human Relations*, *7*, 117-140.

Festinger, L., Schachter, S., and, Back. K. (1950). *Social Pressures in Informal Groups*. Stanford University Press: Stanford, Ca.

Fishbein, M., and Ajzen, I. (1975). *Belief, Attitude, Intention and Behavior: An Introduction to Theory and Research*. Addison-Wesley Publ. Comp.: Reading, Mass.

Fisher, S. (1997). Long-Term Contracting, Sticky Prices, and Monetary Policy: Comment. *Journal of Monetary Economics*, *3*, 317-323.

Ford, D. (1980). The Development of Buyer-Seller Relationships in Industrial Markets. *European Journal of Marketing*, *14(5/6)*, 339-354.

Ford, D. (1984). Buyer/Seller Relationships in International Industrial Markets. *Industrial Marketing Management*, *13*, 101-113.

Friedman, J., and Miller, J. (1965). The Urban Field. *Journal of the American Institute of Planners*, *31(4)*, 312-320.

Fukuyama, F. (1995). *Trust : the social virtues and the creation of prosperity*. Free Press: New York.

Gaertner, S.L., Rust, M.C., Dovidio, J.F, Bachman, B.A., Anastasio, P.A. (1994). The Contact Hypothesis, The Role of a Common Ingroup Identity on Reducing Intergroup Bias. *Small Group Research, 25 (2)*, 224-249.

Gatignon, H., and Anderson, E. (1988). The Multinational Corporation's Degree of Control Over Foreign Subsidaries: An Empirical Test of a Transaction Cost Explanation. *Journal of Law, Economics, and Organization, 4(2)*, 305-336.

Geenhuizen, M. van, B. van der Knaap, and P. Nijkamp (1996). Trans-border European Networking: Shifts in Corporate Strategy? *European Planning Studies, 4(6)*, 671-682.

Gertler, M. (1988). The Limits to Flexibility: Comments on the Post-Fordist Vision of Production and its Geography. *Transactions of the Institute of British Geographers, 13*, 419-432.

Geyskens, I., and Steenkamp, J.B.E.M. (1995). Generalizations about Trust in Marketing Channel relationships using Meta-Analysis. *Research Paper*. Catholic University of Leuven.

Ghoshal, S., and Moran, P. (1996). Bad for Practice: A Critique of the Transaction Cost Theory. *Academy of Management Review, 21(1)*, 13-47.

Giaoutzi, M., Suarez-Villa, L. and Stratigea, A. (1993). Spatial Information Aspects and Communication Barriers in Border Areas. In: Ratti, R., en Reichman, S. (Eds.), *Theory and Practice of Transborder Cooperation*. Verlag Helbing & Lichtenhahn: Basel und Frankfurt am Main.

Giaoutzi, M., and Kamann, D.J.F. (1993). The Role of Corporate Structures in Border regions. In: Ratti, R., en Reichman, S. (Eds.), *Theory and Practice of Transborder Cooperation*. Verlag Helbing & Lichtenhahn: Basel und Frankfurt am Main.

Giersch, H. (1949(1950)). Economic Union Between Nations and the Location of Industries. *Review of Economic Studies, 17*, 87-97.

Glasner, M.I. and De Blij, H.J. (1980). *Systematic Political Geography*. John Wiley and Sons: New York.

Goddard, J. (1973). Office Employment, Urban Development and Regional Policy. *Office Location and Regional Development*. An Foras Forbatha: Dublin, 21-36.

Golledge, R.G., and Stimson, R.J. (1987). *Analytical Behavioural Geography*. Croom Helm: New York.

Gottmann, J. (1961). *Megalopolis*. The Twentieth Century Fund: New York.

Gottmann, J. (1973). *The Significance of Territory*. University Press of Virginia: Charlottesville.

Gottmann, J. (1980). *Centre and Periphery*. London, Sage.

Gould, P., and White, R. (1974). *Mental Maps*. Penguin Books: Harmondsworth, England.

Grabher, G. (1993). Rediscovering the Social in the Economics of Interfirm Relations. In: G. Grabher, *The Embedded Firm; On the Socioeconomics of Industrial Networks*. Routledge: London, 1-31.

Granovetter, M. (1982). The Strength of Weak Ties. In: P. Marsden, and N. Lin (Eds.), *Social Structure and Network Analysis*. Sage: Beverly Hills, Ca, 105-130.

Granovetter, M. (1985a). Economic Action and Social Structure: A Theory of Embeddedness. *American Journal of Sociology*, *91*, 481-510.
Granovetter, M. (1985b). Economic action and Social Structure: The problem of Embeddedness. *American Behavioral Scientist*, *23*, 337-352.
Granovetter, M. (1992). Economic Action and Social Structure: The Problem of Embeddedness. In: Granovetter, M., and Swedberg, R., *The Sociology of Economic Life*. Westview Press: Boulder, Oxford.
Groene, J. de (1995). *Beheersen of Beïnvloeden? De respons van Bedrijven op Milieu Problemen. Het Belang van de Omgeving*. Boekhandel Fanoy: Middelburg.
Gross, A.E. and Crofton, C. (1977). What is good is beautiful. *Sociometry*, *40*, 85-90.
Guichonnet, P. and C. Raffestin (1974). *Géografie des Frontières*. Press. Univ. de France (PUF): Paris.
Gulati, R. (1995). Does Familiarity Breed Trust? The Implications of Repeated Ties for Contractual Choice in Alliances. *Academy of Management Journal*, *38(1)*, 85-112.
Habermas, J. (1996). The European Nation-State - Its Achievements and Its Limits. On the Past and Future of Sovereignty and Citizenship. In: G. Balakrishnan, *Mapping the Nation*. Verso: London/New York, 281-294.
Hair, J.F. Jr., Anderson, R.E., Tatham, R.L., and Black, W.C. (1995). *Multivariate Data Analysis*. Prentice Hall, Inc.: Englewood Cliffs, New Jersey.
Håkanson, L. (1979). Towards a Theory of Location and Corporate Growth. In: F.E.I. Hamilton, and G.J.R Linge, *Spatial Analysis, Industry and the Industrial Environment. Progress in Research and Applications*. John Wiley & Sons: Chichester *Volume I. Industrial Systems*, 115-138.
Håkansson, H. (1982). An interaction Approach. *International Marketing and Purchasing of Industrial Goods: An Interaction Approach*. Wiley: Chichester, 10-27.
Håkansson, H. (Ed.) (1987). *Industrial technological Development- A Network Approach*. Croom Helm: London.
Håkansson, H., and Johanson, J. (1988). Formal and Informal Cooperation Strategies in International Industrial Networks. In: F.J. Contractor, and P. Lorange (Eds.), *Cooperative Strategies in International Business*. Lexington Books: Mass., 369-379.
Håkansson, H., and Snehota, I. (1989). No Business is an Island: The Network Concept of Business Strategy. *Scandinavian Journal of Management*, *5 (3)*, 187-200.
Hansen, N. (1977a). Border Regions: A Critique of Spatial Theory and A European Case Study. *Annals of Regional Science*, *11*, 1-14.
Hansen, N. (1977b). The Economic Development of Border Regions. *Growth and Change*, *8*, 2-8.
Hansen, N. (1983). International Cooperation in Border Regions: An Overview and Research Agenda. *International Regional Science Review*, *8(3)*, 255-270.
Harcourt, A., Waal, F.B.M. (Eds.) (1992). Coalitions and Alliances in Humans and Other Animals. *Oxford University Press*, New York.
Hare, R.M. (1984). Rights, Utility, and Universalization: Reply to J.L. Mackie. In: R. Frey, *Utility and Rights*. University of Minnesota Press: Minneapolis.
Harley, J.B. (1989). Deconstructing the Map. *Cartographica*, *26*, 1-20.

Harrigan, K.R. (1988). Strategic Alliances and Partner Assymetries. In: F.J. Contractor, and P. Lorange (Eds.), *Cooperative Strategies in International Business*. Lexington Books: Lexington, MA, 205-226.

Harris, C.D. (1954). The market as a factor in the location of industry in the United States. *Annals of the Association of American Geographers*, 315-348.

Harris, M. (1993). *Culture, people, nature: An introduction to General Anthropology*. HarperCollins College Publishers: New York.

Hartshorne, R. (1933). Geographic and Political Boundaries in Upper Silesia. *Annals of the Association of American Geographers, 23*, 195-228.

Heigl, F. (1978). *Ansätze einer Theorie der Grenze*. Mitteilungen der Österreichischen Gesellschaft für Raumforschung und Raumplanung (Bd.26): Wien.

Hennart, J-F. (1982). *A Theory of Multinational Enterprise*. University of Michigan Press: Ann Arbor.

Henry, N. (1992). The New Industrial Process: Locational Logic of a New Production Era? *International Journal of Urban and Regional Research, 16(3), 275-396.*

Hill, C.W., Hwang, P., and Chan Kim, W. (1990). An Eclectic Theory of the Choice of International Entry Mode. *Strategic Management Journal, 11*, 117-128.

Hobsbawm, E.J. (1990). *Nations and Nationalism since 1780: Programme, Myth, Reality*. Cambridge University Press: Cambridge.

Hodgson, G.M. (1988). *Economics and Institutions: A Manifesto for a Modern Institutional Economics*. Typeset by Opus: Oxford.

Hofstede, G. (1980). *Culture's Consequences: International Differences in Work-Related Values*. Sage Publications: Beverly Hills/London.

Hofstede, G. (1991). *Allemaal Andersdenkenden*. Contact: Amsterdam.

Hogg, M.A. (1992). *The Social Psychology of Group Cohesiveness: From Attraction to Social Identity*. Harvester-Wheatsheaf; New York University Press: London; New York.

Holton, R.J. (1992). *Economy and Society*. Routledge: London.

Homans, G.C. (1958). Social Behaviour as Exchange. *American Journal of Sociology, 63*, 597-606.

Hosmer (1995). Trust - The Connecting Link Between Organizational Theory and Philosophical Ethics. *Academy of Management Review, 20(2)*, 379-403.

Hotelling, H. (1929). Stability in economic competition. *Economic Journal,*, 41-57.

House, J.W. (1981). Frontier Studies: an Applied Approach. In: A.D. Burnett, and P.J. Taylor (Eds.), *Political Studies from Spatial Perspectives*. John Wiley and Sons: New York.

House, J.W. (1982). *Frontier on the Rio Grande: A Political Geography of Development and Social Deprivation*. Clarendon Press: Oxford.

Houtum, H.J. van (1991). *'The Competitive Advantage of Regions.' Een Kritische Beschouwing en Toepassing van de Analyse van Michael E. Porter: 'The Competitive Advantage of Nations' op Nederlands Regionaal Niveau*. Katholieke Universiteit Brabant: Tilburg.

Houtum, H. van (1993). Het Euregionale Beleid, Stimulans voor een Nieuw Ruimtelijk Elan? In: Boekema, F., *Sociale Economie: Markten, Instituties en Beleid*. Wolters-Noordhoff: Groningen, 67-83.

Houtum, H. van (1994). De Benelux; Een Grenzeloze Economische Unie? In: Boekema, F., Houtum, H. van, en Veraghtert, K., *Benelux, Quo Vadis*? Wolters-Noordhoff: Groningen, 23-62.

Houtum, H. van, and Boekema, F. (1994). Regions Seen as Laboratories for a New Europe: The Applicability of the Flexible Specialization Model. In: Dijck, J.J.J. van, and Groenewegen, J.P.M. (Eds.), *Changing Business Systems in Europe: An Institutional Approach*. VUBPRESS: Brussels.

Houtum, H. van, R. van Kerkhoff, F. Boekema (1994a). De economie van grensregio's, Tilburg en Turnhout: 'verre buren'. *Geografie, 3(2)*, 5-6.

Houtum, H.J., R. van Kerkhoff, F. Boekema (1994b). Het Euregionale beleid, Grenzeloze economie binnen Europese Unie nog ver weg. *Geografie, 3(2)*, 7-9.

Houtum, H.J. van, and Boekema, F.W.M. (1995). Regional Economic Competitiveness; Porter and Beyond. In: Beije, P.R., and Nuys, H.O. (Eds.), *The Dutch Diamond? The Usefulness of Porter in Analyzing Small Countries*. Garant: Leuven/Apeldoorn.

Houtum, H. van, Donkers, M., Boekema, F., Hassink, R., Corvers, F., and Van den Tillaart, H. (1996). Ondernemen over de Grens. *Tijdschrift voor Economie en Management, XLI(4)*, 535-560.

Houtum, H. van (1997a). *De Totstandkoming van Grensoverschrijdende Economische Relaties. Een Onderzoek naar de Vorming van Grensoverschrijdende Economische Relaties tussen Bedrijven in Zeeuws-Vlaanderen, Midden- en Noord-Zeeland en het Gewest Gent/Eeklo in het Kader van het Interreg II-project 'Euregionaal Zakendoen'. Hoofdrapport*. European Regional Affairs Consultants: Boxtel.

Houtum, H. van (1997b). *De Totstandkoming van Grensoverschrijdende Economische Relaties. Een Onderzoek naar de Vorming van Grensoverschrijdende Economische Relaties tussen Bedrijven in Zeeuws-Vlaanderen, Midden- en Noord-Zeeland en het Gewest Gent/Eeklo in het Kader van het Interreg II-project 'Euregionaal Zakendoen'. Samenvatting*. European Regional Affairs Consultants: Boxtel.

Hutchinson, J., and Smith, A.D. (Eds.) (1994). *Nationalism*. Oxford University Press: Oxford.

Hymer, S.H. (1960 & 1976). *The International Operations of National Firms: A Study of Direct Foreign Investment*. MIT Press: Cambridge, MA.

Iacobucci, D., and Ostrom, A. (1996). Commercial and Interpersonal Relationships; Using the Structure of Interpersonal Relationships to Understand Individual-to-Individual, Individual-to-Firm, and Firm-to-Firm Relationships in Commerce. *International Journal of Research in Marketing, 13*, 53-72.

James, J., and Bhalla, A. (1993). Flexible Specialization, New Technologies and Future Industrialization in Developing Countries. *Futures, July/August*, 713-732.

Jenkins, R. (1996). *Social Identity*. Routledge: London.

Johanson, J., and Mattsson, L-G. (1987). Interorganizational Relations in Industrial Systems: A Network Approach Compared with the Transaction-Cost Approach. *International Studies of Management and Organization, XVII(1)*, 34-48.

Johanson, J., and Mattsson, L.G. (1988). Internationalisation in Industrial Sysems - A Network Approach. In: N. Hood, and J.E. Vahlne (Eds.), *Strategies in Global Competition*. Croom Helm: New York, 287-314.

Johanson, J., and Mattsson, L-G. (1994). The Markets-as-Networks Tradition in Sweden. In: G. Laurent, G.L. Lilien, and B. Pras (eds.), *Research Traditions in Marketing*. Kluwer Academic Publishers: Boston/London/Dordrecht, 321-342.

Johanson, J., and Wiedersheim-Paul, F. (1975). The Internationalization of the Firm- Four Swedish Cases. *The Journal of Management Studies*, *XII*, 305-322.

Johanson, J., and Vahlne, J-E. (1977). The Internationalization Process of the Firm- A model of Knowledge Development and Increasing Foreign Market Commitments. *Journal of International Business*, *8(1)*, 23-32.

Johanson, J., and Vahlne, J-E. (1990). The Mechanism of Internationalization. *International Marketing Review*, *7(4)*, 11-24.

Johnston, R. (1984). The World is Our Oyster. *Transactions of the British Geographers*, *9*, 443-459.

Johnston, R.J. (1989). The State, Political Geography, and Geography. In: Peet R. and N. Thrift (Eds.), *New Models in Geography (Volume I)*. Unwin Hyman: London.

Johnston, R.J, Gregory, D., Smith, D. (1994). *The dictionary of human geography*. Blackwell Publishers: Oxford.

Jones, S.B. (1943). Description of International Boundaries. *Annals of the Association of American Geographers*, *33*, 99-117.

Jones, S.B. (1945). *Boundary-making*. Carnegie Endowment for International Peace: Washington, DC.

Kahn, A., and McGaughey, T.A. (1977). Distance and Liking: Moving Close Produces Increased Liking. *Sociometry*, *40(2)*, 138-144.

Kamann, D.J.F. (1989). Actoren binnen Netwerken. In: Boekema, F.W.M., en Kamann, D.J.F., *Sociaal-Economische Netwerken*. Wolters-Noordhoff: Groningen.

Kamann, D.J.F, Krolis, H.P., Van de Laak, P.J.A. (1990). *Kiezen voor evenwicht en ontwikkeling, een economische verkenning en milieu-impact analyse van de Kanaalzone van Zeeuwsch-Vlaanderen*. INRO-TNO: Delft.

Kamann, D.J.F. (1993a). Bottlenecks, Barriers and Networks of Actors. In: Ratti, R., en Reichman, S. (Eds.), *Theory and Practice of Transborder Cooperation*. Verlag Helbing & Lichtenhahn: Basel und Frankfurt am Main, 65-102.

Kamann, D.J.F. (1993b). Cultural differences in business networks. In: P.Nijkamp (Ed.), *New Borders and Old Barriers*. Gordon & Breech: London.

Keeble, D., Owens, P.L., and Thompson, C. (1982). Regional Accessibility and Economic Potential in the European Community. *Regional Studies*, *16(6)*, 419-432.

Kessen, A.L.G.M. (1992). *Bestuurlijke vernieuwing in grensgebieden, intergemeentelijke grensoverschrijdende samenwerking*. Drukkerij Duerinck bv: Kloosterzande.

Kilduff, M. (1992). The Friendship Network as a Decision-Making Resource: Dispositional Moderators of Social Influences on Organizational Choice. *Journal of Personality and Social Psychology*, *62(1)*, 168-180.

Klaue, K. (1985). *Le Rôle de l'Echelle dans les Figurations de l'Espace chez l'Enfant*,: Bern.

Knippenberg, H., en Pater, B. de (1988). *De Eenwording van Nederland: Schaalvergroting en Integratie sinds 1800*. SUN: Nijmegen.

Knoke, D., and Kuklinski, J.H. (1986). *Network Analysis. Quantitative Applications in the Social Sciences, 28*. Sage: London.

Knoke, D., and Kuklinski, J.H. (1991). Network Analysis: Basic Concepts. In: G. Thompson, J. Frances, R. Levačić, and J. Mitchell, *Markets, Hierarchies and Networks*. Sage Publications: London, 173-182.

Knorringa, P. (1995). *Economics of Collaboration in Producer-Trader Relations: Transactions Regimes between Market and Hierarchy in the Agra Footwear Cluster, India*. NWO: Amsterdam.

Koffka, K. (1935). *Principles of Gestalt Psychology*. Kegan Paul, Tench, Trubner: New York.

Kogut, B., and Singh, H. (1988). The Effect of National Culture on the Choice of Entry Mode. *Journal of International Business Studies, 411-432.*

Koomen, W. (1988 (1992)). Relaties tussen Groepen. In: Meertens, R.W. and J. von Grumbkow (Eds.), *Sociale Psychologie*. Wolters-Noordhoff: Groningen, 337-55.

Kosmitzki, C. (1996). The Reaffirmation of Cultural Identity in Cross-Cultural Encounters. *Personality and Social Psychology Bulletin, 22(3)*, 238-248.

Kosslyn, S.M. *et al.* (1974). Cognitive Maps in Children and Men. *Child Development, 45*, 707-716.

Kossmann, E.H. (1976). *De Lage Landen 1780-1940. Anderhalve Eeuw Nederland en België.* Uitgeversmaatschappij Elsevier: Amsterdam/Brussel *Derde, Bijgewerkte Editie.*

Krueger, J. (1992). On the overestimation of between-group differences. *European Review of Social Psychology, 3*, 31-56.

Krugman, P. (1991). *Geography and Trade*. MIT Press: Cambridge.

Kymlicka, W. (1990). *Contemporary Political Philosophy: An Introduction*. Clarendon Press: Oxford.

Lambooy, J.G. (1992a). *Regionale Economische Dynamiek, een inleiding in de economische geografie*. Coutinho: Muiderberg.

Lambooy, J.G. (1992b). Samenleven Met en Zonder Grenzen. In: H. van den Brink (Red.), *Bestuur en Territoir: Opstellen Aangeboden Aan Drs. A. Bours*. Het Spinhuis, 5-14.

Lambooy, J.G., en Verburg, M.C. (1992). *Westerschelde Oeververbinding, Innovatieve Investering, Notitie Inzake de Economische Effecten van de WOV.* Maatschappij voor Nijverheid en Handel, Departement Zeeland.

Lambooy, J.G. (1993). Regional Economic Development in Europe: External or Internal Sources? In: J. van Dijk en M.W. de Jong (Red.), *Steden en Regio's in Europa. Nieuwe Ideeën in Nederlands Ruimtelijk Onderzoek, papers van de RSA Nederland Dag 1992*. Geo Pers: Groningen.

Larson, A. (1992). Network Dyads in Entrepreneurial Settings: A Study of the Governance of Exchange Relationships. *Administrative Science Quarterly, 37*, 76-104.

Lefebvre, H. (1991). *The Production of Space*. Basil Blackwell: Oxford UK & Cambridge USA.

Leimgruber, W. (1991). Boundary, Values and Identity: The Swiss-Italian Transborder Region. In: Rumley, D., and Minghi, J.V., *The Geography of Border Landscapes*. Routledge: New York.

Leimgruber, W. (1980). Die Grenze als Forschungsobjekt der Geographie. *Regio Basiliensis: Hefte für Jurassische und Oberrheinische Landeskunde, 67-78.*

Leonidou, L., and Katsikeas, C. (1996). The Export Development Process: An Integrative Review of Empirical Models. *Journal of International Business Studies, Third Quarter*, 517-551.

Leonidou, L.C., and Katsikeas, C.S. (1995). The Internationalization Process of the Firm: A Critical Assessment. In: M. Bergadaà, *Marketing Today and for the 21st Century. Proceedings of the 24th Annual Conference of the European Marketing Academy*. Essec: Cergy-Pontoise Cedex, France *Volume II*, 625-639.

Levinger, G., and Snoek, J.D. (1972). *Attraction in Relationship: A New Look at Interpersonal Attraction*. General Learning Press: New York.

Levinger, G. (1980). Toward the Analysis of Close Relationships. *Journal of Experimental Social Psychology, 16*, 510-544.

Levitt, T. (1983). The Globalization of Markets. *Harvard Business Review, 61(May-June), 92-102.*

Lewe, A. (1995). *'Invoer te Lande Verboden': Een Verkenning van de Handel over Landwegen tussen Nederland en de Pruisische Provincies Rheinland en Westfalen, 1836-1857.* Uitgeverij Verloren: Hilversum.

Ligthart, P.E.M. (1995). *Solidarity in Economic Transactions: An Experimental Study of Framing Effects in Bargaining and Contracting*. Thesis Publishers Amsterdam: Amsterdam.

Lorenz, E.H. (1991). Neither Friends nor Strangers: Informal Networks of Subcontracting in French Industry. In: G. Thompson, J. Frances, R. Levačić, and J. Mitchell, *Markets, Hierarchies and Networks*. Sage Publications: London, 183-192.

Lösch, A. (1940 (1954)). *The Economics of Location*. Yale University Press: New Haven.

Louter, P.J. (1993). *Internationale Expansie: Een Exploratief Onderzoek naar het Internationale Marketingbeleid van Kleine en Middelgrote Ondernemingen*. Stenfert Kroese Uitgevers: Leiden/Antwerpen.

Lubbers, R.F.M. (1995). *Globalisering: Naar een Nieuwe Kijk op Political Economy*. CentER for Economic Research/KUB: Tilburg.

Lundén, T. (1973). Interaction Across an "Open" International Boundary: Norway-Sweden. In: Strassoldo, R. (Ed.), *Confini e Regioni. Proceedings of the Conference: "Problems and Perspectives of Border Regions"*. Institute of International Sociology: Gorizia, 147-161.

Maillat, D. (1991). Transborder Regions between Members of the EC and Non-Member Countries. In: Quévit, M., *Regional Development Trajectories and the Attainment of the European Internal Market*. Gremi: Paris.

Mann, M. (1984). The Autonomous Power of the State. *Archives européennes de sociologie, XXV*, 185-213.

Manshanden, W.J.J. (1988). Urban Field in Nederland: What's in a Name? *Plan, 3(4), 43-45.*

Manshanden, W. (1996). *Zakelijke Diensten en Regionaal-Economische Ontwikkeling; De Economie van Nabijheid*. Economisch-Geografisch Instituut, Universiteit van Amsterdam: Amsterdam.

Marsden, P.V. (1990). Network Data and Measurement. *Annual Review of Sociology, 16*, 435-463.

Massey, D. (1984). *Spatial Divisions of Labour: Social Structures and the Geography of Production*. Routledge: London/New York.

McAllister, D.J. (1995). Affect- and Cognition-Based Trust as Foundations for Interpersonal Cooperation in Organizations. *Academy of Management Journal, 38(1)*, 24-59.

Meertens, R.W., en Grumbkow, J. von (Eds.) (1988(1992)). *Sociale Psychologie*. Wolters-Noordhoff: Groningen.

Melin, L. (1992). Internationalization as a Stategy Process. *Strategic Management Journal, 13*, 99-118.

Miesenbock, K.J. (1987). Small Business and Exporting: A Literature Review. *International Small Business Journal, 6(2)*, 42-61.

Miles, R., and Snow, C. (1992). Causes of Failures in Network Organizations. *California Management Review, 34(4)*.

Milgrom, P.R., and Roberts, J. (1992). *Economics, Organization and Management*. Prentice Hall: Englewood Cliffs (NJ).

Milward, A.S. (1992). *The European Rescue of the Nation-State*. Routledge: London.

Minghi, J.V. (1963). Boundary Studies in Political Geography. *Annals of the Association of American Geographers, 53*, 407-428.

Minghi, J.V. (1991). From Conflict to Harmony in Border Landscapes. In: Rumley, D., and Minghi, J.V., *The Geography of Border Landscapes*. Routledge: New York.

Ministerie van Economische Zaken (1990a). *Regio's zonder Grenzen, Het Regionaal-Economische Beleid voor de periode 1991-1994*. SDU Uitgeverij: Den Haag.

Ministerie van Economische Zaken (1990b). *Economie met Open Grenzen*. SDU Uitgeverij: Den Haag.

Moles, A. A. and Rohmer, E. (1972). *Psychologie de l'Espace*. PUF: Paris.

Moran, P., and Ghoshal, S. (1996). Theories of Economic Organization: The Case for Realism and Balance. *Academy of Management Review, 21(1)*, 58-72.

Moreland, R.L. and Zajonc, R.B. (1982). Exposure effects in person perception: Familiarity, similarity, and attraction. *Journal of Experimental Social Psychology, 18*, 395-415.

Morgan, R.M., and Hunt, S.D. (1994). The Commitment-Trust Theory of Relationship Marketing. *Journal of Marketing, 58*, 20-38.

Mulder, L. (Ed.) (1994). *Lexicon: Geschiedenis Van Nederland en België*. Kosmos-Z&K Uitgevers: Utrecht/Antwerpen.

Murphy, A.B. (1991). Regions as Social Constructs: The Gap between Theory and Practice. *Progress in Human Geography, 15*, 22-35.

Myrdal, G. (1957). *Economic Theory and the Underdeveloped Regions*. Duckworth: London.

Newcomb, T.M. (1961). *The Acquaintance Process*. Holt, Rinehart and Winston: New York.

Nijkamp, P., Rietveld, P. and Salomon, I. (1990). Barriers in Spatial Interactions and Communications. A Conceptual Exploration. *Annals of Regional Science, 24 (4)*, 237-252.

Nijkamp, P. (1993a). Towards a Network of Regions: The United States of Europe. *European Planning Studies, 1(2)*, 149-168.

Nijkamp, P. (1993b). Border Regions and Infrastructure Networks in the European Integration Process. *Environment and Planning C: Government and Policy, 11*, 431-446.

NIS (1995/1996). *Nationaal Instituut voor de Statistiek.* Brussel, Ministerie van Economische Zaken.

Noorderhaven, N.G. (1994). Transaction Cost Analysis and the Explanation of Hybrid Vertical Interfirm Relations. *Review of Political Economy, 6(1)*, 19-36.

Nooteboom, B., and Noorderhaven, N.G. (1995). *Sources, Measurement and Effect of Trust in the Governance of Buyer-Supplier relations* . Groningen/Tilburg *Research Paper, School of Management & Organization*, 1-33.

Nooteboom, B. (1992). A Post-Modern Philosophy of Markets. *International Studies of Management and Organization, 22(2)*, 53-76.

Nooteboom, B. (1993). Networks and Transactions: Do They Connect? In: J. Groenewegen (Ed.), *Dynamics of the Firm: Strategies of Pricing and Organisation.* Edward Elgar: Aldershot, 9-26.

Nooteboom, B. (1995). *Trust, Opportunism and Governance: A Process and Control Model,*: Groningen *Research Paper, School of Mangement & Organization*, 1-22.

Nordström, K. (1991). *The Internationalization Process of the Firm. Searching for New Patterns and Explanations*, Institute of International Business, Stockholm School of Economics: Stockholm.

Nordström, K., and Vahlne, J.E. (1992). Is the Globe Shrinking? Psychic Distance and the establishment of Swedish Sales Subsidiaries During the Last 100 Years. *Paper Presented at the International Trade and Finance Association's Annual Conference, April 22-25, Loredo, Texas.*

North, D.C. (1990). *Institutions, Institutional Change and Economic Performance.* Cambridge University Press: Cambridge.

Nuesser, H.G. (1985). Die Bedeutung von Hemmnisfaktoren für die Entwicklung des Verkehrsaufkommes. *DFVLR-Nachrichten, 45*, 32-34.

O' Dowd, L. and Wilson, T.M (1996). Frontiers of sovereignty in the new Europe. In: O' Dowd, L. and Wilson, T.M, *Borders, Nations, and States.* Avebury: Aldershot, 1-18.

O'Grady, S., and Lane, H.W. (1994). *The Psychic Distance Paradox.* Paper presented at the AIB annual Conference: Boston, USA.

Oerlemans, L.A.G. (1996). *De Ingebedde Onderneming: Innoveren in Industriële Netwerken.* Tilburg University Press: Tilburg.

Ohmae, K. (1985). *The Triad Power: The Coming Shape of Global Competition.* New York, The Free Press.

Ohmae, K. (1990). *The Borderless World, Management Lessons in the New Logic of the Global Market Place, Power and Strategy in the Interlinked Economy.* Harper Business: USA.

Ohmae, K. (1995). *The End of the National state: The Rise of Regional Economics.* HarperCollins Publishers: London.

Oudenhoven, J.P. van, and Boer, T. de (1995). Complementarity and Similarity of Partners in International Mergers. *Basic and Applied Social Psychology, 17(3)*, 343-356.

Paasi, A. (1986). The Institutionalization of Regions: A Theoretical Framework for Understanding the Emergence of Regions and the Constitution of Regional Identity. *Fennia 164, 105-46.*

Paasi, A. (1991). Deconstructing Regions: Notes on the Scales of Spatial Life. *Environment and Planning A*, *23*, 239-56.

Paasi, A. (1996). *Territories, Boundaries, and Consciousness: The Changing Geographies of the Finnish-Russian Border*. John Wiley & Sons Ltd: Chichester.

Parkhe, A. (1993). Partner Nationality and the Structure-Performance Relationship in Strategic Alliances. *Organization Science*, *4(2)*, 301-324.

Passchier, N.P., en Amersfoort, J.M.M. van (1981). De Sociale Betekenis van de Nederlandse Nationale Grenzen: Twee Onderzoekingen in Midden-Limburg en de Aanliggende Duitse en Belgische Grensgebieden. *K.N.A.G. Geografisch Tijdschrift*, *XV(2)*, 119-130.

Pellenbarg, P.H. (1991). Identiteit, Imago en Economische Ontwikkeling van Regio's. *Inaugurele Rede*. Geo Pers: Groningen, 1-27.

Pellenbarg, P.H. (1985). *Bedrijfsrelocatie en Ruimtelijke Cognitie*. Dissertatie RU Groningen: Groningen.

Penrose, E. (1959). *The Theory of Growth of the Firm*. Basil blackwell: London.

Perroux, F. (1955). Note on the concept of 'growth poles'. In: D.C. McKee et al., *Regional Economics; theory and practice*,: New York.

Pred, A.R. (1967). *Behaviour and Location: foundations for a geographic and dynamic location theory*. Lund Studies in Geography, no.27: Lund.

Pfeffer, J. and Salancik, G.R. (1978). *The External Control of Organizations*. Harper and Row: New York.

Piaget, J. and Weill, A.M. (1976). Die Entwicklung der kindlichen Heimatvorstellungen und der Urteile über andere Länder. In: Wacker, A. (Ed.), *Entwicklung des Gesellschaftsverständnisses bei Kindern*. Frankfurt/New York *127-48*.

Pilkington, N.W., and Lydon, J.E. (1997). The Relative Effect of Attitude Similarity and Attitude Dissimilarity on Interpersonal Attraction: Investigating the Moderating Roles of Prejudice and Group Membership. *Personality and Social Psychology Bulletin*, *23(2)*, 107-122.

Pocock, D., and Hudson, R. (1978). *Images of the Urban Environment*. The Macmillan Press Ltd: London and Basingstoke.

Porter, M. (1990). *The Competitive Advantage of Nations*. Mac Millan Press: New York.

Pounds, N. (1954). France and "Les Limites Naturelles" from the Seventeenth to the Twentieth Centuries. *Annals of the Association of American Geographers*, *44*, 51-62.

Prescott, J.R.V. (1987). *Political Frontiers and Boundaries*. Unwin Hyman Ltd: London.

Proshansky, H.M., Fabian, A.K., and Kaminoff, R. (1983). Place-Identity: Physical World Socialization of the Self. *Journal of Environmental Psychology*, *3*, 57-83.

Raap, R.M. (1995). *Netwerkrelaties van startende ondernemingen*. Katholieke Universiteit Brabant: Tilburg.

Racek, A. (1983). *Philosophie der Grenze. Ein Entwurf*. Herder: Wein.

Raffestin, C. (1974). Éléments pour une Problématique des Régions Frontalières. *L'Espace Géographique*, *1*, 12-18.

Ratti, R. (1988). Development Theory, Technological Change and Europe's Frontier Regions. In: P. Aydalot, and D. Keeble, *High Technology Industry and Innovative Environments*. Routledge: London, 197-220.

Ratti, R. (1993a). Spatial and economic effects of Frontiers: Overview of Traditional and New Approaches and Theories of Border Area Development. In: Ratti, R., en Reichman, S. (Eds.), *Theory and Practice of Transborder Cooperation*. Verlag Helbing & Lichtenhahn: Basel und Frankfurt am Main.

Ratti, R. (1993b). Strategies to Overcome Barriers: From Theory to Practice. In: Ratti, R., en Reichman, S. (Eds.), *Theory and Practice of Transborder Cooperation*. Verlag Helbing & Lichtenhahn: Basel und Frankfurt am Main.

Ratzel, F. (1897). *Politische Geografie oder die Geografie der Staaten, des Verkehrs und des Krieges*. Oldenbourg: München.

Rawls, J. (1971). *A Theory of Justice*. Oxford University Press: London.

Ray, J.J., and Hall, G.P. (1995). Need for Affiliation and Group Identification. *Journal of Social Psychology, 135(4)*, 519-521.

Reynolds, D.R., and McNulty, M.L. (1968). On the Analysis of Political Boundaries as Barriers: A Perceptual Approach. *East Lakes Geographer, 4*, 21-38.

Richardson, G.B. (1972). The Organisation of Industry. *Economic Journal, 82*, 883-896.

Riedel, H. (1994). *Wahrnehmung von Grenzen und Grenzraumen: eine kulturpsychologisch-geographische Untersuchung im saarländisch-lothringischen Raum*. Geographisches Institut: Saarbrücken.

Rietveld, P. and Janssen, L. (1990). Telephone Calls and Communication Barriers, The Case of the Netherlands. *The Annals of Regional Science, 24*, 307-318.

Rijsman, J. (1981). Sociale Motivatie. In: J.M.F. Jaspars, and R. van der Vlist (Red.), *Sociale Psychologie in Nederland; Deel 1, Het Individu*. Van Loghum Slaterus: Deventer.

Rindfleisch, A., and Heide, J.B. (1997). Transaction Cost Analysis: Past, Present, and Future Applications. *Journal of Marketing, 61*, 30-54.

Ring, P., and Ven, A.H. van de (1994). Developmental Processes of Cooperative Interorganizational Relationships. *Academy of Mangement Review, 19(1)*, 90-118.

Ritter, G. (1982). *Die deutsch-deutsche Grenze*. Geostudien (Bd. 7): Köln.

Rokkan, S. and Urwin, D. (1983). *Economy, Territory, Identity: Politics of West European Peripheries*. Sage: London.

Rosenberg, M.J. and C.I.Hovland (1960). Cognitive, affective and behavioral components of attitudes. In: C.I. Hovland en M.J. Rosenberg, *Attitude, Organization and Change*. Yale University Press: New Haven.

Rugman, A.M. (1981). *Inside the Multinationals: The Economics of Internal Markets*. Croom Helm: London.

Rugman, A.M. (1986). New Theories of the Multinational Enterprise: An Assessment of International Theory. *Bulletin of Economic Research, 38(2)*, 101-118.

Rugman, A.M., amd Verbeke, A. (1992). A Note on the Transnational Solution and the Transaction Cost Theory of Multinational Strategic Management. *Journal of International Business Studies, 23(4)*, 761-771.

Rugman, A.M., and Verbeke, A. (1993). Generic Strategies in Global Competition. In: A.M. Rugman, and A. Verbeke (Eds.), *Research in Global Strategic Management: Beyond Porter*. JAI Press: Greenwich, CT, 3-16.

Ruigrok, W. and Van Tulder, R. (1993). *The Ideology of Interdependence, The Link between Restructuring, Internationalization, and International Trade*. Amsterdam.

Rumley, D. (1991). Society, State and Peripherality: The Case of the Thai-Malysian Border Landscape. In: Rumley, D., and Minghi, J.V., *The Geography of Border Landscapes*. Routledge: New York.

Rumley, D., and Minghi, J.V. (1991). Introduction: The Border Landscape Concept. In: Rumley, D., and Minghi, J.V., *The Geography of Border Landscapes*. Routledge: New York.

Rykiel, Z. (1995). European Boundaries in Spatial Research. *European Spatial Research and Policy, 2 (1)*, 35-47.

Sack, R.D. (1986). *Human Territoriality: Its Theory and History*. Cambridge University Press: Cambridge.

Said, E. (1978). *Orientalism*. Routlegde and Kegan Paul: London.

Sarkar, M., Cavusgil, T.S., and Evirgen, C. (1996). The Commitment-Trust Framework in International Collaborative Ventures: The Case of the Construction Contracting Industry. *Submitted for the Conference on Global Perspectives on Cooperative Strategies*.

Sayer, A. (1982). Explanation in Economic Geography: Abstraction versus Generalization. *Progress in Human Geography*, *6*, 68-88.

Sayer, A. (1989). The "New" Regional Geography and Problems of Narrative. *Environment and Planning D: Society and Space*, *7*, 253-276.

Schachter, S. (1959). *The Psychology of Affiliation*. Stanford University Press: Stanford.

Scheer, L.K., and Stern, L.W. (1992). The Effect of Influence Type and Performance Outcomes on Attitude Toward the Influencer. *Journal of Marketing Research, 29(February)*, 128-142.

Scheffer, P. (1996). Land Zonder Spiegel: Over de Politieke Cultuur in Nederland. In: Koch, K, en Scheffer, P. (Eds.), *Het Nut van Nederland: Opstellen over Soevereiniteit en Identiteit*. Uitgeverij Bert Bakker: Amsterdam.

Schutte, G.G., and J.M. Light (1978). The relative importance of proximity and status for friendship choices and social hierarchies. *Social Psychology*, *41*, 260-264.

Scott, A.J. (1988). *Metropolis: From the Division of Labor to Urban Form*. University of California Press: Berkeley and Los Angeles, California.

Shaikh, T, and Kanekar, S. (1993). Attitudinal Similarity and Affiliation Need as Determinants of Interpersonal Attraction. *The Journal of Social Psychology*, *134(2)*, 257-259.

Shapiro, D.L., Sheppard, B.H. and Cheraskin, L. (1992). In theory: Business on a handshake. *Negotiation Journal*, *8*, 365-377.

Sharma, V., and Kaur, I. (1996). Interpersonal Attraction in relation to the Loss-Gain Hypothesis. *The Journal of Social Psychology*, *136(5)*, 635-638.

Simon, H.A. (1961). *Administrative Behavior*. MacMillan: New York.

Simon, H. (1991). Organization and Markets. *Journal of Economic Perspectives*, *5(2)*, 25-99.

Singer, P. (1979). *Practical ethics*. Cambridge University Press: Cambridge.

Singh, R., and Tan, L.S.C. (1992). Attitudes and Attraction: A Test of the Similarity-Attraction and Dissimilarity-Repulsion Hypothesis. *British Journal of Social Psychology*, *31*, 227-238.

Smidt, M. de (1991). Internationalisering: Onderneming en Internationale Arbeidsverdeling. *K.N.A.G. Geografisch Tijdschrift*, *XXV(2)*, 115-123.

Smith, A.D. (1991). *National Identity*. Penguin Books: London.

Smith, J.B., and Barclay, D.W. (1997). The Effects of Organizational Differences and Trust on the Effectiveness of Selling Partner Relationships. *Journal of Marketing*, *61*, 3-21.

Snyder, R.A. (1979). Individual Differences and the Similarity/Attraction Relationship: Effects of Level of Similarity-Dissimilarity. *Perceptual and Motor Skills*, *49*, 1003-1008.

Solocha, A., and Soskin, M.D. (1994). Research Note. Canadian Direct Investment, Mode of Entry, and Border Location. *Management International Review*, *34(1)*, 79-95.

Steiner, M., and Sturn, D. (1993). From Coexistence to Cooperation: The Changing Character of Austria's Southeastern Border. In: Ratti, R., en Reichman, S. (Eds.), *Theory and Practice of Transborder Cooperation*. Verlag Helbing & Lichtenhahn: Basel und Frankfurt am Main.

Stewart, J.Q. (1947). Regional Innovation Complexes. *Papers of the Regional Science Association*, *59*, 29-44.

Storper, M. (1992). The Limits of Globalization: Technology Districts and International Trade. *Economic Geography*, *68(1)*, 60-91.

Storper, M. (1993). Regional Worlds of Production: learning and innovation in the technology districts of France, Italy, and USA. *Regional Studies*, *27 (5)*, 433-455.

Storper, M. (1997). *The Regional World, territorial development in a global economy*. The Guilford Press: New York.

Suarez-Villa, L., Giaoutzi, M., and Stratigea, A. (1992). Territorial and Border Barriers in Information and Communication Networks: A Conceptual Exploration. *Tijdschrift voor Economische en Sociale Geografie*, *83(2)*, 93-104.

Sullivan, D., and Bauerschmidt, A. (1990). Incremental Internationalization: A Test of Johanson and Vahlne's Thesis. *Management International Review*, *30(1)*, 19-30.

Tacq, J. (1992). *Van Probleem naar Analyse: de Keuze van een Gepaste Multivariate Analysetechniek bij een Sociaal-Wetenschappelijke Probleemstelling*. Rotterdams Instituut voor Sociologisch en Bestuurskundig Onderzoek: Rotterdam.

Tajfel, H. (1982). *Social Identity and Intergroup Relations*. Cambridge University Press: Cambridge.

Tajfel, H., Billig, M.G., Bundy, R.P., Flament, C. (1971). Social Categorization and Intergroup Behaviour. *European Journal of Social Psychology*, *1*, 149-78.

Tajfel, H., Turner, J.C. (1979a). The Social Identity Theory of Intergroup Behavior. In: Worchel, S. and W.G. Austin (Eds.), *Psychology of Intergroup Relations*. Nelson-Hall: Chicago.

Tajfel, H., Turner, J.C. (1979b). An Integrative Theory of Intergroup Conflict. In: Austin, W.G., and S. Worchel (Eds.), *The Social Psychology of Intergroup Relations*. Brooks/Cole: Monterey, CA, 33-47.

Tallman, S.B., and Shenkar, O. (1994). A Managerial Decision Model of International Cooperative Venture Formation. *Journal of International Business Studies*, *25(1)*, 91-115.

Taylor, C. (1992). Atomism. In: S. Avineri and A. de-Shalit, *Communitarianism and Individualism*. Oxford University Press: Oxford, 29-50.

Taylor, P.J. (1993). *Political Geography: World-Economy, Nation-State and Locality*. Longman Scientific and Technical: London.

Teece, D.J. (1981). The Multinational Enterprise: Market Failure and Market Power Considerations. *Sloan Management Review, 22*, 3-17.

Teece, D.J. (1986). Transactions Cost Economics and the Multinational Enterprise. *Journal of Economic Behavior and Organization, 7*, 21-45.

Tella, G. di (1982). The Economics of the Frontier. In: C.P. Kindleberger, and G. di Tella (Eds.), *Economics in the Long View*. MacMillan: London/Basingstoke, 210-227.

The Economist (1992). Why Networks Fail. *The Economist, October 10th.*

Thompson, D.L. (1963). New Concept: "Subjective Distance" or Store Impressions Affect Estimates of Travel Time. *Journal of Retailing, 39*, 1-6.

Thrift, N. (1983). On the Determination of Social Action in Space and Time. *Environment and Planning, Society and Space, 1(1)*, p.40.

Tillaart, H. van den, and Busse, G. (1994). *Unternehmer ohne Grenze*? ITS: Nijmegen.

Tinbergen, J. (1991). The Velocity of Integration. *De Economist, 139*, 1-11.

Tolman, E.C. (1948). Cognitive Maps in Rats and Men. *Psychol. Rev., 59*, 389-400.

Turner, J.C., Hogg, M.A., Oakes, P.J., Reichner, S.D., and Wetherell, M.S. (1987). *Rediscovering the Social Group: A Selfcategorization Theory*. Blackwell: Oxford/New York.

United Nations (1993). *Small and Medium-Sized: Transnational Corporations*. United Nations Conference on Trade and Development: Programme on Transnational Corporations: New York.

Veen, P., en Wilke, H.A.M. (1986). *De Kern van de Sociale Psychologie*. Van Loghum Slaterus: Deventer.

Veer, P. van 't (1997). *'Growth Triangles', samenwerking and netwerkvorming in de IMS-GT*. Katholieke Universiteit Brabant: Tilburg.

Veitch and Arkkelin (1995). *Environmental Psychology: An Interdisciplinary Approach*. Prentice Hall: Englewood Cliffs, NJ

Ven, A.H., van de, Emmit, D.C., and Koenig, R. (1975). Frameworks for Interorganizational Analysis. In: A.R. Negandhi, *Interorganization Theory*. Kent State University Press: Kent, 19-38.

Velde, B.M.R., van der, en Th. W.M. Vergoossen (1995). *Kleve en Kranenburg, 'eine Reise wert', grensoverschrijdend koopgedrag vanuit Nijmegen en omgeving*. Nijmeegse Geografische Cahiers, no. 49: Nijmegen.

Velde, M. van der, en E. van de Wiel (1996). Winkelen over de grens, Nijmegen en Kleve vergeleken. *Geografie , 5*, 8-9.

Velde, M. van der, D. Vergoossen en E. van de Wiel (1997). Kleve, Nimwegen und das Einkaufszentrum CentrO Lebendiger Einzelhandel in einem Grenzgebiet. *Geographisches Rundschau, 49(3)*, 164-168.

Vernon, R. (1966). International Investment and International trade in the Product Cycle. *Quarterly Journal of Economics, 80*, 190-207.

Vernon, R. (1979). The Product Cycle Hypothesis in the New International Environment. *Oxford Bulletin of Economics and Statistics, 41*, 255-267.

Von Malchus, V.F. (1975). La Coopération des Régions Frontalières en Europa. *No. AS/Coll. Front(75)*. Council of Europe: Strassbourg.

Weber, M. (1948). The Nation. In: Gerth, H.H. and C. Wright-Mills (Eds.), *From Max Weber: Essays in Sociology*. Routledge and Kegan Paul: London, 171-7, 179.

Weber, M. (1961). *General Economic History*,: New York.

Werlen, B. (1993). *Society, action and space*. Routledge: London, New York.

Wever, E. (1987). The Spatial Pattern of High-Growth Activities in the Netherlands. In: B. van Knaap, and E. Wever (Eds.), *New Technology and Regional Development*. Croom Helm: London, 165-185.

Wever, E. (1991). Bedrijf en Omgeving, Een Ongemakelijke Relatie. *Economisch Statistische Berichten, 23 Oktober*, 1072-1076.

Wiedersheim-Paul, F. (1972). *Uncertainty and Economic Distance - Studies in International Business*. Almquist and Wicksell: Uppsala.

Wilkins, A.L. and W.G. Ouchi (1983). Efficient cultures: Exploring the relationship between culture and organizational performance. *Administrative Science Quarterly*, *28*, 468-481.

Williamson, O.E. (1975). *Markets and Hierarchies: Analysis and Antitrust Implications. A Study in the Economics of Internal Organization*. The Free Press: New York.

Williamson, O.E. (1985). *The Economic Institutions of Capitalism*. The Free Press: New York.

Williamson, O.E. (1991a). Economic Institutions: Spontaneous and International Governance. *Journal of Law, Economics, and Organization*, *7*, 159-187.

Williamson, O.E. (1991b). Comparative Economic Organization: The Analysis of Discrete Structural Alternatives. *Administrative Science Quarterly*, *36*, 269-296.

Williamson, O.E. (1993). Calculativeness, Trust, and Economic Organization. *Journal of Law and Economics*, *XXXVI*, 453-486.

Williamson, O.E. (1996a). Economic Organization: The Case for Candor. *Academy of Management Review*, *21(1)*, 48-57.

Williamson, O.E. (1996b). *The Mechanisms of Governance*. Oxford University Press: New York/Oxford.

Wood, D. (1992). *The Power of Maps*. Routledge: London.

Wusten, H. van der (1997). Het Grondgebied van de Staat. *Facta, Sociaal-Wetenschappelijk Magazine*, *5 (5)*, 8-11.

Young, S. (1987). Business Strategy and the Internationalization of Business: Recent Approaches. *Managerial and Decision Economics: The International Journal of Research and Progress in Management Economics*, *8*, 31-40.

Zajonc, R. (1968). Attitudinal Effects of Mere Exposure. *Journal of Personality and Social Psychology*, *9*, 1-27.

Zucker, L.G. (1986). Production of Trust: Institutional Sources of Economic Structure, 1846-1920. In: B.M. Staw, and L.L. Cunnings (Eds.), *Research in Organizational Behaviour*. JAI Press: Greenwich, CT *8*, 53-111.

Zukin, S. and DiMaggio, P. (Eds.) (1990). *Structures of Capital: The Social Organisation of the Economy*. Cambridge University Press: Cambridge.

Appendix 1 The Questionnaire *(version Zeeland Flanders)*

Inhoudsopgave

We vragen U alle vragen te beantwoorden. Indien nodig, maakt U een schatting. En als een vraag voor uw bedrijf niet van toepassing is, schrijf dan 'Niet van toepassing' erbij en ga verder. In totaal heeft U ongeveer een half uurtje nodig. Opgemerkt zij tenslotte nog, dat overal waar 'hij' staat,'hij/zij' bedoeld wordt. Bij voorbaat hartelijk dank voor het invullen!

Algemene bedrijfskenmerken

1. **Maakt uw bedrijf deel uit van een groter concern ?** *(Toelichting: omcirkel het antwoord)*
   a. Nee, mijn bedrijf is zelfstandig
   b. Ja, met hoofdkantoor in Nederland
   c. Ja, met hoofdkantoor in België
   d. Ja, met hoofdkantoor in ....

2. **Sinds wanneer is uw bedrijf in de regio Zeeuws-Vlaanderen gevestigd?** Sinds 19...............

3. **Hoeveel mensen werken er in uw onderneming in vaste loondienst? (minimaal 15 uur per week)**
   .... *(het aantal noemen)*

4. **Hoeveel procent ongeveer heeft daarvan de Belgische nationaliteit?** :..... ....%

5. **Hoeveel afnemers heeft uw bedrijf ongeveer?** .... *(het aantal noemen)*

6. **Hoeveel zet uw bedrijf (ongeveer) af in de volgende gebieden:** *(in % van de totale afzet)*

Nederland		.... %
Daarvan in:		
Zeeuws-Vlaanderen	..........%	
Midden-en Noord-Zeeland	..........%	
Regio Rotterdam	..........%	
Noord-Brabant	..........%	
Elders in Nederland	..........%	
België		.... %
Frankrijk		.... %
Duitsland		.... %
Overig Europa		.... %
Rest van de wereld		.... %
Totale afzet		100 %

7. **Indien U exporteert naar België, wanneer is uw bedrijf daar mee begonnen?**
In 19..................

Relaties in Nederland en België, juni 1996

8. Deze vraag gaat over de afzet-relaties met andere ondernemingen
Dit zijn relaties om de afzet van uw produkten in Nederland en/of België mogelijk te maken en te bevorderen.
Voorbeelden: transport, opslag, distributie, vertegenwoordiging, marketing.

A. **Heeft uw bedrijf één of meerdere relaties om de afzet van uw produkten in Nederland en/of België te bevorderen?** *(omcirkel het antwoord)*

a. Ja
b. Nee, ga naar vraag 9

B. **Wat voor soort afzetrelaties betreft dit en waar zijn deze gevestigd?**
(Per regio aankruisen, meerdere antwoorden per regio mogelijk)

In Nederland: *(Voor regio-indeling zie eerste blad*-NIET IN DIT RAPPORT AFGEBEELD)

	Zeeuws-Vlaanderen	**Midden en Noord-Zeeland**	**Regio Rotterdam/ Rijnmond**	**Elders in Nederland**
Vertegenwoordiger				
Transport, opslag, distributie				
Marktonderzoeksbureau				
Reclame/promotiebureau				
Anders, namelijk..........................				

In België: *(Voor regio-indeling zie eerste blad)*

	Regio Gent/Eeklo	**Regio Brugge**	**Regio Antwerpen/ St. Niklaas**	**Elders in België**
Agent/Vertegenwoordiger				
Transport, opslag, distributie				
Marktonderzoeksbureau				
Reclame/promotiebureau				
Anders, namelijk..........................				

9. Deze vraag gaat over de dienst-relaties met andere ondernemingen
Dit zijn de diensten die uw bedrijf uitbesteedt. Voorbeelden: schoonmaak, beveiliging, catering, zakelijke diensten, financiële diensten.

A. **Heeft uw bedrijf één of meer dienst-relaties in Nederland en/of België?** (*omcirkel het antwoord*)
a. Ja
b. Nee, ga naar vraag 10

B. **Wat voor soort dienst-relaties betreft dit en waar zijn deze gevestigd?**
(Per regio aankruisen, meerdere antwoorden per regio mogelijk)

In Nederland: *(Voor regio-indeling zie eerste blad)*

	Zeeuws-Vlaanderen	**Midden en Noord-Zeeland**	**Regio Rotterdam/ Rijnmond**	**Elders in Nederland**
Schoonmaak, beveiliging, catering				
Zakelijke diensten (advocaten, adviseurs ed.)				
Financiële diensten (banken, verzekeringen e.d.)				
Anders, namelijk:				

In België: *(Voor regio-indeling zie eerste blad)*

	Regio Gent/Eeklo	**Regio Brugge**	**Regio Antwerpen/ St. Niklaas**	**Elders in België**
Schoonmaak, beveiliging, catering				
Zakelijke diensten (advocaten, adviseurs ed.)				
Financiële diensten (banken, verzekeringen e.d.)				
Anders, namelijk:				

10. Deze vraag gaat over de produktieproces-relaties met andere ondernemingen.

Dit zijn relaties met betrekking tot produktie-activiteiten die uw bedrijf levert of uitbesteedt aan een ander bedrijf. Voorbeelden: Toelevering/uitbesteding van onderzoek & ontwikkeling, toelevering/uitbesteding van grondstoffen, (half)fabrikaten/afvalstoffen, toelevering/uitbesteding van onderhoud of kwaliteitscontrole.

A. **Heeft uw bedrijf één of meerdere produktieproces-relaties in Nederland en/of België?**

(omcirkel het antwoord)

a. Ja

b. Nee, ga naar vraag 11

B. **Wat voor soort produktieproces-relaties betreft dit en waar zijn deze gevestigd?**

(Per regio aankruisen, meerdere antwoorden per regio mogelijk)

In Nederland: *(Voor regio-indeling zie eerste blad)*

Toelevering van:	**Zeeuws-Vlaanderen**	**Midden en Noord-Zeeland**	**Regio Rotterdam/ Rijnmond**	**Elders in Nederland**
Onderzoek & Ontwikkeling				
Ontwerpen en werkvoorbereiding				
Grondstoffen/(half)fabrikaten/ afvalstoffen/restprodukten				
Onderhoud/reparatie/ kwaliteitscontrole				
Anders, namelijk:				

In Nederland:

Uitbesteding van:	**Zeeuws-Vlaanderen**	**Midden en Noord-Zeeland**	**Regio Rotterdam/ Rijnmond**	**Elders in Nederland**
Onderzoek & Ontwikkeling				
Ontwerpen en werkvoorbereiding				
Grondstoffen/(half)fabrikaten/ afvalstoffen/restprodukten				
Onderhoud/reparatie/ kwaliteitscontrole				
Anders, namelijk:				

In België: *(Voor regio-indeling zie eerste blad)*

Toelevering van:	**Regio Gent/Eeklo**	**Regio Brugge**	**Regio Antwerpen/ St. Niklaas**	**Elders in België**
Onderzoek & Ontwikkeling				
Ontwerpen en werkvoorbereiding				
Grondstoffen/(half)fabrikaten/ afvalstoffen/restprodukten				
Onderhoud/reparatie/ kwaliteitscontrole				
Anders, namelijk:				

In België:

Uitbesteding van:	**Regio Gent/Eeklo**	**Regio Brugge**	**Regio Antwerpen/ St. Niklaas**	**Elders in België**
Onderzoek & Ontwikkeling				
Ontwerpen en werkvoorbereiding				
Grondstoffen/(half)fabrikaten/ afvalstoffen/restprodukten				
Onderhoud/reparatie/ kwaliteitscontrole				
Anders, namelijk:				

11. Deze vraag gaat over de zeggenschap-relaties met andere ondernemingen

Hierbij heeft uw bedrijf een vergaande samenwerking met een ander bedrijf. Er is een verdeling naar zeggenschap gemaakt over uw gezamenlijke activiteiten . Voorbeelden: Joint venture, participatie, fusie, overname.

A. **Heeft uw bedrijf één of meerdere zeggenschap-relaties in Nederland en/of België?** *(omcirkel het antwoord)*

a. Ja

b. Nee, ga naar vraag 12

B. **Wat voor soort zeggenschap-relaties betreft dit en waar zijn deze gevestigd?**

(Per regio aankruisen, meerdere antwoorden per regio mogelijk)

In Nederland: *(Voor regio-indeling zie eerste blad)*

	Zeeuws-Vlaanderen	**Midden en Noord-Zeeland**	**Regio Rotterdam/ Rijnmond**	**Elders in Nederland**
Joint venture met ander bedrijf				
Participatie in ander bedrijf				
Fusie met ander bedrijf				
Overname van een ander bedrijf				
Anders, namelijk:				

In België: *(Voor regio-indeling zie eerste blad)*

	Regio Gent/Eeklo	**Regio Brugge**	**Regio Antwerpen/ St. Niklaas**	**Elders in België**
Joint venture met ander bedrijf				
Participatie in ander bedrijf				
Fusie met ander bedrijf				
Overname van een ander bedrijf				
Anders, namelijk:				

Uw relatie in België waarmee U het meest vergaand samenwerkt.

12.A. **U selecteert nu de relatie in België waarmee U het meest vergaand samenwerkt .**

De selectie gaat als volgt: Een zeggenschap-relatie is de meest vergaande samenwerking en staat daarom in rangorde van samenwerking het hoogst, dan volgt de produktieproces-relatie, dan de dienst-relatie en de minst vergaande vorm van samenwerking en dus laagste in deze rangorde is de afzet-relatie. Kies uit de relaties die uw bedrijf heeft in België, op basis van deze rangorde, één relatie in België waarmee U het meest vergaand samenwerkt en geef aan welke vorm deze relatie heeft.

Voorbeeld: *U heeft geen zeggenschap-relatie (=de meest vergaande samenwerkingsvorm), maar wel een produktieproces-relatie, een dienst-relatie en een afzet-relatie in België. Dan kiest U dus de op één na hoogste relatie, uw produktieproces-relatie, U omcirkelt dan vervolgens erachter welke vorm deze relatie heeft en U gaat door naar vraag 12B.*

Mijn meest vergaande samenwerkings-relatie in België is:

1. Een Zeggenschap-relatie, namelijk:
   - a. Joint venture
   - b. Participatie in ander bedrijf
   - c. Participatie in uw bedrijf
   - d. Fusie met ander bedrijf
   - e. Overname van een ander bedrijf
   - f. Anders, namelijk: ....

2. Een Produktieproces-relatie, namelijk:
   - a. Toelevering van Onderzoek & Ontwikkeling
   - b. Uitbesteding van Onderzoek & Ontwikkeling
   - c. Toelevering van Ontwerpen en Werkvoorbereiding
   - d. Uitbesteding van Ontwerpen en Werkvoorbereiding
   - e. Toelevering van afval-of grondstoffen/(half)fabrikaten
   - f. Uitbesteding van afval-of grondstoffen/(half)fabrikaten
   - g. Toelevering van onderhoud, reparatie of kwaliteitscontrole
   - h. Uitbesteding van onderhoud, reparatie of kwaliteitscontrole
   - i. Anders, namelijk: ....

3. Een Dienst-relatie, namelijk:
   a. Schoonmaak, beveiliging, catering
   b. Zakelijke diensten (advocaten, adviseurs ed.)
   c. Financiële diensten (banken, verzekeringen e.d.)
   d. Anders, namelijk: ....

4. Een Afzet-relatie, namelijk:
   a. Agent/Vertegenwoordiger
   b. Transport, opslag, distributie
   c. Marktonderzoeksbureau
   d. Reclame/promotiebureau
   e. Anders, namelijk..........................

5. Geen enkele relatie in België, ga naar vraag 22

B. **Waar in België was de zojuist geselecteerde meest vergaande relatie van uw bedrijf gevestigd?** *(omcirkel het antwoord)*

a. Regio Gent/Eeklo
b. Regio Antwerpen/St. Niklaas
c. Regio Brugge
d. Elders in België

C. *Als U een zeggenschap-relatie geselecteerd heeft:* **Wat was bij de start van deze relatie uw aandeel in de zeggenschap?**
.... %

Als U een andere relatie geselecteerd heeft: **Wat betekende het aangaan van deze relatie voor uw omzet?** *(gelieve aan te kruisen)*

5	4	3	2	1
Zeer sterke toename	*Toename*	*Kleine toename*	*Geen verschil*	*Afname*

De volgende vragen 13 t/m 21 gaan over de tijd dat U in contact kwam met de hierboven geselecteerde relatie.
Probeert U zich die tijd zo goed mogelijk te herinneren. Waar het niet anders kan, maakt U een schatting.

13.A. **In welk jaar kwam U in contact met deze relatie?**
In 19..................................

B. **Hoeveel mensen had uw bedrijf toen ongeveer in vaste loondienst (minimaal 15 uur per week)**
.... *(aantal noemen)*

C. **Hoeveel mensen had deze relatie ongeveer in vaste loondienst (minimaal 15 uur per week) ?**
.... *(aantal noemen)*

D. **Wat was toen de economische hoofdactiviteit van deze relatie?**
(omcirkel het meest passende antwoord)

a. Industrie
b. Bouwnijverheid of installatiebedrijf
c. Handel, horeca of reparatiebedrijf voor gebruiksgoederen
d. Transport-en overslag of communicatiebedrijf
e. Bank-en verzekeringswezen, zakelijke dienstverlening
f. Anders, namelijk..

E. **Welke functie had de persoon van deze relatie, waarmee U toen in contact kwam?**
(omcirkel het antwoord)

a. (mede)Directeur of eigenaar
b. Lid staf/lijnmanagement
c. Agent/vertegenwoordiger
d. Anders, namelijk:..

14. **Wie had er het initiatief genomen tot kennismaking?***(omcirkel het antwoord)*

a. De ander

b. Ik/mijn bedrijf

c. Allebei tegelijkertijd

d. Een derde, namelijk ....

e. Anders, namelijk..

15. **Hebben anderen een informatieve of adviserende rol gespeeld in het totstand brengen van het contact/de relatie?** *(omcirkel het antwoord, meerdere antwoorden mogelijk)*

a. Ja, namelijk:
1. Een andere zakelijke relatie, vb een toeleverancier, klant of adviseur in Nederland
2. Een andere zakelijke relatie, vb. een toeleverancier, klant of adviseur in België
3. Een collega-ondernemer in Nederland
4. Een collega-ondernemer in België
5. Een Kamer van Koophandel in Nederland
6. Een Kamer van Koophandel in België
7. Persoonlijke kennis in Nederland
8. Persoonlijke kennis in België
9. Naaste collega's in uw eigen bedrijf
10. Anders, namelijk: ....

b. Nee, niemand

16. A. **Hoe lang duurde een gemiddelde autoreis naar het kantoor/bedrijf van deze relatie?**

.... Minuten

B. **Hoe vaak bezocht U deze relatie gemiddeld in de periode van kennismaking?** *(gelieve aan te kruisen)*

7	6	5	4	3	2	1
Dagelijks	*Om de paar dagen*	*Wekelijks*	*Om de paar weken*	*Maandelijks*	*Om de paar maanden*	*Om de paar jaren*

17.A. **Had U al andere samenwerkings-relaties in België, toen U in contact kwam met deze relatie ?**

(gelieve te omcirkelen)

a. Ja

b. Nee

B. **Hoeveel <u>zakelijke kennissen</u> had U in België, in vergelijking met Nederland, toen U in contact kwam met deze relatie?** *(gelieve aan te kruisen)*

7	6	5	4	3	2	1
Veel meer			*Evenveel*			*Veel minder*

C. **Hoe vaak bezocht U deze zakelijke kennissen in België in die tijd?** *(gelieve aan te kruisen)*

7	6	5	4	3	2	1
Dagelijks	*Om de paar dagen*	*Wekelijks*	*Om de paar weken*	*Maandelijks*	*Om de paar maanden*	*Om de paar jaren*

D. **Hoeveel <u>persoonlijke kennissen</u> had U in België, in vergelijking met Nederland, toen U in contact kwam met deze relatie?**

(gelieve aan te kruisen)

7	6	5	4	3	2	1
Veel meer			*Evenveel*			*Veel minder*

E. **Hoe vaak bezocht U deze persoonlijke kennissen in België, in die tijd?** *(gelieve aan te kruisen)*

7	6	5	4	3	2	1
Dagelijks	*Om de paar dagen*	*Wekelijks*	*Om de paar weken*	*Maandelijks*	*Om de paar maanden*	*Om de paar jaren*

18A. **Uw omgang met uw zakelijke contacten, in de tijd dat U in contact kwam met de geselecteerde relatie.**
(Gelieve aan te kruisen)

	In welke mate was dit het geval?						
	Zeer sterk het geval						***Niet het geval***
a. Ik had een voorkeur voor projecten met hoge winsten, ondanks een hoger risico.	7	6	5	4	3	2	1
b. Ik had een voorkeur voor vaste, langlopende relaties.	7	6	5	4	3	2	1
c. In de zakelijke contacten zocht ik naar die personen, die zelf veel zakelijke contacten hadden.	7	6	5	4	3	2	1
d. Ik zocht bewust naar nieuwe zakelijke contacten en relaties in België.	7	6	5	4	3	2	1
e. Ik wilde relaties die qua reisafstand dichtbij gelegen waren.	7	6	5	4	3	2	1
f. Ik kende de prijs/kwaliteit verhouding van vergelijkbare bedrijven, voordat ik met een bepaald bedrijf een relatie aanging.	7	6	5	4	3	2	1
g. Ik had een voorkeur voor relaties in Nederland	7	6	5	4	3	2	1
h. Ik voelde me thuis in de Belgische *woon-en leef*cultuur	7	6	5	4	3	2	1
i. Ik voelde me thuis in de Belgische *bedrijfs*cultuur.	7	6	5	4	3	2	1

B. Ieder bedrijf heeft relaties. Waarom koos U er destijds voor om juist in België relaties aan te gaan?

....

....

....

De keuze van deze relatie in België

19. **Waarom juist deze relatie?** Het gaat nog steeds over de relatie in België die U eerder in de vragenlijst heeft geselecteerd. *(gelieve aan te kruisen, meerdere antwoorden kunnen 'zeer belangrijk' zijn)*

	Belang van de reden						
Waarom koos U juist voor deze relatie?	***Zeer belangrijk***						***Zeer onbelangrijk***
a. omdat hij belangrijke zakelijke contacten en informatie had	7	6	5	4	3	2	1
b. omdat U elkaar als persoon goed lag	7	6	5	4	3	2	1
c. vanwege zijn specifieke kennis en know-how	7	6	5	4	3	2	1
d. omdat hij ook met andere bedrijven relaties had	7	6	5	4	3	2	1
e. omdat hij iemand leek waar U van op aan kon	7	6	5	4	3	2	1
f. omdat hij op relatief korte reisafstand gevestigd was	7	6	5	4	3	2	1
g. omdat U zich kon herkennen in zijn zakelijke opvattingen	7	6	5	4	3	2	1
h. vanwege zijn goede reputatie	7	6	5	4	3	2	1

i. omdat een relatie met deze partner voor uw bedrijf een betere marktpositie zou opleveren	7	6	5	4	3	2	1
j. vanwege de lage prijs die hij vroeg	7	6	5	4	3	2	1
k. vanwege de hoge kwaliteit die hij kon leveren	7	6	5	4	3	2	1
l. vanwege zijn specifieke materiële middelen (kapitaal /grondstoffen)	7	6	5	4	3	2	1
m. omdat hij interessante ándere zakelijke opvattingen had dan U	7	6	5	4	3	2	1
n. omdat hij een goede toegang kon verschaffen tot de Belgische markt	7	6	5	4	3	2	1

De keuze voor juist deze relatie was ingegeven door (nog) andere factoren, namelijk:

....

....

De zakelijke besprekingen om tot werkafspraken te komen

20.A. **Deze vraag betreft het verloop van de besprekingen om tot concrete werkafspraken te komen.** Het gaat ook hier nog over de relatie in België die U eerder in de vragenlijst heeft geselecteerd. *(Gelieve aan te kruisen)*

	In welke mate was dit het geval?						
	Zeer sterk het geval						*Niet het geval*
a. Toen U eenmaal de zakelijke besprekingen begon, was het persoonlijke contact met de ander <u>informeel en open</u>	7	6	5	4	3	2	1
b. De communicatie tussen U beiden verliep <u>soepel</u>	7	6	5	4	3	2	1
c. Uw bedrijf moest <u>investeren in kennis/ mensen/middelen</u> om met deze partner tot zakelijke werkafspraken te komen	7	6	5	4	3	2	1
d. Uw bedrijf moest het <u>produktieproces en/of het produkt veranderen</u> om met deze partner tot zakelijke werkafspraken te komen	7	6	5	4	3	2	1
e. U wist precies wat U aan elkaar had	7	6	5	4	3	2	1
f. De zakelijke besprekingen werden gekenmerkt door het <u>stellen van garanties en het wederzijds afdekken van risico's</u>	7	6	5	4	3	2	1
g. In de zakelijke besprekingen deed de ander voorstellen die voor uw bedrijf <u>nadelig</u> waren.	7	6	5	4	3	2	1
h. De uiteindelijk afgesproken samenwerking ging verder dan U vooraf had verwacht.	7	6	5	4	3	2	1

B. **Werden de uiteindelijk gemaakte werkafspraken voor beide partijen op papier gezet ?**

(omcirkel het antwoord)

a. Ja.

b. Nee

Zo ja, wanneer was dat?

In: 19..

21.A. **Is de intensiteit van de samenwerking sindsdien veranderd?***(gelieve aan te kruisen)*

7	6	5	4	3	2	1

Nu veel meer — *Evenveel* — *Nu veel minder*

B. **Beschouwt U de samenwerking vandaag de dag als succesvol?***(gelieve aan te kruisen)*

7	6	5	4	3	2	1

Zeer succesvol — *Zeer weinig succesvol*

De verschillen in relaties tussen Nederland en België

22.A. Ga voor de volgende onderwerpen uit van de Nederlandse situatie en vergelijk de Belgische daarmee: *(gelieve aan te kruisen)*

Het verschil tussen een relatie met een Belgische ondernemer en een relatie met een Nederlandse ondernemer:	*Grootte van het verschil*						
	Veel groter			*Geen verschil*			*Veel kleiner*
a. Het financiële draagvlak dat nodig is, om een relatie in België aan te gaan is:	7	6	5	4	3	2	1
b. Het tijdsbeslag van het vinden van een relatie in België is:	7	6	5	4	3	2	1
c. De tijd die nodig is om een relatie in België goed te leren kennen is:	7	6	5	4	3	2	1
d. Het zakelijke belang van een relatie in België is:	7	6	5	4	3	2	1
e. De onzekerheid over het nakomen van werkafspraken met een relatie in België is:	7	6	5	4	3	2	1
f. De organisatorische aanpassing als gevolg van een relatie in België is:	7	6	5	4	3	2	1
g. Het vriendelijke, informele karakter van samenwerking in België is:	7	6	5	4	3	2	1
h. De succeskans van een relatie in België is:	7	6	5	4	3	2	1
i. Het verschil tussen U en de ander wat betreft zakelijke gewoonten is, in een relatie met een Belgische ondernemer:	7	6	5	4	3	2	1
j. De efficiëntie in de samenwerking met een relatie in België is:	7	6	5	4	3	2	1
k. De verwachte intensiteit van samenwerking met een relatie in België is:	7	6	5	4	3	2	1
l. De verwachte duur van samenwerking met een relatie in België is:	7	6	5	4	3	2	1
m. De kans op communicatie-stoornis is, in een relatie met een Belgische ondernemer:	7	6	5	4	3	2	1
n. Het verschil in zakelijke opvattingen is, in een relatie met een Belgische ondernemer:	7	6	5	4	3	2	1
o. Het belang van een goede marktpositie van een relatie in België is:	7	6	5	4	3	2	1

B. **Geef aan welke knelpunten en problemen U persóónlijk heeft ervaren in het zakendoen met Belgische ondernemers.**

....

....

....

....

Landsgrens en identiteit

23. De aanwezigheid van de landsgrens tussen Nederland en België. Geef uw oordeel over alle stellingen. *(Omcirkel elke keer één cijfer)*

De landsgrens tussen Nederland en België is:

Nutteloos	7	6	5	4	3	2	1	Nuttig
Kunstmatig	7	6	5	4	3	2	1	Natuurlijk
Abnormaal	7	6	5	4	3	2	1	Normaal
Onbelangrijk	7	6	5	4	3	2	1	Belangrijk
Irriterend	7	6	5	4	3	2	1	Niet irriterend
Belemmerend	7	6	5	4	3	2	1	Niet belemmerend
Kostenverhogend	7	6	5	4	3	2	1	Niet kostenverhogend
Beperkend	7	6	5	4	3	2	1	Niet beperkend
Merkbaar	7	6	5	4	3	2	1	Onmerkbaar
Afscheidend	7	6	5	4	3	2	1	Verbindend

24. **Schat de gemiddelde afstand in km per auto over de weg.** *(antwoord zonder op te zoeken)*

Terneuzen-Rotterdam	.... kilometer
Terneuzen-Breda	.... kilometer
Terneuzen-Middelburg	.... kilometer
Terneuzen-Gent	.... kilometer
Terneuzen-Brugge	.... kilometer
Terneuzen-Antwerpen	.... kilometer

25. **De persoonlijke verbondenheid met gebieden.** *(Gelieve per gebied één cijfer aan te kruisen)*

Ik voel me:	*Volledig*					*Geheel niet*	
Zeeuws-Vlaming	7	6	5	4	3	2	1
Zeeuw	7	6	5	4	3	2	1
Nederlander	7	6	5	4	3	2	1
Vlaming	7	6	5	4	3	2	1
Belg	7	6	5	4	3	2	1
Grensregio-bewoner	7	6	5	4	3	2	1
Europeaan	7	6	5	4	3	2	1
Wereldburger	7	6	5	4	3	2	1

26. **Teken op de kaart, de grens tussen Nederland en België, zo nauwkeurig mogelijk in met een lijn.**
Daarbij is het van groot belang dat U spontaan intekent. Raadpleging van een atlas of landkaart maakt ons onderzoek op dit punt zinloos.
U kunt niet goed of fout antwoorden. Teken hieronder in:
Kaart van Nederland en België.
-IN DIT RAPPORT NIET AFGEBEELD -

Slotvragen

27.A. **Welke functie heeft U binnen de onderneming?** *(omcirkel het antwoord)*
a. (mede)Directeur/eigenaar
b. lid staf/lijnmanagement
c. anders, namelijk ....

B. **In welke gemeente woont U:** ....

C. **Welke nationaliteit heeft U?** *(omcirkel het antwoord)*
a. Nederlandse
b. Belgische
c. Anders, namelijk..

D. **Bent U Man of Vrouw?** *(omcirkel het antwoord)*
a. Man
b. Vrouw

28. **Kunt U een aantal suggesties geven hoe de Kamer van Koophandel behulpzaam zou kunnen zijn bij het bevorderen van relaties en contacten in België?**
....
....
....
....

Dit is het einde van de vragenlijst.
Nogmaals hartelijk bedankt!

Appendix 2 Overview of the determinants in the INTERFACE model

This appendix describes the indicator(s) that were used to establish the determinants in the INTERFACE model, as distinguished in this chapter, including their measurement level (see the questionnaire, appendix 1). The measurement level has consequences for the technique of the analyses (see for more information on the choice of techniques in multivariate analyses: Tacq, 1992). Three levels of measurement will be applied (cf. Tacq, 1992): the nominal (N), ordinal (O), and quantitative (Q) level. At the nominal level, no rank or order can be ascribed to the value (one Dutchman is not more than one Belgian or one German). The ordinal scale does allow for ranking; a number of values are thus interposed between two extremes, one of which the respondent selects (criminality in this neighbourhood is very high, high, average, low, very low). The quantitative measurement level, finally, makes it possible to determine the distances between the interposed values (Jack is three years younger than Jill).

In the scheme below, the determinants of the six stages in the INTERFACE model distinguished in section 4.1 are summarised. A distinction is made between independent and dependent variables. The determinants in the stages of 'contact', 'attraction', 'interaction' and 'transaction' are independent variables. 'Economic relationship Yes/No', the number of economic relations, and the success of the economic relationship are dependent variables.

Independent variables

Contact

Variable	**Indicator**	**Measurement Level**
Social network	Number of personal acquaintances in the neighbouring country	Q
	Visiting frequency of these acquaintances	O
Professional network	Number of professional acquaintances in the neighbouring country	Q
	Visiting frequency of these acquaintances	O
Direct or indirect contact	Assistance/advice in establishing the contact with the other in the neighbouring country - Yes/No	N
Indirect contact	Professional relation in the home country - Yes/No	N
	Professional relation in the neighbouring country - Yes/No	N
	Colleague entrepreneur in the home country - Yes/No	N
	Colleague entrepreneur in the neighbouring country - Yes/No	N
	Chamber of Commerce in the home country - Yes/No	N
	Chamber of Commerce in the neighbouring country - Yes/No	N
	Personal acquaintance in the home country - Yes/No	N

	Personal acquaintance in the neighbouring country - Yes/No	N
Relationship preference	Preference for higher profit, despite higher risk Preference for steady long-term economic relationships Preference for economic relations with a broad contact network Preference for conscious search for professional contacts and economic relations in the neighbouring country Preference for economic relations at short distance Preference for knowledge concerning the price/quality ratio of alternative partners Preference for economic relations in the home country	O O O O O O O
Experience	Other economic relationships in the neighbouring country Yes/No	N
Physical distance	Travelling time (in minutes) to the economic partner	Q
Cognitive distance	Estimation of distance to cities in home and neighbouring country (in kilometres)	Q
Mental distance	*The estimation of the differences between the neighbouring country and the home country with regard to:* Required financial resources Time required for finding a partner for an economic relation Time required for getting to know the partner well Uncertainty about respecting agreements Organisational modifications as a consequence of the relationship Chance that the relationship will be successful Differences in professional habits Efficiency in the relationship Expected intensity of the relationship Expected duration of the relationship Risk of miscommunication in the relationship Difference in professional ideas Importance of the other's good market position	 O O O O O O O O O O O O O
'Feeling at home' in the neighbouring country	The degree of 'feeling at home' in the living culture of the neighbouring country The degree of 'feeling at home' in the business culture of the neighbouring country	O O
Spatial identity	Zeeland Fleming Zeelander Dutchman Belgian Fleming Border region inhabitant European World citizen	O O O O O O O O

Border evaluation	Barrier	Irritating - Not irritating Hindering- Not hindering Cost-increasing - Not cost-increasing Restrictive - Not restrictive Perceivable - Not perceivable Dividing - Connecting	O O O O O O
	Relevance	Useless - Useful Artificial - Natural Abnormal - Normal Unimportant - Important	O O O O
Cognitive map		Drawing the state border on a blind map	O

Attraction

Spatial proximity	Importance of short distance to the other Travelling time in minutes to the other Contact frequency with the other	O Q O
Similarity	Sympathy for the other Recognition of the professional ideas of the other The expectation you can count on the other	O O O
Complementation	Professional contacts and information of the other Access to the market in the neighbouring country through the other Economic relations of the other The relation would yield a better market position Diverging professional notions of the other	O O O O O
Physical attraction	Price of the other's resources Quality of the other's resources Specificity of the other's resources	O O O

Interaction

Transaction costs	Necessity of changing production process and/or product Necessity to invest in knowledge/manpower/resources Disadvantageous proposals of the other in professional meetings Professional meetings are characterised by covering risks and setting up guarantees	O O O O
Trust	Communication ease in deliberations Informality and openness of professional deliberations Knowing one can count on the other	O O O

Transaction

Formal or informal	Whether or not make up a contract	N

Dependent variables

Economic relations: Yes or No

Economic relations in the neighbouring country	Economic relationship(s) in the neighbouring country: Yes or No?	Q

The number of economic relations

The number of economic relations	The number of economic relations in the neighbouring country	Q

Success

Degree of success	The evaluation of the actual success of the co-operation since the moment of transaction	O
	Changes in the intensity of the co-operation since the moment of transaction	O

Appendix 3 Factoranalyses

An attempt has been made to reduce the total number of items to a restrained number of dimensions by means of factor analysis (Principal Component Analysis, Rotation Varimax). Dimensions are groups of items under a common denominator. The items within these groups are closely related. The following variables will be dealt with: searching behaviour, mental distance, feeling at home in the culture of the neighbouring country, border evaluation, spatial identity, attraction, interaction, and success.

Table 1 - Dimensions of relationship preference

Factors and items	Factor loadings	Dimensions
Factor 1		
Preference for steady long-term economic relationships	0.794	
Preference for economic relations with a broad contact network	0.737	Networking
Preference for conscious search for professional contacts and economic relations in the neighbouring country	0.719	
Factor 2		
Preference for knowledge concerning the price/quality ratio of alternative partners	0.744	Bold and well-informed searching
Preference for higher profit, despite higher risk	0.724	
Factor 3		
Preference for economic relations at short distance	0.823	Regional/national searching
Preference for economic relations in the home country	0.712	

Table 2 - Dimensions of mental distance

Factors and items	Factor loadings	Dimensions
Factor 1		
The difference in business conventions in a relationship with an entrepreneur in the neighbouring country	0.793	The expected discrepancy with the other's business conventions in cross-border economic relationships
The risk of communication failures in a relationship with an entrepreneur in the neighbouring country	0.737	
The organisational adaptation consequential upon a relationship in the neighbouring country	0.597	
The difference in business habits in a relationship with an entrepreneur in the neighbouring country	0.582	
The uncertainty with regard to the compliance to working agreements with a relation in the neighbouring country	0.499	
The time required for getting to know the relation in the neighbouring country well	0.482	
Factor 2		
The expected superficiality of the co-operation with a relation in the neighbouring country	0.776	The expected negative economic effect of the cross-border economic relationship
The expected transience of the co-operation with a relation in the neighbouring country	0.773	
The expected inefficiency of co-operation with a relation in the neighbouring country	0.712	
The risk that the relationship in the neighbouring country turns out a failure	0.680	
Factor 3		
The financial basis needed for a relationship in the neighbouring country	0.752	The stringency of the financial economic conditions set to cross-border economic relationships
The importance of a good market position of the relation in the neighbouring country	0.718	
The time needed to find a relation in the neighbouring country	0.480	

Table 3 - Feeling at home in the culture of the neighbouring country

Factor en items	Factor loadings	Dimensions
Factor Feeling at home in the living culture of the neighbouring country Feeling at home in the business culture of the neighbouring country	0.926 0.926	Feeling at home in the culture of the neighbouring country

Table 4 - Dimensions of border evaluation

Factors and items	Factor loadings	Dimensions (and Cronbach's alpha)
Factor 1		
Limiting	0.841	The irrelevance of the state border (α=0.87)
Cost-increasing	0.829	
Impeding	0.807	
Noticeable	0.770	
Divisive	0.732	
Irritating	0.591	
Factor 2		
Useless	0.845	The border is a barrier (α=0.78)
Unimportant	0.794	
Abnormal	0.695	
Artificial	0.667	

Table 5a - Dimensions of spatial identity (Zeeland Flanders)

Factors and items	Factor loadings	Dimensions
Factor 1		
Fleming	0.850	Identification with the own regional periphery and the neighbouring country
Inhabitant of a border region	0.760	
Belgian	0.722	
Factor 2		
World citizen	0.910	International/national identity
European	0.898	
Dutchman	0.540	
Factor 3		
Zeelander	0.869	Zeeland identity
Zeeland Fleming	0.794	

Table 5b - Dimensions of spatial identity (Central and North Zeeland)

Factors and items	Factor loadings	Dimensions
Factor 1		
Fleming	0.895	Identification with the own regional periphery and the neighbouring country
Belgian	0.856	
Zeeland Fleming	0.712	
Inhabitant of a border region	0.709	
Factor 2		
European	0.936	International identity
World citizen	0.913	
Factor 3		
Zeelander	0.833	National identity
Dutchman	0.698	

Table 5c - Dimensions of spatial identity (Gent/Eeklo)

Factors and items	Factor loadings	Dimensions
Factor 1		
Zeeland Fleming	0.945	Identification with the own regional periphery and the neighbouring country
Zeelander	0.939	
Dutchman	0.879	
Inhabitant of a border region	0.589	
Factor 2		
European	0.923	International identity
World citizen	0.886	
Factor 3		
Fleming	0.882	National identity
Belgian	0.491	

Table 6 - Dimensions of attraction

Factors and items	Factor loadings	Dimensions
Factor 1		
He had important business contacts and information	0.794	
He could provide good access to the market in the neighbouring country	0.785	Complementation
He had relationships with other companies too	0.771	
He had differing and interesting business notions	0.621	
A relationship with this partner would yield a better market position	0.502	

Factor 2 You could get along well as persons (mutual sympathy) He seemed someone to be able to depend upon The visiting frequency with the other company was relatively high You could recognise his business notions	0.785 0.710 0.505 0.483	Similarity
Factor 3 He had specific material means He could deliver the requested quality He asked a fair price	0.741 0.715 0.683	Price/quality ratio of the commodities
Factor 4 The objective average travelling time to the other company The importance of the relatively short travelling time	-0.798 0.734	Spatial proximity

Table 7 - Dimensions of interaction

Factors and items	Factor loadings	Dimensions (& Cronbach's alpha)
Factor 1 The communication between the two of you went smoothly You both knew exactly what to expect from the other When once you began the business deliberations, the personal contact with the other was informal and open	0.881 0.870 0.837	Trust (α=0.86)

Factor 2 Your company had to modify the production process and/or the product to come to working agreements with this partner	0.787	Transaction costs (α=0.60)
During the deliberations the other made proposals that were disadvantageous for your company	0.752	
Your company had to invest in knowledge/manpower/resources to come to working agreements with this partner	0.641	
The business deliberations were characterised by giving guarantees and mutual safeguarding against risks	0.516	

Table 8 - Dimensions of success

Factor and items	Factor loadings	Dimensions
Factor Change in the intensity of the co-operation since the moment of transaction	0.912	Degree of success of the relationship
Evaluation of the actual success of the co-operation since the moment of transaction	0.912	

FIGURES

TABLES

SCHEMES

Samenvatting en conclusies

Vraagstelling
In deze dissertatie staat de vraag centraal wat de invloed is van de staatsgrens, binnen de Europese Economische Unie, op de ontwikkeling van economische relaties tussen twee bedrijven uit regio's aan weerszijden van de grens. Wat betreft de ontwikkeling gaat het concreet om: het aantal bedrijven dat één of meerdere grensoverschrijdende economische relatie heeft (de frequentie), het aantal grensoverschrijdende economische relaties dat de bedrijven hebben en het economische succes van de grensoverschrijdende economische relaties. Het onderzoek richt zich op de grensgebieden van Nederland en België, te weten Zeeuws-Vlaanderen, Midden-en Noord-Zeeland aan Nederlandse zijde en Gent/Eeklo aan Belgische zijde.

De staatsgrens in relatie tot de *actieve* ruimte, de *affectieve* ruimte en de *cognitieve* ruimte
Om de gestelde onderzoeksvraag te kunnen beantwoorden is eerst onderzocht welke theoretische denkbare invloeden van grenzen op actoren en groepen actoren onderscheiden kunnen worden. Daartoe is een onderscheid gemaakt naar drie soorten ruimten: actief, affectief en cognitief.

De *actieve ruimte* is de ruimte die gevormd wordt door het feitelijk handelen van actoren, hier geoperationaliseerd als de feitelijke spreiding van de economische activiteiten van de ondernemers in de onderzoeksgebieden. Gedacht moet dan worden aan de afzet van de produkten, het contactenpatroon, het wel of niet hebben van en het aantal grensoverschrijdende economische relaties. Verwacht werd dat de handelingen aan de grens een discontinuïteit in het ruimtelijk verloop vertonen.

De *affectieve ruimte* is het tweede soort ruimte welke is onderscheiden. De actoren verdelen de ruimte ook op basis van de affectie, het gevoel. De affectie-ruimte is geconcretiseerd door de mentale afstandsbeleving, het gevoel van thuis zijn in de cultuur, de ruimtelijke identiteit en de evaluatie van de staatsgrens als fenomeen. De assumptie was hier dat de nationale grens in affectieve zin nog altijd sterk aanwezig en merkbaar is.

Actoren verdelen de ruimte niet alleen naar actie en affectie, maar ook naar cognitie. De *cognitieve ruimte* is de ruimte waarover kennis bestaat, hetzij ontstaan door persoonlijke ervaring, hetzij ontstaan door informatie of studie. Deze kennis is in dit onderzoek getest middels de inschatting van fysieke afstanden en de intekening van de grens op een blinde kaart. Beide indicatoren maken deel uit van een cognitieve 'map' die een actor zich vormt over de ruimte. De aanname voor beide maatstaven was dat de precisie van de inschatting/intekening zal toenemen naarmate er meer kennis bestaat over de werkelijke afstanden/grensligging (cf. Riedel, 1994).

De drie soorten afscheidingen van de ruimte (actief, affectief en cognitief) dienen in vergelijkende zin tegenover de staatsgrens geplaatst te worden, die *kunstmatig*, *concreet* en *functioneel* is. De afwijking, de discontinuïteit in het ruimtelijk verloop van de actieve ruimte ten opzichte van de staatsgrens is het *effect van de grens*. In deze dissertatie stond de analyse van juist deze invloed van de grens op de actieve ruimte van de bedrijven in grensregio's centraal. De grensoverschrijdende *actieve* ruimte, voor wat betreft de frequentie en het aantal grensoverschrijdende economische relaties, werd verondersteld sterk samen te hangen met (1) de afwijkingen in de andere variabelen van de actieve ruimte, zoals het informele contactenpatroon en de relatievoorkeur, (2) met de afwijkingen in de *affectieve* ruimte, zoals het thuis voelen in de cultuur van het buurland en de ruimtelijke identiteit en (3) met de *cognitieve* ruimte, zoals de afstandinschatting naar steden in het buurland en de afwijkingen in de tekening van de grens op een blinde kaart.

Economische theorieën over het proces van internationale economische relatievorming
Met behulp van drie dominante economische theorieën op het terrein van internationale economische relaties, te weten de Transactiekostentheorie (TCE), de Internationale Netwerk Benadering (INA) en de 'Psychic Distance' Benadering (PDA), is aangegeven welke elementen van belang moeten worden geacht in het *proces* van *bilaterale* economische relatievorming over de grenzen heen. Het bleek dat de drie geselecteerde economische theorieën, onderling het sterkst verschilden op het punt van de veronderstelling van de kenmerken van '*human nature*' in economische (onder)handelingen.

De *transactiekostentheorie* neemt de 'contractual man' als uitgangspunt van haar zienswijze. De economische actor is volgens deze theorie in principe in staat tot opportunistisch gedrag. De onzekerheid die dat creëert bij de andere actoren, gevoegd bij de veronderstelling van een beperkte mogelijkheid tot volledige informatie-inwinning over de economische actor en de omstandigheden maken dat er contracten moeten worden opgesteld om het risico van de transacties te reduceren.

De bestudeerde *internationale netwerktheorie* stelt daar de aanname van vertrouwen ('trust') tegenover. In de interactie tussen actoren is de economische actor volgens deze visie er niet op gericht zich ten koste van de ander te verbeteren, maar vooral eerst de relatie vorm en inhoud te geven. De economische samenleving wordt in deze theorie opgevat als een netwerk van relaties tussen actoren. De economische relaties verschillen daarbij naar inhoud en diepgang. Het vertrouwen is voor de bestudeerde netwerktheoretici een belangrijke determinant van het bepalen van die inhoud en diepgang van de economische relatie. Het vertrouwen wordt opgebouwd volgens een iteratief, dynamisch proces; economische actoren *leren*.

Het leereffect staat ook centraal in de derde theorie die is behandeld om het begrip grensoverschrijdende economische relaties handen en voeten te geven, de *'Psychic Distance' theorie*. In deze theorie staat niet zozeer de interactie tussen twee actoren centraal als wel de kennis van de actor ten opzichte van de omgeving waarin hij zich bevindt. De aanname is dat de actor beducht is een ander land economisch te penetreren vanwege een sterke mate van kennisachterstand over de samenleving in dat land. Naarmate de actor meer kennis hierover heeft vergaard en ervaring heeft opgedaan in de onbekende, onvertrouwde omgeving van het andere land, zal de mate en diepgang van internationalisatie in dat land toenemen. De 'psychic distance' theorie hanteert voorts een fasenmodel van internationalisatie. Begonnen wordt met export, daarna volgt de afzetrelatie (bijvoorbeeld een 'agent'), vervolgens een produktieprocesrelatie (uitbesteding of toelevering) of zeggenschapsrelatie (bijvoorbeeld een 'joint venture'). Het stapsgewijze internationaliseringsproces mondt tenslotte uit in het opzetten van een eigen vestiging ('foreign direct investment'). Om het verschil in constellaties van samenlevingen te kunnen analyseren wordt in de operationele uitwerkingen van de theorie meestal gefocust op het verschil in cultuur tussen de landen (de *culturele afstandenindex*).

Geen van de drie theorieën bleek, op zichzelf, in staat een afdoende antwoord te geven op de vraag welke invloed de staatsgrens heeft op de ontwikkeling van grensoverschrijdende economische relaties. Het overzicht aan economische theorieën heeft niettemin wel het inzicht opgeleverd dat de in de literatuur belangrijk geachte tegenstelling tussen transactiekosten en vertrouwen, alsmede de tegenstelling tussen de dynamische benadering van de 'Psychic Distance' theorie versus de overwegend statische benadering van de transactiekostentheorie, kunstmatig is en een meer geïntegreerde visie op het internationaliseringsproces blokkeert.

Voorts heeft de studie van de economische theorieën het bestaan van drie leemten in de theorie aangetoond:

1) In economische studies is nauwelijks of geen plaats ingeruimd voor een micro-economische analyse van de betekenis en invloed van de landsgrens op de internationale acties van en interacties tussen ondernemers.

2) Economische studies betrekken nauwelijks of niet de perceptie en attitude van ondernemers in de analyses, alhoewel het belang ervan wel steeds meer wordt onderkend.

3) Economische studies over het proces van relatievorming nemen over het algemeen niet het *gehele proces* van bilateraal contact en attractie tot transactie en relatie in ogenschouw, maar beginnen meestal bij de fase van de interactie, het moment waarbij twee economische actoren gaan onderhandelen over de te maken werkafspraken.

Gezien de vaak verkondigde opvatting dat het belang van afstanden en grenzen in de economie afneemt en er in toenemende mate belang wordt gehecht aan nabijheid en persoonlijke, face-to-face contacten in de economie zijn deze drie leemten in de economische theorie op zijn minst opmerkelijk te noemen. Op basis van deze bevindingen ten aanzien van de economische theorieën van het internationaliseringsproces, is de stelling geponeerd dat een onderzoek naar de economie van grenzen moet worden beschouwd als een studie die veel te maken heeft met een onderzoek naar de grenzen van de economie.

Het INTERFACE model

Op basis van de besproken en geëvalueerde theorieën over de invloed van grenzen en de ontwikkeling van economische relaties is een model ontwikkeld. Dit model had tot doel de ontwikkeling van grensoverschrijdende economische relatie tussen twee bedrijven accuraat te beschrijven en te verklaren. Het model dat is ontwikkeld is het *INTERFACE model* genoemd, wat een acroniem is voor *'INTERnational Formation of Autonomous Co-operation between Enterprises'*. Het INTERFACE model bestaat uit zes fasen:

- contact (de ontmoeting),
- attractie (de keuze van de partner),
- interactie (de onderhandelingen over de werkafspraken),
- transactie (de opstelling van de overeenkomst/het contract),
- relatie (de continuïteit van de samenwerking) en
- succes (de intensiteitstoename en de evaluatie van de samenwerking)

De zes fasen zijn elk nader geoperationaliseerd aan de hand van factoren die in de fasen een belangrijke rol spelen.

In het model wordt aangenomen dat de actoren gekenmerkt worden door wat in de studie is genoemd *contextrationaliteit*. Dat wil zeggen dat de economische rationaliteit niet alleen de strategische rationaliteit bevat, maar ook een weging van affectieve en cognitieve elementen van de context waarin de actie plaatsvindt in zich heeft. Om de frequentie, het aantal grensoverschrijdende economische relaties en het succes van deze relaties te kunnen verklaren, zijn op basis van het INTERFACE model onderzoekshypothesen opgesteld.

Het empirisch onderzoek

In 1992 was reeds het inzicht gewonnen middels ons onderzoek in de grensregio Midden-Brabant (Nederland) en de Kempen (België) dat de grens een breuklijn vormde ten aanzien van het aantal grensoverschrijdende economische relaties van bedrijven in grensregio's (Dagevos *et al.*, 1992). Die eerste verkenning van de rol van de grens in internationale economische vervlechting versterkte het beeld dat er behoefte bestond de werking van de grens nadrukkelijker te belichten en te verklaren. Het onderzoek naar de invloed van de grens op economische vervlechtingen tussen bedrijven in grensregio's was slechts zelden gericht op het ontwikkelen en testen van theorieën en hypothesen.

In deze studie heb ik geprobeerd een aanzet te genereren om deze leemte te vullen. De methodiek en het ontwikkelde theoretische model werden om die reden belangrijke, innovatieve dimensies van deze dissertatie. Om de geformuleerde onderzoekshypothesen te toetsen is een uitgebreide enquête uitgezet onder in totaal 1727 bedrijven in drie regio's aan de grens van Nederland en België, te weten de regio's Zeeuws-Vlaanderen en Midden-en Noord-Zeeland in Nederland en het gewest Gent/Eeklo in België. Alle bedrijven waren afkomstig uit de bouw, industrie en groothandel. In totaal heeft 27,2% van de bedrijven de vragenlijst ingevuld en op tijd geretourneerd.

De enquête startte met de inventarisatie van de spreiding in de *afzet,* het *aantal* en de *typen* economische relaties van de ondernemingen. Deze analyse diende ertoe feitelijk vast te stellen welke invloed de grens heeft op de actie-ruimte, het ruimtelijk handelen van de ondernemingen in de onderzochte grensregio's van Nederland en België.

De spreiding van de afzet en de economische relaties bleek zeer scheef verdeeld te zijn. Het overgrote merendeel van de economische relaties wordt in de eigen regio en het eigen land aangegaan. Het verschil tussen het aantal economische relaties in het eigen land en in het buurland is aanzienlijk. Gemiddeld over de drie regio's heeft een bedrijf bijna vijf keer zoveel economische relaties in eigen land als in het buurland.

De resultaten verschilden daarbij wel sterk naar regio. In deze studie is duidelijk geworden dat handelingen, percepties en attitudes van ondernemers niet los te zien zijn van de regio waarin de ondernemers opereren. Niet alleen hebben de handelingen van ondernemers een invloed op de regio, maar ook de invloed van de regionale context van de ondernemers op hun grensoverschrijdende actie-en affectieruimte is zeer duidelijk waarneembaar. Het maakt nogal wat uit waar, in welke regio, de bedrijven zich bevinden. Zeer sterk bleek die invloed in de regionale analyse van het aantal economische relaties in het buurland. In de dissertatie is de invloed van de grens op de spreiding van de economische relaties ook op kaarten afgebeeld.

De bedrijven uit de regio Midden-en Noord-Zeeland hebben van de drie onderzochte regio's het kleinste aantal grensoverschrijdende economische relaties. De verhouding economische relaties in het buurland ten opzichte van het binnenland ligt op 1:7,4. De bedrijven uit deze regio zijn vooral op Nederland georiënteerd, meer opwaarts dan neerwaarts. Concreet zijn ze, wat betreft hun 'buitenregionale oriëntatie', sterk op de regio Rotterdam/Rijnmond gericht. België is voor deze bedrijven 'een echt buitenland'. Feitelijk hebben de ondernemingen uit deze regio te maken met een dubbele grens, de watergrens van de Westerschelde en de staatsgrens tussen Nederland en België. Niettemin brengt de staatsgrens de sterkste scheiding in het ruimtelijk handelen en in de affectieve ruimte van de ondernemers teweeg.
Buiten de eigen regio richten de bedrijven in regio Zeeuws-Vlaanderen zich vooral op de rest van het binnenland en op de Vlaamse markt. Het is duidelijk geworden dat de bedrijven uit deze regio het meest van alle bedrijven op het buurland zijn gericht. De regio Gent/Eeklo is daarbij voor hen de trekpleister. Het aantal economische relaties dat de bedrijven uit Zeeuws-Vlaanderen in Gent/ Eeklo hebben is zelfs groter dan ze in de regio Midden-en Noord-Zeeland hebben. De belangrijkste reden voor deze relatief sterke oriëntatie op Gent/Eeklo moet gezocht worden in de functionele waterverbinding tussen Gent en Terneuzen, de Kanaalzone. Voor de ondernemingen in Zeeuws-Vlaanderen verkleint de sterk geïndustrialiseerde Kanaalzone letterlijk de afstand naar een relatief grote afzetmarkt in Gent/Eeklo. De verdeling over het aantal economische relaties in het binnenland en het buurland is ook hier scheef, maar veel minder dan bij de bedrijven uit de andere twee regio's, namelijk 1:2,9.
Niettemin moet de relativiteit van deze oriëntatie op het buurland niet uit het oog verloren worden.

Ondanks de relatief sterke oriëntatie op Gent/Eeklo blijkt namelijk, dat, wanneer gekeken wordt naar de afzet en het aantal economische relaties in België, de bedrijven in Zeeuws-Vlaanderen over het algemeen toch duidelijk meer op Nederland gericht zijn. De bedrijven uit Zeeuws-Vlaanderen verkopen en leveren hun produkten daarbij vooral in de eigen regio. Ze zijn relatief meer in de eigen regio economisch actief dan de bedrijven uit Midden-en Noord-Zeeland en zelfs twee keer zoveel als de bedrijven uit Gent/Eeklo. De bedrijven uit Zeeuws-Vlaanderen zijn kortom, wat betreft de afzet en economische relaties, in de eerste plaats zeer sterk op de eigen regio gericht.

De regio Gent/Eeklo blijkt een echt internationaal bedrijfsleven te hebben. De bedrijven uit Gent/Eeklo verkopen hun produkten het vaakst aan consumenten en andere bedrijven buiten hun eigen regio. Maar liefst 73,0% van de bedrijven exporteert bijvoorbeeld naar Nederland. Dat is bijna 6% meer dan de Zeeuws-Vlaamse bedrijven en bijna twee keer het percentage van de Midden-en Noord-Zeeuwse bedrijven. Omdat de bedrijven echter ook relatief vaker en meer naar andere landen exporteren is het exportvolume naar Nederland niettemin over het algemeen klein. Verder blijkt dat de bedrijven gemiddeld meer economische relaties in eigen land hebben dan de bedrijven in de twee Nederlandse regio's. Het aantal grensoverschrijdende economische relaties is bij deze bedrijven significant hoger dan bij de bedrijven uit Midden-en Noord-Zeeland. Het gemiddeld aantal economische relaties in het buurland ten opzichte van het binnenland is 1:4,9. Voorts blijken de economische relaties ruimtelijk beter gespreid dan bij de bedrijven uit Zeeuws-Vlaanderen. De economische relaties zijn niet gericht op één regio in het buurland, maar op het gehele buurland. Evenals voor de bedrijven uit de twee Nederlandse regio's geldt voor de Gent/Eeklose bedrijven dat de grensoverschrijdende economische relaties vooral afzetmarktrelaties en toeleveringsrelaties zijn.

Wat betreft de sectorverdeling kan het volgende gesteld worden. Als het gaat om internationale economische vervlechting blijven de bouwbedrijven duidelijk achter bij de groothandel en industriële bedrijven. Het verschil met de industrie is het grootst. Het zijn vooral deze bedrijven die grensoverschrijdende economische relaties aangaan.

De invloed van de staatsgrens

Na het bestuderen van het spreidingspatroon van de economische relaties, heb ik vervolgens getracht een verklaring te geven van de gevonden resultaten. Daartoe heb ik, op basis van het INTERFACE model, een drietal onderzoeksmodellen aangaande de ontwikkeling van grensoverschrijdende economische relaties geformuleerd. Het eerste model tracht het wel of niet hebben van grensoverschrijdende economische relaties te verklaren, het tweede model probeert het aantal economische relaties te verklaren dat de bedrijven gemiddeld hebben, het derde model tenslotte, zoekt naar een verklaring voor het succes van grensoverschrijdende economische relaties.

De belangrijkste conclusie van de eerste twee modellen is dat de onmiddellijke nabijheid van de grens zelf een groot probleem is in de ontwikkeling van grensoverschrijdende economische relaties. In antwoord op de centrale vraagstelling van dit onderzoek: de staatsgrens blijkt vooral *mentaal* (nog) aanwezig. Het ruimtelijk-economisch gedrag van ondernemers blijkt zich te laten leiden door de abstracte, bestuurlijke grenzen van provincies en landen. De fysieke afstand tot de regio aan de andere zijde van de grens is veelal beperkt, de mentale afstand is vaak veel groter. De markt wordt daardoor in veel gevallen niet alleen ruimtelijk, maar ook in mentale zin gedeeld. De staatsgrens is geworteld in de hoofden van de ondernemers.

Concreet uitte deze mentale impact van de grens zich in de significante verschillen die door de respondenten worden gepercipieerd in de wijze en het succes van economische samenwerking met bedrijven in het buurland vergeleken met economische samenwerking in het eigen land.

De mentale afstand staat niet op zichzelf, maar werkt door in het gedrag. Bedrijven zonder economische relaties over de grens zien grensoverschrijdende samenwerking significant met meer onzekerheid tegemoet dan binnenlandse samenwerking. Ze ervaren een grotere drempelvrees, een grotere mentale afstand. De omvang van de mentale afstand heeft een significant negatieve invloed op zowel de frequentie als het aantal grensoverschrijdende economische relaties. Veelzeggend in dit verband is ook dat de bedrijven zonder grensoverschrijdende economische relaties, welke over het algemeen een grotere mentale afstand hebben, de grens niet zozeer als een barrière opvatten maar juist als een relevante, waardevolle afbakening.

Het aantal grensoverschrijdende economische relaties dat de bedrijven hebben is ook getracht te verklaren door het effect van de grens op de *cognitie-ruimte*. Cognitie-ruimte is in deze studie geoperationaliseerd aan de hand van de nauwkeurigheid waarmee de actoren de afstanden naar omliggende steden inschatten en de nauwkeurigheid waarmee de actoren de ligging van de grens weten in te tekenen op een 'blinde' kaart. De verwachting was dat de precisie van de schatting vooral te maken had met de activiteit over de grens. Voor de inschatting van de afstand naar naburige steden in binnen-en buurland kon deze hypothese niet overtuigend worden aangetoond. Slechts in twee gevallen werd aan deze verwachting voldaan. Ook de vraag met betrekking tot de intekening van de staatsgrens, die opgesteld werd om te toetsen of de vertekeningen van de grensligging samenhingen met het hebben van en het aantal grensoverschrijdende economische relaties, voegde geen overtuigende dimensie toe aan de verklaring van het gevonden grensoverschrijdende actie-patroon. Wel werd door middel van de cognitieve kaart inzichtelijk dat de Belgische respondenten het eigen land systematisch kleiner achten - op Zeeuws-Vlaanderen en Zuid-Limburg na - terwijl de Nederlandse respondenten het eigen land systematisch groter achten. De Belgische respondenten tekenden Zeeuws-Vlaanderen en Zuid-Limburg in als delen van het Belgische grondgebied. Het mag kenmerkend worden genoemd dat juist deze twee gebieden, die een relatief sterk anti-Nederlandse houding hadden ten tijde van de splitsing tussen België en Nederland in 1839 en in Nederland over het algemeen worden beschouwd als gebieden met een sterke mate van affectie met België, geannexeerd worden in de getekende landkaart van België door de Belgische respondenten. Er is aanleiding om in een vervolgstudie de aandacht te richten op het verder analyseren van de invloed van de cognitie-ruimte op de actie-ruimte. Ook een nadere studie van de betekenis van de over-of onderschattingen van de grootte van het eigen land in een cognitieve kaart strekt dan tot aanbeveling.

Uit het onderzoek komt verder naar voren dat de onderlinge zakelijke betrekkingen tussen Nederlandse en Belgische ondernemers door beide groepen sterk verschillend wordt gepercipieerd en beleefd. Op sommige punten bestaat er een duidelijke irritatie. Het beeld dat uit deze analyse naar voren kwam, komt overeen met de algemeen heersende stereo-typering van de onderlinge verhoudingen. De Belgen vinden de Nederlanders arrogant en de Nederlanders de Belgen in sommige opzichten onbetrouwbaar en hun overheid te ondoorzichtig, te gesloten. De ‘mental gap’ zoals die beleefd wordt door de ondernemers van de twee landen, komt overeen met het beeld dat naar voren komt uit de analyses van de algemeen heersende cultuur in de twee landen (zie m.n. Hofstede, 1980, 1991). Uit de analyse van de culturele afstand tussen Nederland en België blijkt dat er grote cultuurverschillen bestaan tussen beide landen. Nederland vertoont cultureel meer verwantschap met landen in Noord-Europa en België meer met landen in Zuid-Europa.

Euregionalisering, of in het algemeen, internationalisering, middels grensoverschrijdende relatievorming moet opgevat worden als een proces dat niet alleen een uitbreiding van de actieve ruimte maar ook van de affectieve ruimte impliceert. De internationale oriëntatie van de beslisser is veelal een leerproces. De ondernemer ‘rijpt’ in het internationaal zakendoen. Ervaring in grensoverschrijdende economische samenwerking stelt de negatieve perceptie en attitude over de ander of over de grensoverschrijdende samenwerking doorgaans bij. Het hebben van zakelijke en vooral persoonlijke contacten in het buurland helpt zeker in het verwerven van economische relaties in het buurland, al is het geen absolute voorwaarde. Ook het zich thuis voelen in de andere cultuur, het vertrouwd zijn met conventies en regels is van belang, maar van een veel groter belang is de perceptie van de ondernemer ten aanzien van het aangaan van grensoverschrijdende samenwerking. Economische subjecten blijken niet altijd volledig in staat te kunnen of te willen zijn de relevante, objectieve informatie te vergaren. Ze blijken eigen ruimtelijke grenzen te trekken en gedragspatronen en bepaalde 'belief sets' te hebben die niet hoeven te sporen met wat economische wenselijk of werkelijk is.

Samengevat, de analyse van de determinanten van het aantal economische relaties in het buurland toont aan dat het in sterke mate internationaal samenwerken gepaard gaat met een relatief sterke nationale economische vervlechting, een hoge exportratio en een open, ‘grensoverschrijdende’ perceptie van de ondernemers. Internationalisering is een proces dat veelal nationaal begint. Wanneer besloten wordt ook economische relaties aan te gaan met bedrijven in naburige of verder weg gelegen regio’s in het eigen land, is vaak de eerste stap op weg naar het buurland gezet.

De analyse van de determinanten het *succes* van grensoverschrijdende economische relaties, het derde verklarende onderzoeksmodel in de dissertatie, bekrachtigde het belang van een open houding en ‘grensoverschrijdende’ perceptie. Het bleek dat de mate van vertrouwen de meest bepalende factor is van het succes van een grensoverschrijdende economische relatie. Verder bleek dat ook de mate van *similariteit* tussen de twee ondernemers, van significant belang is in het bepalen van het uiteindelijke succes van de grensoverschrijdende samenwerking. Deze belangrijke resultaten, welke voortkomen uit het INTERFACE model, leiden tot de conclusie dat de ontwikkeling van een succesvolle grensoverschrijdende economische relatie in feite de overschrijding van een 'dubbele grens' noodzakelijk maakt. Een grensoverschrijdende economische relatie impliceert ten eerste dat de ondernemer de staatsgrens oversteekt en het buitenland betreedt, hetgeen gepaard kan gaan met een zekere mate van 'mental distance'. Daarnaast moet er ook een 'bilaterale grens' worden overschreden. Daarmee wordt bedoeld dat er sprake moet zijn van similariteit en vertrouwen tussen twee ondernemers van verschillende nationaliteiten, wil een relatie tussen beiden succes hebben.

De horizon van ondernemers
Economische vervlechting tussen regio's van naburige landen maakt de samenleving binnen de afzonderlijke regio's complexer en onrustiger. Individuele bedrijven en bestuurlijke instanties worden daar onzeker van. Onzekerheid leidt vaak tot een geringe dynamiek. De regionale netwerken van bedrijven aan beide zijden van de grens in dit gebied blijken nog altijd vooral op zichzelf staand en relatief weinig interactief. Het creëren van een grenzeloze economische zone in de gehele regio Zeeland-Gent/Eeklo, zoals dat in Euregionaal verband gepoogd wordt te doen, is om deze redenen niet gemakkelijk.

Gesteld kan worden dat de onderzoeksregio als geheel haar economische potentie nog niet ten volle benut. De belangrijkste reden daarvoor is dat er door nog ongebruikte mogelijkheden van arbeidsdeling, groei door interdependentie en concurrentie in de gebieden aan de grenzen mogelijk is. Een netwerk waarin tal van contacten mogelijk is, zou tot een doorbraak in de nu veelal begrensde actie-en affectiepatronen kunnen leiden. Wederzijdse openheid van de betrokken actoren in de relaties is daarbij een vereiste. In Zeeland/Gent-Eeklo komt een dergelijk netwerk geleidelijk aan tot stand. De mate van netwerkvorming verschilt daarbij sterk naar gebiedsdeel. Het netwerk voor de regio als geheel is nochtans nog niet in hoge mate structureel en grensoverschrijdend. Deze bevinding staat niet op zichzelf. Andere empirische onderzoeken in Europa zijn tot soortgelijke bevindingen gekomen. Bij beleidsmakers van de Europese Unie is sprake van een groot optimisme over de potentie van de samenwerking tussen grensregio's, maar de realiteit is dat de feitelijke omvang en diepgang van deze samenwerking (nog) te wensen overlaat. In dit onderzoek is getracht een verklaring te vinden voor het patroon en het succes van internationale economische samenwerking tussen bedrijven uit grensregio's.

Als de doelstelling is het (mentaal) belemmerende effect van de landsgrens op de totstandkoming van economische relaties in het gebied te verminderen, moet de vraag beantwoord worden hoe een horizon verlegd kan worden. Theoretisch bezien betekent het stimuleren van grensoverschrijdende economische relatievorming veelal het doorbreken van een patroon, van een vicieuze cirkel. De ondernemer schat in dat grensoverschrijdende economische relaties iets extra's kosten, *i.c.* een grotere mentale inspanning en meer onzekerheid. De drempel, de mentale afstand die wordt ervaren, om in het buurland economische relaties aan te gaan is hoger. Dit draagt bij tot de afhoudende opstelling bij ondernemers. De verschillen in conventies en regels die er bestaan worden groter gemaakt dan ze in werkelijkheid zijn, de kans op succes wordt kleiner geacht en de financieel-economische condities voor de samenwerking in het buurland worden stringenter opgesteld dan nationaal het geval is. De 'drempelvrees' is daarmee zelf een drempel. Dezelfde redenering, maar dan vice versa, geldt voor de ondernemer die gaandeweg ervaart en leert dat grensoverschrijdende economische relaties een positieve meerwaarde kunnen betekenen voor het bedrijf.

In het kort gaat het er om de kosten van economische relatievorming te verlagen en de inzichtelijkheid in en vertrouwdheid met elkaars conventies en regels te verhogen. De kosten zijn hoger en de inzichtelijkheid en vertrouwdheid lager in het geval van een *inter*nationale relatie dan in het geval van een nationale economische relatie. Bij kosten kan gedacht worden aan de kosten van het zoeken naar contacten, het bezoeken van internationale beurzen, de reiskosten, de informatiekosten over mogelijke partners en mogelijke lokaties, de onderhandelingskosten en de contractkosten. Wil er sprake zijn van een duurzaam, inhoudelijk samenwerkingsverband, dan is het sleutelwoord *vertrouwen*. In termen van economisch gedrag betekent dit dat de mentale grenzen van de economische subjecten verruimd zouden moeten worden. Grensoverschrijdende economische communicatie en coöperatie is daarbij een eerste belangrijke stap.

De verbinding tussen macro en micro

Uit deze studie moet de conclusie worden getrokken dat de afstandsinvloed van de staatsgrens, in economisch-psychologische zin, in de theorieën over het grensoverschrijdend economisch relatieverkeer veelal onderschat wordt. De staatsgrens moet, ondanks het bestaan van de economische unie, in dit opzicht nog steeds worden opgevat als een markante afperking van de ruimte. Van een 'ontgrenzing' waarop wellicht werd gehoopt en die wellicht werd verwacht bij de creatie van de Benelux en Europese Unie, is in het onderzochte gebied geen sprake. Het gebied is geen 'ontgrensde' economische zone. Een dergelijke typering doet geen recht aan de grote verschillen in regionale economische oriëntaties van de bedrijven in het gebied. Bovendien onderschat dit de betekenis die de staatsgrens (nog altijd) heeft op de attitude en perceptie ten opzichte van en de daadwerkelijke ontwikkeling van grensoverschrijdende economische relaties. Om diezelfde reden is ook gebleken dat het gebruik van een 'objectieve' maatstaf als culturele afstand alleen, welke vaak in economische studies wordt gebruikt om het belang van culturele verschillen tussen landen in het internationalisatieproces van economische organisaties te benadrukken, niet voldoet. Cruciaal voor het aangaan en verder ontwikkelen van bilaterale economische relaties is niet het 'objectieve' verschil in cultuur, maar het *gepercipieerde* verschil in de formaliteiten en conventies tussen (de actoren van) de betrokken landen en de perceptie van de gevolgen van die verschillen voor het welslagen van een economische samenwerking in dat land.

De staatsgrens die tussen de partners aanwezig is, legt een bijzondere verbinding tussen het macro-en het micro-niveau waarop de studie van grensoverschrijdende economische relaties tussen bedrijven zich beweegt. Op het macro-niveau, het niveau van landen, speelt het proces van het nationalisme een belangrijke rol voor de cohesieve kracht van de nationale samenleving. Nationalisme is de ideologie die toebehoort aan een door staatsgrenzen afgegrensde territorialiteit. De nationale band, gevoed door de cohesieve werking die er van een afgegrensde samenleving uitgaat, die de economische actoren aan de grens scheidt, uit zich enerzijds in het nog altijd relevant vinden van de aanwezigheid van de staatsgrens en anderzijds in 'gedepersonifiseerde beelden' van elkaar. De verhouding tussen landen is in dit verband beschreven in termen van het ontstaan van een 'Wij-Zij' verhouding.

De kracht van de nationale identiteit slaat ook neer op de individuele ondernemers van een land: het micro-niveau van economische activiteiten. Dat de ruimte in affectieve zin lokaal, regionaal of nationaal begrensd kan zijn, is in beginsel een theoretisch probleem. Het wordt eerst een vraag van praktische relevantie als de vraag gesteld wordt hoe er naar gehandeld wordt, hoe dit zich vertaalt naar de actieve ruimte. In deze studie is aangetoond dat op het micro-economische niveau voor de verhouding tussen de economische actoren uit Nederlandse en Belgische grensregio's de 'Wij-Zij' verhouding zich operationeel uit in grotere onzekerheid, een grotere mentale afstand en het gebrek aan vertrouwen in het welslagen van grensoverschrijdende economische relaties in vergelijking met de economische relaties in het eigen land. Met andere woorden, de omvang van het 'Wij-Zij' effect voedt de mentale afstand en reduceert het nationaal gedetermineerde vertrouwen tussen ondernemers in grensoverschrijdende economische relaties.

Binnen de Europese Unie en de Benelux Unie, waarbinnen het gebied valt, bestaat formeel een eenheid van landen waarin geen handelsbelemmeringen meer aanwezig zijn voor goederen, diensten, arbeid en kapitaal. Formeel is er inderdaad sprake van open grenzen in deze zin, in de praktijk is nu gebleken dat er niettemin meer voor nodig is om de formele opheffing van grenzen ook inhoudelijke invulling en diepgang te geven.

Center for Economic Research, Tilburg University, The Netherlands
Dissertation Series

No.	Author	Title
1	P.J.J. Herings	Static and Dynamic Aspects of General Disequilibrium Theory; ISBN 90 5668 001 3
2*	Erwin van der Krabben	Urban Dynamics: A Real Estate Perspective - An institutional analysis of the production of the built environment; ISBN 90 5170 390 2
3	Arjan Lejour	Integrating or Desintegrating Welfare States? - a qualitative study to the consequences of economic integration on social insurance; ISBN 90 5668 003 x
4	Bas J.M. Werker	Statistical Methods in Financial Econometrics; ISBN 90 5668 002 1
5	Rudy Douven	Policy Coordination and Convergence in the EU; ISBN 90 5668 004 8
6	Arie J.T.M. Weeren	Coordination in Hierarchical Control; ISBN 90 5668 006 4
7	Herbert Hamers	Sequencing and Delivery Situations: a Game Theoretic Approach; ISBN 90 5668 005 6
8	Annemarie ter Veer	Strategic Decision Making in Politics; ISBN 90 5668 007 2
9	Zaifu Yang	Simplicial Fixed Point Algorithms and Applications; ISBN 90 5668 008 0
10	William Verkooijen	Neural Networks in Economic Modelling - An Empirical Study; ISBN 90 5668 010 2
11	Henny Romijn	Acquisition of Technological Capability in Small Firms in Developing Countries; ISBN 90 5668 009 9
12	W.B. van den Hout	The Power-Series Algorithm - A Numerical Approach to Markov Processes; ISBN 90 5668 011 0
13	Paul W.J. de Bijl	Essays in Industrial Organization and Management Strategy; ISBN 90 5668 012 9

---

* Copies can be ordered from ThelaThesis,Prinseneiland 305, 1013 LP Amsterdam, The Netherlands, phone + 31 20 6255429; fax: +31 20 6203395; e-mail: office@thelathesis.nl

No.	Author	Title
14	Martijn van de Ven	Intergenerational Redistribution in Representative Democracies; ISBN 90 5668 013 7
15	Eline van der Heijden	Altruism, Fairness and Public Pensions: An Investigation of Survey and Experimental Data; ISBN 90 5668 014 5
16	H.M. Webers	Competition in Spatial Location Models; ISBN 90 5668 015 3
17	Jan Bouckaert	Essays in Competition with Product Differentiation and Bargaining in Markets; ISBN 90 5668 016 1
18	Zafar Iqbal	Three-Gap Analysis of Structural Adjustment in Pakistan; ISBN 90 5668 017 x
19	Jimmy Miller	A Treatise on Labour: A Matching-Model Analysis of Labour-Market Programmes; ISBN 90 5668 018 8
20	Edwin van Dam	Graphs with Few Eigenvalues - An interplay between combinatorics and algebra; ISBN 90 5668 019 6
21	Henk Oosterhout	Takeover Barriers: the good, the bad, and the ugly; ISBN 90 5668 020 x
22	Jan Lemmen	Financial Integration in the European Union: Measurement and Determination; ISBN 90 5668 021 8
23	Chris van Raalte	Market Formation and Market Selection; ISBN 90 5668 022 6
24	Bas van Aarle	Essays on Monetary and Fiscal Policy Interaction: Applications to EMU and Eastern Europe; ISBN 90 5668 023 4
25	Francis Y. Kumah	Common Stochastic Trends and Policy Shocks in the Open Economy:Empirical Essays in International Finance and Monetary Policy; ISBN 90 5668 024 2
26	Erik Canton	Economic Growth and Business Cycles; ISBN 90 5668 025 0
27	Jeroen Hoppenbrouwers	Conceptual Modeling and the Lexicon; ISBN 90 5668 027 7

No.	Author	Title
28	Paul Smit	Numerical Analysis of Eigenvalue Algorithms Based on Subspace Iterations; ISBN 90 5668 026 9
29	Uri Gneezy	Essays in Behavioral Economics; ISBN 90 5668 028 5
30	Erwin Charlier	Limited Dependent Variable Models for Panel Data; ISBN 90 5668 029 3
31	Rob Euwals	Empirical Studies on Individual Labour Market Behaviour; ISBN 90 5668 030 7
32	Anurag N. Banerjee	The Sensitivity of Estimates, Inferences, and Forecasts of Linear Models; ISBN 90 5668 031 5
33	Frans A. de Roon	Essays on Testing for Spanning and on Modeling Futures Risk Premia; ISBN 90 5668 032 3
34	Xiangzhu Han	Product Differentiation, Collusion and Standardization; ISBN 90 5668 033 1
35	Marcel Das	On Income Expectations and Other Subjective Data: A Micro-Econometric Analysis; ISBN 90 5668 034 X
36	Jeroen Suijs	Cooperative Decision Making in a Stochastic Environment; ISBN 90 5668 035 8
37	Talitha Feenstra	Environmental Policy Instruments and International Rivalry: A Dynamic Analysis; ISBN 90 5668 036 6
38	Jan Bouwens	The Use of Management Accounting Systems in Functionally Differentiated Organizations; ISBN 90 5668 037 4
39	Stefan Hochguertel	Households' Portfolio Choices; ISBN 90 5668 038 2
40	Henk van Houtum	The Development of Cross-Border Economic Relations; ISBN 90 5668 039 0